Garland Studies
in Medieval Literature

Editors

Christopher Kleinhenz
University of Wisconsin–Madison

Paul E. Szarmach
State University of New York at Binghamton

Garland Studies
in Medieval Literature

1. Kimberlee Anne Campbell, *The Protean Text: A Study of Versions of the Medieval French Legend of "Doon and Olive"*

2. Vincent A. Dunn, *Cattle-Raids and Courtships: Medieval Narrative Genres in a Traditional Context*

3. Barbara Nelson Sargent-Baur, *Brothers of Dragons: "Job Dolens" and François Villon*

4. Rachel Bullington, *The* Alexis *in the Saint Albans Psalter: A Look into the Heart of the Matter*

5. Theodore L. Steinberg, Piers Plowman *and Prophecy: An Approach to the C-Text*

6. Jay Ruud, *"Many a Song and Many a Leccherous Lay": Tradition and Individuality in Chaucer's Lyric Poetry*

7. H. Wayne Storey, *The Transcription and Visual Poetics of Early Italian Lyrics*

8. Robert L. Kindrick, *Henryson and the Medieval Arts of Rhetoric*

9. Nancy Bradley-Cromey, *Authority and Autonomy in* L'Entrée D'Espagne

AUTHORITY AND AUTONOMY
IN *L'ENTRÉE D'ESPAGNE*

NANCY BRADLEY-CROMEY

Volume 9
GARLAND STUDIES IN MEDIEVAL LITERATURE

Garland Publishing, Inc.
New York & London
1993

Library of Congress Cataloging-in-Publication Data

Bradley-Cromey, Nancy.
    Authority and autonomy in L'entrée D'Espagne / Nancy Bradley-
Cromey.
      p.   cm. — (Garland studies in medieval literature ; vol. 9)
(Garland reference library of the humanities ; vol. 1730)
    Includes bibliographical references and index.
    ISBN 0–8153–1332–2 (alk. paper)
    1. Entrée d'Espagne.   2. Roland (Legendary character)—
Romances—History and criticism.   3. Epic poetry, French—History
and criticism.   4. Chansons de geste—History and criticism.
5. Authority in literature.   I. Title. II. Series. III. Series: Garland
studies in medieval literature ; v. 9.
PQ1459.E75B73   1993
841'.1—dc20   93–20545
                                                          CIP

Printed on acid-free, 250-year-life paper
Manufactured in the United States of America

For my husband

Preface of the General Editors

Garland Studies in Medieval Literature (GSML) is a series of interpretative and analytic studies of the Western European literatures of the Middle Ages. It includes both outstanding recent dissertations and book-length studies, giving junior scholars and their senior colleagues the opportunity to publish their research.

The editors welcome submissions representing any of the various schools of criticism and interpretation. Western medieval literature, with its broad historical span, multiplicity and complexity of language and literary tradition, and special problems of textual transmission and preservation as well as varying historical contexts, is both forbidding and inviting to scholars. It continues to offer rich materials for virtually every kind of literary approach that maintains a historical dimension. In establishing a series in an eclectic literature, the editors acknowledge and respect the variety of texts and textual possibilities and the "resisting reality" that confronts medievalists in several forms: on parchment, in mortar, or through icon. It is no mere imitative fallacy to be eclectic, empirical, and pragmatic in the face of this varied literary tradition that has so far defied easy formulation. The cultural landscape of the twentieth century is littered with the debris of broken monomyths predicated on the Middle Ages, the autocratic Church and the Dark Ages, for example, or conversely, the romanticized versions of love and chivalry.

The openness of the series means in turn that scholars, and particularly beginning scholars, need not pass an *a priori* test of "correctness" in their ideology, method, or critical position. The studies published in GSML must be true to their premises, complete within their articulated limits, and accessible to a multiple readership. Each study will advance the knowledge of the literature under discussion, opening it up for further consideration and creating intellectual value. It is also hoped that each volume, while bridging the gap between contemporary perspective and past reality, will make old texts new again. In this way the literature will remain primary, the method secondary.

For the ninth volume of this series, Nancy Bradley-Cromey provides the first extensive literary study of the *Entrée d'Espagne*, the most important romance epic in the Franco-Italian tradition. In the late thirteenth and through all of the fourteenth century a rich literary tradition—known variously as Franco-Venetian, Franco-Lombard, or, more generally, Franco-Italian—was developing in Northern Italy. While the comprehensive history of this corpus (over one hundred literary texts, including, among other genres, *chansons de geste*, chronicles, and romance epics) has yet to be written, critical and philological interest in these texts continues to increase. One group of texts presents material related to the expedition of Charlemagne to Spain and provides the "background" for the first part of the Old French *Chanson de Roland*. The *Entrée d'Espagne*, composed by a well-educated Paduan, is the best known romance epic in this group and has received more critical attention than most of these generally neglected works.

Bradley-Cromey's intent is comprehensive and multifaceted, just as the text of the *Entrée d'Espagne*, which assumes the shape of a sort of literary *summa* and which, in her words, "offers to its public a complex dialogical arena where a host of issues—literary, political, hermeneutic, religious—enter into communication, and frequently in confrontation, with one another." With masterly skill and authority Bradley-Cromey situates the *Entrée* in the historical, political, ideological, and cultural context of its composition, i.e., in the vibrant intellectually oriented university town of Padua, where pre-Humanist scholars such as Lovato Lovati "recuperated, largely in the study of the primary *auctores* of the Middle Ages, the *Romanitas* of the city's past, key to its illustrious pre-Renaissance future." Bradley-Cromey's meticulous and insightful examination allows the *Entrée* to emerge from its long and deplorable state of critical obscurity and to receive, finally, its proper recognition as one of the major and enduring products of the late Middle Ages.

Christopher Kleinhenz   Paul E. Szarmach
Univ. of Wisconsin-Madison   SUNY-Binghamton

Contents

Preface   xi

Abbreviations   xiii

Introduction   3

Chapter 1: Roland as *baron révolté*?   27

Chapter 2: Nobles: In Search of Foundations   57

Chapter 3: The Dialectic of Ideologies   81

Chapter 4: Discourse and Ideologies   135

Chapter 5: Signs of *Sententia*   215

Conclusions   255

Appendix   269

Selected Bibliography   277

Index   305

Preface

This book, initiated as a doctoral dissertation, initiated its author as well into an area of medieval literature unexplored by the majority of medievalists and still virtually unknown in the United States.

Given my dual interest and longstanding commitment to both French and Italian medieval literature, the dissertation proved subsequently to be the point of departure for continued research on the remarkable literary and cultural phenomenon of the Franco-Italian corpus and of *L'Entrée d'Espagne* in particular. The present work thus offers major conceptual revisions, broadened discussion of questions concerning text/context, and deepened analysis of the entire text.

An earlier version of chapter 1 appeared in *Olifant* 5.4 (May 1978), and parts of chapter 5 appeared in *Romance Epic: Essays on a Medieval Literary Genre*, ed. Hans-Erich Keller (Kalamazoo: The Medieval Institute, 1987).

Translations for all *Entrée* passages have been added. Given the linguistic complexities of the text, these were in some instances problematic to render in an English at once accurate and readable. In order to respect the inherent linguistic breadth of Franco-Italian, I have in certain instances added brackets providing clarification of translated material, and an alternate or complimentary reading, indicated by slashes, where the reader might benefit from such additions.

Abbreviations

Journals and Series

AIV	*Atti dell'Istituto Veneto*
CCM	*Cahiers de Civilisation Médiévale*
CN	*Cultura Neolatina*
EC	*L'Esprit Créateur*
MA	*Moyen Age*
PRF	Publications Romanes et Françaises
Rom	*Romania*
RPh	*Romance Philology*
SATF	Société des Anciens Textes Français
Spec	*Speculum*
SM	*Studi Medievali*
VR	*Vox Romanica*
YFS	*Yale French Studies*
ZRP	*Zeitschrift für Romanische Philologie*

Collective volumes

Charlemagne et l'Epopée romane: Charlemagne et l'Epopée romane., Actes du VIIe Congrès international de la Société Rencesvals (Liège, 28 août-4 septembre 1976), Bibliothèque de la Faculté de Philosophie et Lettres de l'Université de Liège 225 (Paris: Les Belles Lettres, 1978).

Essor et fortune: Essor et fortune de la chanson de geste dans l'Europe et l'Orient latin. Actes du IXe Congrès international de la Société Rencesvals pour l'étude des épopées romanes. Padoue-Venise, 29 août-4 septembre 1982, 2 vols. (Modena: Mucchi, 1984).

Mél. Delbouille : Mélanges de linguistique romane et de philologie médiévale offerts à M. Maurice Delbouille, 2 vols. (Gembloux, 1964).

Mél. René Louis: Mélanges offerts à René Louis, publiés par ses collègues et ses élèves à l'occasion de son 75e anniversaire, ed. André Moisan, 2 vols., Bibliothèque du Musée Archéologique Régional (Saint-Père-sous-Vézelay, 1982).

Romance Epic: Romance Epic: Essays on a Medieval Literary Genre, ed. Hans-Erich Keller , Studies in Medieval Culture 24, Medieval Institute Publications (Kalamazoo: Western Michigan UP, 1987).

SCV : Storia della cultura veneta, ed. Gianfranco Folena, 6 vols. (Modena: Neri Pozza, 1976-): vol. 3, *Il Trecento.*

Testi, cotesti : Testi, cotesti e contesti del franco-italiano, Atti del primo simposio franco-italiano (Bad Homburg, 13-16 aprile 1987), ed. Günter Holtus, Henning Krauss, Peter Wunderli (Tübingen: Niemeyer, 1989).

Authority and Autonomy in
L'Entrée D'Espagne

INTRODUCTION

Li quens Rollant se jut desuz un pin,
Envers Espaigne en ad turnet sun vis.
De plusurs choses a remembrer li prist:
De tantes teres cum li bers cunquist,
De dulce France, des humes de sun lign,
De Carlemagne, sun seignor, kil nurrit.

Count Roland lay beneath a pine tree,
He has turned his face toward Spain.
He began to remember many things:
The many lands he conquered as a brave knight,
Fair France, the men from whom he is descended,
Charlemagne, his lord, who raised him
(*La Chanson de Roland* 2375-80).[1]

Vos voil canter e dir por rime e por sentençe
Tot ensi come Carles el bernage de Françe
Entrerent en Espagne, et por ponte de lançe
Conquistrent de saint Jaqes la plus mestre habitançe.
Ne laserent por storme ne por autre pesanze:
S'il n'aüsent leisié par une difirnanze
Que lor fist Gaenelonz, le sire de Maganze,
Coronez eüsent, n'en soiez en dotançe,
Roland, par chi l'estorie et lo canter comanze,
Li melors chevalers que legist en sianze.

3

> I wish to sing and tell you in rhyme and in sentential
> language all about how Charles and the barons of
> France made their entry into Spain, and by the point
> of the spear conquered the greatest shrine of St.
> James. They would not have abandoned [the mission]
> on account of battle or for any other difficulty, if they
> had not ended it because of a "difference"/quarrel
> which Ganelon, lord of Maganza, brought upon them.
> They would have crowned Roland, concerning whom
> the story and song begin, the best knight whom men
> read about when they gather together; have no doubt
> about it (*L'Entrée d'Espagne* 9-18).[2]

Of things remembered as Roland lies dying at Roncevaux, the
Oxford narrator names lands conquered, homeland, family, and
Charlemagne. Verses remembered, perhaps, by the *Entrée* narrator
outlining, more than two hundred years later, his narrative agenda: how
Roland and Charles began the expedition to Spain. He also mentions
conquests in the recovery of the route to Compostella ("E le chemins
l'apostre saint Jaqes **recovrer**" 29; "Molt avoit grant mester ch'ele fust
recovree" 39; emphasis added), the global mission common to both
texts. In addition to mention of narrative form, methods, and meaning,
the *Entrée* narrator immediately recalls for his northern Italian
reader/public why Roland lay dying: the elliptical, elusive "difirnanze"
between him and Ganelon, of which virtually nothing more will be
said. The nearly sixteen thousand verses of the extant *Entrée*, then,
recovers for its medieval and modern public the tales comprising the
substance of memory as it conjoins two major literary components of
the Rolandian macrotext.

With current international interest in *francophonie* and what we in
the late twentieth century term "artificial" languages, the neglected area
of Franco-Italian language and literature may, if somewhat vicariously,
acquire the increased scholarly notice it has long been denied. Although
inclusion of Franco-Italian into these dual areas requires a somewhat
broadened definitional base, a renewed perspective permitting this
medieval phenomenon its merited place in the dissemination of French
language and letters can contribute significantly to our understanding of
related activity centuries thereafter. The first exclusively Franco-Italian
international symposium was held in 1987, a year after the first
francophone summit in Germany, its published communications
introduced by an article entitled "La 'renaissance' des études franco-
italiennes. Rétrospectives et prospectives."[3] A small but active group

of scholars continues to make available new, not infrequently first editions, as well as literary and philological studies of the more than one hundred works in the corpus.

It is no longer acceptable to classify the *Entrée* as a late, i.e., decadent product of the French chanson de geste, a *post quem*, nor on the other hand, to relegate it to the precursory stages of the masterworks of Italian epic literature, e.g., pre-Pulci, pre-Boiardo, pre-Ariosto. Outdated scholarly biases still run deep. William Kibler, who has done a great deal to revive interest in the fourteenth and fifteenth-century chanson de geste, notes even among preeminent French medievalists a decided reserve:

> Ces critiques, nourris du roman réaliste français depuis Flaubert, avec sa vision sceptique de la condition humaine et son souci de réalisme, cherchent tous une unité et une beauté classiques. Et, dans le domaine de la littérature médiévale, ils persistent à comparer ces épopées tardives à la chanson de geste dite 'traditionnelle,' représentée presque toujours en fait par la seule *Chanson de Roland* du manuscrit d'Oxford. [4]

With more informed perspectives on medieval and Renaissance literature available through new critical methodologies and technologies, it is time to eliminate facile, traditional categorizations which have hindered recognition of this remarkable text. The *Entrée* is an important component in our understanding of the developmental processes of literature. Critical to our comprehension of narrativity and intertextuality, it has much to add to our increasing knowledge of letters both French and Italian.

Although the *Robert* dictionary definition of "francophonie" is limited to its oral communicational aspects, major interest focuses also on the literary production of regions generally associated with French colonialism of the seventeenth to twentieth centuries. Pertaining to a francophone language community, *Robert* predicates one in which "le francais est pratiqué en tant que langue maternelle, officielle ou véhiculaire (même si les individus ne parlent pas tous le français)." It is at this latter vehicular or transmissional level of orally-produced and orally-disseminated French texts that one may mention the complex and disparate Franco-Italian linguistic phenomenon.

"Véhiculaire" as a communicational mode, in that Franco-Italian was among the first modes of transmission devised, as early as the twelfth century, to disseminate French texts, not merely chansons de geste, but romance, history, and hagiography in non-French-speaking regions. Franco-Italian is likewise "artificial" in the literal sense, insofar as we have no irrefutable evidence of its use as a non-literary system. Nonetheless, the issue is still unresolved; one can plausibly maintain, as does Geoffrey Robertson-Mellor, that "derrière la littérature il se trouvait toute une civilisation qui pensait—et même parlait—d'une façon qui n'était ni française, ni italienne, ni même vénitienne" ("Langue et littérature franco-italienne" 787). Yet so far as present evidence indicates, orality was restricted to performative situations. Further, delimited by rather specific parameters of time and space, its energies appear to spring from a purely cultural source, the phenomenon of Francophilism in northern Italy, and to flourish for some 200-250 years. With these fundamental elements in mind, we may, in the introductory overview here, begin to refine initial perceptions.

Since the Carolingian conquest of the Lombards and coronation of Charlemagne in Rome (AD 800), legends about him had circulated throughout Italy. With the diffusion of the chansons de geste in "France" came their *mouvance* southward to the Italian peninsula, where the Veneto-Lombard region seems to have provided the most enthusiastic cultural climate for the initially epic material in the Italian peninsula.[5] From the latter twelfth century, powerful lords/princes of the region were apparently welcoming to their opulent courts poets and performers narrating tales about the (usually) heroic deeds of French knights. In the great courts of the region, perhaps as many as 15 to 20, such narratives were enthusiastically received among the aristocracy and rising merchant classes emulating their values and interests.[6] The *Entrée* poet speaks of the "joiose Marche del cortois Trevixan" (10,976) ("the joyous march of the courtly region of Treviso") in which he lived.

Not all reception of French epic tales was so enthusiastic. The disruptive behavior of some performers aroused the censorious wrath of a thirteenth-century Bologna lawyer:

> . . . unde domini ioculatores qui ludunt in
> publico causa mercedis habende et domini orbi,
> qui vadunt in curia comunis Bon. et cantant de
> domino rolando et oliverio si pro precio faciunt
> sunt infames ipso iure quia mercedis causa
> ludibrium sui corporis faciunt.
>
> . . . whence gentlemen jongleurs who
> perform/entertain in public for the purpose of
> obtaining alms, and gentlemen who go about under
> the porticos of the Palazzo del Comune and sing of

lord Roland and Oliver, are punishable by law if they
do so for remuneration, since they obtain alms on
account of the scandalous gestures of their own
bodies.

And in 1289, the elders of the Bologna commune passed a decree
outlawing public gatherings of those listening to the tales:

> Cum igitur sermoni divino multa reverencia
> debeatur, quod placeat conscilio et masse
> populi quod huius modi lussores açardi et
> bescaçarie et incisores caesi . . . nec eciam
> cantatores françiginorum in platea comunis ad
> cantandum nec in circonstançiis platee et
> pallatii comunis omnino morari non possint.

> Therefore since great reverence is owed to the divine
> word, may it please the council and mass of the
> people that [no] gamblers, roustabouts, and cheese
> cutters . . . nor especially the singers of French tales,
> be permitted to loiter in the communal square or
> stairways for the purpose of singing or in other
> circumstances.[7]

In acknowledging an element of "valore snobistico," [8] we should
remember that a number of Italy's medieval authors chose to write in
French as well as in Italian (and Latin, of course): Brunetto Latini;
Marco Polo; Martin da Canale, author of an early *Estoires de Venise*;
Tommaso da Celano, the first biographer of Saint Francis of Assisi,
who claimed that the saint sang praises to the Lord "in lingua
francigena." [9]
   Several of these authors provide some explanation of their choice
of language: Nicholas of Verona's is particularly energetic: ". . . tels, qi
en premier l'aprent / Ja n'i pora mais autrement / Parler ne autre langue
aprendre." (" . . . Such that he who learns it as a first language will no
longer be able to speak or learn another language").[10] Dante, the first
major apologist of the nascent Italian *volgare*, finds the French
language particularly suitable for prose narration of epic or Arthurian
romance:

> Allegat ergo pro se lingua *oïl*, quod propter
> sui   faciliorem   ac   delectabiliorem
> vulgaritatem quicquid redactum sive

> inventum est ad vulgare prosaycum, suum
> est: videlicet Biblia cum Troianorum
> Roman-orumque gestibus compilata et
> Arturi regis ambages pulcerrime et
> quamplures alie ystorie ac doctrine. .... (*De
> vulgari eloquentia* 1.10:7-11).

> The *langue d'oïl* may allege for itself, since it is the
> easiest, most pleasant, and most widely known,
> whatever is written in or translated into vernacular
> prose as most particularly its own, that is, biblical
> compilations with the histories of Troy and Rome,
> and the lovely digressions in the fables of King
> Arthur, and other works of history and knowledge.[11]

Given the considerable linguistic and literary differences between
works in the corpus, a three-part classification has been established
delineating levels of distanciation from French models:

a.   copies of French texts, with slight modifications (*Aliscans,
     Aspremont, Chanson de Roland V⁴*, etc.)
b.   more liberal *remaniements/rimaneggiamenti* (*Codex Marciana
     XIII, Le Roman de Hector et Hercule, Macaire, Anseïs de
     Carthage*)
c.   essentially original texts by Italian authors writing in Franco-
     Italian: (*L'Entrée d'Espagne, Aquilon de Bavière, Pharsale, La
     Passion du Christ*, and *Prise de Pampelune* of Nicolò da
     Verona, *Huon d'Auvergne/Ugo d'Alvernia*).[12]

With many questions of transmission still unresolved, we may
safely conjecture that Carolingian and Arthurian material brought to
Italy by early French jongleurs was transcribed and illuminated in the
Veneto-Lombardy plain, and, further to the south, in Bologna.
Manuscript studies reveal increasing degrees of originality, until, with a
text such as the *Entrée*, scholars concur that one is referring to a text
conceived in Franco-Italian and composed in Italy by an Italian author.
While the work is clearly affiliated with the larger Rolandian macrotext
and to other works, the *Entrée* and works of the third group are
considered autonomous.

While earlier scholarship tended to stress affronts wrought upon the
French linguistic infrastructure, recent studies have more effectively
examined the interaction between French usage in epic texts going back
to the twelfth century, and the more contemporary usage level of the
suprastructure Italianizing element. Günter Holtus, who has done much
of the finest research to date, affirms that Franco-Italian must no longer

be viewed "come tentativo più o meno riuscito di imitazione della lingua francese" combined "in maniera non sistematica." On the contrary, it emerges "come il prodotto di un adattamento intenzionale della lingua e della forma francesi alla situazione dell'Italia settentrionale" and must be seen accordingly:

> . . . allora il complesso dei testi franco-italiani può essere visto come esempio di una mescolanza linguistica che è condizionata da diversi fattori, come la conoscenza del francese da parte dell'autore o del compilatore, la valutazione del pubblico, il prestigio del modello francese, il desiderio di mantenere le caratteristiche formali della tradizione dei generi letterari, ed infine la nascita e i primi sviluppi di una tradizione letteraria autoctona e di lingue scritte regionali.[13]

Considering the pluralistic nature of the corpus from a cultural, literary, and linguistic perspective, it is not surprising that even naming it has been the subject of considerable debate. While "Franco-Italian" was the original term adopted (i.e., G. Paris, A. Thomas, G. Bertoni, A. Viscardi, etc.), there are regional dialectical differentiations which terms such as Franco-Venetan or Franco-Lombard more clearly identify; the term Venetan is used here to designate the whole Veneto region, not merely the area adjacent to the city. A second fundamental problem remains at the descriptive level. Although polyglossia and hybridism are common to the nascent Romance tongues, Franco-Italian must still be considered "un phénomène *sui generis*." Unusually complex and endowed with "une richesse extraordinare," it cannot be reduced to the status of dialect, pidgin, or creole. Further, its "artificiality" is not that of esperanto, for example, principally because Franco-Italian was crafted purposefully on the model of a living language, while esperanto is a systematic, yet entirely synthetic system. "Le franco-italien a un status incomparable."[14]

The present study is to date the most extensive literary examination of the *Entrée d'Espagne* (see Appendix for detailed summary of the plot). The late Alberto Limentani considered the text a *summa:*

> Il Padovano ha forzato al massimo il vecchio strumento formale della *chanson de geste* verso una strutturazione di poema: ne è risultato un 'poema sacro' con forma, spirito e scopi suoi propri, ben

> distinto in questo dagli antecedenti come dai posteriori
> sviluppi della materia carolingia. *L'Entrée* ha diritto a
> un suo posto di rilievo non solo nella storia culturale,
> ma al livello degli apprezzamenti qualitativi senza i
> quali questa storia non può che risultare deformata.
> Quella consistenza di poema stacca *L'Entrée* dalle
> *chansons* post-rolandiane, e le consente di accostarsi
> al gruppo delle opere poetiche tardo-medievali a
> carattere di *summa*, quali inanzitutto il *Roman de la
> rose* e la *Commedia* . . . .[15]

As I hope to demonstrate, the *Entrée* is also characteristic of major
works of late medieval literature in the Bakhtinian sense that:

> there lies at their heart an acute feeling for the epoch's
> contradictions, long overripe; this is, in essence, a
> feeling for the end of an epoch. From this springs
> that striving toward as full as possible an exposition
> of all the contradictory multiplicity of the epoch.[16]

Of primary interest to me is also the text's constant challenge to its
reader/public, medieval or modern, to question ideas and canons
previously taken for granted, whether as correct or incorrect. The *Entrée*
offers to its public a complex dialogical arena where a host of issues—
literary, political, hermeneutic, religious—enter into communication,
and frequently into confrontation, with one another.

A brief overview here may help to underline the importance of
contextuality to the *Entrée*. Although information concerning date of
composition remains conjectural, scholars now generally concur on the
first half of the fourteenth century, with Limentani positing a date in
the 1330's.[17] The proud "je sui patavian" of an otherwise elusive author
provides a city, but more importantly, a broad region of northern Italy;
association with the Veneto conjoins with a number of allusions to
Lombardy, to help delineate an extensive territory in which the text was
composed and circulated.

The founding of Padua's Studium in 1222 (to become Europe's
fourth oldest university) initiated an important "rinnovamento culturale"
in both the secular and clerical populations. Originally comprised of
scholars migrating from Bologna, the Studium rapidly became an
intellectual center of the study of law and the Trivium. Paduan civic
humanism, which we now recognize as the Prehumanist movement
leading directly to the Florentine Renaissance, originated with a group
of young scholars intent on exploring various aspects of Graeco-Roman

Antiquity. Lively epistles, translations, recovery of long-lost manuscripts in churches and monasteries of the region, bear witness to inexhaustible intellectual energies. Their archeological research was rewarded in 1274 when Lovato Lovati announced the rediscovery of the ruins of ancient Patavium, founded, as the *Aeneid* claimed, by Antenor after the fall of Troy:

> hic tamen ille urbem Patavi sedesque locavit
> Teucrorum et genti nomen dedit armaque fixit
> Troia, nunc placida compostus pace quiescit
> (I: 247-49).

> Yet here he set Padua's town, a home for his Teucrians, gave a name to the race, and hung up the arms of Troy; now, settled in tranquil peace, he is at rest.

A monumental tomb of Antenor was erected a decade later to remind Paduans of their illustrious origins. As Michelangelo would do centuries later in Rome, Lovati and his Studium recuperated, largely in the study of primary *auctores* of Antiquity, the *Romanitas* of the city's past, key to its illustrious pre-Renaissance future.

Lovati, hailed by Petrarch as the finest of his generation of scholars, was a strong apologist for classical Latin, wrote a *Tristan* in classical hexameter, and argued that epic, for its nobility of subject and style, should only be written in Latin.

Originally the pupil of Lovati, Albertino Mussato is perhaps the Studium's most prominent member, called the finest Latinist of his century. Humanist and notary, reflecting the legalistic training common to the Paduan Prehumanists, Mussato has also been named "the first republican philosopher-statesman since Cicero" and was crowned the city's poet and historian with the traditional laurel wreath in 1315. His *Historia Augusta* chronicles regional events of the *Entrée* epoch; his *Eccerinis* (also written *Ecerinide*), tracing the infamous career of the regional tyrant Ezzelino da Romano and stressing the lessons to be learned from a twenty-year reign of terror, earned Mussato the encomium "father of Renaissance tragedy."[18]

Many others contributed to an exceptionally fertile cultural/intellectual climate which was almost certainly known to the exiled Dante, residing in nearby Verona under the patronage of Can Grande della Scala. There is a strong case to be made, as Limentani has demonstrated, of the *Entrée* poet's knowledge of Dante's *Commedia*; I have likewise found several areas of communication between the two texts, as well as to the *De vulgari eloquentia*.

Regional political history of the *Entrée* period, broadly delineated here as mid-thirteenth to mid-fourteenth centuries, likewise requires brief introductory remarks in terms of the several ideologies inscribed within the text and examined in more detail in chapter 3. During the period in question, Padua (like other cities in the region) witnessed a particularly turbulent series of experiences in civic governance: from commune to tyranny; restoration of the commune; the Da Carrara *signoria*; then, takeover by the less benevolent *signoria* of Can Grande della Scala. Thereafter the city fell to Venetian forces in 1405, reducing it to the provincial periphery of *La Serenissima*.

The Paduan commune, among the most flourishing of the region, represented what historians call the most innovative experiment in civic governance of the Middle Ages. Although not a democratic system in twentieth-century terms, the commune enunciated an ideology based on a broad system of citizen representation summarized in the phrase "ubi multa consilia, ibi salus." Communes were established throughout the Veneto-Lombard area in the twelfth-thirteenth centuries; the case of Padua is both connected to global new mentalities behind the experiment and unique in itself. Traditional modes of civic governance and their representative institutions, whether imperial, Church, or feudal, were challenged and exposed to change, in some instances successfully negotiated, but more often vigorously resisted. Pervasive and irresolvable instability marked the "contradictory multiplicity" of time and place.[19]

Of an undoubtedly sizeable quantity of *Entrée* manuscripts existing in the fourteenth century, the *unicum* remaining today is nonetheless the most elegant and elaborately illuminated of all those (French, Italian, and Franco-Italian) representing Rolandian material. Appearing in a group of six entries of the vast private library holdings of Francesco Gonzaga of Mantua at his death in 1407, it appears Latinized as item 53, along with its sequel text *La Prise de Pampelune* (item 58):

> 53. LIBER INTROITUS YSPANIE. Incipit: En onor et em bien et in gran remembra[n]ce. Et finit: chasa vie disponue. Continet cart[as] 308.
> 54. LIBER INTROITUS YSPANIE. Incipit: Molt fu luoco illuc datons li milon oir. Et finit: ne sognent cum linfrange. Continet cart[as] 284.
> 55. LIBER INTROITUS YSPANIE. Incipit: Grant fu la prese entor le duc d'Anglent. Et finit: tu nola respondus. Continet cart[as] 154.

56. LIBER INTROITUS YSPANIE SECUNDUM
MINOCHIUM. Incipit: En onor en bien in gran
reverenza. Et finit: non trovera falanza. Continet
cart[as] 246.
57. LIBER INTROITUS YSPANIE. Ut supra incipit.
Et finit: en virum tuti franzosis. Continet cart[as]
116.
58. LIBER SECONDUS YSTORIARUM ISPANIE.
Incipit: Con fu la sbare auerte le valaynt roy lombard.
Et finit: e de strinte e man misse. Continet cart[as]
101.

A summary of interpretations of the other entries in the 1407 Gonzaga
inventory is provided in the notes.[20]
    Recent research by André de Mandach illuminates additional aspects
of the rather lively history of the manuscripts, intending to explain for
whom the *Entrée* was composed, where, and how it came into the
possession of Mantua's Gonzagas. Among the extensive library
holdings of Padua's Da Carrara dynasty, he has found an item catalogued
as *"Liber Introitus" Magnifici domini*. According to de Mandach, the
inventory in question was hastily drawn up under the direction of
Francesco il Novello da Carrara in 1404 while the city was under attack
by Venice, then confided to the care of a city administrator. When Padua
fell in 1405, the Da Carraras were taken prisoner, their magnificent
manuscripts among the most prized of Venetian booty. To explain the
manuscript's passage from Padua to Mantua, de Mandach suggests that:

> le chef des troupes vénitiennes à l'assaut de Padoue est
> nul autre que Francesco Gonzaga en personne. C'est
> lui qui investit Padoue et le château des Carrara en
> novembre 1405. C'est lui qui pénètre dans ce palais
> où figure le superbe manuscrit de l'*Entrée* . . . rien
> n'est plus facile donc, lors du pillage, de faire main
> basse non seulement sur l'*Entrée* fr. XXI, mais aussi
> sur d'autres exemplaires de cet ouvrage, en un ou deux
> volumes.[21]

    In addition to ms. 53, now known as Codice francese XXI in
Venice's Biblioteca Marciana, two manuscript fragments have been
discovered since the publication of Antoine Thomas' *editio princips* in
1913. The first, found in 1925 in the library of the Château de
Châtillon (Val d'Aosta), derives from another manuscript of the *Entrée*.
Estimated at over ten thousand verses in its entirety, it appears to have

begun at the point when the Paduan interrupts the narrative at 10,939
for the second prologue. The remaining segments seem to fall within
the major *lacuna* between folios 269-270 and within the Hermit
episode. [22]

In 1960, another set of fragments was published by Angelo
Monteverdi. Found in Reggio Emilia, the two folios date from the
fourteenth century; the first begins with a verse corresponding to
12,309 of the extant Marciana fr. XXI, while the second appears to be
part of the major *lacuna*, although not from the same portion of the text
as the other fragment.[23] It is to be hoped that additional manuscripts
may come to light.

The sole, elliptical indication of authorial identification, "Mon
nom vos non dirai, mai sui Patavian" (10,974) has aroused the curiosity
of many scholars since the mid-nineteenth century. Léon Gautier first
combined the Paduan with the "Nicolais" of the 131-verse
"continuation" appended to ms. fr. XXI=257 ("Ci tourne Nicolais a
rimer la complue / De l'Entree de Spagne, qe tant est stee escondue"/ to
hypothesize a Nicholas of Padua; the theory was adopted by Gaston
Paris, Paul Meyer, and others. Thomas subsequently proposed two
authors: one an anonymous "Patavian," the other a "Nicolais," who
continued the unfinished work and, as Nicolò di Verona, authored the
Entrée's (Franco-Italian) sequel *La Prise de Pampelune*, plus a *Pharsale*,
and *Passion du Christ*. [24]

An impressive authorial profile emerges from the text, noted
universally by *Entrée* scholars. Thomas affirmed evidence of formal
training in the classics, a *"bagage intellectuel"* considerably superior to
most secular French poets of the time: "c'est un clerc assurément, et à
qui il ne déplaît pas de faire parade de son latin." Comfortable
familiarity with a number of Latin authors including Horace, Seneca,
Ovid, and Virgil is clear, as well as an unusual knowledge of warfare
(the Nobles episode and "war machine" to assail Pamplona), astronomy,
and astrology (*Entrée* 1: xliii-lxi; Limentani, "Astronomia, astrologia, e
arti magiche nell'*Entrée d'Espagne*"). Limentani adds that emphasis on
events, texts, and authors of Antiquity conveys the impression "che
l'esemplarismo del Padovano si discosti da quello del romanzo francese e
in qualche modo tenda al tipo più erudito che i padri dell'umanesimo,
alla metà del Trecento, portavano a così alto grado." Sense of "una
missione morale-letteraria può far pensare al più vicino poeta della
Commedia (Limentani, "Epica" 342-52). Profound theological
knowledge is consistently in evidence.

The Paduan is well-read in medieval French epic and romance,
despite his disdainful claim of the superiority of his text over "les flabes
d'Artu" (367). His knowledge of the *Chanson de Roland* may have come

from a Franco-Italian version similar to V^4 and V^7 (Limentani, "Epica" 348), but it seems plausible that he knew original French versions of the *Roland*, as well as *Girard de Vienne*, *Renaud de Montauban*, *Beuve d'Aigremont*, and the *Chanson d'Aspremont*. The *Roman d'Alexandre* becomes central to the *Entrée*'s ideological position on secular leadership (see ch. 4, locus i: Typologies Re-viewed). His text shows familiarity with the Tristan legend and Arthurian Round Table literature, including Grail quest texts.[25]

Three professional affiliations may be provisionally hazarded: first, that the Paduan was a well-educated professional working as author, teacher, and/or secretary to regional princes and magnates; secondly, a notary or legal professional; thirdly, a Churchman. In each case we should envisage close connections to the regional courts. For Limentani, a court setting such as an:

> aula carrarese o gonzaghesca o viscontea fu certo la sede dell'audizione o lettura . . . se non da subito, certo presto, come attestano appunto i cataloghi gonzagheschi del 1407. Questa letteratura può essere classificata come 'epica delle Signorie padane': ma il ristretto pubblico di queste aule, cosa poteva cogliere delle relationi inter-testuali che con tanta incertezza abbiamo cercato di individuare qui addietro? ("Presenza di Virgilio" 310-11).

For Henning Krauss, also taking consideration of the *Entrée's* extraordinary complexity, it becomes necessary to distinguish between the earlier public(s) of works such as the *Chanson de Roland*, on which the text made relatively few intellectual demands, and the *Entrée* public(s), of which a great deal more receptor competence is required. It is within the rising protocapitalist bourgeoisie, as enthusiastic by the early Trecento for acquisitions of an intellectual/cultural nature as for those merely material, and mingling closely with the old nobility, that Krauss situates the *Entrée*'s first narratees (*Epica feudale* 226-28).

According to the theory of E. Carrara, the Paduan was "un di quegli 'uomini di corte' tra il pedagogo e il segretario dei Signori, de' quali conosciamo più d'un esempio; e rappresenta quella classe di mezza cultura, né laici né umanisti, che al pari di quella dei 'notai' formò la 'massa di manovra' nella conquista della nuova civiltà italiana" (48).

Two recent studies by André de Mandach offer new hypotheses. According to his "*L'Entrée d'Espagne*: six auteurs en quête d'un personnage," those contributing narrative material include Turpin, the two "bons clers" Jean le Gras and Gautier d'Aragon of Prologue II (see ch. 2), Nicholas of Verona, and the unknown "Minocchio" mentioned in the Gonzaga inventory; the primary author and architect of the extant Ms. fr. XXI is identified as the prominent Paduan judge Giovanni di Nono. A second publication, "Sur les traces de la cheville ouvrière de l'*Entrée d'Espagne*: Giovanni di Nono," lists three Latin works on the history of his native Padua written by the latter in the early fourteenth century. Adding that the di Nono family considered itself descended from Roland, de Mandach cites in their genealogy individuals named "Milon," "Ol[i]vradum," and a "Rolandus ioculatoris." Taking into consideration scribal errors and inconsistencies, the Swiss scholar offers a possible corrected reading of line 10,974, rendered by Thomas as "Mon nom vos non dirai, mai sui Patavian," with the only variant noted by Thomas as "fui." If one reads instead "Mon nom jo no (bar over n) dirai. . . ," the first segment of the verse becomes an abbreviated rendering of Franco-Italian "Mon nom Jo. de Non dirai," i.e., "I will tell you my name, Giovanni di Nono/Jean de Non" (48-64).

De Mandach's argument is meticulously documented and compelling. Virtually all Padua's Prehumanist writers were notaries or lawyers: "the notaries were the most numerous representatives of the new, urban, literate laity." Included in the 1287 list of urban guilds, notaries exercised considerable political and cultural influence, seeing themselves as curators of currently-reviving Roman law and letters. Hélène Nolthenius finds notaries frequently in the company of the established nobility, for whom they performed legal services, and by whom they may have been commissioned to compose literary works. Part of the upwardly-mobile population developing in the communes, the best-known of Padua's notaries/authors (Lovati, Mussato, Rolando da Piazzola, Gambone d'Andrea, and others) were self-made men. [26]

But desire for anonymity may stem from a cleric directly associated, though we cannot say in what function, with the Church. Ample textual evidence supports this view, from the *Entrée*'s opening dedication, to the doctrinal elements in the Ferragu combat and the quasi-mystical tonality of the Hermit episode.

The opening chapter, "Roland as *baron révolté*?" seeks to establish the microstructure of the *Entrée*'s two major segments: I. The Expedition to Spain; IIA. Roland in the Near East; IIB. The Hermit episode. A series of nine increasingly serious confrontations between Roland and Charlemagne concerning Roland's aspiration for some measure of autonomy, countered by the emperor's desire to retain total authority, is identified as the text's essential organizational strategy. A pattern emerges, wherein Roland appears to prevail in conflicts one through five, Charles in seven through ten. Midway in the conflict structure occurs a critical, if brief, incident where Charles permits Roland to keep and to use freely at his own discretion a magnificent horse offered to Roland as a gesture of gratitude and respect by the young Saracen prince Isoré, whom Roland had taken prisoner in the battle for Nájera. If what I call the "plateau phase" seems in an initial reading to suggest a voluntary relaxation of imperial authoritarianism, subsequent confrontations require re-examination of the complex heteroglossia of Charles's discourse in 6,662-71. Increasingly irresolvable differences culminate in the violent rupture of the Roland-Charles relationship following Roland's unauthorized departure for the city of Nobles, which he reconquers in Charles's and his own name for Church and Empire. When Charles accuses Roland of treason for leaving the field at Pamplona without permission and subsequently strikes him with a mailed glove, an infuriated and vindictive Roland abandons the expedition. An intertextual link is thus established between the *Entrée* and *baron révolté* cycle, several of whose texts are clearly familiar to the Paduan.

It becomes evident that a reader of the *Entrée* cannot presume a symbiotic Charles-Roland relationship, nor that either individual is wholly right or wholly wrong. Among issues raised are those of Roland's pride and *démesure*, particularly in the Pamplona Reinforcement episode with its parallels and divergencies from the *scènes du cor* in the *Chanson de Roland*.

Thus while part I generally appears to justify the feudal acts of a wronged vassal, and persuasive arguments can be made in defense of either man, the more important truth is the threat posed to the global mission by the inability of its two major agents to resolve their differences. The blow, which radically alters the text and Rolandian canon, does violence to the expectations of both narrative and authorial publics. It shatters what both assumed to know about the indissolubility of the Charles-Roland bond.

In IIA, Roland is in the Near East; forging new, curiously ambiguous identities, he regenerates his heroic status in *consilium* and *auxilium* for the sultan of Persia. Comparisons are made between the respectively negative/positive interactions with Charles and Daïre in an effort to understand why one relationship fails, while the other proves viable and produces important military victories.

Given the length (over two thousand verses), site, and centrality of the Nobles episode, it is unlikely that the Paduan introduced it simply as an amplification of two passing mentions in the *Chanson de Roland*. Chapter 2 opens with an exploration of the chronological and geographical *mouvance* of the Nobles episode in medieval texts from Norway to northern Italy over a period of two hundred years. In all

instances, Nobles is a site—the only one in the geographical repertoire
of the chansons de geste—which is consistently linked to serious
conflict between Charles and Roland concerning methods of pursuing
the reconquest of Spain. In my opinion, it was precisely the
iconoclastic nature of the tale which determined its inclusion and
centrality to the *Entrée* by an author whose public could be expected to
relate to broader extra-narrative issues of order and authority.

Chapter 3, "The Dialectic of Ideologies," examines the evolution of
selected theories of social order in relation to the complex realities of
thirteenth- and early fourteenth-century northern Italy. The primary
trifunctional Model I is shown to be incompatible with the era's new
methods of governance. Some acknowledgement of changing notions of
social order appears in Alain de Lille and Humbert of Romans; a more
reality-oriented perspective is examined in the theories of Thomas
Aquinas, while the case for radical secularism is made by the author's
compatriot Marsilius of Padua.

The aim of chapter 4, "Discourse and Ideologies," based on the
nearly exclusively theoretical perspective of ch. 3, is to explore the
Entrée as a dialogical arena where multiple languages and ideologies are
deployed. Franco-Italian polyglossia immediately signals the
intersection of dual language and culture systems and serves to alter our
expectations of content and meaning. In its French epico-feudal
infrastructure, the *Entrée* meets that part of reader/public expectation
anticipating a prologue to the *Chanson de Roland*. The canonic literary
and political discourse of the chanson de geste seeks to posit itself as
the correct, authoritative way of thinking and speaking the world.
However, that authority is challenged by other discourse systems
entered into the arena: literarily, those of romance and hagiography;
politically, those concerning organization of the human community.
The *Entrée* initially adopts an established, yet foreign and ideologically
predetermined discourse system; repeatedly tested in part I, it fails. In
IIA, a somewhat modified Roland-Daïre relationship reverses that
failure. The text becomes a forum, raising, exposing, disputing issues
pertinent to its particular public, among whom are the "retors de tere"
and "om soveran" addressed in Prologue II. A series of twelve textual
loci more closely probe literary and political dialogism in the following
sectors: the ethics of human *labor*; Roland as Christian *orator*; the
Paduan as *orator* of his own textual doctrine; notions of hierarchy;
ethical considerations of warfare; compromise; uses of authority;
orgueil reconsidered; typologies re-viewed; autonomy enacted; women,
marriage, status; the new *bellator*.

Chapter 5, "Signs of *Sententia*," examines the polysemous motifs
of forest and voyage in *Entrée* II to demonstrate the text's transcendance

of its epic and romance axes. *Sententia* as *profundior intelligentia* announced in Prologue I is enacted in the corrective quest of both hero and text; both Roland and the text enter those worlds and experience directly their imperfect, i.e., incomplete and flawed nature. When Roland departs the Near East, he has recovered his own heroic identity and introduced or restored Christianity to much of the region. When urged to remain and pursue the conquest of the Tower of Babel, Roland recognizes that his unresolved conflict with the Emperor must claim priority. Text and character must re-examine their trajectory thus far and determine their future direction.

Judged by "la loy Deu," those acts in Part I which set Roland against a superior representing *lex aeterna* are violations of an authority not open to compromise. Hero, poet, and public must acknowledge the inadequacy of any societal model based solely on *lex humana*. We now see Roland's vindictive wrath after the blow as "parole vaine," the erroneous language of pride "qi li fu sempres un poi germaine" ("which was always a little germane in him"), and his authority-challenging actions as what the text terms "mespreison," a mis-taking of his proper function. As Roland himself acknowledges, he lost the knowledge of all good, particularly the sometimes difficult truth that it is Charles's sacralized function to represent the *bonum comune* and to maintain order within the human community. In the Malquidant and Dionés episodes, Roland fulfills his own expressed desire that his voyage serve to teach him to honor a higher law. When he leaves the Mideast, Roland has acquired the "sens et nature atenpree" ("sense/wisdom and temperate nature") necessary to fulfill the significance of his own name, explained to him as derived from "*rotholandus*," "wheel of knowledge and wisdom." He thus reappropriates the name of which he is now worthy, abandoning the pseudo-identities invented after his departure from Spain.

When the converted Persians urge Roland to remain with them and lead their attack on the Tower of Babel, an earlier query about the youth, "qe senefie?" ("what does he mean?") is resolved. In the course of his several years' odyssey, Roland has corrected his own "parole vaine" and is now sufficiently competent in the use of language to correct the confusion of human communication which is the source of global disorder. Further, he is now prepared to comprehend the Word as it is presented in the hermit's narrative of his own existential trajectory. A *mise en abyme* of Roland's experience, the récit stresses the dangers of pride and rejection of hierarchism. Culminating in the sacralization of Roland as "le ome beneoit," the episode closes with the final stage of Roland's journey toward reconciliation with Charles. Returning to Pamplona, he can now affirm in a deeper sense that he knows where he is (" 'Je sai bien ou je sui venus et arivés' "). He now possesses a *profundior intelligentia* of his own experience.

NOTES

1. *The Song of Roland: An Analytical Edition*, ed. and trans. Gerard J. Brault, 2 vols. (University Park and London: Pennsylvania State UP, 1978) 2: 146-147. All citations will be from this edition unless otherwise noted.

2. *L'Entrée d'Espagne, chanson de geste franco-italienne publiée d'après le manuscrit unique de Venise*, ed. Antoine Thomas, SATF, 2 vols. (Paris: Firmin-Didot, 1913) 1: 1, 9-18. All cited material is from this edition. All translations from the *Entrée* are mine.

3. Günter Holtus, Henning Krauss, Peter Wunderli, eds., *Testi, cotesti e contesti del franco-italiano, Atti del primo simposio franco-italiano* (Bad Homburg, 13-16 aprile 1987 (Tübingen: Niemeyer, 1989) 3-19.

4. "Relectures de l'épopée," *Au Carrefour des routes d'Europe: la chanson de geste, Xe Congrès international de la Société Rencesvals pour l'étude des épopées romanes, Strasbourg 1985*, Senefiance 20, 2 vols. (Aix-en-Provence: Publications du CUER MA, 1987) 1: 105.

5. Although the chanson de geste seems to have provided the earliest models for Franco-Italian adaptations, Arthurian romance texts were also in circulation to a lesser degree, the earliest known Franco-Italian work being Rustician of Pisa's *Meliadus*. Drawn largely from French *Tristan* and *Palamède* parent texts, it recounts adventures of knights from the generation of Uther Pendragon to Arthur and the Round Table. Edmund G. Gardner, *The Arthurian Legend in Italian Literature* (London: Dent, 1930) 45. However, as Gardner mentions and the *Entrée*'s somewhat disdainful disclaimer of similarities to the "flabes d'Artu" reinforces, acceptance of the "matter of Britain" was less enthusiastic than for the chanson de geste. According to Holtus, although the first evidence of literary propagation dates to the late twelfth century, dissemination was slow, not reaching its culmination until over a century later. "La 'matière de Bretagne' en Italie: quelques réflexions sur la transposition du vocabulaire et des structures sociales," *Umgangssprache der Iberomania: Festschrift für Heinz Kröll* (Tübingen: Narr, 1984) 325-42.

6. For discussion of northern Italian socio-political and cultural conditions relative to receptivity of French epic material, see Henning Krauss, *Epica feudale e pubblico borghese: per la storia poetica di Carlomagno in Italia*, ed. and trans. Andrea Fassò, Ydioma Tripharium 6 (Padua: Liviana, 1980) 11-24.

7. See N. Tamassia, *Odofredo, studio storico giuridico, Atti e memorie della R. Deputazione di storia patriotica per le provincie*

di Romagna, 3rd ser. (Bologna, 1894) 176. The second quotation appears in Ezio Levi, *I cantari leggendari del popolo italiano nel secolo XIV e XV, GSLI* supp. 16 (1914): 6. See also Meyer, "De l'Expansion de la langue française en Italie pendant le moyen âge," *Atti del Congresso internazionale di scienze storiche* 4 (Rome: n.p., 1904) 69.

8. Ruggero M. Ruggieri, "Temi e aspetti della letteratura francoveneta," *Atti del Convegno di studi 'Dante e la cultura veneta': Venezia, Padova, Verona: 30 marzo-5 aprile 1966* (Florence: Olschki, 1966) 153.

9. Cited in Giuseppe Della Giovanna, "S. Francesco d'Assisi, giullare," *GSLI* 25 (1895): 2. For reservations concerning the claim, see Meyer, "Expansion," 68.

10. Cited in Giulio Bertoni, *Storia letteraria d'Italia: Il Duecento* (Milan: F. Vallardi, 1911) 1: 50.

11. *De vulgari eloquentia, Dante's Book of Exile*, trans. and ed. Marianne Shapiro, Regents Studies in Medieval Culture, U of Nebraska P (Lincoln, 1990) 57.

12. Antonio Viscardi, *Letteratura franco-italiana*, Istituto di Filologia Romanza dell'Università di Roma, Testi e manuali a cura di Giulio Bertoni 21 (Modena: Società Tipografica Modenese, 1941) 50. The second group includes the Laurentian Library (Florence) and Udine manuscripts *Bovo d'Antona/ Beuve d'Hanstone*. See also Peter Wunderli, Günter Holtus, "La 'renaissance' des études franco-italiennes," *Testi, cotesti* 9-10:

> . . . . En partie, ces trois phases se recoupent, mais ceci ne change rien au fait qu'elles jalonnent en principe les étapes d'une succession chronologique. Si l'on fait abstraction de quelques textes tardifs (et par là atypiques) tels le *Huon d'Auvergne*, l'évolution aboutit à l'*Aquilon de Bavière* qui . . . tenait aux *cantari* in *ottava rima* et aux versions toscanes en prose. . . .

> See also Geoffrey Robertson-Mellor, "Langue et littérature franco-italiennes: état des études et problèmes," *Essor et fortune de la chanson de geste dans l'Europe et l'Orient latin, Actes du IXe Congrès international de la Société Rencesvals pour l'étude des épopées romanes, 29 août-4 septembre 1982*, 2 vols. (Modena: Mucchi, 1984) 2: 786-88.

For a complete international listing of *chansons de gestes* and related texts, see John Robin Allen, "Index de la chanson de geste romane et textes apparentés du moyen âge: brouillon du 17 août

1984 " (copyright 1984 by J.R. Allen, Saint John's College, University of Manitoba) and André Moisan, *Répertoire des noms propres de personnes et de lieux cités dans les chansons de gestes françaises et les œuvres étrangères dérivées*, Publications romanes et françaises 73, 5 vols. (Geneva: Droz, 1986).

13. G. Holtus, "Etimologia e lessico franco-italiano," *Etimologia e lessico dialettale, Atti del XII Convegno per gli Studi Dialettali Italiani* (Macerata, 10-13 aprile 1979) (Pisa: Pacini, 1981) 153-63.

14. Wunderli, Holtus, " 'Renaissance' des études franco-italiennes" 4-8. L. Renzi, noting the *Entrée*'s prevalence of Lombard elements, suggested the term "francese di Lombardia" in "Per la lingua dell'*Entrée d'Espagne*," *CN* 30 (1970): 59-87; Joseph Palermo introduced the term "italo-français" in "La Langue franco-italienne du *Roman d'Hector et Hercule*," *Actes du Xe Congrès international de linguistique et philologie romane, Strasbourg 1962*, 2 vols. (Paris: 1965) 2: 687-95. Given the restrictive aspects of such terminology, necessarily expanded to include French from the Piedmont, Ligurian, and Tuscan regions, it is perhaps best to retain the traditional term, with identification *in situ* of specific regional components.

15. Alberto Limentani, "L'epica in 'lengue de France': L' 'Entrée d'Espagne' e Niccolò da Verona,"*SCV*, 6 vols. *Il Trecento*, (Vicenza: Neri Pozza, 1976) 2: 360.

16. M. M. Bakhtin, *The Dialogic Imagination: Four Essays*, trans. Caryl Emerson and Michael Holquist, ed. Michael Holquist (Austin: U of Texas P, 1981) 156 and *ad passim* 151-67; and his chapter "Epic and Novel: Toward a Methodology for the Study of the Novel," 3-40.

17. Scholars have traditionally assigned the *Entrée* to the period from the last quarter of the thirteenth century to the first half of the fourteenth. More recent scholarship moves the *Entrée* closer to the end of the period, but before 1343: Limentani in the 1330's; André de Mandach as well, with the author Giovanni de Nono leaving his 20,000-verse work to Nicolò da Verona for completion after 1337. Alberto Limentani, "L'epica in 'lengue de France,' " 2: 342-43; Limentani and M. Infurna, eds., *L'epica*, Strumenti di filologia romanza 3 (Bologna: Mulino, 1986) 40-43. De Mandach, "*L'Entrée d'Espagne*: six auteurs en quête d'un personnage," *Studi Medievali* 3rd ser. 30, 1 (1989): 207-08. For further information see bibliography.

18. See John Kenneth Hyde, *Padua in the Age of Dante* (Manchester: Manchester UP, 1966) 295ff. See also F. Novati, "Poeti veneti del trecento," *Archivo storico per Trieste, Istria e Trentino* (1881):

216. Essential also are two contributions to *Storia della cultura veneta: Il Trecento*: Girolamo Arnaldi, "Il primo secolo dello studio di Padova,"1-18; Guido Billanovich, "Il Preumanesimo padovano," 19-110. Other articles in this volume are also useful: Rino Avesani, "Il Preumanesimo veronese," 111-41; Luciano Gargan, "Il Preumanesimo a Vicenza, Treviso e Venezia," 142-70; Franco Alessio, "Filosofia e scienza. Pietro da Abano," 171-206; Girolamo Arnaldi and Lidia Capo, "I cronisti di Venezia e della Marca trevigiana," 272-337; Lino Lazzarini, "La cultura delle signorie venete e i poeti di corte," 477-516.

19. A good overview, with attention to specific communes in the Veneto-Lombard region, is provided in Daniel Waley, *The Italian City-Republics*, 3rd ed. (London and New York: Longman, 1988) especially ch. 3, "Government," 33-68. The prescriptive "ubi multa consilia, ibi salus" is cited from the thirteenth-century *Oculus pastoralis*, the earliest extant manual pertaining to the flourishing genre of the *ars dictaminis*, providing model speeches, in this case, for orators in the communes. In Lodovico Muratori, *Antiquitates*, 6 vols. (Milan: 1751; Bologna: A. Forni, 1965), diss. 46. See ch. 3 for further references to the *Oculus pastoralis*.

20. Initial publication of the Gonzaga inventory was by Willelmo Braghirolli, "Inventaire des manuscrits en langue française possédés par Francesco Gonzaga I, Capitaine de Mantoue, mort en 1407," *Romania* 9 (1880): 504. Regarding interpretation, see Thomas, *Entrée*, 1: xxix-xxx and *Nouvelles recherches sur l'Entrée de Spagne, chanson de geste franco-italienne*, Bibliothèque des Ecoles françaises d'Athènes et de Rome 25 (Paris, 1882) 1-65. Two variations in the otherwise similar titles should be noted. Number 56 adds "secundum Minochium," while 58 mentions a *"liber secondus."* Entry 53, corresponding to Marciana XXI, is the only surviving manuscript of the *Entrée*, and is itself incomplete (see Appendix). The final 58 represents the extant *unicum* manuscript of *La Prise de Pampelune*, which continues the *Entrée*'s narration of the lengthy battle for that city and 11 others on the Compostella route. Its initial 131 verses have been added to ms. 53. In efforts to order the series, Thomas considered that the Gonzaga family had originally commissioned two copies of the *Entrée* at the time of its composition (53 and 57); subsequently, at the completion of *La Prise de Pampelune*, they commissioned a complete copy of both works, comprising the remaining four entries. At the time of the 1407 inventory, then, there were three copies of the *Entrée* in the Gonzaga library in Mantua.

There are further elements to consider. The *incipit* of 53 and 56, both of which appear to represent the beginning of the extant *Entrée*, are not the same: "remembra[n]ce" in 53 becomes "reverenza" in 56, indicating a greater degree of Italianization. According to Dionisotti, these indicate different authors and texts; Ruggieri, on the other hand, considered that the "Minochium" of 56 was either the author or "rifacitore" of 54, 55, and 56, which together contained not only the *Entrée* and *Pampelune*, but a somewhat modified version of the *Chanson de Roland*. Ruggieri added that a missing volume filling in the *lacuna* between the 131 verses added to *Entrée* 53 and the opening of the *Pampelune* 58 belonged to the Gonzaga collection before the 1407 inventory.

In 1982, René Specht proposed that the scribal change at *Entrée* 15,805 does not mark the close of the Paduan's text, which continues through 124 of the 131-verse "suite" ending with elaboration of the reunion scene between Charles and Roland. Nicholas of Verona then begins his "continuation" of the *Entrée* known as *La Prise de Pampelune*. Specht also hypothesizes a now-missing volume of the *Pampelune* between verse 131 and the *incipit* of Marciana V, which he entitles *Liber primus istoriarum Ispanie*, companion to the *Liber Secundus* of that title entered in the 1407 inventory. Reconstruction of the lost volume can be attempted via consultation of *La Spagna*, a fourteenth-century Tuscan work, and *Li fatti de Spagna*. Its narrative material would largely be concerned with events surrounding the usurpation of Charles's throne and queen by his appointed vicar, and the exploits of Guron de Bretagne. Since the extant *Pampelune* manuscript is incomplete, it becomes impossible to supply those missing portions which would connect it to the *Roland*, of which both *Entrée* and *Pampelune* form a vast prologue.

For additional discussion, see André de Mandach, "Le Destinataire de *L'Entrée d'Espagne* de Venise (Marciana fr. XXI): Francesco il Vecchio da Carrara?", *Atti dell'Istituto Veneto. Classe di Scienze Morali, Lettere ed Arti* 148 (1989-90): "en préparation." Carlo Dionisotti, "*Entrée d'Espagne, Spagna, Rotta di Roncisvalle*," *Studi in onore di Angelo Monteverdi*, 2 vols. (Modena: Mucchi, 1959) 1: 209-13; Ruggero M. Ruggieri, "Dall'*Entrée d'Espagne* e dai *Fatti di Spagna* alla 'materia di Spagna' dell'inventario gonzaghesco," *CN* 21 (1961): 186-88; René Specht, *Recherches sur Nicolas de Vérone. Contribution à l'étude de la littérature franco-italienne du quatorzième siècle*, Publications Universitaires Européennes, Series 13, Langue et littérature française 78 (Berne, Francfort: Peter Lang, 1982) 47-87.

21. "Le Destinataire de *L'Entrée d'Espagne* ," 9-10, in press .

22. Paul Aebischer, "Ce qui reste d'un manuscrit perdu de *L'Entrée d'Espagne*," *Archivum Romanicum* 12 (1928): 263.

23. The fragment has been studied by René Specht, "Cavalleria francese alla corte di Persia: L'episodio dell'*Entrée d'Espagne* ritrovato nel frammento reggiano," *Atti dell'Istituto Veneto di scienze, lettere ed arti* 135 (1976-1977): 489-506 and "Il frammento reggiano dell'*Entrée d'Espagne*: raffronto filologico col codice marciano francese XXI (=257)," *Atti dell'Istituto Veneto* 136 (1977-1978): 407-24.

24. Léon Gautier, "*L'Entrée en Espagne*, chanson de geste inédite, renfermée dans un manuscrit de la bibliothèque de Saint-Marc, à Venise. Notice, analyse et extraits," *Bibliothèque de l'Ecole des Chartes*, 4th ser., 4 (1858): 220ff; Gaston Paris, *Histoire poétique de Charlemagne* (Paris, 1865) 173-74; Paul Meyer, "Expansion" 89-90; Thomas, *Nouvelles recherches* 6.

25. See also Anna Maria Finoli, "Personalità e cultura dell'autore dell'*Entrée d'Espagne*," *CN* 21 (1961).

26. Hyde, *Padua* 285-86 and Appendix I; Hélène Nolthenius, *Duecento: The Late Middle Ages in Italy*, trans. Darton (London: Longman & Todd, Ltd., 1962; rpt. 1968) 48.

CHAPTER 1

ROLAND AS *BARON RÉVOLTÉ* ?

Of the many chansons de geste in which Roland appears, the most widely known is the *Chanson de Roland*; it is here that we perceive the model for other texts, which will fill out the career of Charlemagne's illustrious vassal, from his birth and childhood in the Franco-Italian *Rolandino* and *Mainet* and the *Enfances Roland* to the meeting with Olivier and Aude at Vienne and the voyage to the East in the *Pèlerinage*. Although much chronological and geographical distance separates the appearance of these texts, their portrayal of Roland is, nonetheless, surprisingly uniform. He is, most frequently, the favored nephew, the faithful vassal, the valiant and invincible knight.[1]

However, there are variants in the portrait, of which perhaps the *Entrée* offers the most radical example. Here, the character transgresses the anticipated model; indeed, the essence of the *Entrée*'s Roland is escalating conflict with Charles, whose expectations of authority become increasingly incompatible with the hero's desire for some measure of autonomy. The frequently-cited spirit of epic solidarity characteristic of the *cycle du roi* and exemplified in the Oxford text is radically undermined here by discord threatening the viability of the entire community and enterprise. The result is physical violence and rupture of the Charles-Roland relationship.

For those accustomed to see in the *Roland* a text "qui magnifie les rappports parfaits, idéaux, absolus, du vassal et du seigneur," the *Entrée*'s iconoclasm may be puzzling (Aebischer, *Rolandiana* 218). How—and why—did the anonymous Paduan conjoin the *baron révolté* theme with Roland, the "destre braz" of the emperor? Analysis of the nine-stage structure of conflict, developed over the initial ca. eleven thousand verses, will offer responses in chapters one and two.

27

The Structure of Conflict

1. The Roland-Ferragu combat

Friction initially arises as the multi-national imperial armies reach Nájera, site of the first encounter with the Infidel in this "entry"—or, less euphemistically, invasion—of Spain, which will culminate at Roncevaux. Roland, marshal of the imperial armies, has organized the 100,000-man force. Conflict arises when Roland wishes to accept the offer of single combat which the giant Ferragu makes to him and Olivier to decide the fate of the city, 10,000 defenders of which "por l'entree defandre d'Espaigne sunt garni" (805) ("are armed to defend the entry into Spain"). Ferragu is well aware of the critical nature of the encounter: should Nájera fall, all of Saracen Spain will lie open to Christian penetration. Given his size and quasi-invincibility, descended from Goliath and invulnerable except at the navel (*Pseudo-Turpin*, ch. 17), Ferragu calculates his chances for victory greater in a one-on-one encounter:

> 'Se moi conquirent, quitemant lor otroi
> 'L'entrer d'Espaigne; afiez sunt de moi.
> 'Et se je pus abatre lor bofoi,
> 'Aquitez soit le païs Espainoi' (932-35).

> 'If they vanquish me, I will pose no obstacles to their
> entry into Spain; they may have confidence in me.
> And if I can crush their arrogance, may Spain be freed
> of this invasion.'

Charles, rejecting without explanation the *combat singulier*, predicts that Nájera will see "storme e bataille" (1058) before the Christians proceed on the route to Compostella.

2. Return to France

After witnessing Ferragu's defeat and imprisonment of 11 *pairs*, Charles is unwilling to risk Roland as well: " 'Se je vos pert, ensi remanri sos / 'Cum pobre dame quant a perdu l'espos' " (1595-96) (" 'If I lose you, I shall be alone, like a poor woman when she has lost her husband' "). Rather, he apparently prefers to abandon the expedition altogether and return to France, " 'Car cist païs commance estre anoios' " (1598) (" 'For this country is beginning to be bothersome' "). In order to persuade Roland, Charles reminds him that, as his sole heir, Roland will inherit the position of emperor and king of the French (1599-602). Roland mounts a four-part rebuttal of Charles's defeatism: *a.* what will Aude say; *b.* what will Gerard say, who entrusted his nephew to Roland (1606); *c.* Ferragu will hang Ogier and the remaining *pairs* who came to Spain for Roland's sake; *d.* the specter of "male chançun" (" 'nus de moi ne dira / 'Che fuïs soie, se caisons ne sera.' ") (1611-12) (" 'No one will say of me that I fled, if there be no cause.' ") Commending the French to God and himself to their prayers, Roland departs for a three-day combat with Ferragu.

3. Coronation of Roland

Roland's victory at Nájera enhances his heroic status in the eyes of the Christian armies as well as for the Emperor, who triumphantly enters the city and "gives" it to his nephew. Curiously, the narrator chooses this seemingly golden moment to introduce further friction between uncle and nephew; Charles, overjoyed by this auspicious *entrée de Nájera*, declares that Roland shall be king of Saracen-occupied Spain forthwith (4441-44). Protesting the premature and prideful implications of such an act, Roland refuses, stating that his coronation, as well as his wedding to Aude, will occur only after the successful completion of the entire mission, when all Spain shall have been reclaimed for Christendom.

4. Victory celebrations at Nájera

Upon their triumphant *entrée de Nájera*, the French find the population eager to welcome both their new masters and new faith. Six days of baptism follow in an atmosphere of celebration on both sides. The emperor's newfound optimism, in which the narrator comments on Charles's "aut entendiment" (4481) ("profound understanding"), renders him impatient to continue the expedition, and of decidedly "mal talent" (4486) one evening upon seeing Roland and the *pairs* riding elegantly through the streets "looking at the ladies who were on their balconies" (4486). In a protracted (30-verse) diatribe protesting their " 'trop long repouser' " (4522) and that " 'trop desiromes ci la joie e li sbanoi' "

(4526), Charles articulates one of the text's principal enunciations of chivalry:

> 'baron qe feit enprise
> 'D'autre terre conquerre vuelt sens e maïstrise
> 'E haïr le repos et sa pelice grise
> 'E costumer le cald e le froid e la bise
> 'Quand il a un castel o une terre prise,
> 'Ne doit por vane glorie entrer en druerise,
> 'Mais prés l'une vuelt este mantinant l'autre asise,
> 'Car qi altrui offend penser doit por certise
> 'Qe le offendus porchaçe comant il l'en merise'
> (4504-12).

> ' . . . the baron who undertakes the conquest of
> another land requires good sense and self-mastery and
> must detest leisure and its (luxurious) grey fur and
> accustom himself to heat and cold and the cold north
> wind. When he has taken a castle or a piece of land,
> he must not out of vainglory enter into a spirit of
> frivolous amusement, but must immediately follow
> up the first conquest with another, for he who offends
> another man must consider it certain that the offended
> party will hunt him down [seek vengeance] as he
> merits.'

Essential are a spirit of vassalic self-sacrifice and perseverance, discourse familiar from the parent *Chanson de Roland*, plus constant alertness of adversary response to one's actions. Unacceptable are duties postponed or abandoned before completion and the temptations for a victorious knight to enter into courtly dissipation. That a touch of authorial irony may color Charles's discourse in the light of his own recent chastisement by St. James and Conflict 2 is heightened by the introductory "aut entendiment." On Charles's insistence, which places him in the somewhat unappealing posture of *trouble-fête* following this first critical victory, the expedition departs with all haste for Pamplona.

5. Ransom of Prince Isoré

Isoré, newly-knighted son of King Maugeriz, fights valiantly at Pamplona but is captured, as is Roland's cousin Hestout. Refusing to surrender to anyone except Roland, Isoré is dispatched to Charles under

Roland's instructions that he be treated as a royal prisoner, proper treatment of whom " 'puet molt son honor avancier' " (5509) (" 'can greatly increase his [Charles's] honor' "). However, appearing to associate Isoré with his own lack of military success thus far in the battle for this major city, Charles vows to hang the youth. Later, he adds a second rationale for killing the prisoner: he will thus avenge the capture, and possible death, of Hestout (5670). The Charles-Roland confrontation broadens to include agreement or dissent from a number of individuals and focuses on chivalric ethics, with frequent use of words such as *honor* and *loi*. A " 'chevaler novel' " (5464) true to the ideals of his *ordo*, Isoré is first to express dismay at Charles's intention:

> 'Je ai si grant fiançe en le vostre renom,
> 'Qe portez de bontei le gant e le baston,
> 'En l'amor qe portez Rolant, vostre baron,
> 'Qe ce qe il a promis, s'il fust plus rice don,
> 'Nel desoutroierez, anchois vos ert de bon'
> (5546-50).

'I have such great faith in your renown, that you bear in good faith the glove and scepter, in the love which you bear for Roland, your baron, that what he has promised, even if it were a more important request, you will not fail to grant, as soon as it will be appropriate for you.'

When Roland arrives, he reminds Charles that Isoré is his prisoner and states his position:

> 'Qu'il n'avra mal, mais si le retindron
> 'A loi de pris, si com feire devon.
> 'Pensés, biaus sire, s'il m'est honor o non
> 'S'oncir le lés: nenil, por saint Simon;
> 'Nel sofreroie por je perdre Clermon' (5677-81).

'That he will suffer no ill-treatment, if we retain him from now on according to law, as we must do. Consider, kind sire, whether it is honorable or not for me, if I allow him to be killed: no, by Saint Simon; I would not tolerate it by losing [giving up, voluntarily] Clermont.'

Not only is Roland absolutely opposed to harming the prisoner, but rejects such infamy even if his cousin is dead and if Isoré had killed Roland's own father (5682-84). Highly displeased with what he perceives as insubordination, Charles delivers a lengthy reminder to Roland of his authority, which the narrator introduces with the Aristotelian notion of primary authority: "Si com le home qu'en sa propre maison / Ne veult de rien avoir contrediçon" (5689-90) ("Just as man in his own home does not wish to suffer contradiction"). In another rather dramatic articulation of domestic hierarchism, Charles declares: " 'Home qui taise et sofre orguel sa hoisor / 'Si li mete hon sor le chief le raisor, / 'Car il subjete liberté et honor' " (5693-95) (" 'the man who is silent and tolerates the pride of his wife thus places upon his own head the razor, for he surrenders liberty and honor' ") and orders Roland to relinquish the prisoner.

The latter, now barely suppressing his anger, makes an appeal to Charles's chivalry: " 'Mais si vos pri por la vostre douçor / 'Qe non facés, biaus sir enpereor, / 'Rien qui vos tourt ni a moi desenor' " (5713-15) (" 'I beg you more strongly for the sake of your sense of the humane that you do nothing that may bring dishonor to you or to me' "), shortly thereafter adding: " 'Plus n'avrai onte por sofrir longement' " (5761) (" 'I will not have to suffer shame any longer' ").

The *pairs* now take sides. Olivier comments: " 'Le roi feit vilanie' " (5764) (" 'The king is acting disgracefully/beneath his station' "), while Ogier and Richard of Normandy urge Roland to yield. Their argument is initially expressed as a generalized statement on vassalic subservience: " 'Celui a tort qui son droit contrelie' " (5777) (" 'He who resists his rightful authority is in error' "); then, in more direct warning that others may see envy as the root of Roland's behavior in this quarrel with Charles. Their advice: " 'Portés vostre oncle onor e cortesie' " (5782) (" 'Grant your uncle honor and courtesy' "). Roland, however, is not prepared to compromise his principles, protesting that he is not acting inappropriately: " 'Da moie part n'i a nul estralois' " (5794) (" 'On my part there is no unlawful behavior' "). For the first time, Roland threatens to abandon Charles (5807-08).

Charles now initiates a series of negotiations for settlement of the conflict, which fluctuate from one statement to another, but which essentially center on demands that Maugeriz convert, yield Pamplona and/or exchange Hestout for Isoré. When Charles finally agrees to delegate the matter entirely to Roland, the youth congratulates him: " 'Parlés avois a loi de jantils hon' " (6017) (" 'You have spoken according to the standards of a gentleman' "). The narrator adds his approbation: "De bieux servis e de grace complie / Servi li roi son neveu cele fie" (6246-47) ("In [a spirit of] fine service and accomplished grace, his nephew served the king this time"). The prisoners are returned, although Maugeriz refuses both conversion and surrender.

Again, discord has arisen over Charles's autocratic posture, resisted in this instance by Roland's demand that a decision regarding a prisoner he considers his own be made according to established chivalric ethics. Roland's position, of course, is more humane, particularly to a fourteenth-century northern Italian public directly acquainted with the problematics of ethics in government. Should the *Entrée* public perceive insubordination in Roland's position, it is worth recalling that one of the major goals of the expedition is to elevate him to the ranks of the highest leaders of the human community, a privileged status which will require independent judgment and the ability to act with autonomy. Yet it is this very autonomy which Charles appears both to proffer and to thwart, creating an aura of confusion reflecting the inconsistency of his own thinking.

In this fifth occasion of conflict, Roland acquires new heroic dimension. Less monolithic, more humane, he recognizes enemy valor and rejects what he perceives as unjustifiable violence.

It is clear at this point that the Charles-Roland relationship is perilously close to the breaking point. In five increasingly serious conflicts, Roland has successfully resisted positions taken by Charles which he considers unacceptable. Midway in the conflict structure, then, the narrator offers a pause, in which both narrative and authorial public may stand back and reflect on what appears to be a collision course.

6. Plateau phase: rhetoric or speech act?

Upon the release of Isoré and return of Hestout, the latter brings with him a horse offered as a gift from the Saracen prince to Roland, against whom Isoré still hopes to test his prowess on the battlefield. Hestout, whose name is curiously similar to OF *estolt/estoltie*, meaning foolish(ness) or lacking in sense, implies that one should beware of gift horses, perhaps offered to a Roland who had been overly amicable with their foes at Pamplona. Roland thereupon offers the horse to Charles, who insists that his nephew keep it.

In discourse pertinent to the episode at hand but equally suggestive of a broader *prise de position* on the part of a Charles who has been compelled to yield in each of the five preceding occasions of conflict, the narrator offers to him the voice of appeasement. In an eloquent and extended simile, Charles compares Roland to the merchant's son who has earned his father's trust and his own independence. Explaining that he prefers that Roland keep the magnificent gift, he announces:

> 'mais de vos entendons
> 'Feir come feit li mercheant prodons
> 'Quant oit noric fil o niés grant e lons:
> 'Se il feit bien e ne le voit felons,
> 'Sa merchandise le met tot a bandons,
> 'Aler l'en laise e por vals e per mons;
> 'E cil porchase, chi bien soit sa raisons.
> 'Da Deu, bel niés, e de ma nuriçons
> 'Vos voi si feit che desor vos metons
> 'Les fais des armes che porter solions' (6662-71).

'But we intend to do with you as the honorable merchant does, when he has raised a son or nephew for a long time: if the youth behaves well and [the father/uncle] does not see in him an evil character, he grants him free disposition of/full authority over his merchandise/property. He lets him go through mountains and valleys; and the youth goes his way freely, he who well knows his reason [for his comings and goings]. By God, fine nephew, and as the young man whom I have raised, I see you formed in such a way that to you we grant the feats of arms which we were accustomed to bear ourselves.'

In addition to the tangible act of granting to Roland the insignia of his own authority, Charles acknowledges confidence in Roland's discretionary judgment. On the evidence of Roland's conduct thus far, Charles appears to be prepared to grant, with the horse, unlimited freedom of movement, i.e., a greater degree of autonomy not incompatible with Roland's future role as king of Spain.

It appears, then, that Charles is likewise acknowledging the necessity of compromise on his part, as well as the requisite largesse soon to be emphasized by Naimon. Where he had previously yielded with reluctance and without grace, his words here appear to be uttered in good faith. Further, conscious of the undesirability of continued antagonism, Charles may be prepared to relax some of his authoritarian rigidity. The issue of Charles's authoritarianism, generally unquestioned in earlier texts of the *cycle du roi*, emerges as a central thematic in the *Entrée*.[2] In subsequent episodes, however, the appearance of compromise in the above passage becomes a major problem as the second half of the conflictual structure emerges. A more detailed analysis of this passage will be given in chapter 4.

7. The Thiois rebellion

At dinner immediately following the above, Charles is informed that his front-guard has been attacked at Nobles, the city next on the Compostella route; he is advised to fortify his position at Pamplona before undertaking a full-scale attack on Nobles. Tasks are assigned: the Parisians are to cut wood, the "Tiois de Polaine" to haul it. As if anticipating their resentment, Charles urges that " 'they not consider it [the task] as an insult or dishonor . . . For they are large men and do not fear labor, but live by hard work and sweat' " (6782; 6786-87). Humiliated, the Thiois plan to desert "et unt feit sagrament / de non servir le roi a son vivent" (6838-39) ("and have sworn an oath not to serve the king for the rest of his life"). When a Thiois spy reveals the conspiracy to Charles, the emperor conceives his revenge. Confiding (falsely) to a small group of trusted knights that Marsile is planning a surprise attack in the forest, he orders a secret interception operation; he then assigns night watch to the Thiois, who appear to accept. After one turn around the camp, the Thiois ride off according to plan, innocent, however, that the oliphant blast Charles now sounds is the signal to begin the ambush of the non-existent enemy force. "The Germans thought that they were pagans, and Salamon's men are of the same opinion " (6986-87): Charles has mounted a nocturnal massacre of Christian against Christian in which he alone knows the truth of what the narrator terms this "contance si pesme e si vilaine" (6985) ("so evil and so villainous struggle"). When daylight reveals reality, Charles's desire for vengeance is unspent; he orders his men to pursue the Thiois traitors, whom he despises more than the Saracens. When Charles accuses Salamon, leader of the ambush party, of ceasing the assault when he realized the "enemy" were relatives and coreligionists, Salamon declares that since Charles was in error by concealing the truth of the encounter, the knight's moral responsibility takes precedence over his chivalric duty of *auxilium* :

> 'N'a home en l'ost, se au roi forfesist
> 'En tel mainere, e le roi me disist,
> 'Se je pooie, che je ne l'onciis.
> 'Mal fist mon sire quant il bien ne m'aprist,
> 'Car tot celor che pont deshobeïst
> 'A tort son sire, Deable ert ses minist' (7103-08).

'There is no man in the army whom I would not kill,
if he wronged the king in such a manner, and if the
king told me about it. My lord did wrong when he did
not inform me correctly, for he who does not disobey
his lord [when the latter is] in the wrong, the devil
will be his minister.'

A major role in this event is assumed by Naimon, maintained in
his traditional voice of sage moderation ("cil qe fu filz de sciance sa
mere," (780), ("he who was the son of wisdom, his mother"). His
condemnation of Charles's conduct is unmitigated by his usual
diplomatic discourse, in part because one of the Thiois leaders, Herbert,
was his cousin. He tells Charles: " 'Une si grant folie ne feïstes
anchor' " (7024) (" 'A greater folly [than this] you have not yet
committed' "). In addition, Naimon formulates a hypothetical portrait of
the qualities essential to the good leader, an abbreviated *miroir du
prince*. The wisdom and strength necessary for the proper use of power
are qualities inherent in the good leader, who is able to see beyond the
immediate incident in his appraisal of events and in his function as
justicier. Thinly-veiled censure of Charles, who insists on the
justification of his vengeance, is offered by the character traditionally
portrayed as the embodiment of wise counsel:

'Sor li sers doit avoir un avantaje
'Le grant baron chi ame signoraje:
'Plus rich doit estre e plus fort e plus saje.
'Se son baron, plen de aut vasalaje,
'Feit un defaut en trestoit sun aaje,
'Nel doit tantost destruir par un folaje,
'Mai segunt l'euvre li doit estre salvaje'
(7120-22).

'The great baron/lord who loves seigniory must have
an advantage over the serf: he must be more
rich/powerful and more strong and more wise. If his
[vassal] baron, full of a sense of lofty vassalage,
makes a mistake once in his life, the lord must not
destroy him for one act of folly, but according to the
particular circumstances, he must be severe'.

Here, additional suggestion of an increased flexibility of judgment
issuing from consideration of the individual case serves as the
conclusion of Naimon's counsel. Perhaps it is an aspect of *caritas*

which permits the wise leader to avoid vindictive punishment for an isolated act of vassal "folaje" offset by so many previous acts of heroism; perhaps it is that same *caritas* in which a sovereign's "avantaje" ultimately lies. The episode concludes as Roland, who participated in the ambush but who articulates little overt criticism of Charles here, asks pardon for both the Thiois and Naimon in the interests of mediation (7132). Charles yields, delegating further decisions in this matter to Naimon.

8. Saracen reinforcements at Pamplona

The next conflict offers intertextual parallels with the plight of Roland at Roncevaux. In the *Entrée*'s Pamplona Reinforcement episode (7420-992), Roland is dispatched from the Christian camp outside Pamplona with a small force of men to prevent Saracen reinforcements from entering the city. Informed that the enemy is receiving massive reinforcements due to converge imminently outside the walls, Roland is encouraged by one of his men to send for aid. His initial response, like the response to Olivier in the first *scène du cor* in the Oxford *Roland*, is blatant refusal due to fear of *male chançun* :

> -Sir', dit Berart, 'il ne ferait folie
> 'Mander a Çarles a la barbe florie
> 'Ch'il nos envoi Richart de Normandie
> 'E Salemons, chi ne nos heite mie.'
> Respont Rolant: 'Dehait chil vos otrie!
> 'Honte n'avroie de ceste coardie,
> 'Si feit l'avoie, en tretote ma vie;
> 'Vos voleç bien che dan Hestous s'en rie'
> (7643-50).

> 'Sire,' says Bernard, 'it would not be folly to send a message to Charles of the flowing beard, that he send us Richard of Normandy and Salomon, who hates us not.' Roland replies: 'May he who grants that to you fall ill! I could not bear the shame of that cowardice, if I had done it, for all my life; you really want sir Hestout to make fun of such a thing'.

Not long thereafter, however, when Roland sees the urgency of the situation, he acts immediately to send for aid, adding that it would be helpful if Charles himself were to come. In the meantime, Roland means to fight on: " 'Proieç nos sire, por Deu, che il tost vagne, / 'Car entreç somes de marchié en bragagne' " (7688-89) (" 'Pray for us, sire, for God's sake, that he come soon, for we have entered into combat' ").

Unlike the *Chanson*'s Roland, whose vehement and persistent rejection of Olivier's pleas has been among the most debated aspects of epic heroism, the *Entrée*'s hero hesitates only momentarily between self-preservation and self-image. Rather, Roland willingly steps down from the *Chanson*'s super-being pedestal to defer to the better-informed appraisal of his companion Girard, who, like Olivier, has seen the reality of the situation. Here, as in Roland's earlier refusal to accept the Spanish crown, the narrator explicitly exonerates him of the possible charge of *orgueil* commonly levelled in the parent text.

As battle is engaged, however, the vastly outnumbered Christians (8000 vs. 87,000 Saracens) begin to flee, and Roland himself receives some twenty wounds. In another intertextual moment, Olivier meets Roland briefly as battle rages about them, lamenting: " 'Perduç vos ai, flor de civalerie. / . . . / 'Haï! Rolant, vestre douç compagnie / 'M'unt Seracins hui tolte e ravie' " (7826; 7829-30) (" 'I have lost you, the flower of chivalry / . . . / Ah! Roland, the Saracens have taken from me and robbed me of your sweet companionship' "). Parallels continue with the latter phases of the battle at Roncevaux; in a second encounter of the *compagnons*, Roland decries the shame of dishonor and defeat: " 'De la jent Çarles ai feit mauvés regart; / 'Honiç me voi e tenuç a cohart' " (7857) (" 'I have done a poor job as guardian of Charles's men; I see myself shamed and considered as a coward' ").

The conflict itself arises with Charles's belated arrival, after the Saracen reinforcements have succeeded in entering the city. Here, it is a Roland smarting from the shame of retreat who reproaches Charles and the others for failing to come to his aid in time: " 'Signor' . . . 'mout saveç bien dormir: / 'Dormant quidés vos nemis desconfir?' " (7913-14) (" 'Sire, you certainly know how to sleep well: do you think you can conquer your enemies by sleeping?' "). In turn, Charles reprimands Roland for relinquishing the fray, but enlarges his chastisement to condemn his nephew's uncontrollable pride:

> 'Orguel fist ja mant pros homes morir,
> 'Sire Rolant; . . . .
> . . . .
> 'Une sol home ne poit le munt conquir,
> 'Soit beus quant veult, fort e de grant haïr,
> 'Che s'il pur veult a l'orgueil consentir,
> 'La ou doit pros estre, orgueil li feit fuïr.

. . . .
'La vostre fam, chi tot cuide anglotir,
'Aprés mangier vos fera mal geisir'
(7921-22; 7926-29; 7935-36).

'Pride has made many a brave man perish, Sir Roland
. . . / . . . / one man alone cannot conquer the world,
as fine a knight as he wants to be, strong and full of
ardor; nonetheless, if such a man is willing to yield
to pride, there in circumstances where he ought to be
courageous, pride makes him flee. / . . . / Your
hunger, which considers it can devour all things, will
make you lie uncomfortably after eating.'

Roland, controlling his anger (cf. Roland's volatile temper cited by
Olivier in the *Chanson* as justification for not appointing him as
ambassador to Marsile), does not escalate the conflict, but, rather,
reiterates his submission to Charles: " 'Sire' , . . . or dites vos plaisir, /
'Car je sui senpre a vos ire seguir : / 'Quant che m'est greu a autre home
sofrir / 'Me feit contant, soul par vos hobeïr' " (7939-42) (" 'Sire, now
state your pleasure, for I am still yielding to your wrath: as much as it
is difficult for me to tolerate [such behavior from any other man], it
makes me happy just to obey you' "). Yet Roland's sense that Charles
is in the wrong persists: " 'Signor, veois se l'emperer me feit a tort
sordois' " (7961) (" 'Sire, see whether the emperor wrongly behaves
most badly toward me' "). His increasing anger is reaching an explosive
level. Charles, quick to reassert authority, reminds his nephew that
" 'hobedïence senpre orgueil venqui' " (7982) (" 'obedience always has
vanquished pride' ").

9. Assignment refusal

The penultimate phase in the degenerating Charles-Roland
relationship occurs as a direct consequence of the above. Gathering the
armies for the next encounter at Pamplona, Charles orders his nephew
to organize the military units in a capacity which Thomas identifies as
marshal (*Entrée*, Introduction xv). In a vehement statement refusing the
assignment, Roland declares that he will not assume the role of
commander ("bailior" 8312) of any men except his own, over whom he
has authority, from the Pope, as "senator" and "condutor" (8306- 8307).
Further, he adds, having donated " 'de mes cités la meilor' " (8308)
(" 'the finest of my cities [fiefs]' "), he is unwilling to risk the

"desonor" of commanding another's troops in battle. Charles's wrath is
quick to erupt, at least partially in frustration because Roland does not
appear to be altering his insubordinate behavior: " ' . . . trop estes plain
d'ardor, / 'Tiel cum vos fustes senpre vos trov ancor' " (8315-16) (" 'you
are too full of ardor [overzealous independence], such as you always
were I find you still' "). In reprisal, Charles deprives him of the "onor"
of engaging the enemy on that day and assigns him to the rear guard.

The existence of this "private" militia, mentioned in the *Pseudo-
Turpin* and other texts, serves in the *Entrée* to underscore the autonomy
already possessed by Roland and recognized by the Pope, the highest
leader of the Christian community. Establishing him as a military
leader of the Church ("capitaine de l'Eglise") clearly capable of victories
more grandiose than a small militia might suggest, the Paduan adds the
military function to the political—Roland is, as the text frequently
repeats, also "senator de Rome." His authority issues from the power
center of Church and empire, reminding us that the *Entrée*'s Roland,
unlike his previous incarnations, is more than the mere vassal knight
whose obligations of obedience and submission were considerably less
complex. In a sense, the Paduan's Roland, with sanctioned claims to
authority himself, replicates, albeit on a lesser scale, the political and
religious functions of Charles. It is with this recognition that audience
perception (narrative and authorial) must appraise the escalating
confrontations between the two.

10. Nobles

The Nobles episode is thus the culmination of a progressive
augmentation of tension, acquiring its significance from the gradual
accumulation of prior events. In order to trace its introduction and
integration into the narrative, we return to events leading up to the
Thiois massacre (conflict 7), at which time Charles had emphasized the
urgency of taking nearby Nobles, strategic for its wealth, power, and
location. Advised to fortify Pamplona before proceeding to Nobles, he
has temporarily postponed the defense of his front guard at Nobles,
presently under attack.

During the ensuing battle at Pamplona and only after another fierce
encounter, Christian victory at last appears imminent to both Charles
and Roland, who are at different points on the field. It is at this critical
moment that Roland's scout Bernard, a Noblian himself, returns from a
reconnaissance mission and assures him: " 'Car Noble vos donrai
demain a le maitin' " (8991) (" 'For I shall give you Nobles tomorrow
morning' "), since the city's defense troops are all at Pamplona.

Expressing his gratitude to God, St.Thomas, and St. James for this opportunity to further the Christian crusade, Roland nonetheless initially hesitates to heed Bernard's insistence that he leave immediately for Nobles:

> 'Volenter i veroie, mais je redoit le roi
> 'Qi est en la bataille (mais au meillor le voi:
> 'A la ville s'en veit), e si le feit por moi.
> 'Se riens lui mesvenist en icistui tornoi,
> 'Jameis ne m'ameroit, je le pains bien e croi.
> . . . .
> 'Je venrai. . . mais bien sai q'i foloi' (9007-16).

'I would come gladly, but I fear the king, who is in battle (but I see him in the best [strongest] position: he is leaving for the city), and he is doing it for me. If any accident were to befall him in this battle, he would never [again] love me, I truly think and believe so. / . . . / I will come, but I know well that I am acting foolishly.'

Roland then delegates the *oriflamme* to Ogier and encourages the small force of men he will employ, some of whom express hesitation to leave for an unknown destination without orders from the emperor. Roland reminds them of their feudal and Christian responsibility to endure hardship in the cause of honor (9038-40). And, without notifying Charles, whom he sees heading toward the city but is not close by, Roland gathers his own militia and departs for Nobles.

The two-week battle there is successful, though more difficult than Bernard had claimed. Nobles won and the dual banners of Roland and Charles raised over its ramparts, Roland returns to Pamplona.

Unfortunately, Roland's absence has radically altered French prospects for a *prise de Pampelune*. Indeed, no sooner did the Christian armies learn of Roland's unexplained departure than they began to retreat; there will be no present victory here. Charles, assuming somehow that Roland has deserted, declares that the "traïtor" (9224) has failed to accept the risks which everyone else has assumed for Roland's sake: " 'Mout m'a renduz bon cange qe sui en sa conqeste / 'E par lui honorer su je an peril d'estre / 'Perdanz, moi e mes homes, ou de membre ou de teste.' " (9226-28) (" 'He certainly has repaid me well, my men and me, who are in danger of losing life and limb in order to honor him in his conquest' "). In his vindictive (and didactic) wrath ("enseinemens Carlon" 11,063), Charles sees only one way to enlighten others on the perils of unapproved departures: Roland shall be hunted

down and hanged, along with all his kin. Charles inwardly relishes the
anticipated scene, the moment when Roland enters his tent; he himself
will strike the first blow, whereupon his barons are to rise and slay the
faithless nephew with their swords (11,049-62). The barons, however,
seeing the self-destructive irrationality of such an act and defending
Roland as champion of peace and reason, refuse to obey:

> 'Par saint Donis', font il, 'qe ne feron.
> 'Qi a soi meïsme feit onte e mespreison,
> 'L'en le devroit pandre come leron.
> 'E donc n'est il Rollant li canpion
> 'Qe nos mantient en peis et en reison?
> 'Par cui somes nos ci se par lui non?'
> (11,066-71)

> 'By Saint Denis,' they say, 'we will not do that.
> Whoever does unto himself shame and error, they
> should hang him like a thief. And thus is not Roland
> the champion who maintains us in peace and reason?
> In behalf of whom are we here if not for him?'

Thus when Roland comes into the tent laughing and lighthearted
("si feit chiere riant" 11,103), confident that the victory and wealth he
can present to Charles will compensate for any anger which his uncle
may harbor, he is hardly prepared for the reception that awaits him.
Raising a mailed glove and again condemning the incorrigible *orgueil*
which has jeopardized the lives of Emperor and all the Christian host,
Charles strikes Roland, vowing simultaneously to hang him (11,108-
16). Roland, bloodied and confused, but restraining the impulse to
strike back only by recalling the bond of the *nourri*, leaves the tent. The
two will not meet again for many years.

Summary

Several points may be made regarding the issue of (overlord)
authority versus (vassal) autonomy as it is presented in *Entrée* I. First,
in crowning Roland king of Spain, Charles will not only augment his
nephew's authority, but his requisite autonomy as well, albeit within
the established parameters of the lord-vassal hierarchy. As noted above,
Roland, "senator de Rome," already belongs to the ranks of global
governing authority apart from his immediate obligations to Charles.
Peter Wunderli comments on a similar element in *Aquilon de Bavière*,

where Roland is likewise "senateur de Rome et chef des Chrétiens de l'Eglise." Elevated to that dual function, Roland "semble garantir la continuité et le succès de l'idée de l'Empire" and he "assure la protection et la défense du Christianisme contre les multiples attaques des païens" ("La Théologisation de Roland" 761).

Narratorial approbation throughout *Entrée* I seems, upon an initial reading, significantly, if not absolutely, on the side of Roland, most of whose actions are justified by a narrator who emphasizes the injustices perpetrated upon a wronged hero. Beyond narratorial empathy, Charles is indisputably in violation of feudal ethics when he raises his hand in violence against Roland; closely related to *exfestucatio*, this semiotically charged gesture automatically marks the annulment of the feudal contract, releasing its victim from all further feudal obligation. (see ch. 4). In the case of *Raoul de Cambrai* and *Renaud de Montauban*, texts familiar to the Paduan, the gesture of violence also signalled initiation of open hostilities and the vassal's initiation into the ranks of the *barons révoltés*.[3]

It is simplistic to claim, as earlier scholars have done, that Roland is guilty of abandoning Charles at Pamplona "in cerca di gloria." (Bertoni, *Duecento* 57). The text indicates Roland's awareness of the dilemma presented by the *prise de Nobles*. Yet, characteristic of medieval epic, it posits the polarities of conflict with minimal analytical amplification:

'Volenter i veroie'	vs.	'je redoit le roi'
'au meillor le voi'	vs.	'Se riens lui mesvenist . . . '
		'Jameis ne m'ameroit . . . '

'I would come willingly'	vs.	'I fear the king'
'I see him bettering [the enemy]'	vs.	'If any mishap should happen to him . . . '
		'Never again would he love me . . . '

If we refer back to the merchant analogy of the plateau phase, we can say, unequivocally, that Roland's departure for Nobles specifically enacts the autonomy apparently granted to him immediately before. Further, Roland departs at a moment when he (unlike Charles) perceives no military risk for the emperor or his troops, and at no point expresses any motivation except that of furthering the Christian and imperial cause. Thus Roland states: " 'Vencuz a l'anperere les cuvers maleïs; /

'Par le partir de nos ja nun sera maumis' " (9126-27) (" 'The emperor
has vanquished the evil wretches; by our departure he will not [no
longer] be harmed' "). Despite some indisputably irregular aspects of
Roland's departure for Nobles, he perceives it as another act of feudal-
Christian service.

Similarly, the Paduan is not guilty, as Henning Krauss has
suggested, of a less than successful fusion of dissonant portrayals of the
Rolandian character in the *Entrée*:

> Ci si deve dunque chiedere perché l'autore volesse
> unificare le due tradizioni concorrenti, quelle di un
> Rolando *soltanto* impulsivo e l'altra di un Rolando
> valoroso *e* avveduto, operazione che in questo punto
> non gli riesce affatto persuasiva, e che forse non era
> qui ancora perseguita come sintesi ideale (*Epica
> feudale* 221).

However, although there is no doubt regarding the honor of
Roland's stated intentions, neither narrator, other characters, nor Roland
himself sees his Nobles expedition as totally blameless. As the
character himself states, the "folloie" which he acknowledges centers on
his unsanctioned departure and the unforeseen, yet not entirely
unpredictable, jeopardy of the entire expedition, subsequently stalemated
at Pamplona.

The narrator, inserting a characteristic note of ambiguity here,
describes Roland en route to Nobles: ". . . qe ne garde a mesure:/
Comant il en port bleisme, segir veult sa nature" (9408-09) ("Roland,
who does not have regard for / is not concerned about moderation; how
he bears the blame for it, he wants to [insists on] following his
nature' "). This "nature," cited by Ganelon in the Oxford text also in
relation to Roland's unauthorized conquest of Nobles, seems to imply
here (a perception of) tendencies toward excessive behavior in the
execution of vassalic *auxilium* leading to acts of unlicensed
independence. Indeed, a lively debate springs up en route to Nobles,
when Olivier, Gerard, Anseïs, and Hestout question the expedition.
Although Olivier initially describes it as "mout savage" (9105) and
urges Roland to send a message back to Charles of their destination, he
accepts Roland's assurances of good faith:

> 'Ne fust par avantaje q'avrai sor mes nemis,
> 'Si com je croi avoire, nen seroie partis
> 'Ne n'avroie mun oncle a bataille garpis,

> 'Car plus l'aim de coraje d'ome dou siegle vis'
> (9122-25).

> 'Were it not for the advantage that I will have over
> my enemies, just as I believe I have, I would not
> have left. I would not have abandoned my uncle in
> battle, for I love him more than any man alive.'

Yet both Olivier and Hestout refer to Roland's "follage," a judgment which may be calculated more on the present precarity of the Charles-Roland relationship than on the act of departure in an objective sense. Roland himself weighs risk against reward in terms of the global mission: " 'E se folie faiz, encor amenderai' " (9159) (" 'And if I am committing an act of folly, I shall nonetheless make amends for it' "). In predicting his ability to make rapid retribution for his absence-without-leave by presenting a reconquered Nobles to Charles, the vassal-knight Roland is placing his departure within the context of possible, yet remediable error; even if the means (i.e., timing) may be problematic, the results will justify the undertaking. More significantly, Roland is innocently expressing a profound sentential truth of this text which will be the focus of our attention in chapter 5.

In raising the issue of *démesure* in Roland's character, the narrator invites our recall of earlier Rolands, that of the *Aspremont*, for example, or possibly of the *Chanson* itself. The question, not entirely resolved at this point in the *Entrée*, yet presented with apparent pro-Roland empathy, re-emerges as a major problematic, one to which no immediate textual solution is offered. Indeed, the only unambiguous, and perhaps the only profoundly important reality for a fourteenth-century Italian public well familiar with the complexities of balance of power, is that the position of both men is subject to debate. While sufficient justification of actions and decisions may be cited in defense of either man individually, their positions are at present incompatible, with potentially dire effects on the mission. Yet since few medieval theorists would dispute the Aristotelian tenet that the interests of the global political organism are always more important than any part thereof, traditional, or even modern justification of any political behavior is automatically invalidated if it threatens the commonweal. It is thus less significant that either Charles or Roland thinks or acts according to a given code of ethics than the simple fact that their behaviors are mutually abrasive. At such a point, the position of both men is subject to review.

A distinct pattern emerges in the course of the ten-phase conflict. In 1-5, Roland "wins"; that is, his will prevails over Charles's. Thus:

1. Charles does not wish Roland to fight Ferragu; Roland fights.
2. Charles wants to abandon the expedition; the expedition, at Roland's insistence, is pursued.
3. Charles wishes to crown Roland king of Spain at Nájera; Roland refuses.
4. Charles disapproves of victory celebrations at Nájera; Roland enjoys the festivities nonetheless.
5. Charles threatens to hang Prince Isoré against Roland's will; Isoré is safely returned to his family.

In the last confrontation, Roland's victory is particularly significant; it involves not merely his own interests, but those of honor and justice. However, following plateau phase 6, conflicts 7-10 display a reversal in Roland's capacity to prevail; he is either humiliated and/or "defeated" in his confrontations with Charles, who continues to deny the autonomy apparently extended. The following schema may be applied:

7. Charles, enraged at the insubordination of the mutinous Thiois, plans and executes a violent revenge. None of the pairs is consulted; their role, including that of Roland, is reduced to post facto protest and efforts to remedy damage already done.
8. Roland fails to execute orders to prevent Saracen reinforcements from entering Pamplona; he is wounded and forced to cease battle. Charles thereupon condemns his *orgueil* for retreating too quickly.
9. Roland refuses the appointment as marshal, explaining that henceforth he will command only his own forces; Charles humiliates him further by denying him action on the field and expelling him to the rear guard.
10. Roland reconquers Nobles for Charles and Christendom; the emperor condemns him as a traitor and publicly strikes him.

Nonetheless, Charles's "victories" in these confrontations contain an undeniable element of ambiguity and might be termed Pyrrhic, since the net results do not achieve any end beyond maintenance of an impotent autocracy. On the contrary, the real results serve rather to weaken both the emperor's military strength and his effectiveness as head of the mission; the barons had said as much in refusing to slay Roland. In conflict 7, he incurs loss of respect among his followers for excessive vindictiveness. In 9, where there is no visible need for his finest knight to lead the rear guard (as there was in the *Chanson*), public humiliation of Roland only weakens Charles's military effectiveness. Finally, in 10, Charles incurs both loss of respect and military effectiveness by physically striking Roland, thereby causing the young hero to abandon him. This ill-conceived gesture leads inexorably to rupture of the feudal bond and disorder within the Christian armies. It could also, within the global scope of epic vision, grant decisive advantage to the enemy and jeopardize both the expedition and all of Christendom. The interdependence and thus necessity of harmonious collaboration between lord and vassal, governor and governed, those parties whom Thomas M. Greene calls the director and executor of action (*Descent* 19) is the essential, ultimate reality of the *Entrée*'s secular ethos.

In *Entrée* I, the text deploys the discourse of feudalism, while demonstrating in the dialectical structure of conflict the nonviability of a system no longer suited to a more complex world. A Trecento northern Italian public, familiar with the incompatibility of the seigniorial system and expanding urban communities, can readily recode the problematics of the Charles-Roland relationship into those of methods of governance more pertinent to its own experience. While there will be more to say on this subject in chapter 3, it is now clear how critical that relationship is. From the equilibrium and stability of that bond derives that of the entire community and all its enterprises: political, military, and religious.

In order to assess whether the *Entrée*'s Roland can be characterized as a *baron révolté*, we must follow his actions beyond the point of rupture with Charles. To what extent does he resemble the protagonists of *Girard de Vienne, Raoul de Cambrai, Renaud de Montauban*? Is Roland to become a *renoyé* or *rénégat*, then a *repenti* as several of those models prescribe?[4]

Entrée II, introduced by a second protasis outlining 13 additional episodes following Roland's departure from Pamplona, offers further innovations in the portrait. The blow of 11,117 is the dynamic force which serves to motivate the final ca. 5000 verses. The text, radically altered by the blow, begins again in different and, for those accustomed to the Rolandian repertoire, scarcely recognizable directions. The blow violates the expectations of both narrative and authorial publics; it shatters what both assumed to know about the Charles-Roland relationship from centuries of texts inscribed with a common message, the indissolubility of that bond. Even if tested in other chansons de geste, it had held firm. In the *Entrée*, it is tested, too, methodically, meticulously, relentlessly. And it fails.

Charles's vociferous oaths to slay Roland without benefit of a hearing, not to mention trial, contribute to our perception of the closure of *Entrée* I. Further, the blood drawn by the mailed glove suggests the symbolic death of the Roland we have known to this point, in this and all those texts related to it. What the blow has destroyed is, precisely,

Roland's function as hero, defender of the faith, "destre braz" of the Emperor and Christian community. It has also destroyed our knowledge of him, rendered him a stranger whose actions recall other knights, some problematically heroic, whose careers are not at all like that of the conventional Roland. Since a significant part of his delineation was dependent on the relationship with Charles, he can no longer be predicated as the favored *nourri*, the cherished nephew. The blow is a quasi-parody of the feudal *paumée*, the ritualistic gesture marking the moment of entry into the institution of chivalry. Rather than to "create" the knight by a mock gesture of violence, the *Entrée* blow in fact annuls, in an act of real violence, the hero's essential functions and his established identity as well. And as it annuls the contractual bond between Charles and Roland, it likewise eradicates the traditional bond between character and public; our expectations of Roland's actions, established and sanctioned in so many previous texts, no longer apply.

As in some texts in the *baron révolté* cycle, the *Entrée*'s rupture involves vows of vengeance on the part of both litigators. In Roland's case, it is vengeance for what he sees as undeserved condemnation of his Nobles victory. He has not been deprived of a fief or wife like Raoul de Cambrai or Girard de Vienne (see Calin, *Revolt*). Yet he has been publicly dishonored, his well-intentioned *auxilium* "mis-taken" and condemned. Acutely conscious of the shame which such a public gesture invites, Roland's discourse indicates responses of both shame and guilt. Yet stronger than both, or stemming from them, is his desire for vengeance and vindication.

Vengeance and vindication are behaviors involving a minimum of two parties and two acts. In the case of vengeance, an initial act perpetrated by agent A is negatively received by B, who then conceives a retaliatory second act in direct response to A's perceived misconduct. In fact, A's appraisal of his own action is not important; he may consider it laudable, blameworthy, or neutral. The critical factor is B's perception and desire for retribution. In the case of vindication, an initial act is perceived by A as justifiable, but as culpable by B, somehow affected by the act and assuming a judgmental function. Here, phase two involves a second act staged by A with the purpose of reversing the negative response of judge B. A's task is to change B's vision, to demonstrate the blameless intentionality of the initial act via another/other act/acts, which must be carefully conceived and executed to accomplish that goal. Only when the power of A's second act brings about B's acknowledgement that his initial judgment was wrong will the vindication be successful. In each instance it may be language which is the substance of action.

Both are educative behaviors. *Entrée* II is thus essentially the process by which Roland enacts both vengeance and vindication, retaliation via desertion as well as demonstration, via the sequence of his actions, of the justifiability of his *prise de Nobles* and the necessity that Charles change his condemnation thereof. Roland's statement immediately following the blow well illustrates the didactive intention in his departure: " 'Mielz veul morir qe je ni li **ensaigne** / 'Se je riens li valloie en la gere d'Espagne' " (11,151-152; emphasis added) (" 'I prefer to die [if necessary] in order to teach him whether I was worth nothing to him in the war for Spain' "). Yet as if to underline that his means of vengeance/vindication will not imitate *ad litteram* the *baron révolté* model, Roland alerts us that it will be " 'en stragne guise' " (11,132) (" 'in strange form' "). The hero himself states that deviation from canons will inform this text henceforth.

As for Charles, it is not the ends, but the means by which the city was taken which constitute willful disregard of that aspect of *auxilium* which required Roland's presence on the field at Pamplona until specific orders should release him. He cannot fault Roland for *auxilium* in the fight for either city; the vassal's service per se is not in question. For Charles, however, Roland's failure to secure authorized permission to depart Pamplona is more immediately important than his victory at Nobles. It would seem that ends are less important than means, results less critical than form. If Roland is more intent on reconquest of these cities as steps in the re-establishment of acceptable religious and political systems in Spain, Charles in the present instance insists on the maintenance of his authority regardless of altering circumstances (i.e., necessity of seizing Nobles immediately). Seen in this light, Roland is more the pragmatist, receptive to new ways of achieving goals, sufficiently flexible to change strategies where circumstances dictate. Charles, on the other hand, remains attached to traditional courses of action and mentalities, too old, perhaps, to alter his vision.

Regeneration of the Hero

Three principal episodes comprise the exile portion of the text: Roland's victory over the Persian Prince Pélias, his triumph as commander-in-chief of the Persian armies over a rebellious noble, and his conquest of Jerusalem (part of the *lacuna* in ms. XXI. In the first of these episodes (11,904-13,466), Roland defends the Persian Princess Dionés, who is protesting a political marriage contrived by her father to the aged but powerful Malquidant. Roland enters the sultan's service and emerges victorious from combat with Malquidant's nephew Pélias. He is named "baillis" and "avoheor" (13,494, 10,954; Thomas and Holtus *défenseur* < Lat. *advocator*) of Persia, a position of leadership partially analogous to his privileged status under Charles. (cf. his rejection of the "bailior" role in conflict 9). But, faithful as ever to Aude, he declines the victor's prize, marriage to the princess with its attendant personal and political advantages.

The second Mideastern episode is a military encounter with the armies of Malquidant. Interrupted by a sizable *lacuna* (see Introduction), it narrates Malquidant's defeat, coronation of Anseïs de Blois in a re-Christianized Jerusalem, and closes with Roland's imminent return to Spain after an absence of seven years. Dionés has been converted and her father engaged to build churches in "paganie."

It is clear that the Paduan has altered the patterns characteristic of the Doon de Mayence cycle, of which only the *Chevalerie Ogier* was apparently adapted into a Franco-Italian version. Although Roland and Charles reach an impasse where they become virtually enemies, and where both seek reprisal, the hero avoids the bellicose postures of Raoul de Cambrai, Girard de Vienne, Isembart, and Renaud de Montauban. The *Entrée*'s Roland is spared the dishonor of the *renoyé* or *renégat*.

The vindication he enacts is, instead, the attempt to reconquer via his own chivalry the heroic identity which he has lost. In a textual society where (at least in Roland's case) birth is not the inevitable determinant of rank, Roland enters the sultan's service in a formal investiture ceremony; subsequently, as commander-in-chief of the Persian forces in the war against Malquidant, he receives the "verger" marking his leadership status and is finally named governor of Persia. In a structure tracing the creation and rise of a new hero, Roland demonstrates the ability to adapt comfortably to the structures of Persian authority and to develop a non-agonistic relationship with superiors. Finally, Roland's acts in *Entrée* II demonstrate that the essence of heroic action is his in whatever context he is placed.

This heroism is existentially predicated; it generates and perpetuates itself with each of Roland's feats in the Orient. In his quasi-feudal service there, he adopts the same responsibilities of *auxilium* and *consilium*, enacts to all appearances the same loyalty to Daïre as to Charles. However transferable these secular roles may be, the apostasy of Roland would radically alter his poetic destiny, and might banish him from the empathies of his medieval public. Thus, although conformist on the social and chivalric planes in the Mideast, the character carefully conceals the Christian identity which he inwardly maintains while professing militant Moslem convictions.

An innovative kind of dualism is thus established as Roland's strategy for survival and heroic reincarnation in the Mideast. Without this *être/paraître* doubling, the author's strategy to integrate him into a new society, demonstrate his ability to interact harmoniously with peers and superiors, and merit the honor and privilege of the hero, would not be possible. Having abandoned the French at Pamplona, he does in fact verbally recreate himself as the enemy of Charles in inventing a series of new national, religious and political identities and supposed loyalties. The authorial public knows that Roland does not abjure his faith; on the contrary, the solidity of his Christian convictions is emphasized even more in *Entrée* II by the increased frequency and length of his prayers. While Roland's equivalent of *exfestucatio* represents a radical alienation from his secular past, the internalized Christian identity, source of all else, is never altered. By retaining the notion of Christian verticality, the poet preserves the essential integrity of the character and facilitates his repredication as hero among the Christians.

Unlike Isembart or Ogier, for example, the orientalized Roland never does battle with a Christian foe. Neither does he, formally, in a speech act, renounce his vassalage to Charles. The blow is the propellant sending him beyond the Christianized world on an epico-romance quest for lost identity. The blow as rupture point in the problematic Charles-Roland relationship creates a crisis not only for them, but for the intra- and extra-textual community. The Paduan has disturbed the essential relationship upon which rests the stability of epic society. His final task, then, following the reaffirmation of Roland-as-hero, must be redemption of that relationship and reintegration of the hero within the original community. In the Dionés and Malquidant episodes, Roland, reappearing under a series of pseudo-identities, achieves these ends; by his two triumphs, he becomes the sultan's "right arm" and universally acclaimed hero of the adopted community. In both the Marciana text and Reggio fragment, Roland stresses the (feudal) service he renders to the sultan (Reggio f. 2c, v. 144: "che [ ]. . . se doit pener s[er]vir sempre autre"; Specht 494). Further, in Marciana XXI when Dionés speaks of rewarding Lionés/(Roland) directly following his defeat of Pélias, he reaffirms a commitment to the feudal contract: " 'Petit hai fait, mais a le sustinance / 'De vostre peres moi met in oferance; / 'Jamais in moi non trovera falance' " (13,195-97) (" 'I have done little, but I offer my services in support of your father; he will never find failure in me' ").

When Roland reveals his true name toward the close of his prolonged stay in the Near East, it is to Pélias in the course of their duel, with the confidence that the latter will be unable to repeat the information. In this critical encounter which assures Roland the status of hero, he shows himself superior to the finest, most seasoned, and most feared of Persia's knights. Prevailing over Pélias, acting in the service and for the honor of the sultan, Roland has become, once again, the valiant warrior, faithful and invincible knight—and almost the adopted son-in-law. He has once again shown himself worthy of his name in terms of epic literature:

> His life as a hero is devoted to informing his name
> with meaning. Because, unlike an animal, he can
> accomplish a distinctive, personal thing, and unlike a
> god, he has no past accomplishments, the hero must
> discover and demonstrate at the outset what meaning
> his name may have. He is impelled to act, and as
> action among men is agonistic, he is plunged into a
> contest of *areté, virtus,* capacity—a struggle to
> impose his being on his world. He can do this by
> demonstrating his control over a piece of his
> world. . . . To remain a hero he must continue to
> demonstrate control, and so his career imitates the
> expansiveness of the epic imagination. But at the end
> of that movement, implicitly or explicitly, his
> inescapable limitations await him (Greene, *Descent*
> 16).

Further, Roland's reappropriation of heroic status in the Mideast has not been clouded by accusations, or even insinuations, of what Bertoni decried as "ricerca di gloria" or pride. In ms. XXI, Dionés urges her father to accept "Lionés's" offer to serve him: " 'Retenés Lionés, a le voutre cherine, / 'A lui dounés les armes, li vair et li ermine; / 'Gardés qu'en lui amer ni ait nule volpine' " (13,575-77) (" 'Retain Lionés in your care, give him arms, blue-grey fur, and ermine; note that in loving him there is no treachery' "). The narrator in the Reggio fragment reinforces this, following the ceremony in which, by the sultan's request, Roland anoints Prince Samson as chevalier: "Car . . . . ne dote[n]t . . . . .orgoi/ M. . . . . . . .che fir(n)t Persians/ [Seulem]a(n)t po(r) l'amor de le niés K(arl)ema(n)s" (F 20, 178-80).

The *Entrée*'s reconciliation between Charles and Roland is presented in a spirit of mutual contrition. Charles, still unsuccessful after many years at the walls of Pamplona, now confronts the imminent desertion of two hundred of his barons unless Roland returns. While maintaining the justifiability of the blow on a theoretical basis, Charles has come to recognize the act as pragmatically untenable if he is to maintain his own status as defender of the faith and leader of his people. He acknowledges to Roland on his return that " 'Se je vos fi oltraje ne sordois, *l* . . . je conois / 'Que senz vos bras non valdroie un pois' " (15,798-800) (" 'If I committed an outrageous or despicable act toward you, I recognize that without your support I would not be worth anything at all' "). In a parallel gesture, Roland admits to transgressive behavior in the Nobles affair, submitting himself to the emperor's judgment. Handing his sword to Charles, he states: " 'A vos plaser prenez de moy justisse, / 'Car enver vos ai fet plus grand fantise / 'D'ome del secle . . . ' " (15,767-68) (" 'Carry out justice on me as you wish, for I have committed an act of greater deception toward you than any man alive' "). The death-rebirth motif suggested by the blow and Roland's subsequent regeneration in the Mideast is repeated by Charles, who declares that he, too, suffered a symbolic death by destroying Roland's heroic identity. Reunited with his nephew, he says "with a humble voice": " ' . . . resuresi m'avois / 'Da mort a vie; vesqui n'aüse un mois' " (15,791-93) (" 'You have resurrected me from death to life; I would not have lived a[nother] month' "). Moved by "la piété" of Charles, the entire host weeps for joy.

At the feudal level, the theme of lord-vassal interdependence stresses that the two function best when no friction distracts from the common task confronting them. Nonetheless, it is clear that the hero is the indispensable member of this pairing; while Charles is quite literally immobilized at Pamplona, Roland's chivalric ability and adaptability are without limitation. Ironically, it is the long period of separation, during which each is compelled to reformulate his alliances, which ultimately stabilizes the Charles-Roland bond for sequel texts such as the *Chanson de Roland.*

In *Entrée* II, the Paduan alters the outcome of the feudal conflict. Claiming that the material is his own, he fashions Roland into a *chevalier errant* not engaged in open warfare with an unjust overlord, but in search of his own 'mis-taken' identity. If the Roland of *Entrée* I bears distinct resemblance to some of the rebellious barons, the character and narrative are then significantly modified to incorporate material and strategies borrowed from romance. Reader/audience considerations may have been the poet's primary concern; it can be expected that an early Trecento Italian public, engaged in what has been called one of the Middle Ages's most audacious experiments in human governance, would be less interested in the intricacies of feudal conflict than in the more general—and more pertinent—issue of interrelations

between a citizen and his leaders. There will be more to say on this
issue.

Notes

1. Noteworthy variants in the portrait include the *Chanson d'Aspremont*, in which Roland follows the imperial armies to Italy and performs his first chivalric feats, and the *Quatre fils Aymon*, where Roland temporarily abandons Charles out of sympathy for Renaud de Montauban, with whom Charles is at war. Regarding the *Chanson de Roland* as a model chanson de geste, this is a common perception based on the relatively small number of canonic texts which are generally the subject of discussion. It is also true that the *Roland* is unique, different from other works. See the interesting discussion of this and other aspects of epic literature in "1977 Annual Meeting of the Société Rencesvals, American-Canadian Branch: Proceedings," *Olifant* 5.3 (March 1978): 203-30, especially the comments of William Kibler, 218:

    > ... there tends to be a monolithic understanding of chansons de geste derived almost uniquely from studying the *Chanson de Roland*. Yet we have so many other texts that are so different. The *Roland* stands out as different from all the others, yet we establish binary relationships and paradigmatic structures based on the *Song of Roland* and then show how all the others do not fit. Maybe we should start looking at them and see how they fit and say that the *Song of Roland*, on the other hand, might be the exception.

2. Cf. W. T. H. Jackson, *The Hero and the King: An Epic Theme* (New York: Columbia UP, 1982), a comparative study of western European epic based on the thesis that opposition between an established ruler and an independent, usually intrusive warrior is a significant theme in the *Iliad, Aeneid, Beowulf*, the *Niebelungenlied, Chanson de Roland, Guillaume d'Orange* poems, and *Le Cid*. Conflicts generally center upon loyalty, and bring in issues such as age and conservatism vs. personal ambition characteristic of the younger man. Jackson identifies Roland among the models of the exiled hero; as I understand his argument, Roland is in an "exile" largely determined by "his opposition to Charlemagne and hence to the ruling establishment" predicated in the initial *conseil*, where they disagree over continuation of the war. From this opening episode, Jackson sees the development of a confrontational relationship of the "self-

centered hero as contrasted to the responsible king" (58). However, Charlemagne is then said to represent "the classic situation of the ruler unable to control a situation," leading to the tacit recognition that it is the subject, not the ruler, who is in control (60). Although Charles and Roland do disagree in the initial *conseil* in the *Chanson*, there is no evidence of antipathy beyond the immediate situation; to see Roland as an "exile" is, in my judgment, erroneous. In his brief examination of the *Guillaume* poems, Jackson locates the oppositions in the "paradoxical picture of hero and king in conflict for the king's own good" (74); i.e., the ruler's apparent inability or unwillingness to fulfill his sovereign functions.

3.   For discussion of the results of conflict between lord and vassal, see Reto R. Bezzola, "De Roland à Raoul de Cambrai," *Mélanges de philologie romane et de littérature médiévale offerts à Ernest Hoepffner* (Paris: Les Belles lettres, 1949) 195-213 and William Calin, *The Old French Epic of Revolt: Raoul de Cambrai, Renaud de Montauban, Gormond et Isembard* (Geneva: Droz, 1962).

4.   See Florence Callu-Turiaf, "Notes sur une version disparue de 'Renaut de Montauban' en franco-italien," *Moyen Age* 68 (1962): 125-36.

CHAPTER 2
NOBLES: IN SEARCH OF FOUNDATIONS

The literature concerning Nobles, the Spanish city briefly mentioned in the Oxford *Roland*, has long been a lively forum for differing opinions on sources, philology, geography, and historicity. The following pages, themselves testimony to continuing exploration of the city's foundations, will identify a corpus of Nobles references in order to examine closely a group of seven core texts in which evidence of a récit can be perceived. These core texts disclose a narrative and thematic structure revolving around the problematics of the Charles-Roland relationship. It is this common element, the dialectic of overlord authority and vassal autonomy, which explains the *inventio* and *dispositio* of the episode's most extensive treatment in *L'Entrée d'Espagne*, more than 2000 verses of the total 15,805, approximately 12 percent of the entire text.

In the Digby manuscript, earliest of the extant poems to mention Nobles, the city first appears in a list which Roland recites to enumerate his Spanish conquests:

> Set anz ad pleins que en Espaigne venimes.
> Jo vos cunquis e Noples e Commibles,
> Pris ai Valterne e la tere de Pine
> E Balasgued e Tuele e Sezilie (197-200).

> We have been in Spain full seven years.
> I conquered Noples and Commibles for you,
> I took Valterne and the land of Pine,
> Balaguer, Tudela, and Sezille.

The purpose of Roland's récit, cataloguing eight sites including Galne in 662, is to persuade Charles that he must reject Marsile's peace proposals and lay siege to Saragossa until total victory in Spain is achieved. Roland counsels Charles to pursue the war "a tute vostre vie" (212), if necessary; as we know, his advice is rejected. The victories are credited to the agent's prowess ("jo"), but syntactically juxtaposed to

articulate Roland's subservience to the seigneur: i.e., the subject acting
for the beneficiary dative "vos," the latter also the director of events.
Syntax serves to foreground Roland's awareness of feudal hierarchism,
the context in which his acts are accomplished. The catalogue itself is
tangible, as well as temporal evidence of the apparent viability of the
relationship as perceived by the vassal.

Later, Ganelon will offer a rather different, dissonant récit of the
seizure of Nobles when he attempts to persuade Charles to disregard
Roland's oliphant message from Roncevaux:

> Guenes respunt: 'De bataille est nïent!
> Ja estes veilz e fluriz e blancs,
> Par tels paroles vus resemblez enfant.
> Asez savez le grant orgoill Rollant,
> Co est merveille que Deus le soefret tant.
> Ja prist il Noples seinz le vostre comant;
> Fors s'en eissirent li Sarrazins dedenz,
> Sis cumbatirent al bon vassal Rollant.
> Puis od les ewes lavat les prez del sanc,
> Pur cel le fist ne fust aparissant.
> Pur un sul levre vat tute jur cornant.
> Devant ses pers vait il ore gabant,
> Suz cel n'ad gent ki l'osast querre en champ.
> Car chevalcez! Pur qu'alez arestant?
> Tere Major mult est loinz ça devant.' AOI. (1770-84)[1]

> Ganelon replies: 'There's no battle!
> You're old now, you're grizzled and white-haired,
> Yet such words make you seem a child.
> You know Roland's great folly perfectly well,
> It's a wonder God suffers him so.
> He took Noples without your orders;
> The Saracens inside came rushing out,
> They fought the good knight Roland.
> Then he washed the blood from the meadows with streams
>   of water,
> He did this so it wouldn't show.
> He sounds his horn all day long for a mere hare.
> He's showing off now before his peers,
> No force on earth would dare challenge him in the field.
> Ride on! Why are you stopping?
> The Fatherland is very far ahead of us.' AOI

These 15 verses conclude the 24-verse total of laisse 134, which opened with narration of Roland's last, fatal, oliphant call. We are thus at a critical moment, when audience attention can be expected to be at its peak.

One notes immediately that both utterances can be rhetorically classified as *genus deliberativum*: their goal is to persuade the same interlocutor to act/react in a specific fashion. The structure and tonality of their arguments, however, differ significantly. Roland argues, first, that Charles should not accept Marsile's overtures because past experience has proven the latter untrustworthy. As evidence, he cites the case of Basin and Basile, an incident in which Charles's credibility cost him more than the loss of two ambassadors; more significantly, the emperor lost the respect of the French ("Loërent vos alques de legerie" 206). In a cultural context where one strives to save face at all costs, Roland's reminder should have some effect on Charles's decision. Secondly, Roland argues, Charles should pursue the war because his own past record is sufficient proof that Saragossa will soon be won and all Spain reconquered.

Ganelon's arguments are more numerous and complex, but less coherent. Yet Roland and Ganelon share one fundamental element with Roland's: both men place Charles's judgmental faculties into question. While *consilium* is a major vassalic function, persuasion depending on denigration of the lord's perceptions is probably not the best strategy. Here, Ganelon blatantly attributes Charles's poor judgment to the irreparable failings of age. He had already cast the burden of the long war in Spain on Roland alone, in another récit related to Blancandrin on their journey to Saragossa. To characterize the youth's consuming pride, Ganelon recalls the scarlet apple ("vermeille pume") which, just the day before, Roland had offered to his uncle as a symbol of all the conquered crowns which "I present to you" ("vos present" 388). Whether intended in jest or not, the act is recounted by Ganelon not as vassalic *auxilium* colored by the ebullience of youth, but to focus the threat to Marsile's Spain on one man alone: the next apple/crown to be incorporated into Charles's possession may be Marsile's. The polysemous "vermeille pume" also bears the *Genesis* association of the forbidden fruit offered by Satan: a similarly diabolical Roland tempts others to claim what they should not take. Roland's "orgueilz" should someday be the death of him (Jenkins 39, n386)—and could be now, suggests Ganelon, if Blancandrin sees that the end of war is as simple as the elimination of Roland. Further, given the recklessness with which Roland "abandons himself" to danger every day, his removal should be rather easy to accomplish. In our mutual interests, Christian and Saracen, of course: then, only, "tute pais puis avriumes" (391).

Both men seek to persuade Charles of the error, real (Basin-Basile) or potential (acceptance of the peace offer and misinterpretation of the oliphant message) of his perceptions. Both use Nobles as an elliptical *récit exemplaire* to praise or vituperate Roland. The oliphant resounding across the mountains is a communicative act, with narrator, narratee, and text; comprehension of its code and context are impossible without correct interpretation by the recipient. In themselves, the sounds are void of signification. Yet although the blasts may seem to be a totally open genotext, the listener/reader knows that within the parameters of the French chanson de geste, their correct decodings in the present instance can be narrowed to two: the oliphant is blown either in circumstances of the hunt or of combat. Given the fact that Roland, guiding the rear guard in perilous isolation through mountain passes, is unlikely to be enjoying the pleasures of the hunt, the probable correct decoding indicates that a military encounter is involved.

Ganelon's immediate goal is to prevent Charles from interpreting the oliphant message as a call for help, to incapacitate and invalidate his readerly skills. He wishes to divest the oral/aural text of signification, or at least of that signification which Charles instinctively perceives and which the audience/reader knows is correct. In opposition to Charles's interpretation of crisis, Ganelon will thus offer an antithetical reading: Roland has been chasing rabbits all day, as he frequently does, and at this very moment is, literally, "blowing his horn" in the jubilation of the hunt. Of the three individuals involved in sending and decoding the message, the sender (Roland) and the author of the situation creating the message (Ganelon), know its correct meaning. Yet on Ganelon's intentionally *wrong reading* depends the success of his whole scheme to destroy Roland; if the ambush is to succeed, Ganelon must lead Charles, at least temporarily, to discredit his intuition and thus delay his return to Roncevaux. Ganelon can also hope to play upon Charles's war-weariness in this seventh year of the struggle and on his profound desire for an end to the war. On this issue, Ganelon and Charles are in agreement, both opposed to Roland's zeal for protracting the conflict.

While Roland had previously utilized Nobles to illustrate his chivalric superiority, Ganelon amplifies the same récit to establish a decidedly negative characterization of his stepson. According to Ganelon, it is, once again, precisely what Roland did (probably several years ago) at Nobles that reveals what he really is, certainly not the ironically lauded "bon vassal" of 1777:

    a. a transgressor of authority ("seinz le vostre comant"), implying that Roland acted autonomously in the absence of, perhaps, rather than contrary to, orders (see below);

    b. devious, in washing the field to conceal evidence of bloodshed, and conscious of wrongdoing;

    c. frivolous (nb. Ganelon's accusation of Charles's "legerie" as well) and irresponsible (blowing the oliphant all day for a mere rabbit!);

    d. and of course, prideful and arrogant.

Curiously, the final element in this intended defamation ("Suz cel n'ad gent ki l'osast querre en champ") shifts and clouds the argument, despite grave character flaws; Roland has no equal on the field of battle. Verses 1780-82 lend themselves to different readings according to how one phrases or punctuates them. Digby, with its full stops after each verse, is of no assistance, so interpretation as to where semantic units are to be understood will depend on oral delivery or editorial intervention. My inclination is to see 1780-81 as a self-contained statement attempting to provide evidence of Roland's boisterous, boastful nature: "for the sake of a mere rabbit he goes about blowing his horn all day long, and so, even now, he is going about bragging before his *pairs*." In the next verse, 1782, Ganelon concludes his argument with the darkly ironic declaration that, despite all his failings, Roland has always shown himself invincible: no need, then, to be concerned. This reading seems more in keeping with Ganelon's argument than to render 1782 an instance of *discours indirect (libre)*: i.e., at this very moment he is boasting in front of the *pairs* (he is boasting that) there is no one on earth who would dare seek him in battle. Ganelon, of course, means to reinforce his previous arguments in order to deter Charles from returning through the mountains. Yet this hyperbolic statement also serves to justify elements in Roland's character which Ganelon has just decried. If no one "under heaven" would dare to challenge Roland in battle, then the "orgoill" of 1773 is certainly more understandable, and from a military standpoint, possibly excusable. At that point his *gabs*, verbal manifestations of pride, move within the range of acceptable-to-pardonable behavior as well. Moreover, Ganelon's concluding praise of his stepson contains an inconsistency: in 1776, he stated that the Saracens came outside the walls of Nobles to do battle with Roland; they did, then, dare to "querre en champ" the young knight. In attempting to evoke a negative response in Charles to the sound of the oliphant, Ganelon cites/recites the Nobles text as the focal point of his suasive efforts, the irrefutable illustration which crowns his case. Yet unlike the economy and efficiency with which Roland presented his petition, Ganelon's disordered narration tends to undermine the effectiveness of his argument.

In the initial decoding which narratee, medieval auditor/reader and modern reader need to do, Ganelon claims that Roland is a superb warrior, but not an equally good vassal in terms of respect for authority. The narrator, however, counters this charge in 1094 when he asserts that both Roland and Olivier "unt merveillus vasselage." But with the Nobles episode as an immediate analogy, Charles may think that Roland has willfully, without orders, undertaken battle in the Pyrenees. Now, the oliphant may be communicating danger (Roland attacked) or unauthorized action (Roland attacking). The resulting message is more likely to confuse than to calm Charles's apprehensions.

In a second decoding, Ganelon's assignment of the hyperbolic 1782 to Roland himself as self-aggrandizement is a more insidious form of attack. By not risking inconsistency in praising Roland himself at this critical moment, Ganelon's discourse is not logically incoherent; rather, his argument cites his stepson's faults and transgressions with the conclusion that just as the good knight/bad vassal triumphed in the past, he will prevail once again. Nobles thus becomes not only the sign of Roland's vassalic transgressions, but, ironically, of his invincibility as well. This reading, stressing Roland's own decidedly arrogant, yet accurate self-image, is more likely to appease Charles's anxiety. If Ganelon can convince him that Roland sees himself as thoroughly self-confident and competent in the present circumstances, why should Charles worry, eager as he is to believe in Marsile's offer and an imminent end to the war?

The two Oxford allusions may be used as guides in analysis of the Nobles récit as it reappears in some twenty-one additional works, which I have divided into two groups.[2] In the first, the city may be merely an item in an enumeration of Frankish conquests: *Aiol, Gaydon, Floire et Blancheflor, Gui de Nanteuil*, the *Ruolantes Liet*.[3] Alternatively, some few details are added to a minimal allusion. In Jean Bodel's *Chanson des Saisnes*, for example, Nobles is named as a Spanish city seized by Charles from its King Forré; it was here that he acquired his *eaume*. In *Aimeri de Narbonne*, Charles left soldiers in the vanquished city and "a retenu Forré." In *Gui de Bourgogne*, Nobles is taken and Forré killed.[4] In the *Karlamagnús Saga* Branch 4, the episode is mentioned, although the city not named. However, a Bernardus de Nobilis is listed among the leaders of Charles's host. The emperor slays King Furra of Navarre at Mt. Garzdin with 4000 troops. No Christians perish in battle, because Charles's prayer that God sign those destined to fall is answered: Frankish knights marked with a red cross are then sequestered in a chapel and not permitted to fight. Nonetheless, they die in the chapel.[5]

To these texts should be added the *Chronique dite Saintongeaise*, compiled in the latter twelfth century and containing interpolations which its editor, André de Mandach, identifies as earlier epic sources. The brief Nobles episode in "Interpolation C" recounts Roland's seizure (with Arnaux de Beaulande) of the city and massacre of reluctant converts. It adds the flight of King Forrez and the innovation that "fit Karles une chapele de Saint Vincent et fit hi evesque e mist hi chenoines e mist hi assez sanctuaire en l'outer de Saint Vincent. A Guaisfier de Bordeu comanda Nobles."[6] Finally, there is the dubious allusion by the Poeta Saxo to Pamplona as a "nobile castrum" and the conquest of "Nobele" by Guillaume in the Franco-Italian *Mort Charlemagne*.[7]

In the second group of texts, the episode includes additional and/or variant narrative units. The Franco-Italian *Roland* V[4] approximates the second Oxford passage, with two modifications. The O verses concerning purgation of the battleground are omitted, as they are in C and V[7]; secondly, the order of O's 1780-82 has been altered in all three texts so that there is less doubt that affirmation of Roland's invincibility comes from Ganelon, not Roland:

> 'Çà prese'l Noble sença vost comant,
> Fora insì Saraçin ch'era davant
> Sì conbaté al bon cont Rollant,
> Rollant i ancis cum Duridarda el brant.
> Soto el cel no è çent chi olsasse durer avant,
> Per una levorxella va tut li çorno cornant,
> Cun li François se'n va ore gaband!
> Ber Çarlo, çivalça, no alé demorant,
> Terter et mont sì aleron passant!' (1886-94).[8]

'He already took Nobles wihout your command; the Saracens who were in front [of the city?] went out and fought the good Count Roland. Roland killed them with the sword Durendal. Under heaven there is no one who would dare oppose him. For a small rabbit he goes about blowing his horn all day; he is going off to amuse himself with the French right now! Mighty Charles, ride on, do not delay, we shall go on, passing hills and mountains!'

At the close of the *Pseudo-Turpin*, Roland has spent seven years besieging Gratianopolis (Granopolim) when Charles, unable to win his separate war to the north against the rebellious Saxons, summons Roland to his aid.[9] Upon receipt of the message, Roland debates whether to persist at Gratianopolis or to abandon immediately this "urbem pro qua tantos labores passus ferat" in order to rescue his uncle. The three days and nights devoted to prayer and fasting are the narrator's means of depicting a mind divided between desire for some measure of autonomy and the awareness of the vassalic duty of *auxilium*. Roland must decide whether to pursue his own mission independently, now in violation of Charles's wishes, or yield his autonomy and reassume the familiar role as "destre braz." The dilemma is not minimized: ms. A.6 reads: "Tunc nepos, avunculi sibi dilecti anxietate moestus, fluctuabat anxius quid magis eligeret . . . O virum per omnia laudabilem, pietatem redundantem, inter duas fortunas ita angustiatum!" (Meredith-Jones 236-37). Resolution comes when, on the third day, the walls of the city conveniently fall à la Jericho (a miracle which had already occurred at Pamplona and Lucerna). Roland thereupon departs for Saxony. In the Meredith-Jones edition, chapter 16 relates the war against Furre, Prince of the Navarese at Mt. Gazim. In chapter 24, the Spanish toponym Nobles, altered from Naples / Naupalos / Nauples, is rendered adjectival and applied to the French cities Orthez and Dax. In a similar process, the comparative form is used to extol Roland in the epitaph on his tomb: "Nobilis antiqua decurions (?) prole parentum / Nobilior gestis nunc super astra manet" (144-47).

The issues surrounding Nobles are important to three other branches of the *Karlamagnus saga*: 1, 5, and 8. In 1, the reconquest of the city is first on the expedition to Spain; it is also interlaced with narration of other military enterprises to the east. The episode proceeds, somewhat sporadically, as follows:

    a. Charles sends Roland and Olivier ahead to Nobles with 200,000 men to besiege the city with its king Fulr, "who was prepared to defend the city for twenty years" (Hieatt 1: 134-38; 143-49; Aebischer, *Textes norrois* 1: 17, and 2: 3-5; 20-28);

    b. Charles leaves France for Saxony, but is unable to cross the Rhine (ch. 48); he recalls Roland and Olivier from Nobles to assist him. They join his armies, construct a bridge, and occupy the major Saxon cities;

    c. St. Gabriel tells Charles to pursue the reconquest of Spain; a host departs after two years of preparation (ch. 51);

    d. Charles again sends Roland and Olivier ahead to surround Nobles, *with orders not to kill the King;*

        1) Roland comments to Olivier on his uncle's "foolish order" not to kill Fulr, "who's not yet taken!" Olivier replies: "It would be a marvel . . . for him [Charles] to take care of him [Fulr], if I can capture him" (ch. 52);

e. In the course of battle, Fulr attacks Olivier, Roland comes to the aid of his friend, striking and dehorsing Fulr; Olivier delivers the mortal blow to Fulr (Hieatt 3: 16-17, 25-30, 39-42, Aebischer 1: 17).

f. The *compagnons* take the city, killing many; they then wash the field so that Charles will not see the evidence of bloodshed;

g. When Charles arrives, Roland reports that it was he who killed Fulr;

h. Infuriated because "he had ordered them to bring him to him alive," *Charles strikes Roland* (ch. 52).

Karlamagnus saga Branch 5, the *Saga af Guitalin Saxa* also, opens with the Nobles récit, narrated in less detail. In outline:

a. Charles and Roland, in Spain besieging Nobles for three months, are as yet unsuccessful in taking the city;

b. A messenger informs Charles that Cologne, among other Saxon cities, has been attacked by King Guitalin; Charles proposes immediate departure for the new front;

c. Roland is reluctant to leave Nobles until it is won, and says so: " 'Your thought is a strange one. We have been here for scarcely three months (ms. Aa: one month), and I thought it most likely that I would not leave for all the gold in the world, if it were to be brought to me, until I had conquered this city' " (ch. 1).

d. Infuriated, Charles strikes him, declaring: " 'You are a coward, kinsman. You say much, but show little wisdom and deliberation.' " Roland controls his anger; he "would have avenged this direly if the king had not been his kinsman and his ruler" (ch. 1);

e. Roland remains in Nobles; Charles, subsequently besieged himself in a Saxon castle, begs Roland to rescue him;

f. Receiving the letter, Roland wishes to aid Charles as soon as possible. To hasten events at Nobles, he immediately mounts a major assault, vowing that " 'we will either conquer this city or never escape' " (ch. 8);

g. Roland takes Nobles, leaves a garrison there, and sets out for Saxony;

h. A messenger meanwhile informs Charles that:
   1) Roland is on his way
   2) Nobles has been won
   3) Nearly all its inhabitants have been slain and "Roland has killed the leader" (Ms. Bb: " 'we killed' ") and sent his head to Charles (ch. 16);

i. Charles praises his nephew as a " 'remarkable warrior;' " a
joyful reunion ensues Hieatt 3: 16-17; 25-30, 39-42, Aebischer
1: 17.

In Branch 8, known as the *Saga af Runzivals bardaga*, there are two
mentions of Nobles corresponding to the Oxford text. Roland lists it
among his Spanish conquests. Hieatt (3: 28) stresses Roland's sense of
his accomplishments in the catalogue of cities won: " 'Seven winters
have now passed since we came to this land, and I have endured many
pains in your errand. I won for you Nobles and Morinde, Valterne and
Pine, Balaguer, Crudele, Sibilie, Port, and Pailart . . . . Ganelon tells
Charles, anxious upon hearing the oliphant across the mountains:

> 'You are easily misled . . . you speak like a child. You
> know the valour and arrogance of Roland. It is a great
> wonder that God will endure him *when he took Nobilis*
> *without your leave* and drove out the heathens in the
> city and had some blinded, some hung, some cut down,
> and no man dared fight against him. He would always
> ride after an army blowing his horn to amuse himself,
> rather than out of fear' (ch. 31, emphasis added).

Hieatt's translation reflects O's "seinz le vostre comant," while
Aebischer renders the preposition "sans" in one instance, but "contre la
volonté" of Charles in another (1: 13, 44). In all the texts which
include this phrase or an approximation thereof, *Roland took Nobles
without orders, or without permission.*[10]

By far the most extensive treatment of the Nobles conquest is in
the *Entrée*. Of the extant 15,805 verses in Marciana XXI, *Entrée* I
consists of eleven principal episodes, of which three occupy more than
one thousand of the more than eleven thousand total: the "prise de
Nájera," the Isoré episode, and the "prise de Nobles," interlaced into the
narrative after the initial counsel five times for a total of more than two
thousand verses (see Appendix). A summary of its structure follows:

a. Charles summons a *conseil*; rendered aware of the wealth and
strategic position of Nobles, he is advised to take it (6678-767).
He assigns troops, to be dispatched following the securing of
fortifications and supplies at Pamplona (6768-806);
   1) Meanwhile, his front guard is already under attack at Nobles
(6684-89);
   2) Roland is sent to the rear guard after refusing Charles's
assignment as marshal (8301-21);
b. Victory at Pamplona appears certain (8773 and 9007-09);

c. Bernard, returning from a reconnaissance mission to Nobles, informs Roland that the city can, and must be taken immediately, if at all: " 'Car Noble vos donrai demain a le maitin' " and " 'Car bien porois perdre, se avant ne lor vais' " (8991-99);
d. Without informing Charles, Roland leaves for Nobles with 20,000 rear guard troops of his own militia; he thanks God for this opportunity to complete the Christian mission[11];
e. The French, learning of Roland's absence, retreat, lessening hope for rapid victory there (9183-98);
f. Charles declares Roland " 'cest feluns traitor' " (9224) and vows revenge; the youth is to be found, then hanged and all his " 'jeste' " slain (9226-40);
g. Roland captures Nobles, raises his own and Charles's banners over its walls, and returns to Pamplona with booty and hostages for Charles (9410-938);
h. Charles orders his barons to slay Roland as he enters the imperial tent; when they refuse, he himself strikes Roland with his mailed glove (10,997-11,130).

In the first group of texts above, narration of the episode is either too elliptical or abbreviated for any significant intertextual relationships to be analyzed. In the second, however, a number of observations can be made. Comparison of the four Norwegian versions reveals that the first branch is the only one to include all the motifs scattered elsewhere:

1. Roland's siege of Nobles
2. Conquest of Nobles
3. Death of King Fulr
4. Massacre of army and citizenry
5. Cleansing of the field
6. Charles's wrath toward Roland
7. Charles's striking Roland when told that Fulr is dead.

Aebischer thus concluded that Branch I, with its violent confrontation between Charles and Roland, was the source of all other extant versions in the *KS*. In itself, *KS* I formed what he entitled a *Vie et chronique guerrière, mondaine et scandaleuse de Charlemagne et de sa cour*, to which had been added a series of six "épisodes épiques" which "ne sont que des accidents, ou mieux des incidents et des fioritures dans le contexte plus vaste constitué par la chronique de la vie de Charlemagne" (1: 48; 2: 20-28). The last of these insertions is identified as an *Entrée d'Espagne*, opening with the Nobles episode. Aebischer hypothesized an earlier *Vie romancée de Charlemagne* as the source of the French compilation, the *Vie et chronique*:

> Notre compilateur, en un mot, avait devant lui, au
> moment où il a entrepris de rédiger ce qui, traduit plus
> tard en norrois, est devenu la première branche de la
> *Karlamagnús saga* . . . un texte, vraisemblablement en
> prose . . . que j'appellerai la *Vie romancée de
> Charlemagne*. Texte qu'il a truffé, lorsqu'il en avait
> l'occasion et que cela lui semblait opportun, de détails
> complémentaires qui lui étaient connus par d'autres
> sources.

The epic insertions, predating the Oxford *Chanson de Roland*, would
have been added in France by the "compilateur" or "arrangeur";
thereafter, the entire work was translated by an anonymous Norwegian
cleric (1: 32; 2: 54).

In an effort to reconstruct a more logical, coherent "prise de
Nobles" from the disparate elements of *KS* I, Aebischer posited different
evolutionary phases:

> Que la version du chapitre 52 soit loin d'être parfaite,
> nous le savons; qu'elle représente une Prise de Nobles
> déjà réduite, c'est ce qui est plus que probable. Il suffit
> d'ailleurs de peu de chose pour lui rendre un aspect plus
> logique, un sens plus continu: imaginer que Roland et
> Olivier, chargés de l'opération contre Nobles, avaient
> l'ordre non seulement de ne point tuer Fulr, mais de
> s'emparer de la ville sans effusion de sang. Et peut-être
> avons-nous là un ultime indice, dans les récits français
> relatifs à l'expédition d'Espagne, que Charles savait que
> ces vallées navarraises étaient chrétiennes, et qu'il
> importait en conséquence de les épargner le plus
> possible. Mais ce détail étant sorti peu après de la
> mémoire commune, on tenta en un premier moment
> d'expliquer la colère de l'empereur en faisant état d'une
> obéissance de Roland, ou relative à Forré, ou au siège
> même de la ville; puis, le sens du thème se perdant de
> plus en plus, tout l'épisode a fini par être noyé dans la
> série des conquêtes de Charlemagne (I: 48).

The essential point was, then, to explain Charles's anger regarding
some misdeed of Roland in the taking of Nobles. Although one has
difficulty in deciphering the sequence of all the details in the above
reconstruction, the reason for sparing Fulr and his subjects because

there were Christians in the region is interesting. One wonders, however, why a "pagan" ruler should be spared, even in such circumstances.

In Aebischer's theory, as well as in all works in my Group II texts (and most of Group I), the common, striking element concerning the taking of the city is friction between Charles and Roland. In O, Roland used Nobles to illustrate his military success as executor of seigniorial orders, while Ganelon cited the act in an attempt to prove the contrary. In *KS* V, the issue is *which* orders Roland is to obey, those sending him initially to seize Nobles, or subsequent, contradictory commands that he leave the task unfinished to depart for another front. Elsewhere, Charles dispatches Roland to Nobles, but considers his authority violated when the king is slain, blood shed, or even the bordering river crossed. In the versions involving the death of the king, the question of disobedience remains ambiguous: Roland does not initiate the duel, nor should he be blamed for defending himself and protecting his companion. Yet whether it was imperative to kill the king, and whether Roland or Olivier should be held responsible, is left unresolved. Nonetheless, Charles's orders have not been scrupulously followed. The question thus arises: were those orders reasonable? And is Roland actually guilty of violation of authority, disobedience, or insubordination?

That the Paduan's sources in *Entrée* I, in addition to the *Pseudo-Turpin*, were the "bon clerges" "Çan de Navaire" and "Gauter d'Aragon" (2780) has been frequently dismissed (Thomas xxxvii-viii; Limentani, "Epica," 347; cf. de Mandach, *Chronique* 136-39). That his material in *Entrée* II includes extensive originality is clearly to be taken more seriously (Thomas xxxii-xlii; Limentani "Epica" 345, Holtus, Krauss). While the undeniable veracity of the second claim does not guarantee the integrity of the first, perhaps we should reexamine the role of these two unidentified sources.

It is plausible to equate the term "bons clerges" with an "écclésiastique et historien" (de Mandach 137). There are four additional epithets applied to "Çan de Navaire" and "Gauter d'Aragon": "dos barons" 2769), "le dui troveor" (2810), "ces dos prodomes" (2781) and, considered with Turpin, "ces troi otor" (2791-92). The predications divide into two referential pairs: on the one hand, the feudal/epic/chivalric field of the order of the *bellatores*, and on the other, the author/cleric of the remaining three. They are insistently differentiated from "les foibles jogleor" (2812), whose tales of the Spanish war are, according to the narrator, unworthy of serious consideration. The Paduan painstakingly distinguishes the contributions of each of his sources. While Jean de Navarre and Gautier d'Aragon terminated their texts with Ganelon's treason, Turpin continued the narrative to include that infamous event. Nonetheless, the narrator claims that Gautier's is the longest version ("Mais cil Gauter dist plus de nus autre on," 2793). In any case, the *Entrée* offers the definitive text, insofar as it will tell the whole story as it should be told, profiting from and perfecting the work of its predecessors. From the Paduan's authorial/authoritative self-presentation in Prologue B, it is clear that he might well describe himself, too, as "clerge," "otor," and "troveor." Indeed, Prologue B specifies that he is the "houtor" of post-Noblian events, and even the most naïve component of his public will quickly recognize the cleric/scholar in his text (Finoli; Limentani, "Epica"; Krauss, Holtus). Given a detailed delineation of sources and the quality of the work, it may be ingenuous on the part of the twentieth-century reader to dismiss his claims as merely another medieval cliché, more germane to seek the presence of intertextual borrowings from sources known to, and utilized by the Paduan.

The chronologically and geographically varied allusions to the "prise de Nobles," from the c. 1130-1170 Digby manuscript to David Aubert's 1458 *Croniques et conquestes de Charlemaine* and from the north of Italy to Norway, are indicative of the vitality and *mouvance* of the tale. Gaston Paris (*Histoire poétique* 261), Bédier (*Légendes* 120), R. Guiette ("Notes" 67), R. M. Ruggieri ("Titolo e protasi" 287), and André de Mandach (*Chronique* 127-33), among others, have argued that other medieval texts once existed relating various pre-Roncevaux phases of the Reconquest: specifically, that a *Prise de Nobles* was among them. Perhaps the strongest affirmation comes from A. Roncaglia, claiming that in the mid-twelfth century:

> una canzone, la quale narrava l'assalto alla misteriosa città nei termini poi sostanzialmente ripresi dall'*Entrée* francoveneta, doveva godere d'una fortuna non inferiore a quella della canzone di Roncisvalle, da poter essere oggetto d'un'allusione che la colloca praticamente sullo stesso piano e quasi come parte d'una *Chanson de Roland....* (" 'Les Quatre eschieles' " 203).

Yet Antoine Thomas, while noting the striking correlation between the episode in the *Entrée* and *KS* I, dismissed it as a "coincidence singulière," concluding that "l'épisode de la prise de Noble, auquel il [the Paduan] a donné une si grande place ... peut être sorti d'une allusion qui se trouve au v. 1775 de la *Chanson de Roland*: 'Ja prise il Noples seinz le vostre comant" (Introduction xlv).

While it is highly unlikely that the over two thousand lines in the *Entrée* had such humble origins, Aebischer's contention that it was merely part of an early French *Entrée d'Espagne* is not entirely satisfactory either. In his reconstruction of the *KS* I *Entrée*, he cites five segments:

1. Gabriel orders Charles to Spain > convocation of the host
2. Miracle of the "biche blanche" at the Gironde
3. The Nobles episode
4. Capture of Montjardin and Cordres
5. Arrival at Saragossa, where Marsile feigns submission, then slays Basin and Basile ("Deux récits" 15-16).

It is strange, then, that in the sole extended descendant of this hypothesized epic, part one, a topical opening of any chanson de geste, and part three, the "prise de Nobles," are the only episodes retained. Further, it is odd that such minimal correlation exists between the model text and its major surviving descendant.

On the contrary, it seems more likely that an independent poem, a *Prise de Nobles*, was indeed in circulation prior to the redaction of the Oxford *Roland*. What is more compelling, unlike mention of other cities upon which scholars have theorized the existence of lost epics, is the common thematic core of serious Charles-Roland conflict converged around the many tales of Nobles.

Gustave A. Beckmann finds that the episode in its various manifestations combines two discrete but coherent elements, the "réalité topographique" of the thermal springs at Dax with what he terms "le tempérament fougueux de Roland" ("L'Identification Nobles = Dax" 22-23). Wunderli likewise notes Roland's "frequentes accès de rage" as his only serious flaw in the *Aquilon de Bavière* ("Roland théologien" 761n11). Thus it was Roland's impetuous character which would have denied the Noblians what eleventh-century Christian epic normally offered, the possibility of pre-battle surrender and conversion. Roland's transgression, then, would be this specific decision and its subsequent act—counter to the expectations, and perhaps the orders of Charles (Beckmann 22-23). Aebischer, too, noted that it was the Nobles episode which originally established the poetic character of Roland, identifiable by its somewhat excessive temerity and "capable de pousser le courage jusqu'à la désobéissance, ou presque . . ." (*Textes norrois* 2: 90).

The "jo"/"vos" juxtaposition in O 1778 now assumes further potential resonance. In Roland's articulation of the feudal relationship, the self-assertive "jo" preceded the dative "vos." It is not implausible that the enunciation could retain its anaphoric impact by reversing

pronominal sequence: "you" ordered "me" [to conquer]. . . ." Rather, the
first person takes precedence while retaining established feudal
hierarchism. Nonetheless, an active/passive character polarity is
suggested, which, if enacted by a knight with character traits such as
Roland's, might develop into potential confrontation with the overlord.
Ganelon certainly perceives it so.

Apart from events at Nobles, the feudal relationship between
Charles and Roland in the Oxford text works well, with any
disagreement (pursuit of the war, appointment of the messenger)
amicably resolved. Yet inclusion itself of the episode signals authorial
transgression of what we perceive as normative presentation of the
relationship within the *cycle du roi*. The mere mention of serious
conflict in the past, conflict utilized by a third character to orient a
major decision, disrupts public/reader response conditioned to see the
Charles-Roland rapport as unshakeably stable. The Nobles episode,
then, proposes transgressive behavior on two axes: the intratextual
personage acting in defiance of feudal authority, and the narrator acting
in defiance of onomastic expectation/authority.

There are other chansons de geste in the cycle which suggest less
than total harmony on the authority/autonomy issue. In the *Chanson
d'Aspremont*, an adolescent Roland disobeys Charles and manages to go
to Italy with the French armies; his transgressions (theft of a horse and
murder of a guard) are punished by a blow from the avuncular hand. In
the *Quatre fils Aymon*, he abandons Charles temporarily in support of
the brothers' assertion of their autonomy.

The archetypal *Prise de Nobles* would have been thematically
related to such poems. The potentially dialectical nature of the Charles-
Roland rapport is mentioned by Ruggieri ("Titolo" 270ff.), who sees
allusions to Roland's increasing power and autonomy in the *Chanson* as
well as in other works. The *Pseudo-Turpin*, for example, already
establishes Roland as commander of his own armies, "dux exercituum,
comes cenomannensis et Blavii dominus, cum quatuor millibus
virorum bellatorum," (Meredith-Jones 17; nb. Olivier and others had
their own militia, too) a trace of which might be seen in the "jo"
assertiveness of Digby 23. A similar syntactical structure occurs in
Roland's second catalogue of his conquests, repeating the "jo . . .
cunquis" throughout; Charles is here relegated to the third-person
absentee (O 2322-34). Such elements establish Roland in the function
of a second protagonist at least, one who might possibly become
agonistic to a power-sensitive leader.

In Charles's *planctus* at Roncevaux, for example, he omits all
mention of Roland's victories, citing only the threat of future uprisings.
Further, Charles strongly asserts his own sovereignty in *his*

pronominal choices: "Morz est mis nies ki tant me fist cunquere" (2920). Ruggieri comments: "Il tema della guerra vittoriosa di Carlo sta dunque in stretto rapporto con quello della sua assoluta indiscussa sovranità." He finds that silence regarding the Compostella pilgrim route in the *Chanson* and veiled allusions such as those regarding Nobles suggest deliberate narrator reticence "su taluni antecedenti della *Chanson* di cui era a conoscenza, e da cui emergeva un notevole antagonismo tra Rolando e Carlomagno . . . delineatosi durante le prime fasi dell'azione bellica" ("Titolo" 269-71). Charles's regret regarding his own behavior might be seen in O 2900 addressed to the dead Roland: "Cum en Espaigne venis [a] mal seignur!" If this is another unexplained Oxford allusion, it has its counterpart amplification in the *Entrée*, where Charles is contrite upon his reunion with Roland: "Davant son niés engenolé seroit / Mercé crier de ce che feit li oit" (15,757-58).

Regarding the augmentation of Roland's power, Ganelon informs Marsile that, as future vassal of Charles, he will have to share the Spanish fief with Roland, a "mult orguillos parçuner" (O 474). In the *Ruolantes Liet,* Roland claims all Spain and the barons actually crown him (Mortier, *Textes* 10: 3150-51), while in the *Entrée*, Charles proclaims at the outset that one of the two reasons for the expedition is to crown Roland King of Spain. Ruggieri comments:

> Insomma il processo di ascesa per cui il poema francoveneto attribuisce a Rolando un titolo e una dignità ("re di Spagna") che lo rendono di poco inferiore al re Carlo, e ce lo presenta come glorioso 'comprimario' nella conquista del suolo iberico, è già decisamente in atto più di centocinquant'anni prima ("Titolo" 280).

Yet all the extant Nobles récits, including the *Entrée*, avoid the eruption of the conflict into open war. Instead, a reconciliation is achieved within each text, albeit after years of alienation in the *Entrée*. Prologue B announces anticipated audience reception of the Charles-Roland reunion: "Mais sor tot autres coses vos pora abellir / La joie q'en fist Carles quant le voit revenir" (10,989-90).

Because the Oxford poet did not choose to undermine seriously the Charles-Roland bond, he attributes the accusation of Roland as traitor to the least credible of his characters, a traitor himself. His source, some now-unidentifiable form of a *Prise de Nobles*, was also known by the Paduan and incorporated into his work precisely for its exploitation of the authority/autonomy theme. Gaston Paris cited a version of the

Nobles episode in which Olivier kills Forré in vengeance for the latter's murder of his father: Charles thus strikes Roland when he defends Olivier's act (*Histoire poétique* 263-64). Hieatt, referring to this version, writes:

> If these details were part of the original story, they would certainly make a more consistent tale than any we can put together from the scattered evidence about the taking of Noples available in the Norse sagas . . . . That is, the original story might have been that Forré, king of Noples, had killed Olivier's father; thus, when Charlemagne ordered Roland and Olivier to take the city without bloodshed and to capture its king alive, Olivier, moved by the need to avenge his father, disobeyed orders. General bloodshed ensuing, the French tried to wash away the evidence before Charlemagne arrived. When Charlemagne found the truth, Roland defended his comrade, thus angering the emperor to such an extent that he slapped Roland (*KS* 1: 48-49).

In Gaston Paris's reconstruction, Roland and Olivier, returning from Italy, leave Charles with orders to lay siege to Fourré at Nobles. Recalled by the emperor to construct a bridge across the Rhine so that Charles can avenge the bishop of Mutersborg, who has been slain by the Saxon King Vitakind, the two leave Nobles, quell the Saxon uprising, and subdue the city of Dortmund in the same manner in which Turpin recounts the fall of Gratianopolis. Meredith-Jones, remarking on the connection between Fourré and Nobles, remarks: "Le roi Fourré est rélégué à un autre épisode, la chute miraculeuse des murailles de Dortmund est attribuée à Grenoble; l'empereur, qui ne s'occupe plus de la construction du pont, est enfermé dans une autre ville assiégée" (*Historia Karoli Magni* 336-37).

This theory posits no overt allusion to Charles-Roland conflict. The problem would seem to arise at one or two junctures, either at the initial moment of separation on the return from Italy, or, as in the *Turpin*, in Roland's decision whether to relinquish the siege of Nobles immediately when ordered to Saxony. Yet because the nucleus of the tale is unmistakably Charles-Roland conflict, Hieatt's reconstruction is more plausible. In either case, the Paduan, preferring to place lord and vassal in more open conflict, modified his source so that the timing of the attack within the larger context of the expedition becomes the issue leading to crisis. The Aebischer reconstruction would have been altered in the extant *Entrée*: the city is distinctly "pagan" and the death of its king not at issue. Nor does Roland cleanse the site, knowing that Charles will not be arriving to disapprove of the signs of combat.

In order to serve his apparent narrative ends, however, the *Entrée* poet had to place Charles in a decidedly unfavorable light, similar to the authority figures in the *baron révolté* epics. Thus its second protasis opens with an authorial announcement of the blow: "Por quoi [Roland] parti de lui a loi de corocé, / Dont mout en fu le rois de ses barons blasmé / Et il meïsme en fu irez et adollé" (10,942-44). Public/reader sympathy is apparently oriented to align with the vassal knight seeking to loosen the excessive curtailment of an autonomy which he appears to merit. Thus the narrator renders Charles inconsistent and extremist, possibly even abusive of his authority.

Karl-Heinz Bender has traced six thirteenth-century Franco-Italian chansons de geste to show how they progressively, if sporadically, transform the Charlemagne figure from its mythic status to a purely literary one. Bender claims that moralistic, rather than legalistic, treatment of Ganelon's act in these works testifies to Italian disinterest in things feudal: "L'accomplissement du devoir du vassal ne pose plus de problèmes, et c'est parce que les relations des barons avec le roi ne sont plus problématiques qu'elles ne décident plus de l'évolution de l'action." Evidence can be cited in the Franco-Italian *Chevalerie Ogier*, where Karloto is prepared to suffer three blows from the hand of his vassal in order to obtain the latter's military *auxilium*:

> Un tel châtiment corporel du seigneur aurait été inconcevable pour un public imprégné de l'esprit féodal; car le code d'honneur de la féodalité ne permettrait ni au seigneur de battre son vassal, ni au vassal de lever la main contre son seigneur ("Métamorphoses" 164-69).[12]

The *Entrée* (not included in Bender's study) has clearly eroded the Charles portrait still further; the blow renders him a transgressor of the feudal contract (see ch. 4). Within an epico-feudal reading of the text, the *Entrée* leaves little doubt that Charles is a negative model in the exercise of seigniorial authority. Roland, in his desire for some degree of vassal autonomy, is the undeserving victim of contractual abuse. In the Franco-Italian poems, as in those concerning the rebellious barons:

> ce sont la colère et la fierté de Charlemagne, traits de caractère habituels du roi, qui déclenchent, puis aggravent la lutte féodale dans laquelle les qualités traditionnelles du mythe de Charlemagne sont niées ou changées en leur contraire ("Métamorphoses" 166).

The conquest of Nobles in the *Chanson de Roland* was a parenthesis, a brief but critical moment of remembered dissension, where its quality of story-within-a-story did not disturb the essential viability of the lord-vassal bond. Credit for the apparent stability of the relationship must be granted to Charles, of whom Gerard J. Brault affirms that he "possède la sagesse depuis le début jusqu'à la fin de la *Chanson de Roland* par la grace de Dieu et en tant que *basileus*" ("Sapientia" 113). The Oxford Nobles parenthesis alerts us to other, more profound dimensions to the agonistic relationship with roots in other texts. An earlier *Prise de Nobles*, transgressive and iconoclastic, may have been rather swiftly relegated to a marginal position in the *cycle du roi*, then neglected and finally, nearly forgotten. It is the use to which the Paduan has put its thematic base which offers our best evidence of its existence and content.

Notes

1. Brault discusses problems in the reading and interpretation of Digby laisse 134, noting manuscript damage, scribal errors and revisor's alterations: "In short, this passage is so corrupt that we should be doubly suspicious of any aberrant word or line. . . . This suggests that v. 1778 in the Oxford version, which is doubtless incorrect, represents an original: 'Puis od les ewes lavat s'espee del sanc,' which may be translated as follows: 'Then he washed the blood on his sword in a stream.' " The purging of the field with the explicit intention to conceal the bloody signs of battle, presumably under Roland's orders, is not mentioned in any other version of the *Roland*, except in *KS* I (2: 216-17, 427-28).

2. Of the various spellings of the city (Nople, Noples, Noble, Nable, etc.), only those clearly pertaining to the site in question are examined here. Works considered predate the *Entrée*, although mention will be made of texts appearing after the mid-fourteenth century. See Moissan, *Répertoire* 1.2: 217.

3. Raynaud, Gaston and J. C. L. Normand, eds. *Aiol: chanson de geste* (Paris: Firmin Didot, 1877) 236: 8087-88. F. Guessard and S. Luce, eds., *Gaydon: chanson de geste*. Les anciens poètes de la France (Paris, A. Franck, 1862) 2: 28, 35-37. Nobles is besieged by Charles after Roland's death. E. du Méril, ed., *Floire et Blancheflor, poème du XIIIe siècle* (Paris, P. Jannet, 1856). In its first version, Floire is raised at the Spanish court of Gaydon at Naples. James McCormack, ed., *Gui de Nanteuil, chanson de geste*. Textes littéraires français 161 (Geneva: Droz, 1970) 1: 294; 2; 127. The city is entered as "Naples," rendering identification with Nobles dubious. Mortier, Raoul, *Les Textes de la Chanson de Roland*, trans. Jean Graff, 10 vols. (Paris: La Geste Francor, 1941-1944) 1211, 8047. The name given is "Nobiles," a pagan country, and "Nables" or "Mables," a Moslem city.

4. Jehan de Bodel, *La Chanson des Saisnes*, ed. Annette Brasseur (Geneva: Droz, 1989) 5484-86. Bertrand de Bar-sur-Aube, *Aimeri de Narbonne*, ed. Louis Demaison, 2 vols., SATF (Paris: Firmin Didot, 1887) 2: 105-106, 280-82. F. Guessard and H. Michelant, eds., *Gui de Bourgogne, chanson de geste*, Les anciens poëtes de la France (Paris: F. Vieweg, 1859) 1854-61.

5. I have consulted three versions of the *Karlamagnus Saga ok Kappa Hans* in translation. Paul Aebischer, *Textes norrois et littérature française du moyen âge*, 2 vols. Société de publications romanes et françaises 54 and 118 (Geneva: Droz, 1954 and 1972). Constance B. Hieatt, ed. and trans., *Karlamagnús Saga: The Saga of Charlemagne and His Heroes*, Mediaeval Sources in Translation

13, 3 vols. (Toronto: The Pontifical Institute of Mediaeval Studies, 1975). Gaston Paris, "La Karlamagnus-saga," *Bibliothèque de l'Ecole des Chartes*, 5th ser. (Paris, 1864) 5: 89-123, and 6th ser. (Paris, 1865) 6: 1-42.

6.   André de Mandach, ed., *Chronique dite Saintongeaise*, Beihefte zur Zeitschrift für Romanische Philologie 120 (Tübingen: Max Neimeyer Verlag 1970), ch. 10, especially verses 127-41 and 296-300.

7.   Gianfranco Contini, "La canzone della *Mort Charlemagne*," *Mélanges de linguistique romane et de philologie médiévale offerts à M. Maurice Delbouille*, 2 vols. Gembloux: Duculot, 1964) 2: 105-26. *Poeta saxo, The Saxon Poet's Life of Charles the Great*, Mary Emma McKinney, ed. (New York: Pageant P, 1956) 97.

8.   Giuliano Gasca Queirazza, ed. and trans., *La Chanson de Roland nel testo assonanzato franco-italiano* V[4], L'orifiamma: collezione di testi romanzi o mediolatini 1 (Torino: Rosenberg & Sellier, 1952)100: 1886-94.

Mortier's reading of V[4] is essentially the same; however, he punctuates 1886-90 as follows:

> 'Soto el cel non e çent chi olsasse durer avant.
> Por una levorxella va tut li çorno cornant;
> Cum li François s'en va ore gaband.
> Ber Çarlo, çivalça, no alé demorant!
> Terter et mont si aleron passant.'

His reading of Châteauroux 3089-3101 is:

> 'Ja prist il Nobles tot sanz le vostr comanz.
> Fors s'en issirent li Sarazin as chans;
> Tuit s'entrocissent a lor espiez trenchant.
> .R. li fers, li hardi combatanz,
> Se fist lever enz es pré verdoianz,
> Saisi les cors a toz les combatanz
> Q'il volst li sans en fust aparisanz.
> Sor toz les pers est il ore gabanz,
> Apres une lievre est tote jor cornanz.
> Chevauchez, rois, ne soiez atarianz!
> Terre Major, qi tant par est vaillanz,
> Loinz est encore, ne soiez destrianz;
> A mot grant piece ni serez sejornanz.'

See also G. Robertson-Mellor, ed., *The Franco-Italian Roland V⁴* (Salford: University of Salford Reprographic Unit, 1980). The corresponding passage in V⁷ is essentially the same.

9. Gratianopolis appears in the Codex Calixtinus, Granopolis in ms. A.6. C. Meredith-Jones, ed., *Historia Karoli Magni et Rotholandi ou Chronique du pseudo-Turpin* (Geneva: Droz, 1936) 234-39. Meredith-Jones considers that the original text ended with the death of Charles in the previous chapter, whereas in this edition it is the final chapter before four appendices. The city is in France, conquered by Roland "antequam ingrederetur Hispaniam"; the same is true in the *Grandes croniques de France*, where it is called Granople. See Mortier, *Textes* 3. Yet Meredith-Jones affirms that this is the "correct" Nobles: "Tout le monde sera d'accord pour voir à la base de cette prise de Gratianopolis, Granople, la légende, mutilée et déformée, de la mystérieuse ville de Nobles, Noples." It is curious that the *Pseudo-Turpin* does not include Nobles among cities conquered in Spain in ch. 3, although a Bernardus de Nublis appears in ch. 11 among leaders of the Carolingian armies. These points apply also to ms. BN 17656.

10. Brief mention should be made of three works appearing after the *Entrée* which contain a Noples episode: ch. 29 of *Li fatti de Spagna*, ed. Ruggero M. Ruggieri (Modena: Mucchi, 1951); laisse 12, v. 39 through laisse 14, v. 37 of *La Spagna, poema cavalleresco del secolo XIV*, ed. Michele Catalano, Collezione di opere inedite e rare, Commissione per i testi di lingua, 3 vols. (Bologna: Carducci, 1939); David Aubert's *Croniques et conquestes de Charlemaine;* see Robert Guiette, "L'Entrée de Charlemagne en Espagne et la tradition des *Croniques et conquestes de Charlemaine (1458)*," *CN* 21 (1961): 206-13.

11. Regarding the importance of Roland having his own army, see Ruggieri, "Il titolo e la protasi dell'*Entrée d'Espagne* e dei *Fatti di Spagna* in rapporto alla materia della *Chanson de Roland*," *Mélanges de linguistique romane et de philologie médiévale offerts à M. Maurice Delbouille*, 2 vols. (Paris: Gembloux, 1964) 2: 281ff. Several other texts grant Roland this privilege; Ruggieri sees it going back to the rear guard troops originally assigned to him, which subsequently become his personal militia. In *Entrée* 8304-13, Roland declines to assume responsibility for any but his own troops. See ch. 1. here. *La Spagna* models its Nobles episode closely upon the *Entrée*'s, while emphasizing even more strongly Roland's autonomy. The youth claims that he took only his own men to Nobles; when confronted with Charles's wrath, he declares that he is subservient not to Charles, but directly to Rome. He

has to be physically restrained from returning the blow which
Charles deals him. Catalano, laisse 14, v. 10. See also Aurelio
Ronclaglia, " 'Les quatre eschieles de Rollant,' " *CN* 21 (1961):
191-205.

12.   "Les Métamorphoses de la royauté de Charlemagne dans les
      premières épopées franco-italiennes," *CN* 21 (1961): 164-69.
      Bender is citing Marc Bloch: *La Société féodale: les classes et le
      gouvernement des hommes* (Paris: A. Michel, 1940) 352.

CHAPTER 3
THE DIALECTIC OF IDEOLOGIES

Medieval Models of Society

A. The Primary Model: Sources and Evolution

> We must show . . . that our hierarchy is inspired by
> God and that it implies a divine and deifying science,
> activity, and perfection.[1]

In the notions of order, hierarchy, and the sanctity of each is
posited a mentality which was to dominate Western Europe throughout
the Middle Ages, and upon which was erected the model of Christian
society articulated in eleventh-century France. Because both its
ideological foundations and operative mechanisms are fundamental to
subsequent discussion here of its manifestations in northern Italy and in
the social modelling within the *Entrée*, these initial pages recover its
essential tenets.

It is Pseudo-Dionysius the Aeropagite, writing c. AD 500, who
introduces the sacralization of societal *hierarchia*: "The source of this
hierarchy is the Trinity, the fountain of life, the essence of goodness,
the one cause of things that are" (*Ecclesiastical Hierarchy* 20).
Augustine expresses a similar theory in *City of God,* 19.13 : "Pax
omnium rerum tranquillitas ordinis. Ordo est parium dispariumque
rerum sua cuique loca tribuens dispositio." ("The peace of the whole
universe is the tranquility of order—and order is the arrangement of
things equal and unequal in a pattern which assigns to each its proper
position.") For Pseudo-Dionysius, the universe consists of two
hierarchies, celestial and earthly, united and epitomized in the
Incarnation. In establishing His Church, God offered to mankind a
model of the superior celestial order. And, through "divinely transmitted

scriptures," " . . . the first leaders of our hierarchy transmitted to us the supracelestial in sensible figures. . . . They transmitted the unified in variety and multiplicity, the divine in the human, the immaterial in the material, the super-essential on our own level, making use of both written and oral instructions" (*Ecclesiastical Hierarchy* 21). Every Christian, then, by virtue of his/her confirmation, becomes a *déchiffreur* of signs and symbols, charged with seeking the *significata* of observable phenomena in the world, as well as within his/her own existential experience. Yet such knowledge and understanding was not to be divulged except to privileged individuals. As Pseudo-Dionysius immediately cautions his fellow bishop: "Be prudent and respect the hidden things of God by using spiritual and obscure notions" (*Ecclesiastical Hierarchy* 17).

In the first triadic church hierarchy are the initiators, who interpret God's signs: in ascending competence, they are the lower clergy, priests, and bishops. The bishop, whose title derives from the term hierarchy itself, is the person "learned in all sacred knowledge," in whom "the whole hierarchy is plainly perfected and recognized." Next are those whom the bishops initiate, called perfectibles; in ascending order, they are the penitent, faithful, and finally, the monks. In this description the latter are considered unsuited for "pontifical" roles within the Church and remain subject at all times to the authority of the priestly orders (*Ecclesiastical Hierarchy* 19, 62-63, 73-74).

In 595, Gregory the Great reinforced these tenets in a letter to the bishops of the kingdom of Chilperic:

> Providence has established various degrees [*gradus*] and distinct orders [*ordines*] so that, if the lesser [*minores*] show deference to the greater [*potiores*], and the greater bestow love [*dilectio*] on the lesser, then true concord [*concordia*] and conjunction [*contextio*] will arise out of diversity. Indeed, the community [*universitas*] could not subsist at all if the total order [*magnus ordo*] of disparity [*differentia*] did not preserve it. That creation cannot be governed in equality is taught us by the example of the heavenly hosts; there are angels and there are archangels, which are clearly not equals, differing from one another in power [*potestas*] and order [*ordo*] (*Ep.* 54, *PL* 77: 785-87 cited in Duby, *Orders* 3n1).

More than four centuries later, between 1023 and 1031, with social equilibrium in northwestern France jeopardized by proliferating heretical sects, dissension within the Church, a weakened monarchy, and ominous signs of social change, the theories of Pseudo-Dionysius and Gregory were resuscitated, recombined and recast. The trifunctional model of society was first articulated by two bishops, countered by competing models for a century and a half, finally adopted in a modified form in the latter twelfth century to dominate until the Revolution of 1789.[2]

The two bishops articulating the system, Gerard of Cambrai and Adalbero of Laon, were cousins to one another, descendants of Charlemagne, and part of the long Carolingian tradition whereby the episcopate kept a counselling and corrective eye on secular rulers. Such bishops, the guardians of classical rhetoric, "tenue par les intellectuels des chapitres cathédraux pour un moyen de gouverner," were quite naturally the generators of ideology (*Ordres* 29, 31). The link between rhetoric and politics was significant; the function of both was the optimal organization of language and of people for the purpose of recreating perfect order on earth (*Ordres* 95).

Gerard's model has been transmitted to us in three separate segments distinguished here by the places with which each is associated: Compiègne, Arras, Douai. Each transmission is part of, and closely related to, a context of time and events in both an immediate and broader sense. For the bishop of Cambrai, the broader themes concern the definition and use of power and how it is that peace can be achieved—in essence, "une réforme générale de la société chrétienne" (*Ordres* 39). His theses, recorded by his canonical secretary, were subsequently integrated in the *Gesta episcoporum cameracensium* written in 1024 and recast thirty years later after Gerard's death.[3] The bishop initially identifies two *ordines*, a term which contains at least two major meanings as it was used at that time in reference to social groups. In its concrete sense (a), *ordo* indicated the ceremonial procedure (ordination) by which an individual acquired membership in a given group or organization; by analogical implication, the word indicated "un corps privilégié, isolé du reste, investi de responsabilités particulières, manifestant au regard sa cohésion, sa supériorité, sa dignité par le rang qui lui était attribué dans les défilés religieux militaires ou civiques." In its more abstract sense (b), *ordo* referred to the proper ordering or organization of the universe "ce que la morale, la vertu, le pouvoir ont mission de maintenir" (*Ordres* 95).

In his speech at Compiègne, Gerard employs the term to classify the functions of the two leaders charged with the rhetorical and military ordering of the state: *oratores* and *pugnatores*. On the one side the bishops, closest of all humans to the Divinity and mediators between them, to whom are entrusted the several powers of the verb *orare*: to pray, i.e., to communicate with and beseech God for aid in the maintenance of order, stability and harmony in the world; second, to preach, thus to disseminate the Word. The *pugnatores* are kings and emperors (not *milites*, who are not mentioned in Gerard's model but roundly chastized in other parts of the *Gesta* for their rapacious behavior, responsible for the defense and governance of the human community). The two orders are not to be considered equal: *orare* also encompasses an instructional function, and in this sector the king is subject to the bishop's *sapientia* (*Ordres* 28-29). Thus it is from the bishops that kings are to receive their swords, a statement behind which lurks the interminable medieval debate on secular vs. ecclesiastical authority culminating in the Investiture conflict.

In the Arras text, the second and most extensive enunciation of the model, Gerard again quotes Gregory to buttress the thesis of *inegalitas* as the will of God. It is also true, he says, that man has brought social inequality upon himself as a result of the Fall:

> Although nature creates all men equal [or: although all
> men are born equal by nature], error [*culpa*] subordinates
> some to others in accordance with the variable order
> [*ordo*] of merits; this diversity arising from vice is
> established by divine judgment so that, since man is not
> intended to live in equality, one may be ruled by another
> (*PL* 77: 34, *Regula Pastoralis* II: 6 cited in *Orders* 35
> n18).

Gerard could have cited others on the subject of submission to authority—the formulation, rather than the idea, was new.[4] In fact, responding to specific regional situations, he needed authoritative precedents to justify his position on an urgent problem, a heretical sect nearby. Likewise seeing the need for social reform, the group had adopted its own social micro-model, based on the most orthodox of Christian tenets—*contemptus mundi*, chastity, pardon of wrongdoing, manual labor, and fraternal love. The difficulty lay in the sect's elimination of all the sacraments, thus of the clergy itself, as mediators. This was clearly unacceptable.

As the basis of the anathema proclaimed against them, Gerard had to prove that there is no way to salvation except via the sacraments administered, according to Divine Will, by a particular *ordo* of men set apart from, and above, the rest of humanity. The priesthood, serving a mediating function between the earthly and celestial cities, was hierarchically ordered itself; the anointed hand of the bishop, sacralized by ordination and thus an extension of the hand of Christ, was empowered to transmit to other clerics the holy signs, Gerard's use of the term *sacramenta*. All authority flows from Christ, the supreme *orator* and *pugnator*; it is the ordering of the human population enacted by his earthly *ministri* which brings about peace (*Ordres* 46-48).

It is not until the bishop's address at Douai, in the peace proposal of 1024, that the third element in the ideological structure is mentioned—almost parenthetically, in order to reinforce his argument of providential *inegalitas*, then under serious challenge by a group of bishops advocating the elimination of social differentiation in three arenas.[5] In his discourse on *otium* and *labor*, in which Gerard wishes to justify the "holy leisure" of the *oratores* (or *sacerdotes*), he explains that it is the labor of both *pugnatores* and *agricultores* which ensures that requirement. The passage opens with a statement of the bishop's adherence to a threefold functional division of mankind into men of prayer, men of war, and farmers, a schema which he claims has been part of the Divine model since the Creation. To the *agricultores* fall the tasks of the verb *decernere*: to serve the social order by working the land, providing food, and carrying out the myriad related chores involving the existential needs of the other orders. According to Jacques Le Goff, this burgeoning third sector, identified by the more general term *laboratores* in other sources, likewise designated a peasant "élite économique, celle qui est au premier rang de l'essor agricole de la Chrétienté entre le IXᵉ et le XIIᵉ siècles" (*Temps* 90). However, as evidence of the potential menace feared by both the monarchy and Church, a dream of King Henry I of England in 1130 portrayed the *laboratores* and the other orders physically attacking the monarch. "Mais alors les *laboratores* ont pris l'aspect non plus d'élite collaboratrice, mais d'une masse hostile, d'une classe dangereuse" (*Temps* 90). The term *laboratores* is not used anywhere in the *Gesta*; in the early eleventh century, the third function is still classified as exclusively agricultural. In fact, the Douai text emphasizes *divisio* rather than *hierarchia*; the *bellatores*, still kings and princes, are mentioned last, after the *agricultores*, in any enumeration of the orders.

The landworker is assured that he, too, profits from the system in the protection he receives from the warriors and the prayers offered for him by the priests. Social order, and the peace so ardently desired, would come from the collective enactment of a willing exchange of services (*alterutrum*) carried out in a spirit of charity and mercy. The orders, dividing social sectors according to function, express the perennial laws of inequality and interdependence.

Elsewhere, Gerard clearly recognizes, but does not accommodate, other segments of society in the model:

> Conditioned as they are by their different social
> backgrounds, men will devote themselves to pursuits of
> the most varied kinds. Young soldiers delight in waging
> arms and waging war; lawyers take pleasure in putting
> on their gowns and arguing cases; others strive
> anxiously to accumulate riches and see wealth as the
> supreme good (*Itinerarium Kambriae*, "Prefatio prima"
> 3-4, cited by Nichols, "Fission and Fusion" 25).

From the beginning, the model was incompatible with social realities; articulated as a response to specific regional situations, it imposed an ideological grid on a world which it sought to control, with perhaps the tacit acknowledgement that such control was slipping ominously away.

The trifunctional model of Adalbero of Laon reiterates key elements of its predecessor, but in a complex poetic text, the *Carmen ad Robertum regem*. A century later, the Laon cathedral school would attract students from around the world, the largest number of Europeans from Lombardy, who would scrutinize the bishop's text and those from which he drew inspiration (*Temps* 84-90).

Adalbero construed a model based on the same trifunctional division of labor. The earthly community, he reasons, requires two leaders, the bishops and kings, who interpret God's signs and codify them as laws for the human community. Thus it is they who have the all-important charge of determining the human composition of the orders and maintaining the *divisio* between them. The kings are responsible for law enforcement and all aspects of civic justice, as well as matters of war and peace. Since king and bishop are unable to execute their responsibilities singlehandedly, each is permitted to exercise vertical delegation of authority, thus extending the orders to a specified degree. The bishops, for example, may delegate some aspects of their power to diocesan priests, though not to monks, who remain excluded from roles drawing them into worldly concerns. Kings are permitted to appoint *rectores* as governors, who must be of noble blood (*Ordres* 239); such *rectores* may in turn apppoint military "captains," also perforce of noble extraction. There is no warrior order per se: the military function is a component of the king's two charges, which Adalbero formulates as "Rex, lex, pax." Since effective execution of these duties requires the king's communicative access to the people, he is also granted the *facultas oratoris*, but, in Adalbero's cautionary words, it is a right best exercised under the guidance of the bishops. "Roi des *oratores*, le monarque participe d'une certaine façon de la nature et des privilèges ecclésiastiques et religieux et d'autre part entretient avec l'ordre clérical les relations ambivalentes de protecteur et de protégé de l'Eglise que le clergé carolingien a mises au point au IXe siècle" (*Temps* 84-85).

Adalbero also divides men into *nobiles* and *servi* according to their place in the power structure. To the former pertains a condition of independence and leisure, to the latter one of service and obedience. Both *oratores* and *bellatores* are to be exempted from the "indelible stain" and degradation associated with manual labor. To the *servi*, then, once again fall all manner of thankless tasks, both domestic and agricultural. In depicting the lot of the *rusticus*, little effort is made to mitigate its hardships; it is likely that Adalbero's poeticized epithet "labor, sudor, dolor" accurately summarizes the life of the lowborn. Similar conditions prevailed in Italy: "Il potere signorile di banno era resoluto a trarre il massimo profitto possibile dalla protezione esercitata sui rustici" (Tabacco 251).

Thus a whole network of essential subjections is conjoined. Since the earthly model is divinely ordained, all men must accept their allotted function without question, and must not, above all, seek to alter that assignment. Impenetrable barriers stand between the social groups to prevent transgressive mobility, tantamount to disobedience and, literally, error.

Binary pairs illustrate a judgmental system of both human activity and spatiality. The optimal locus in the human community is the church, where closed, sanctified space minimizes the temptations of transgression; the public square, seductively open, is denounced as a locus of sin. Additional pairs can readily be drawn: + immobile / - mobile; + inside / - outside; + order / - disorder; + Divine / - earthly (historical)[6].

As Le Goff notes, the tripartite model represented "un instrument d'action sur une société nouvelle, et d'abord, au niveau de l'action la plus évidente, un instrument de propagande" (*Temps* 81). Maintenance of social order, i.e., of inequality and, according to some, of exploitation (Duby, Le Goff), was the primary duty of the secular function. Unquestioned submission of the *agricultores/servi* was imperative; the insistence of both Gerard and Adalbero on this point suggests that obedience was not guaranteed by the third decade of the eleventh century.

The Gerard/Adalbero model was articulated at a time when the threat of disorder stemming from an unruly knightly class was as real as the freedom demanded by the new urban communes. While the model does not integrate the increasing population of vassal *milites* except to charge the royal *bellatores* with controlling their violent and disruptive conduct, the Peace of God movement and the Crusades represent efforts to channel chivalric energies into a positive force for Church and society. From c. 1015, a moral code was drawn up for the *calabrius*, the more popular term for the armed horseman, according to which this all-important sector of the nascent seigniorial system was gradually integrated with the specified functions of the *bellatores* to perform (*Ordres* 171-172). The lexicon used to describe feudalism in the early eleventh century is a curious adaptation of oral vernacular terminology translated, sometimes hesitantly, into Latin for written texts. Commenting on a "breakdown" in the French sociolect around the second decade of the eleventh century, Duby says that "feudal society is revealed to us by the renovation of this vocabulary" to the extent that at last we can see previously concealed realities regarding social organization. By c. 1025, the term *milites* designated the large groups of armed horsemen in the service of the *bellatores*, the vassal warriors pledged to serve the *dominus*. By the last third of the following century, the process of linguistic "correction" was complete in France; the knight was a member of the nobility, acceding through birth and sacralized initiatory rites (*sacramentum militiae*) into the order of knighthood (*Ordres* 183ff.).

The trifunctional schema of Gerard and Adalbero was not adopted as either a descriptive or prescriptive model at the time of its conception. Curiously, it was to lie dormant for 150 years, to re-emerge in the last quarter of the twelfth century with a decidedly different ideological thrust. Commissioned by Henry II to write a panegyric of the Plantagenet dynasty, Benedict of Sainte-Maure composed his *Chronicle of the Dukes of Normandy* in and for one of the great courts of the period. Perhaps it was the brilliance of the court or the royals themselves who inspired Benedict to consider that environment and that form of governance as the best model of social order; in any case, the tripartite system he erected eliminated the primacy of the episcopate, replacing it with the prince as its highest authority. Most noteworthy in this model is the secularization of the entire social construct, from its conception by the *princeps* to the omission of all transcendance. The prince stands at the head of all three functions, foregoing any ceremonial sacralization of his office; for assistance in executing the royal charges, he looks to his *milites* rather than to the *oratores*. The knight is also charged with the defense of the realm; elevated and institutionalized, the knight is the "destre braz" of the king, a sort of extension of the monarchical function. As for those who pray, the *Chronicle* justifies their frequently comfortable existence by their abstention from worldly pleasures. The lot of the *laboureur*, or *paysan*, is essentially unaltered, with the added negativity of the term *vilenie* describing behavior characteristic of the third order and its uncourtly baseness (*Ordres* 335).

Thus, by the last quarter of the twelfth century, there were two trifunctional models, the one with its roots deep in Scripture and Church doctrine, the other supplanting Church with royal sovereignty, and bearing more than a superficial resemblance to the arguments for imperial sovereignty. That Benedict's system disparages communal government comes as no surprise. It will be in the Italian versions of these prototypes that we shall look for models in the thirteenth and early fourteenth centuries when the *Entrée* first appeared.

B. The Communes of Northern Italy: Formation

The northern Italian communes owed their existence to a significant degree to the weakening authority of both Church and empire, and to the profound changes in the social order resulting therefrom:

> il grande conflitto tra papato ed impero . . . scosse l'ordine stabilito, scardinò situazioni locali che parevano immutabili . . . aprì insperate prospettive di rinnovamento religioso, sociale, politico (Fasoli, *Città* 38).

In an era of extensive Church reform, dividing the episcopate and weakening its hold on urban centers, emperors in the early twelfth century were compelled to grant certain civil liberties ("privileges") to the cities, which in turn permitted the landowning nobility an opportunity to play a more active role in the organization and operation of urban government. The processes by which communal governments were formed, which are essentially those of liberation from older authorities and acquisition of citizen autonomy, can be summarized in sequential phases. It goes without saying that each of these steps might involve considerable degrees of resistance from those who perceived their interests placed into jeopardy:

1. formation of the consulate as a permanent executive body. This group, initially drawn for the most part from the nobility, might also include clerical candidates and members of the lower sectors. It was charged with creating a stable magistrature for the maintenance of peace and order, and arose "con un esplicito significato politico e territoriale, dalla volontà dei maggiorenti di rappresentare l'intera collettività cittadina;" (Tabacco 232)

2. gradual accession to jurisdictional authority by the communal body over already-established episcopal, papal, feudal, and/or imperial authorities. This was a complex, lengthy and inevitably uneven process. But in the eyes of the nascent communes, "*libertas* significava prima di tutto la libertà di eleggere i magistrati che dovevano eseguire i mandati della collettività" (Fasoli, *Città* 49);

3. acquisition of communal authority over the surrounding territory on which the city depended economically and agriculturally;

4. establishment of its own institutions for administration, defense, and diplomatic relations. Oaths of obedience and fidelity to the commune and its officers, not unlike the feudal *sermentum*, were exacted from both governors and governed.

By the twelfth century, the term *comune*, initially adjectival and lexically linked to classical forms of political organization, came to indicate "il complesso degli abitanti di una città o la lora assemblea"; subsequently, the word would identify a particular form of governance (Fasoli, *Città* 43). Otto of Freising, visiting Italy in 1154 with the emperor, marvelled at the autonomy of north Italian towns:

> The entire land is divided among the cities, scarcely any noble or great man (*magnatus*) can be found in all the surrounding territory who does not acknowledge the authority of his city. . . . They are aided by the absence of their princes, who are accustomed to remain on the far side of the Alps (Waley 34 citing *MGH SS*, 20: 396-97).

Among the more interesting aspects of the communal experiment was its ideology of power-sharing between social strata with differing, and, inevitably, often conflicting interests. In Milan, for example, establishment of one of the earliest communes represented an effort to reconcile class conflicts escalating since the eleventh century. In addition to the city's collective defense against imperial intrusions, the Milanese commune was typical in having to confront resistance from external authorities as well as internal dissension between the *magnati* and the *popolo*, each of whom demanded representation in government. A glimpse of the social order of the period illustrates the point.

Until the twelfth century, Italian social organization in the Veneto-Lombard region consisted of three broadly-defined groups, *maiores*, *mediocres*, and *minores*: a socio-economic classification is substituted for functionality. The *maiores* were knights and nobles, often large seigniorial landowners; most of the consuls in the early communal period came from this group, although some might also be recruited from wealthy merchant families, creating what Tabacco calls an "aristocrazia consolare" (233). Included among the *maiores*, and indicative of the prestige of the legal profession in the region were lawyers, judges, and with a lesser degree of prestige, notaries. The latter, though often of modest background, like Lovato Lovati and Albertino Mussato in Padua, were to assume a prominent role in communal affairs. Theirs was a major contribution not only in the civic function, but in the Prehumanist movement of the thirteenth and fourteenth centuries.

Classified as *minores* were those who lived on and worked the land in the various capacities described by the terms *agricultores*, *laboratores*, *villani*, or *rustici*. They might be small landowners and/or agricultural laborers, but their distinguishing trait was the manual toil by which they survived, either in the countryside or in the towns. The condition of these individuals was probably analogous to that described in the Cambrai/Laon model in its stipulation of subjection and obedience. As late as 1170, the Milanese commune issued legislation requiring such persons to remain on the land and "reverentiam exhibere" to their masters (Waley 80).

Between these two groups, ironically identified like the Middle Ages itself by exclusion from sanctioned terminology, was the undifferentiated yet highly portentious segment of the population known as the *mediocres* whom we shall have to examine more closely.

However, the rapidly changing configuration of these societies from the twelfth to the mid-fourteenth centuries in northern Italy rendered such descriptions largely obsolete by the time the *Entrée* was written. In addition to large-scale immigration bringing country dwellers into the cities, where they could hope to find employment in the increasingly varied trades and professions, it is probable that most individuals (Waley claims it is the "absolute majority") combined more than one professional activity, and so elude classification in one of the conventional "orders." The usual combination was commercial or industrial work with some aspect of agricultural production: " . . . to have both a warehouse or shop and a holding in land, so being by income and outlook neither fully rentier or peasant nor artisan-shopkeeper, was thus extremely common and any census which placed

men in one category alone would be seriously misleading."
Accordingly, the classes "shaded into one another," so that the peasant
might also own land and moneylenders might claim the more
prestigious profession of banker or financier (Waley 11).

The degree of social mobility in northern Italian cities at an early
date is striking in relation to the prohibitions against transgression in
virtually all prescriptive models. Mercantile activities, essential to
growing prosperity, were too vital to be either ignored or thoroughly
scorned; nonetheless, sometimes ambiguous distaste and disparagement
of such pursuits were frequent throughout the period. Dante renders Hell
the city of wealth ("città di Dite"), and thunders throughout the *Inferno*
against the temptations of money and power, which, in *Paradiso*
15:118-20, he appears to associate with the absence of his fellow
Florentines pursuing mercantile fortunes in France. It is his noble
ancestor Cacciaguida who most eloquently identifies the several crises
in contemporary Florence with the evils of commerce and the disruption
of social order which they engender. One case in point is a now-
obscure, but apparently heinous "man of business" ("tal fatto è
fiorentino e cambia merca" *Par.* 16:62), who either "came from
nothing" or from a family of peddlers, to whom Cacciaguida traces the
rise of the Cerchi family, leader of the Bianchi involved in the
escalation of intraurban hostilities. When Cacciaguida adds: "Sempre la
confusion de le persone / principio fu del mal de la cittade" (16:67-68),
he appears to condemn the violation of the primary social model in
which social mobility was forbidden, and in which the merchant classes
had no role. Dante's source is Aristotle (*Politics* III,3,1277^b-1278^b),
where social order is discussed in terms of the functions of slave,
citizen, or ruler(s) within different constitutional systems.

With most of the changes in the primary model issuing from the
strata of the *minores* and *mediocres*, the nobility tended to display
increased self-consciousness of what it perceived as its inherent,
divinely sanctioned superiority, resenting encroachment of its privileges
by those considered their inferiors. Dante's lengthy discussion of what
constitutes nobility in the *Convivio* is one of many testimonies to the
shifting of the social lexicon. Declining to accept the imperial
definition of Frederick II, he argues for God-given nobility of individual
character unrelated to accidents of birth or wealth (4.7-10; 15-22).[7]

The *milites* sector provided the all-important military function of
the communes; yet there, as well, earlier models proved inadequate.
Originally drawn from the landowning aristocracy, this sector broadened
with the appointment of *milites pro comune*, knights raised to the order
rather than born into it, generally for pragmatic reasons of manpower

requirements in time of war. Otto of Freising again offers the opinion of a Germanic feudatory on the Italian "violation" of the noble *ordo*:

> That they may not lack the means of subduing their neighbors they do not disdain to give the girdle of knighthood or the grades of distinction to young men of inferior station and even some workers of the low mechanical crafts, whom other people ban like the plague from the more respected and honorable pursuits (Waley 24 citing *MGH SS*: 20: 397).

Although the knightly sector was extended according to the needs of individual communes, it was the *popolo* which was to undergo the most dramatic expansion. A proliferation of new terms appeared after 1150 to designate its increasing stratification:

a. *boni homines de populo, convenienter divites* (wealthy *popolani* of good family; cf. original term *boni homines* for *maiores*)
b. *grandi e possenti popolani*
c. *antico e nobile popolano e ricco e possente*
d. *grandi e nobili popolani*
e. *nobiles populares* (Waley 26, Hyde 84-85).

Apparent oxymoronic heteroglossia here is another sign of social models in evolution, underlining the inadequacy of the earlier prescriptive models to describe these communal societies. That such mobility was not always readily accepted is evidenced in the patently cacophonic term *gente nuova*. Dante's diatribe against the newcomers to Florence expresses the scorn with which these immigrants were regarded, concluding: "Sempre la confusione de le persone / principio fu del mal de la cittade" (*Par.* 16:67-68). Also subject to the derision of the same epithet were the newly wealthy, an interesting prejudice, given the probability that a large proportion of the economically prosperous must surely be enjoying very new money. As Waley notes, no matter who you were, the *gente nuova* was always someone else (31).

C. Communes and their Context

The introduction of communal government in northern Italy remains the single most important change in the organization of the human community during the latter Middle Ages. However, formation and survival of the communes must be seen in relation to the long-established institutions of Church and empire, as well as the peculiarly

Italian manifestations of the feudal system. History of individual communes was to depend largely on their success in dialogic interactions with these already-established authorities.

Just as each commune was unique in its formation and development, all shared common ideological elements identifying them with the aspirations for liberty and autonomy which lay behind the experiment. Portrayed by the chronicler Landolfo Seniore, the population of Milan was "fortissimo nell'aspirazione alla libertà, desideroso di richezza, ma più solicito di essere libero" by the latter eleventh century (Muratori, *RIS* sec x cited in Tabacco, *Egemonie* 227). And Henning Krauss, commenting on the role of economic prosperity in the formation of the northern communes, writes: "Uguaglianza e libertà come leggi fondamentali dell'economia implicano necessariamente nella sfera politica, il rifiuto di ogni autorità eteronoma, lo sforzo per un' autodeterminazione entro una forma statale sia pur limitatamente democratica" (*Epica feudale* 18).

D. Communes and the Church

The communes emerging in the late eleventh to mid-twelfth century were formed in an epoch when both Church and empire laid their separate claims of sovereignty to the Veneto-Lombardy region, but at a time when their own conflicts regarding investiture had weakened the viability of their influence. Far more profoundly than elsewhere in Europe, the struggle between *sacerdotium* and *imperium* transformed social and political relationships in northern Italy, where a four-party dialogical process saw its earliest and most complete evolution, and where a new social and political order was in evidence by the first half of the twelfth century (Appelt 24).

While one can generalize that alliances between the Lombard communes and the papacy were one of the constants of Italian political life following the establishment of the Lombard League in 1167, this is not to say that the relationships were unproblematic or that the communes perceived the Church's encouragement or even toleration of their unrestricted autonomy. In the bull *Non Est Dubitum* (1170), Alexander III emphasizes papal support of the cities' efforts to liberate themselves from the imperial "yoke of servitude," which he characterizes by the incomprehensible language imposed on the Italians by such "brutal foreigners." The Pope affirms the common interests of League and papacy, declaring that the cities are fighting for the "freedom of Italy and of the Church" (Pacaut, *Papauté* 35). Nonetheless, it would be misleading to read into the document the papacy's commitment to communal autonomy as proposed by Guelph partisans. Some thirty years later, Innocent III issued a distinctly different document, reiterating the necessity of eliminating the "insupportable tyranny" of imperial intervention in the region, but requiring that the communes virtually abrogate their freedoms for the papal effort to succeed. He adds, ominously, that freedom can be and sometimes is the source (cause) of anarchy (Pacaut 39). This is a remark attributed to Innocent, who, by the early '200, was very ambivalent regarding alteration of the Church-established hierarchy. Clearly, the pope desired "liberation" of the communes from "imperial servitude," yet their continuing submission to Church authorities. Such a comment hedges the question to expose self-interest as a primary motivation of "liberation" ideology. The caveat is clear: hierarchy > order: freedom > anarchy.

On the conflict between communal aspirations for autonomy and Church desire to maintain its strong influence in the operation of the new governments, Tabacco states: "Gli spunti di autentica autonomia delle città erano stati riassorbiti, spontaneamente o coattivamente dall'autorità vescovile"; he adds that dissension between communes and Church were often veiled or concealed in the documents (410). At the local and regional level, it was of course episcopal authority which claimed to represent Church interests. Between the twelfth and thirteenth centuries, the north Italian bishops, extending their temporal power, were broadening their hegemony over the rural areas adjacent to the towns, many of them becoming large seigniorial landowners; in many cases, their secular interests were abetted by private militia. Since the bishops were *in situ* members of the community familiar with details of the political arena, it is not surprising that in the early phases of communal government a close albeit frequently agonistic relationship tended to prevail. The bishops were available for counsel and assistance concerning problems of the emerging communes, particularly those problems involving the incessant intraurban hostilities and imperial intervention. Yet at the same time, there was resistance to temporal extensions of episcopal intervention, particularly regarding the appointment of commune officials (Tabacco 276).

Despite such resistance, it is essential to acknowledge the increasingly tolerant policies of Gregory IX toward the mid-thirteenth century and the full recognition of communal autonomy by Innocent IV, lauded as "champion of urban liberties and communal rights." It is Innocent who first expresses confidence in the political sphere, "dans les forces bourgeoises et populaires . . .[and] au plan doctrinal, la pensée arrêtée que les communes ont des droits propres and doivent s'administrer elles-mêmes, ce qui a pour conséquence de situer cette fois

le guelfisme originel dans les intentions des pontifs plus que dans celles
des villes" (Pacaut 44).

E. Communes and the Empire

The relationships between the empire and the Lombard/Venetan
communes were far more problematic; indeed, they have been
characterized as the most bitter conflict between bourgeois and
monarchical power of the Middle Ages (Appelt 23). Considering that
the traditional Germanic conception of the state no longer sufficed to
effect the annexation of the *Regnum Italicum* to the *Imperium*,
Frederick Barbarossa desired a more authoritative act of legitimization;
this he managed to acquire from legists at the University of Bologna
(Diet of Roncaglia, 1158), who composed the ideology of the *Sacrum
Imperium* from elements of the Justinian Code, feudal and Lombard
law. Thus Frederick, who claimed to be the successor of the Lombard
monarchs as well as of the Roman emperors, acquired a legal
ideological foundation for establishing the monarch as the epicenter
from which all power derives and emanates.

Further, in the belief that enforcement of a more Germanic feudal
order would check the increasing autonomy of the Lombard cities, by
now the wealthiest trade centers in the West, Barbarossa reclaimed in
the Diet of Roncaglia a number of aspects of imperial authority
unobserved since Henry IV. Opinions differ regarding the feudal aspect
of Frederick's Italian policy. On the one hand, it is claimed that he
intended to instate a more or less Germanic model: "fu un sistema
approssimativo di autonomie, già disordinatamente cresciute in un
intreccio di giustaposizioni e sovraposizioni, e ora immesse in una
gerarchia formale, convergente nel re" (Tabacco 268). Others argue that
he was neither so ingenuous nor reactionary to even contemplate such a
policy; rather, he was prepared to adopt whatever means might ensure
his interests. Accordingly, policy might accommodate certain
communal freedoms, provided that these were not incompatible with
imperial hegemony (Appelt 26-27). Frederick thereby assumed the right
to name, or at least to invest in office, all consuls, plus counts, dukes
and marquises, and to appoint within every city a *podestà* who was not
to be a local citizen and would not counter imperial policy (Davis 329).
Further, in recognizing the need to secure the alliance of the landowning
nobility in the confrontations which both were experiencing with the
communes, Frederick remodelled the network of fiefs in such a way as

to draw up explicit legal contracts between the established feudal lords and the empire (Tabacco 263-64).

The northern feudal nobility, in competition for the maintenance of its authority with the communes and, not infrequently, one another, had developed a "confusa e discorde rete nobiliare di poteri" (Tabacco 288). Unwilling to see their power diminished, the nobles adapted in often ingenious ways to social and political change. Originally defenders of the tripartite models to the extent that these models valorized their privileged way of life, the nobles were inevitably drawn into the affairs of the emerging communes, where they were to play a critical role. According to Waley, feudal lordship, however, was the greatest obstacle to the judicial, fiscal and military development of the emerging communes.

Apparent gestures of imperial largesse, however, were not executed to further the autonomy of such powerful regional dynasties as the Montferrato, Malaspina, and Estensi, but rather to put the feudal system to the service of imperial policies and to secure the *regnum* (Tabacco 268). From the communal point of view, the concessions granted by the emperor might restore some measure of law and order, but at the unacceptable sacrifice of independence and self-governance (Tabacco 328). Milan was first to revolt in 1160-62, and as a lesson of the dangers of resisting imperial authority, was razed to the ground by imperial forces. Shortly thereafter, the first six-member regional alliance was formed to resist imperial intervention, with the much larger *Societas Lombardie* drawn up in 1167. The chronicler Ottone Morena states its raison d'être from the communal perspective:

> . . . the Milanese, more oppressed than other Lombards
> and seeing themselves unable to liberate themselves and
> to live, convened a colloquium with the citizens of
> Cremona, Bergamo, Brescia, Mantua, and all relating in
> turn the evils which they were suffering at the hands of
> imperial procurators, determined to die with honor rather
> than to live in anguish and dishonor; as a result they
> soon united in a league, with the pact and sworn oath
> that each city would aid the others if the emperor or his
> officials should bring harm to any of them (cited in
> Brezzi ,"Uomini della Lega" 252; translation mine).

In its first act of self-assertion and self-defense, the League constructed the city of Alessandria on its western flank in the Alps, selecting a name flaunting its papal affiliation. The League emerged victorious from its first military encounter with Frederick at Legnano

(1176), seen as the turning-point in Barbarossa's Italian fortunes. Forced
to negotiate a disadvantageous peace with both Church and League, he
chose to settle first with Rome; then, having restored wrongly
appropriated Church property and acknowledged Alexander III as sole
bishop of Rome, Frederick performed one of history's dramatic gestures
of submission in St. Mark's square, casting off his imperial robes and
prostrating himself at the feet of the pope. The secular peace was
concluded at Constance in 1183: it virtually restored the autonomy of
the Lombard communes while stipulating the sworn feudal allegiance to
the empire of all adult citizens and of all consuls of the communes,
who were to submit to periodic formal investiture. The imperial *podestà*
were eliminated. Although defeated and compelled to sue for peace,
Frederick clearly retained a significant measure of imperial authority.

If Barbarossa had permitted some degree of flexibility in his
transactions with the cities, Frederick II held a decidedly more negative
view of both the privileged Italian nobility and the freedoms sought by
the communes. In an effort to break the communal alliances with the
papacy, he aligned himself with the latter in disputes regarding fiscal
and judicial immunity claimed by the Church (Appelt 29). More
significantly, his absolutist claims to sovereignty interpreted any past
or present accord negotiated with the communes as an act of imperial
"clemency," thus without binding legal foundation and subject to
revocation. Not long after his coronation in 1220, Frederick revoked the
Treaty of Constance, reinstating complete dominion over the cities and
reintroducing the imperial *podestà*. With strong papal encouragement,
the second Lombard League was soon invoked; by this point, a
characteristically pragmatic attitude on the part of the communes
viewing the empire as a "subversive force" (Tabacco 273) was
strengthening the communal alliances with the papacy. And to counter
the increasingly militant ideology, further enunciation of Church
sovereignty continues to appear toward mid-century.

Interrelationships between papacy, empire, and communes become
increasingly problematic with Frederick's renewal of imperial claims on
Lombardy in 1226. This was the period in which he appointed imperial
princes to control the northern cities, among them Padua, where
Frederick installed the infamous Ezzelino da Romano. The latter had
been a member of the anti-imperialist league until 1232, when he
reversed his allegiance "merely because he had concluded that Frederick
II would make a more satisfactory ally than the anti-imperialists"
(Waley 91). Ezzelino also became son-in-law to Frederick. In the war
which he then declared against Lombardy (1235), Frederick succeeded in
devastating the Milanese at Cortenuova and in shattering the League.
He then increased imperial appointments in the region, naming a

capitanus in each city accountable to a regional *vicarius generalis*, thus assuring him virtual control over the region. With his second excommunication of Frederick the following year, the pope annulled all feudal obligations contracted by the cities, formally prohibiting any feudal services to be honored. The excommunication was to last for nine years, until the Synod of Lyons voted Frederick's deposition in 1245 and initiated a crusade against him. The emperor's defeat at Parma effectively broke his power over northern Italy, whose cities ceased to be the fulcrum of confrontations between papacy and empire at his death in 1250. Thus, at mid-century, the imperial obstacle to communal autonomy was much diminished; by then, however, it was dubious whether the communes themselves, ravaged by war and internal dissension, could survive.

F. Internal Dissension within the Communes

As the above begins to suggest, even if/when communal autonomy was established and recognized by external institutions, there were often major problems due to internal conflicts between classes and factions. In more than a few instances, Padua among them, the eventual failure of the commune was due more to internal difficulties rather than to pressures from without. Albertino Mussato's *Ecerinide* (1314) decries such incessant infighting as source of the Ezzelino tyranny: "O feroci odi dei nobili, o furore del popolo! / Ecco la fine dovuta alle vostre liti, ecco il tiranno che la vostra rabbia ha creato . . . " (2.1).

In its simplest outlines, social conflict present prior to the communal era in cities such as Milan was exacerbated by the *popolo*'s perception of unjustified discrepancies between their contribution to the commonwealth and the representation granted them in the operations of government. The *popolo* itself, once a fairly homogeneous group, had proliferated and subdivided into multiple economic and professional groups, the all-important guild associations being central to the dynamic growth and prosperity of the cities. The communal governments, as explained above, had been formed by, and tended to remain largely in the control of the *maiores* unless pressures from below, not infrequently violent, compelled relaxation of their authority.

The ways in which the *popolo* challenged the oppressive authority of the *magnati* were several and varied. Its initial response, quite logically, was the formation of professional associations to protect and foster its own interests. Such "protection" was literally realized in many instances by the popular militia which counterbalanced the official communal army under the *pars nobilium*. With the establishment of its own armed force, the *popolo* had taken a major step toward claims for its autonomy within the parameters of the communal system. In duplication of the communal governing structures, it frequently elected its own councils and *capitanus*. Thus a curious government-within-a-government arose in many cities during the Duecento, broadening the power base of the *pars populum*, but often leading to other problems. For, as mentioned above, the *popolo* was already a multi-faceted group whose interests would, under the best of circumstances, be difficult to unify beyond the fundamental demand for increased representation. Yet to be granted recognition, it must assume a unified voice; the *popolo* must operate as a self-contained unit while simultaneously participating in the larger communal government.

The history of many northern communes is closely tied to the relentless, often violent ascent of the *popolo*:

> La peculiarità di quella lotta, per gran parte del XIII secolo, fu nei modi in cui una complessa organizzazione armata di 'popolo' si andò ovunque costituendo e politicamente operò; fu nel sorgere di un potere autonomo, coesistendo con il potere 'comunale' nella città, ambiguo dunque istituzionalmente rispetto al 'comune,' non cioè riducibile a pure strumento di concorrenza coi nobili per l'inserimento dei ceti popolari in organi già costituenti il 'comune' e già operanti ufficialmente in nome della città (Tabacco 284).

There are interesting analogies in the modelling tendencies of the three power groups. Just as the urban noble *consorterie* formulated their own authority on the basis of seigniorial experience of the tenth and eleventh centuries, gradually acquiring control of urban politics, so the *popolo* followed the imitative process, setting up its own autonomous institutions for handling both internal and external relations.

Within the incessant conflicts between upper and lower social strata, the mercantile sector played an oscillating role characteristic of its ambiguous place in the social order. The third function was no longer *labor*, but primarily *negotium*. We have noted that commercial activity was not viewed as incompatible with one's identification as *miles* or membership in associations of the nobility. At the beginning of the thirteenth century, relationships between the mercantile and financial sectors and the noble *consorterie* were often close and harmonious, obliterating the "impenetrable barriers" of most prescriptive models. These two sectors were to be pivotal in the class struggle, especially in the early communal era, due to their associations with both *popolo* and nobility and the flexibility with which they handled social transactions and political alliances.

As the *popolo* succeeded in acquiring some measure of authority, divisions within its own ranks tended to increase, as resentment arose among the *popolo minuto* against the greater economic and political fortunes of its compatriots. In fact, anti-magnate legislation, widespread in the region during the '200 and '300, was directed not only against knights and nobles, but against those *popolani* perceived as overbearing. The term *magnati* was always loosely defined, largely based on perceptions of socio-economic "grandezza" and power, a threat by such "prepotenti" to the harmonious operation of government. To diminish such manifestations associated with the feudal system, many communes passed legislation requiring the *magnati* to reside within the city, where their activities could better be monitored.

G. Authority/Autonomy: The Paduan Experience

In Padua and those cities finally able to liberate themselves from the Ezzelino tyranny after the mid-thirteenth century, the reconstitution of communal government played a major role in their ensuing "golden age." It comes as no surprise, then, to find in the documentary and literary texts of the period a pervasive caution and ambivalence toward authority (Hyde 2).

Two aspects of this ambivalence stand out. First, a profound fear of tyranny: from the chronicler Rolandino to the Prehumanist Mussato, Ezzelino's despotic reign is the dreaded past from which the city must learn better how to delegate authority and regulate power. As only one city with similar lessons to learn, Padua adopted controls within the restored communal government; one of these prohibited the office of *podestà* to any Paduan citizen, on the premise that self-interest and ambition might hinder optimal performance of duties. New stipulations also involved closer scrutiny of activities while in office and full accountability at the end of tenure.

Second, Venetan-Lombard politics of the latter '200-early '300 testify that a commune successful in acquiring a satisfactory degree of autonomy remained vulnerable to the more insidious threat of internal division. As a governance system intentionally exercising bias against the very wealthy and very poor (as potential threats of unlawful usurpation of power or rebellion), the commune theoretically extended its policy of citizen participation to a sizable sector of the male population. In theory, its viability was to be insured by the communality of shared interests within this sector. In Padua as elsewhere, events were to reveal the vulnerability of theory: increasingly divided by internal partisan conflicts, themselves exacerbated by virtually constant threats of Church and/or imperial encroachment into local affairs, the commune ultimately disintegrated from within, its stability eroded by an inability to reconcile the interests of discrete groups with the common good of the whole. By the second decade of the fourteenth century, communal governance had been compromised in Padua, first by the appointment of the local magnate Giacomo da Carrara as *podestà* with powers more suggestive of the *signore*, then progressively debilitated to the extent that seizure by the imperial vicar Can Grande della Scala in 1328 was virtually unavoidable.

It is within the chronological parameters of two tyrannies (i.e., 1256-1320), a reality in Padua and throughout the Marca Trevigiana, that the *Entrée*'s ideological orientation should be sought. We need now to examine issues of tyranny, internal discord, and the desire for liberty and autonomy, as they are articulated in other texts of the period.

The sizable corpus on theory and practice of government from the mid-thirteenth to mid-fourteenth centuries expresses a strong aversion to external imposition of authority such as the Lombard League was intended to prevent. Yet tyranny might also arise from within the state. Brunetto Latini's *Tresor*, after describing what kind of individual should be named *podestà* or *signore*, emphasizes the restrictions to be placed on the individual appropriating excessive judicial authority. Written in Franco-Italian and dedicated to Galeozzo Visconti of Milan, Brunetto's text stipulates the necessity of accountability to the law:

> Porquoi je di que s'il trespasse aucunefois outre ce que
> bon soit, u en ses dis u en ses commandemens, il n'est
> pas honte d'amender le, ains est grans vertus que
> chascuns chastie son erreur et retour au millor; et ce doit
> li sires faire, selonc ce que la lois commande (3.90.4).

Comparing the Italian communal system of elected representatives governing the "commun proufit" with hereditary monarchy in France, Brunetto clearly prefers the former:

> 5. Et cil sont en .11 manieres; uns ki sont en France et
> es autres pais, ki sont sozmis a la signorie des rois et
> des autres princes perpetueus, ki vendent les provostés
> et les baillent a ciaus ki plus l'achatent (poi gardent sa

bonté ne le proufit des borgois); 6. l'autre est en Ytalie,
que li citain et li borgois et li comunité des viles elisent
lor poesté et lor signour tel comment il quident qu'il
soit plus proufitables au commun preu de la vile et de
tous lor subtés (3.73.5-6).

Strong aspiration for freedom runs throughout one of the major
chronicles of the time, the *Cronica in factis et circa facta Marchie
Trivixanie* (1262). Its author, Rolandino, a distinguished professor of
grammar at the Studium in Padua and member of the Prehumanist
circle, contributed significantly to the exceptional intellectual
productivity of the city. His text is a largely eyewitness account,
concentrating on the processes and effects of Ezzelino's tyranny, with
frequent mention of nearby Lombardy. The preface underlines the
Paduan character, "que semper libertatem dilexit et diligit" (Muratori
167-68; c.2v,4) ("which has always prized and chooses liberty").

Rolandino heightens the impact of nearly two decades of tyranny
by framing his narration with scenes of the Marca before Ezzelino's
takeover. An entry for 1229-1230 extols "tantum gaudium et leticia
inter gentes, ut a pluribus crederetur quod amodo nulle sediciones esse
debeat in Marchia, nulle werre" (1.19, 40) ("such joy and happiness
among the people, that it might be believed by many that in any
circumstances there should be no sedition in the March, no war").

In Mussato's tragic drama, the *Ecerinide*, Ezzelino is the child of a
monstrous union between Satan and his mother, "un adultero ignoto"
(1.1.38), quite delighted with his "origine divina," thoroughly
committed to his role as enemy of God and good governance (1.2.93-
113). Dante portrays him, nearly submerged in boiling blood, among
history's most infamous tyrants, condemned as basest of those guilty of
violence against others; Ezzelino lives in *Inferno* 12:109-112, along
with another contemporary regional despot, Ferrara's Obizzo II d'Este.
Villani characterizes him as "il più crudele e ridottato tiranno che mai
fosse tra' cristiani. . . . E sotto l'ombra di una ruda e scellerata giustizia
fece molti mali, e fu uno grande flagello al suo tempo nella Marca
Trevigiana e in Lombardia. . . . (*Cronaca* 6.72-73).

As cities one by one yield to Ezzelino, Rolandino's narrative
recounts Padua's futile attempts to prevent the inevitable. On 24
February 1237, the citizens agree to the "peaceful entry" of imperial
legates, ingenuously accepting reassurances that their autonomy is
uncompromised. After all, the risk seems acceptable: Ezzelino belongs
to one of the region's oldest feudal dynasties, and presides over one of
its most brilliant courts. Yet the following day, when Ezzelino and the
legates enter the city, Rolandino sees an ominous sign:

> Tunc est data civitas comiti Geboardo recipienti
> eam nomine imperatoris et vice eius. Set in
> consiliis et arenis loquendo postmodum addebat et
> loquebatur dompnus Ecelinus—nec perpendebat
> aliquis qua de causa, dicebat enim—verum esse
> quod Padua data era dompno Geboardo pro
> imperatore et nunciis imperatoris cum ipso; unde si
> qua fiebant vel tractabantur ulterius in Padua pro
> communi, nullius valoris erant, nisi facta forent de
> consilio et consensu dompni Ecelini (3.16,18-28).

> Then the city was given to count Geboardo [Ezzelino]
> receiving it in the name of the emperor and as his vicar.
> But, speaking to the councils and in the arena presently,
> lord Ezzelino added and spoke—nor did anyone question
> why, indeed he was saying—it was true that Padua had
> been given to lord Geboardo in behalf of the emperor
> and to the ambassadors of the emperor with himself;
> whenceforth, if anything were done or negotiated in
> Padua in the interests of the commune, they [the
> negotiations/transactions] were of no value, unless they
> had been done upon the advice and with the agreement
> of lord Ezzelino.

Despite several attempts in subsequent years to overthrow him via inter-communal alliances, the "Antichrist" and "flagellum Dei" (Boni 213) retains control; in *Ecerinide* 1.2, Mussato's Ezzelino boasts: "Negai sempre Cristo a me avverso e sempre odiai il nome nemico della Croce." Rolandino characterizes the tyrant in Aristotelian terms, as one who rules solipsistically, without regard for the common good. "Studiosus namque totis viribus Ecelinus Paduam deformare, non ponebat curam minimos; quamvis eciam et de illis aliqui perierunt" (7.11, 107-08) ("For Ezzelino, determined to damage Padua by doing harm to all her citizens, cared nothing for the least of them; however many of them might perish").

Mussato's *Historia augusta de gesta Henrici VII Caesaris* foresees the horrors of tyranny revisited in Can Grande, and attempts to issue warnings by drawing analogies between the two, both in service to the Emperor. In 1313 Can Grande:

> . . . incussit Paduanorum animos tanta in se
> Caesaris animaversio, tamque dirae pronuntiationis
> asperitas, magisque Seniorum Ordines, qui adhuc
> acceptae cladis a Friderici de Stoph de infanda

tyrannide memoria non abolita, veluti facti nova
imagine torquebantur. Eadamque & filiorum, ac
nepotum conquestio paterna, avitaque monimenta
reminiscentium, haec non ob aliud sibi contigisse
dijudicantium, nisi quod Canem Grandem adimstar
infandissimi Eccerini de Romano ad se vorandos
non excepissent . . . sic fata poscere, ut tractim
longa refecta pace hujusce Imperii flagello
alternatim nunc floreat, nunc arescat Paduana
Civitas (6:545).

Struck so greatly the minds and souls of Paduans in
their hostility to Caesar, sometimes the harshness of
his cruel pronouncements, and more the Order of the
Elders who, still not having abolished the memory of
the destruction wrought by Frederick's abominable
tyranny, were being tormented by a new image of such
a deed. The complaint of the city fathers, of their sons
and grandsons, remembering the ancestral monuments,
judging that these things would not have happened
because of anything else, unless they captured Can
Grande, following upon the most abominable Ezzelino
da Romano, consuming/devouring them . . . Thus to
ask the fates, that gradually, peace having been restored
from the scourge of the Empire, the Paduan city-state
[which] now on the one hand might flourish, now
might perish.

H. Summary

The communal governments contained built-in mechanisms for
resolution of internal conflicts, in the two major councils and others
added not infrequently in other forms. Multiple advisory bodies
necessary to the check and balance of power are praised in the well-
known prescription for communal well-being, "ubi multa consilia sunt,
ubi salus" (*Oculus pastoralis* 4,103). Thus it is unfortunate that, to a
great extent, internal conflicts were only resolved by recourse to
violence, which constantly threatened civic order and the viability of

government. Historians are unanimous in citing this fundamental and uncorrected instability.

After the mid-twelfth century, selection of a *podestà*, also cited as *rector*, was tacit admission that the councils were unable to maintain order. Entrusted with broad executive and police powers, but constitutionally circumscribed even to the minute details of his personal activities, the *podestà*'s absolute impartiality was to be ensured by his "foreign" origin. Yet even this measure, the potentially dangerous conferral of broad authority on one individual, was to prove insufficient to sustain the system. By the late thirteenth century, most of the northern communes were yielding to the one-man rule of the *signoria*, which once again radically diminished the liberties and autonomy each had struggled to achieve:

> E dunque lecito dire che il comune cittadino, il quale pur
> si definisce come 'res publica' e opera come ente
> territoriale, impiega pressoché un secolo per condurre a
> compimento, in rapporto con la residua concorrenza
> vescovile o del potere comitale o viscontile della città,
> la costruzione di un proprio assetto istituzionale, e che a
> questo assetto il comune perviene quando i suoi organi
> sono già violentemente investiti, dall'interno della
> compagine stessa della città, da forme nuove di lotta di
> vecchie fazioni e dalla concomitante esplosione di forze,
> capaci di generare centri di potere di struttura
> nuovissima: quasi a mostrare una volta ancora, dopo
> secoli di libera germinazione di nuclei politici, la
> precarietà di ogni ordinamento che aspira a chiudere in
> un apparato di potere la società medievale (Tabacco
> 277).

Models in Evolution: Descriptive and Prescriptive

Comparison of the Cambrai/Laon and Plantagenet models with the preceding summary account of northern Italian social structures discloses the inability of those ideological systems to contain radical social change erupting throughout Europe, nowhere more dynamically than in northern Italy. The canonization of such models, predicated on the immutability of authority descending from a monologic source, is perhaps in itself an acknowledgment of the fragility of their authority. Drawn up on the eve of one of Europe's most profound renascences, the models were hardly inscribed before their limitations and anachronisms were in evidence. Attempts were made from the twelfth century to accommodate some of the discrepancies between model and reality; beginning in a conservative vein, these palimpsest texts of socio-cultural theory establish a dialogic relationship among themselves as well as with the primary models.

Progress toward articulation of new models can be discerned in the *Summa de arte praedicatoria* of Alain de Lille in the last quarter of the century. The *Summa* consists of model sermons, with suggested themes and exempla for the use of the preaching clergy. As mediating instruments between established models and inevitably divergent realities of individual parishes, the importance of sermon literature cannot be overestimated. Its most useful contribution for our purposes lies in its focus on lexical differentiations as indices of changing social realities. Rather than addressing members of the congregation in terms of *ordines*, Alain stipulated that sermons be selected according to their *status*. A progressive, if sometimes inconsistent, shift in terminology first evidenced in the latter twelfth century from *ordo* to *status* is an acknowledgement of the gradual erosion of the primary system; "the first shift toward the margins of the model occurs when hierarchic relationships are not transgressed, but changed in function and meaning" (Lotman, "Dynamic Model" 349). Whereas *ordo* stipulated immutability and inviolability, *status* referred to

> ce qui ne dépend pas de l'ordre ni de la nature, beaucoup plus flottant par conséquent, s'élévant, s'abaissant selon les mouvements de la roue de fortune—et relatif comme le sont la 'noblesse' ou la 'pauvreté'—tout le mobile, l'indécis, le jeu, introduit précisément dans les rigidités de l'engrenage social par la croissance économique. Et le multiple (*Ordres* 382).

As a referent to reality rather than ideology, the increasing number of *statutes* implied the flexibility of manmade structures necessarily sensitive to change.[8] Alain included two additional terms of social differentiation. *Conditio* referred to the individual's degree of dependence on others, with particular reference to whether one was "in service" to others, i.e., in subjection either voluntarily or not. Finally, there was *gradus*, grade or rank within one's own group (*Ordres* 380-82).

The *Summa* includes seven categories of *status*. Listed after the *milites* come the *oratores*, who now are the *advocati*, those expert in judicial oratory with training in the related fields of law and rhetoric as was common in the Studium of Padua. The order of "communicators"

is no longer restricted to disseminators of the Word; the languages of
the social body are many and varied. Thereafter, all but one of the
statutes are secular: princes, judges, monks and priests, married couples,
widows, and virgins. Princes are no longer *bellatores*: judges,
proliferating in urban centers, are named before clergyman, themselves
no longer differentiated. The last two categories allude to states of
secular activity and, for the first time, include women.

However, if the above suggests a radical liberalization of
mentalities, two fundamental aspects of the trifunctional model persist.
Using the state/body metaphor, Alain states that, just as everything in
the body has an order imposed upon it, human salvation can only be
achieved if each individual remains within the place allotted to him/her
by the Deity. Duby concludes:

> L'ordre social et moral que la prédication entend
> raffermir, repose sur un mythe, la réciprocité des
> services rendus par les divers organes d'un corps, et sur
> une réalité, le pouvoir, détenu par le prince, appliqué
> pas les chevaliers, étendu sur le 'peuple', lequel n'a qu'à
> 'obtempérer' (*Ordres* 381).

Further motion away from the primary models appears in the
Sermones vulgares ad omnes statutes of Jacques de Vitry (d.1240). In a
hybridization of the model which Maria Corti describes as an index of a
semiotic structure in crisis, Jacques avoids the term *ordines* altogether,
and includes among his addressees women, now entered within the
system independent of their relationships to men. Corti calls the Vitry
model "clamorosamente ibrido," "una voluta contaminazione fra schema
gerarchico verticale includente e schema orizzontale incluso"
("Ideologie" 231). Disseminators of official culture had come to realize
that previous models were descriptively inadequate and prescriptively
impotent. The thirteenth century thus sees "conflict and theoretical
hybridism," followed by a genuine attempt, especially by Dominicans
Thomas Aquinas and Humbert of Romans, to adapt to the new society
"a general 'signifier' or articulated model," capable of depicting
contemporary realities and still conforming to the primary trifunctional
models (Corti, "Models" 345).

Horizontal expansion at the lower echelons of Model I is aptly
illustrated by the one hundred *statutes* identified by Humbert of Romans
(d.1272), whose importance among medieval Dominicans has been
assessed as inferior only to Saints Dominic, Aquinas and Albertus
Magnus (Brett 3). Master of Arts from the University of Paris and fifth
Dominican General, expert in techniques of Aristotelian analysis,

Humbert makes another conscious attempt to accommodate social innovations—with curiously paradoxical results.

The dilemma confronting Humbert was probably shared by many clerics responsible for composing model sermons for others to preach in congregations whose heterogeneity presented serious difficulties of choice of material and manner of delivery. The 347 sermon samples attempt to communicate to a diversified public in comprehensible language. For example, in the classification *laici in civitatibus*, Humbert distinguishes 27 types from the highest, *rectores* (NB *Entrée* prologue addresses the "retors de tere"), in descending order to the *officiales civitatis*, *maiores*, and *turba popularis*, and lowest servants, *familia divatum*. Immediately evident here is a reiteration of previous vertical hierarchism, with the omission of guilds and trades. Reflecting on this evidence of Lotman's "minus device," Corti correctly judges that their inclusion would have been tantamount to sanctification within the official model, a step which Humbert, like most of his contemporaries, found too threatening to contemplate, although John of Salisbury had already acknowledged the *mechanical arts* a century earlier (Corti, "Ideologie" 233-34).

In a second series of sermon patterns, Humbert makes a curious concession (or confession?) regarding the tradesmen and guild members; they are entered into the system under the heading *negotia*, but described relative to their locus rather than their status. In Humbert's codification of social functions, the merchant element retains its assignation of 'low', 'outside', 'mobile', and of course 'disorderly', an ambivalent acknowledgement, to be sure. Cultures tend to "forget," i.e., to omit or eliminate those elements which do not integrate into the officially sanctioned models (Lotman, "Dynamic Models" 193-210);[9] in "forgetting" the most dynamic, innovative sector of thirteenth-century society, Humbert produces an ambiguous new/old model modifying the earlier one and rendering it less repetitive and anachronistic, but ultimately reproducing its fundamental ideologies. He superimposes partially new classifications on the old grid, so that the result is a conjoining of traditional power structures with emerging social realities. The vertical hierarchism of the tripartite models is unchanged, as is the hermeticism of its component sectors.

Sermon writers like Humbert of Romans stand in a delicate position as mediators between the ideologies they are charged to proselytize and defend, if necessary, and the unavoidable realities of profound social change. To the modern mind, Humbert's ambivalence or avoidance stategies may appear evasive or even cowardly; yet we should keep in mind the conflicts presented to such individuals who only

partially comprehend the global nature of such change and tend to view
it as a threat to the status quo and to their own authority.

Placing Humbert within the 150-year period 1125-1275, this
paradox of stated intentional accommodation of social change versus
tenacious resistance to it becomes more comprehensible. Duby, looking
at the era in terms of changes in value systems, finds less substantive
change than long-term evolution. Advocacy of reason as an essential
cognitive tool is already in place in the early part of the twelfth century
with Anselm and Abelard, while other "revolutions" turn out to be less
so under close scrutiny. Duby finds that a relativist mentality,
particularly with reference to matters of faith, may be the most radical
change in value systems. Humbert, for example, meditating on
resistance to Church authority, decline of imperial power, plus the
diminishing role of Latin in the East, found it impossible to continue
to believe in the unity and necessity of the history of God's people. In
the intellectual realm, where study of recently-recovered Aristotelian
texts was viewed less askance, schoolmen were compelled to recognize
that:

> la découverte progressive de l'immensité de la diversité,
> de la complexité de la création, la conscience nouvelle
> que l'univers est rempli d'hommes qui refusent
> d'entendre le message du Christ obligent les plus lucides
> à penser que la chrétienté n'est peut-être pas située au
> coeur du monde, ou du moins qu'elle n'en occupe qu'un
> secteur limité. De même qu'il leur faut bien reconnaître
> que la pensée chrétienne se trouve incapable d'absorber
> ou de dissocier le bloc cohérent du système aristotélicien
> (Duby, "L'Histoire des systèmes de valeurs" 21).

A. Aquinas and the *Civitas terrena*

A major target of castigation and site of that least original of sins,
superbia, was of course the city/city-state. The human *civitas* had been
viewed disparagingly at least since Augustine's *De civitate Dei*:

> . . . thus we find in the earthly city a double
> significance: in one respect it displays its own presence,
> and in the other it serves by its presence to signify the
> Holy City. But the citizens of the earthly city are
> produced by a nature which is vitiated by sin . . . the
> earthly city is generally divided against itself by

litigation, by wars, by battles, by the pursuit of
victories that bring death with them or at best are
doomed to death. For if any section of that city has
risen up in war against another part, it seeks to be
victorious over other nations, though it is itself the
slave of base passions. . . . Thus the quarrel that arose
between Remus and Romulus demonstrated the division
of the earthly city against itself; while the conflict
between Cain and Abel displayed the hostility between
the two cities themselves, the City of God and the city
of men (15.2,4,5).[10]

Aquinas's theories on the human *civitas* are integrated into a
number of his works and present some difficulties of interpretation and
synthesis. Views on social order, authority, hierarchy, forms of
government, and the individual in relationship to the state are frequently
articulated in discrete statements of principles and theories from which
one can attempt to construct a system. Such a system must originate
with the fundamental conviction that "Quidquid est in mundo, totum
ordinatum est" (1 *Sent.*, d.39, qu.2, art.1, 2, ad 5um.). As a model of
perfect order, it follows that the Thomist universe is perfectly good.[11]
Supreme Author/Authority of the universe, the Deity is also its
supreme Governor and Legislator. In this dualist model, spiritual
authority granted to the Church is superior to its temporal counterpart.
Under ordinary circumstances, the powers remain separate. "However,
prelates having spiritual power sometimes interfere in matters for the
secular power. Therefore usurped judgment is not unlawful " (*ST* 2a,
2ae, qu.60, art. 6, ad 3um). The point of convergence of spiritual and
temporal powers is in the person of the Pope, "whose power is supreme
in matters both temporal and spiritual, through the dispensation of Him
who is both priest and king. "(*CPL*, dis. 44, qu. 3, art. 4). The divine
regimen completes [perfects and valorizes] the human. Now, to govern
is to impose order: "Nihil autem aliud est gubernare aliqua quam cis
ordinem imponere" (*CG* 3, 64.9). So God governs all things by His
intellect, will, and reason, particularly through the person of His son,
the most perfect of human creatures who became a member of the
civitas terrena in order to correct the disorder wrought by the Fall:
("Christus habet judicium . . . etiam super administratione in totius
creaturae:) (*ST* 3a, qu.59, art.6 ad 3um).

A fundamentally positive appraisal of human nature is reflected in
Aquinas's conception of the human community. Discussion thereof
naturally leads to consideration of the nature of man, since " . . . it is
natural for man, more than for any other animal, to be a social and

political animal, to live in a group" (*DR* 1.1,4). Aquinas's addition to the Aristotelian tenet is critical: to exist is to co-exist. "Man is unthinkable without the State because it is only within the State and through the State that he can achieve perfection" (D'Entrèves xvii).

Community living is necessary not only to provide the *vitae sufficentia*, but is described by Aquinas as the *perfecta communitas*, an earthly microcosm of the Divine model conceived by human intelligence, will, and reason (*DR* 1.1,14). The importance of reason as the power to move to action from the will pervades every aspect of Aquinas's social theories. His model *civitas*, conceived within the political context of the Duecento, is to be associated with the individual sovereign city-state, a human structure created by rational man for the common good of the group. Yet it is neither self-contained nor autonomous, for activities of the state, participating hierarchically in the natural order of the world, must be determined by, and subservient to, divine governance.

Aquinas, too, posits a trifunctional model: "secundum diversos actus, nam alius est ordo judicantium, et alius pugnantium et alius laborantium in agris et sic de aliis." *Podestà* and councils govern the state as the "retors de tere," to whom the *Entrée* addresses admonishing counsel. Aquinas also differentiates sectors of society in a hierarchical but non-functional classification: the *supremi ut optimates*, the *medii ut populus honorabilis*, and the *infimi ut vilis populus* (*ST* 1a, qu. 108, art. 2). In stressing the necessity of social order, Aquinas writes that whoever, or whatever, promotes it is acting as an instrument of God. Following the Justinian Code, Aquinas affirms that all men are created equal as creatures of God, but immediately qualifies this to cite the natural inequality and hierarchism which prevails in all forms of life throughout the universe:

> Now in the operations of nature it is necessary that higher things move the lower in virtue of the pre-eminence of natural powers conferred upon them by God. So also in human affairs it is necessary that superiors impose their will upon inferiors, in virtue of the authority established by God (*ST* 2a, qu. 104, art. 1).

Order within the *civitas* depends upon a *triplex ordo* of human subjection: first, the individual to his own rational faculty; secondly, to civic authority; finally to the ultimate authority of the *lex aeterna*. In specifying what comprises the well-being of the community, Aquinas identifies unity of purpose, harmony in orientation to the well-being of the majority, and sufficient material goods.

There are essentially two kinds of individual subjection to civic authority: *subiectio servilis* and *civilis*. The former, resulting directly from the Fall, is that non-voluntary servitude of one man to another, condemned by Thomas as contrary to nature. *Subiectio civilis*, however, is the necessary subordination of individuals and groups to other forms of secular authority; freely offered and consonant to natural order, it does not contradict man's essential freedom. Because the individual loves the common good, he also loves the authority of those who govern (*ST* 1a, 2ae, qu. 92, art. 1, qu. 96, art. 3-4). Contemporary testimony to unconditional individual freedom may be cited in a 1257 Bologna decree prohibiting slavery, and a 1289 Florentine proclamation of absolute individual freedom (Krauss 20).

In the hierarchy of secular authority, functions of governance, both the *principes* and communal officials, are best executed by those endowed with *praeeminentia intellectus*. Citing both Scripture and Aristotle's *Politics*, Aquinas posits the natural leadership of the intellectually superior ("qui intellectu praeeminent naturaliter dominantur"); those less intelligent but of more robust physique seem intended by nature to act in service functions ("a natura videntur instituti ad serviendum," *CG* 3, 81). The optimal form of government is a constitutional monarchy which fulfills requisite relationships of order. Thus:

$$\frac{\text{king}}{\text{kingdom}} = \frac{\text{soul}}{\text{body}} = \frac{\text{God}}{\text{universe}}$$

Broad authority is granted to the prince or king: "Rex in regno suo est imperator; civitas sibi princeps" (*DR* 1.2;*CG* 4, 76). As the *principium unitatis*, and thus analogous to God in his directive function, the king is charged with the obligation to defend the city, wage the just war, and seek the peace without which the *civitas* cannot thrive. Very significantly, then, the good of the city is in the king.

Of equal, if not greater importance, is the new function of law, the common obligation of each sector to adhere to the particular legal codes determined by the community pertinent to its welfare ("et ideo istis hominibus specialia quaedam iura aptantur" (*ST* 1a, 2ae, qu. 95, art. 4, ad 4um). Law, which has "as its first and principal object the ordering of the common good," has greater authority than the individual, just as the whole is always more important than any part thereof and the commonweal of the city takes precedence over the citizen. Expanded

importance of the establishment and maintenance of social order is
assigned to a judicial system devised and directed by human will and
reason. Laws possess coercive power, impelling citizens toward the
virtuous living necessary to the preservation of the community. They
serve the well-being of the *civitas* if they meet specific conditions: if
they are directed toward the common welfare; if they do not exceed the
powers of the person or body executing them; if the burdens imposed
"are distributed in such proportion as to promote the common welfare"
(*ST* 1a, 2ae. qu. 95, art. 4).

No one is above the law, neither monarch, *podestà*, or councils.
Witness to the tyrants abounding in Duecento Italy, Aquinas is well
aware that unchecked one-man rule, even elective, easily degenerates
into tyranny; he thus prescribes restrictions on executive authority.
With regard to positive law, however, the legislative agent, whether
individual or collective, is superior to legislation itself, since it is the
authority of the agent which engenders and activates the law. This agent
may, in case of emergency threatening the community, change or
dispense with the law. Nonetheless this, like all authority, is valid only
if enacted *ratione regulata* :

> There are two things to be observed concerning the right
> ordering of rulers in a state or people. One is that all
> should have some share in government; this makes for
> peace among the people, and commends itself to all, as
> Aristotle says. The other regards the kind of
> government. Hence the best system in any state or
> kingdom is one in which one man, as specially
> qualified, rules over all, and under him are others
> governing as having special endowments, yet all have a
> share inasmuch as those are elected from all, and also
> elected by all. This is the best form of constitution, a
> mixture of monarchy, in that one man is at the head, of
> aristocracy, in that many rule as specially qualified, and
> democracy, in that the rulers can be chosen from the
> people and by them (*ST* 1a, 2ae, qu. 105, art. 1, 5).

Thus in a model significantly altered from the Cambrai/Laon and
Plantagenet prototypes, Thomas's prescription for ideal government
combines qualities of aristocracy, monarchy, and democracy (*potestate
populi*), "in that rulers may be elected from the people and the whole
population has the right of electing its rulers." Such (apparent)
advocacy of universal suffrage and participation in government
represents another innovation in the Thomist model; yet elsewhere,

servi were excluded even from membership in the community, since "the city is a community of free men, the slaves not being citizens at all" (*Comm. Pol.* 3, lect. 5-8). The excluded (-low, -outside) are relegated to the "ad serviendum" function. If in this model the *servi* are so assigned due to physical, intellectual, or moral deficiencies rather than inherited and inviolable *ordo*, their lot remains similar to that of the *agricultores* or *laboratores*: unquestioning submission to their betters. "Lower must remain beneath the direction of the higher; . . . inferiors are bound to obey superiors according to the order established by natural and divine law." However, the obligation to obey one's superiors extends to all sectors of the community: "it is necessary that superiors impose their will upon inferiors, in virtue of the authority established by God " (*ST* 2a, 2ae, qu. 104, art. 1).

At the origin of the doctrine of obedience is the Pauline dictum: "Let every person be subject to the governing authorities. For there is no power but of God" (*Rom.* 13, 1-4). Aquinas, whose position on this question is "witness to a deep transformation of the Christian notion of obedience," affirms that since civic obedience is a religious obligation, "the Christian faith does not dispense the faithful from the obligation of obeying temporal princes" (D'Entrèves xxx). In general, the citizen should heed again the cautions of Paul: "Those who resist authority bring upon themselves damnation" (*Rom.* 13, 1).

Yet there are instances where resistance is justified, even necessary. An individual may disobey the orders of a secular authority, for example, a *podestà* or *signore*, when those orders contradict a higher authority, such as a prince. Secondly, and equally germane to Duecento northern Italy, disobedience is justifiable if the command pertains to something beyond the authority of the individual or group promulgating it. Thirdly, authority not only may, but must be resisted if it issues commands incompatible with Christian morality.

Similarly, where authority becomes abusive of the well-being of the group, the individual may refuse to submit. Thus the necessity of moral excellence in the governing authority is critical; that authority must not only be exemplary in his/its respect of reason and will as articulated in civil law, but must be able to move others to obedience of divine law by his/its example. It is the governing body or agent alone which may determine the common interest (*ST* 1a, 2ae, qu. 96, art. 4).

The right to resist unjust authority should nonetheless be exercised only in the event of extreme circumstances, i.e., if a monarchy appears to be degenerating into tyranny. Even then, the sanctioned deposition of a government abusive of its authority and noxious to the interests of the people becomes an act of sedition if the disorder produced by the rebellion creates a more serious threat to the community (*DR* 1.6).

The limitations of sovereignty have an immediate
bearing upon the problems of obedience and resistance.
...Allegiance cannot and must not be unconditional. It
is circumscribed with remarkable precision by the very
nature of political authority, as a means to achieve the
common good, and by the fundamental constitutional
laws which determine the position and the powers of the
ruler within the body politic. The emphasis is on law
and on the legal basis of authority.

We should also note that:

John of Salisbury taught that a ruler who broke with
custom and his promises could be removed;
Polycraticus 3, 15; 8, 20. This accepted principle in the
twelfth century was backed by the deposing powers of
the Church. St. Thomas agreed that subjects can
actively resist injustice, but his later writings seem
more in favour of the office held by existing authority;
perhaps from the tragic experiences of his family when
the Angevins replaced the Hohenstaufens in Naples.
Already Greek philosophy and Roman law were forming
a picture of the State more defined and majestic than
that of a feudal system (D'Entrèves xxx).

A tyrannical ruler, by definition one who exercises authority solely
for his own benefit, dislikes excellence and virtuous conduct in his
subjects as well as any threat to his position suggested by their power
and wealth. He rules by fear rather than by love, a weak foundation for
civic stability, though an issue which will find another spokesman in
Machiavelli. The ensuing disorder disrupts the *perfectam
communitatem*, but is permitted by a God who allows evil to exist in
the world; in the chain of reckoning, however, just as the king punishes
those who rebel unjustly against him, God punishes the king abusive
of his authority. Finally, in a statement less charitable than one might
hope, Thomas concludes that citizens deserve tyrants as punishment for
their sinful ways, "for it is by divine permission that wicked men
receive power to rule as a punishment for sin" (*DR* 1.6).

Aquinas stresses the diversity of men comprising a community, as
well as their differing interests and pursuits. While functionality of the
clerical and knightly sectors is reiterated and mention made of *servi*,
vilis populus, and *populus infimis*, the latter groups are neither entered

into the model as an order nor explicitly designated for agricultural or manual labor. Aquinas's descriptions of the social body acknowledges the increasing importance of the commercial element, albeit introduced in the *Summa Theologiae* under the negative heading of *fraudulentia*, since "the way will be opened to many vices," such as greed, loss of good faith, and the inevitable corruption of civic life (*DR* 2.8). *Negotiatores* are "those who apply themselves to the exchange of goods," divisible into two categories. Those who engage in trade in the interest of survival ("propter necessitatem vitae") and not necessarily involving monetary exchange are innocent of wrongdoing; others, trading for profit ("propter lucrum") and solely out of *cupiditas*, are condemned by Aquinas, just as they were by Aristotle. However, Thomas goes on to qualify that profit in itself does not automatically imply evil or immoral conduct; although commercial activity "always implies a certain baseness" ("quandam turpitudinem habet"), it becomes acceptable if the profit motive is directed toward assisting the common good, the poor, or even the upkeep of the individual's own household. Likewise, Aquinas roundly condemns usury, but recognizes the complexity of the issue in '200 Italy and accommodates an evil admittedly central to the description of contemporary society:

> Human laws allow certain sins to go unpunished because of the imperfection of man's condition which brings it about that much which is useful would be prevented if all sins were separately punished by explicit penalties. Therefore human law permits usury, not as though considering it to be just, but to avoid interference with the useful activities of many persons (*ST* 2a, 2ae, qu. 77, art. 4, qu. 77, art. 1).

In a tone of pragmatic reconciliation between prescriptive and descriptive models, Aquinas relaxes some of the strictures binding society to outmoded and outdated classifications. Thus human law silences the anathema of natural law to tolerate activities potentially harmful to the community's moral and spiritual well-being, yet vital to its material prosperity.

B. Marsilius of Padua

If Aquinas enunciates the most influential prescription of the theocratic model's *ordinatio ad unum* for the late Duecento and Trecento, the secular model had its own powerful, if controversial, spokesman in Marsilius of Padua. A contemporary and compatriot of the *Entrée* poet, Marsilius's *Defensor pacis* (1324) draws on lengthy experience as a citizen of the Paduan commune in its post-Ezzelino era; his treatise appears some fifty years after the death of Aquinas and just three years after the death of Dante. Marsilius stands at a radical ideological distance from both, as well as from the primary models, and from some of the promulgators of an imperial model; two centuries later, "Marsilianism" was tantamount in some circles to social iconoclasm. Yet if we view him not only as a major voice in the global conflict between Church and state, but also as "the authentic spokesman for the North Italian cities," Marsilius's views of Italian society through the first quarter of the Trecento help to illuminate another segment of the *Entrée*'s ideological dialogism.[12]

The fundamental (Aristotelian) thesis opening the *Defensor pacis* is the notion that peace and tranquillity are the conditions without which "the greatest good of man, sufficiency of life," cannot be attained (*DP3*; dis.1,1). Indeed, Marsilius was called "homo magis aristotelicus quam christianus" (Quillet 51). Although reiterating Aristotle's theory that all men are drawn toward community living by necessity and instinct, he pursues the argument differently; following the thesis that "man is born composed of contrary elements, because of whose contrary actions and passions some of his substance is continually being destroyed," Marsilius reaches the real thrust of his argument, which is that strife and discord are the unavoidable conditions of social existence and must, somehow, be controlled. The state "came into existence for the sake of living, but exists for the sake of living well"; such is its final cause, supported by all "normal" human beings (those not "deformed" mentally or morally). The dialectic of (+) necessary tranquillity and (-) inevitable discord forms the keystone of the entire Marsilian model (*DP* 12-13; dis. 1, 4).

Since nature and art proceed from the imperfect to the perfect, the human community, likewise, is a perfectible entity within the prescriptive model he proffers. Yet if order and tranquillity lead to peace, Marsilian notions of order are entirely devoid of transcendental reference and consist solely of "transient" human actions and events. Establishment and maintenance of social order depend upon the cooperation of each part of the state in the execution of operations proper to its function. And, as Gewirth notes: "It is the peace of Padua's burghers, not that of her clergy" (97-98).

Marsilius divides his model state into six *partes* (or *officia civitatis*) according to function:

1. the judicial: *pars principans*, the first, most vital element, whose function it is to "regulate matters of justice and the common benefit" (*DP* 64-67; dis.1,15);

2. the military: defender of liberty, which also executes "in a coercive manner," if necessary, sentences of the judges (*DP* 58-59; dis.1, 14);

3. the priestly: about which introductory comments in the *Defensor* anticipate subsequent revolutionary theses:

> All men have not thought so harmoniously about this as they have about the necessity of the other parts of the state. The cause of this difference was that the true and primary necessity of this part could not be comprehended through demonstration, nor was it self-evident.

Marsilius concedes, however, that the religious sector exists in all nations for the purpose of "worship . . . and for the benefit resulting therefrom for the status of the present or the future world" (*DP* 18-19; dis. 1, 5);

4. the financial: the commercial and treasury office;

5. the "mechanical" or artisan: functions include "spinning, leathermaking, shoemaking, all species of housebuilding. . ." and other arts "which moderate not only men's touch or taste but also the other senses." Such activities (including art and medicine) are said to exist more for pleasure than from necessity. Individuals engaged in this sector are compelled to apply all their energies to provide the necessities of life to themselves and family, and so they enjoy no leisure, which significantly determines human character and abilities (*DP* 17; dis. 1, 5 and 59; dis. 1, 14);

6. the agricultural: the first three *partes* are members of the "honorable class" (*honorabilitas*), and in a strict sense, comprise the *civitatem*, while the others make up the *vulgarem* and are called *officia* only insofar as they fill functions indispensable to the group (*DP* 52-53; dis. 1, 13 and Gierke 134n88). Differentiation among men in terms of aptitudes and inclinations is the work of nature, generating "prudent" men for the judicial and deliberative functions, strong and courageous

men for the military. Natural diversity provides the state with individuals competent to ensure its preservation and prosperity (*DP* 25-26; dis. 1, 7).

The state is a community of free men comprised of adult males (children, slaves, aliens, and women are excluded); a citizen is someone who participates at some level in the operation of government (*DP* 45-46; dis. 1, 12). The critical elements distinguishing the "best men" (called *prudentes* in the communes) are that they are more educated and enjoy the leisure for "liberal functions in which are exercised the virtues of both the practical and the theoretic soul" (*DP* 12; dis. 1, 4). It is this leisure which permits such *vacantes* to hold leadership positions in government; the more numerous common masses have less education and experience, although they are competent in the comprehension and judgment of ordinary civic concerns (*DP* 53; dis. 1, 13).

Since the whole is greater than its parts, both in quantity and quality, Marsilius names as head of state what he terms the "human legislator." In one of the most radical aspects of his model, he identifies this "primary authority" as "the whole population of citizens," or "the weightier part" (*pars valentior*) thereof. If an individual or collective ruler is elected, he/they remains in a subordinate position to the legislator, since:

> The aforesaid whole body of citizens or the weightier part thereof is the legislator, regardless of whether it makes the law directly by itself or entrusts the making of it to some person or persons, **who are not and cannot be the legislator in the absolute sense, but only in a relative sense and for a particular time and in accordance with the authority of the primary legislator** (*DP* 44-45; dis. 1, 12; emphasis added).

The legislator (adopted from Aristotle's *Politics*), then, corresponds to the *pars judicialis*, assuming primacy over all other sectors; it is the "first part," (*DP* 67; dis. 1, 15) which must both generate and approve any action relative to civic law. This human agent, whose authority is coercive and absolute, is the efficient cause of the state, solely entitled to bestow authority on the law, while at the same time being subject to it (Gewirth 166). What Quillet terms the "primauté, nécessité [et] continuité" embodied in the legislator extends to other powers invested in that function (102). First, the legislator enjoys both temporal and spiritual power. Without its approval, no regulations can be made regarding "other human acts," from consumption of meat to marriage within certain degrees of kinship, and including canonization and veneration of saints (292-93; dis. 2, 21).

The legislator, considered "more noble and more perfect in prudence and moral virtue," is elected by the citizens and entrusted with the ordering of the social body. Of particular interest here is what Marsilius terms the "norm or law of well-established policies," the charge to "establish and differentiate the parts and offices of the state from the appropriate matter"; thereupon to assign men to professions or trades according to their talents and to provide young men the training and education required to prepare them for their functions in society. The final responsibility for efficient and harmonious operation of the offices and their effective cooperation lies with the ruling part of the state, since all parts :

> are ordered by and toward the ruler as the first of all the parts for the status of the present world. For in the civil community that part is first which has to establish, determine, and conserve the others in and for the status of the present world or the civil end (65-67).

Symmetry in the body politic and regulated, proportionate growth of any part thereof again falls to the ruling sector, which is determined electively by the legislator. Strict control in makeup and size of any of the six parts is essential to prevent unnoticed, excessive increase of the number of the poor in democracies, or of the priesthood, as happens in the "law of the Christians" (66-67). Although the initial comment appears to target pejoratively the politically and economically problematic, accommodation of the *vulgus* is an important aspect of the Marsilian model. Identified principally by a lack of opportunity to acquire the education and skills of the *vacantes* rather than any sacralized and immutable ordination, the *vulgus* is a member of the *pars valentior*. Despite less education and, hence, less competence as experts in civic affairs than the *honorabilitas*, its numbers can be increased "to such an extent that they would judge about these things equally as well as, or even better than, the few who are more learned" (*DP* 52-53; dis. 1, 13). Rejecting spiritual vs. secular polarity, the *Defensor* renders all six parts of the state pertinent to the human soul: even farmers moderate the "acts of the nutritive part of the soul." The less-educated sectors are not to be understood as the "infinite number of the stupid" as in *3 Eccles.* and in fact "virtuous poor men" may be elected to political office and even to leadership positions. In such a case, it would be necessary to provide such individuals the requisite leisure associated with the honorable class. In theory, power-sharing is the most rational means of governance, since the collectivity of the people is "more ample, and consequently its judgment is more secure, than that of some part taken separately" (50-59). The actualization of Marsilian theory was the commune, Padua or any other, in Duecento and Trecento Italy.

When Marsilius names the priesthood as one *universitas* among six, he radically disrupts traditional Church, and many imperial models. As a result, "the priesthood loses its political or institutional authority to the whole body of the faithful, and its religious or sacramental authority to God" (Gewirth 265). For it is the functions of the clergy, not Christian doctrine or the Deity as supreme authority, which Marsilius means to alter. Citing Christ's voluntary submission to the secular legal system which was to condemn him, the Paduan insists not only on the absolute separation of temporal and spiritual power, but on the subordination of the clergy to civic authority (*DP* 124-25; dis. 2, 4 and Gewirth 262).

Particular vehemence is focused on the episcopate: "No bishop has immediately from Christ any authority over anyone else." More specifically, no bishop

> can authorize or decree the alteration, augmentation, diminution, suspension, interpretation. . . or total revocation of the ordinances and decisions made by the general council, whether concerning the faith or the meaning of the evangelic law or concerning church ritual or divine worship, as well as all other ordinances in any way (*DP* 113-26; dis. 2, 4).

The *Defensor* "subverts . . . [the] entire hierarchic structure" by means of a three-part revolution whereby it reduces the mediating function between the priesthood and Divinity, renders the whole body of the faithful superior to the clergy, and equalizes priests, bishops, and pope (Gewirth 262). Marsilius effects this by denying the existence of any divine Order on which the institutional Church can claim its foundation, employing both the argument of Christ's desire for equality and humility among his apostles and the contention that the fallibility and instability of human nature would have prevented God from appointing any mere human as absolute authority over His Church (*DP* 140-47; dis. 2, 6). Nonetheless, the *Defensor* recognizes the greater "zeal and ability" of some clergymen over others as well as the need for organization within the institution. In order to avoid, or at least minimize, the discord inevitable within any human group, a "head bishop," or pope, may be elected. However, "the Roman bishop has no more essential priestly authority" than any other bishop; furthermore, neither he nor any cleric has any coercive power in secular affairs of the state. In civic matters, and even in the spiritual realm, the *pars sacerdotalis* is to be strictly constrained by the surveillance of the law and its executors (*DP* 233-38; dis. 2, 15).

Conclusions

To complete our examination of social models in the era of the *Entrée* with Marsilius of Padua is of course to maximize the distance from the eleventh-twelfth century primary models to the "democratic radicalism" of the *Defensor pacis* (Gierke 46); differences are many and great, beginning with the diminution of episcopal power from the nearly limitless functions of ideologue and governor to the strictly controlled, non-coercive custodian of the spiritual. It would be a mistake to see the Paduan's theories as a sanctioned model of the early '300, an epoch fertile with theories of social governance; it would also be an error to dismiss his theories a priori without due consideration. The *Defensor* model is a prescriptive semiotic system constructed for the purpose of establishing order, peace, and harmony by a specified distribution of societal functions. In the broadest terms, medieval models of society trace their origins to either the religious or the secular community, and it is there, in their separate claims of "potestas soluta est," that their ideologies are to be found.

Beyond discrete claims for sovereignty, however, lies a vision of the universe shared by Church and state and joining them as members of the human *universitas*, the unity of which precedes any plurality. The universal earthly community, one articulated whole within which every being, whether a collectivity or an individual, is both a part of the whole and a whole unto itself (*minor mundus*), reflecting in every aspect of its operation the same principles which the Deity has chosen to govern the world (Gierke 7-9, citing Dante, *De mon.* and Aquinas *CG* and *DR*). Accordingly, the principle of inclusion accommodating all created matter is governed by the One; in doctrine reiterated from Augustine to Aquinas, *omnis multitudo derivatur ab uno*.

At the apex of the trifunctional pyramid of the primary models are those entrusted with the supreme privilege of articulation and mediation of the Word, the *oratores*; in the *Entrée*, it is Roland who will emerge as the bearer of the Word, and will participate in the establishment of a new social order in the East. Conversely, the orderers of the world, the

narrator's "retors de tere" and "hom soveran," are counselled to sharpen
their linguistic faculties in order to better comprehend and enact the
power of words. Brunetto Latini requires those who govern to be "trés
bons parliers," learned in the art of ordering language and, consequently,
entrusted with the ordering of human society, since language is the
living expression of social order (*Tresor* 393).

Given the likelihood that most prescriptive social models are
enunciated as bulwarks erected to ward off already-invasive change, it is
not surprising that discrepancies between the *res-signum* levels of the
primary models were not long in appearing. Each of the models
described here, from Alain de Lille thenceforth, is an acknowledgement,
tacit to be sure, that the old system no longer "fits" the changing
configurations of medieval society. The forces straining the old models
were several and relentless; according to Otto Gierke, they emerge from
all sides of the social body, slowly, subtly weakening its resistance.
They include canonists promoting papal absolutism, as in Boniface
VIII's *Unam Sanctam* of 1302; the ponderous influence of recuperated
Aristotelian theories and of the Justinian Digest, the ensuing claims of
imperial sovereignty predicated by the Hohenstaufens, and, most
patently, Church-state conflict preparing the Reformation; Aquinas,
too, "unconsciously labored in a work of destruction and innovation"
(Gierke 5-8). On a more abstract level, the relativist mentality emerging
as men lived and conceived their lives in a changing world proved an
irreversible process.

The doctrine of monarchical government runs throughout medieval
political theory. Among its most eloquent apologists is Dante in the
De monarchia, where he argues that since the principle behind the *unum
regens* is Divine will, the single will of one individual best represents
the unity of all (1.5-6). This was as true for the Church as for the
empire: "in every Body which is a Member of the Church or Empire,
and consequently every human group, a monarchy appeared to the
Middle Age [sic] as the normal form of government" (Gierke 32). But
the recovery of Aristotelian and Roman political theories compromised
that monologism, inviting consideration of other forms of government:
Aquinas, for example, revalorizes Aristotelian republican constitutions;
the francophile Brunetto Latini, dedicating his *Tresor* to Milan's
Galeozzo Visconti, weighs the advantages of Italian communal
government over French monarchy (392), aligning himself with
corporative theorists such as Henry of Ghent. A lively debate developed
in the late Middle Ages regarding forms of governance. It wasn't long
before publicists were writing that alternative forms of government
offered advantages over monarchy; further, that republicanism might be
preferable within certain contexts. At least one Italian theorist, Ptolemy

of Lucca, concluded that republicanism was the only viable alternative to tyranny within the context of his own experience, and thus should be adopted. Humanists studying classical texts found Roman republicanism attractive, then began to argue that the principle of unity is as safe within a republic as within a monarchy (Gierke 113, 33). Theoretical hybridism had arrived.

Conceptions of the human community had long been under the influence of Augustine's hospital metaphor; popes from Gregory VII to Innocent III quite naturally reiterated the opinion that human government exists because of man's inability to live within the perfect environment initially offered him. Imperfect by nature, then, the human community was perceived as rife with internal division, lust for power, abuse of authority, all generated by the heresy of self-love. Society, then, was established "under divine sufferance" either by an act of human violence or "extorted from God for some sinful purpose" (Gierke 12). Elaine Pagels discusses at length the radical nature of Augustinian theories of human nature and the process by which that mentality came to dominate Christian ideology.

Decidedly more positive theories of human nature and society begin to appear in the twelfth century, undoubtedly coterminous with the renascence of urban corporations and the new mentalities which they helped to engender. Preeminent are the praises of St. Thomas, particularly the conviction that the human community exists through Divine desire, the replica, not antithesis of the heavenly *civitas*. Theories proposing the divine origin of the state were in circulation: canonists insisting on the Church's role as mediator, imperialists and legists on immediately Divine origin (Gierke 31-32; John of Salisbury, *Policraticus* 4.1: 208-09 and 6.25: 391-95).

At another level, terminology used in reference to the *ordines* was to change in the evolving models examined above. First came the substitution of *statutes* for *ordines* by Alain de Lille; then the shifting of functions as well, whereby the earlier warrior sector (*bellatores*) was elevated to the ranks of the nobility (*milites*), and *oratores* were no longer confined to the episcopacy, but broadened to include the secular *advocatores*, now vital to the increasingly important judicial sector. For Aquinas, a man's status was defined by the degree of personal autonomy he enjoyed. The term *sacerdotes* still delineates the religious function, while the multiple charges of secular governance belong to the *principes*, normally performing their functions separately from the Church. The earlier third function of the landworker was redefined as the dynamic new *negotium* sector circulating the goods—and undoubtedly the ideas—of changing societies, a group probably as important in the function of communicators as the *oratores* themselves. The ambivalence of Aquinas (and most theorists) toward this group, constantly subdividing in order to multiply further, illustrates the reservations held by a Church which still saw Satan as king of the marketplace. And in 1327, Marsilius proposed the complete divorce of Church and state, granting virtually all authority of governance to the latter, alone.

From the revalorization of reason in the twelfth century and the Aquinate premise of its immanence in all individuals and communities, one can predict new attention, and controversy, directed toward definitions and distinctions of law in its several manifestations: "le propre de la raison est de découvrir la loi des choses" (Lagarde 1: 65). At a time when customary systems were patently inadequate, a potent dialogic arena was opened by theorists both clerical and secular concerning the relation of state to law. At the apex of the hierarchy was *lex aeterna* or *ius divinum* pre-existing and prevailing over all earthly constructs, eternal and immutable above pope, emperor, sovereign people and all human institutions. While natural law had been given to man for use in earthly matters, divine law was given "in a supernatural way and for a supramundane purpose," divided into old and new law; we might recall the *Entrée*'s textual self-predication as "*canticum novum*." The law of nations (*ius gentium*), was likewise transmitted to man by the Divinity, thus sacralized, but not immutable.

Delineation of the operational sphere of natural law fostered lively debate in its relation to civil and Church jurisdiction. Aquinas responded by saying that natural law can be divided into first and second principles, the former being absolute and unchanging, the latter, due to the fallen state of mankind, subject to modifications "ex causa." Subdivision resolved the question of lordship and ownership as possibly contrary to natural law. He also held that private ownership is not contrary to natural law, provided it is exercised with reason; one might recall Charlemagne's claim in the *Entrée* to immutable lordship countering Roland's claim for lordship as control over his own militia. There was general agreement that secondary principles of positive law regulating civic affairs (*ius civile*), divine law and the law of nations were, if necessary, subject to intervention. In stressing the relativity of all law (except *lex aeterna*), legal systems exist as *artes* fashioned by human reason, interacting, sometimes conflicting one with another: "le droit est *rationis ordinatio* dans un rapport de relation à d'autres choses . . . il est toujours un 'ad aliquid', un 'rapport' " (Lagarde 1: 66).

The theory of sovereignty whereby any monarch, religious or temporal, stands above any human legislation decreed by him or his predecessors, can be traced to Roman law revived in the twelfth century. Focus of considerable debate thenceforth, *principes legibus solutus est* renders the ruler a law unto himself, empowered to alter or annul any civic law (Gierke 77). Roman dominion decreed by Divine will made its initial appearance with the God-man Christ; subsequently transferred to the Greeks in the time of Constantine, final *translatio imperii* delegated to the German emperor authority over all earthly communities (Gierke 19). The Hohenstaufens claimed unlimited power on the basis of the (convenient) doctrine of abdication of the people; i.e., it was by popular will that the monarch ruled without limitation. It was this authoritarian absolutism which distinguished the monarch from a republican magistrate. It should be remembered that a contract of subjections is the basis of any medieval state, which either enacts or assumes the consent of the whole people (Gierke 43 and n265). Buttressed by *de iure* and *de facto* claims of insolubility, the medieval empire claimed the sovereignty of its judicial system over any law or individual, rendering null and void any act diminishing the Empire, even if perpetrated by the incumbent emperor himself (Gierke 20).

Opposing publicists and legists extolled popular sovereignty, rendering any ruler accountable to the law(s) which originated in the consent of the community (Gierke 77-78). Marsilius champions this thesis, rendering the law as the will of the sovereign people, theirs to create, alter, or eliminate.

Among the innovations of medieval theory, and naturally compatible with communal society, was the law of corporations and its effort to refine further the relation between governor and governed. In the event of dissension, the latter were represented by a group of its chosen spokesmen; any action taken was as legally binding as that of the entire community. In the Church, the *consilium* became the representing body; in the secular sphere, elected councils exercised the collective will, optimally transferred to them by election by the whole community (Gierke 64-66). Medieval epics and romances are replete with reflection of the law of corporations as one of the two principal modalities by which action is taken.

To the above summary of the dialogic nature of matters of law and governance in the latter Middle Ages should be added the increasing authority of law, perhaps best illustrated by Aquinas's tripartite model, with principal emphasis no longer on the inviolability of the orders, but on adherence to laws pertinent to the general good. And of Marsilius's six societal functions, the *pars judicialis* is most important. Thus a certain levelling takes place in communities where both ruler and ruled are bound to, and optimally, wish to comply with the law. In contrast to the proponents of the quasi-divine monarch, Aquinas speaks for those viewing political authority as duty with given rights and responsibilities corresponding to the *officia* binding each citizen to his leader(s). The contractual nature of the relationship stressed that rulers exist for the sake of the people, not peoples for the sake of rulers; Dante, Petrarch, and Aquinas underline the idea that the good ruler provides peace, justice, and maximum freedom for his subjects (Gierke 125). When the ruler fails in any respect to honor these duties he brings upon himself the charge of tyranny, at which point the legality of his governance is put into question. As stated by Gierke, the "doctrine of the unconditioned duty of obedience was wholly foreign" to the medieval mind (34-35); rather, it was the propriety of any given law or command which determined the citizen's response, either to comply or to resist.

Significantly, according to Aquinas, active resistance was *required* of any citizen upon whom a governor imposed commands inappropriate to his office; more precisely, and with the circumspection we may see as caveat, disobedience was permitted, even required, in cases where "human laws which are directed against God's commandments . . . or when a law inflicts an unjust grievance on its subjects, . . . if without scandal or greater damage he can resist" (*ST* 1a 2ae, qu. 96, art. 5 ad 2um, ad 3um). Coercive enforcement of an unjust order was further grounds for disobedience. Henry of Ghent, an apologist for the communes, held that revolt is better than passive disobedience (Lagarde 324); Coluccio Salutati adds that a tyrant may be lawfully resisted, even, in extreme circumstances, assassinated: "resistance against a ruler who abuses his rightful power through *superbia* is lawful." Nonetheless, Salutati criticizes John of Salisbury's theory of tyrannicide, because "his illustrations prove, not that the murder of a tyrant is right, but that it is frequent" (85-90). And, while in a forceful statement he praises Dante for placing tyrants in the deepest wastes of Hell, Salutati weakens the impact of his conviction: "it would be a presumptuous, nay, a *superbum* act to rebel against a ruler while all the rest were willing to endure him, were he a Nero, **an Ezzelino**, a Phalaris or a Busris" (cited in Lagarde 85-90, 92, 110; emphasis added).

The stridency of *plenitudo potestatis* claims by both Church and empire was to open the dialogic arena questioning and ultimately challenging such doctrines, leading to alternative theories entrusting increasing authority to the people, or certain segments thereof. The process, seen retrospectively from the comfortable distancing of time, appears logical, even inevitable: by the schism of the fourteenth century, the doctrine of conditional obedience formulating the right of resistance to unlawful government and eventually even to revolution evolved quite naturally to the acknowledgment of *potestas limitata* of pope and emperor (Gierke 35-37 and n134 regarding Ockham on papal limitations). Increasingly, the advantages of elected authority and power-sharing were entered into the dialogue.

The processes of democratization and secularization are most aptly demonstrated in the northern Italian communal experiments examined in this chapter. Separation of Church and state, a perennially problematic state issue, took its first hesitant steps at this time, with the optimistic anticipation that harmony in the human community would be more attainable thereby. Still, one cannot overlook the distinct signs of ambivalence coursing throughout these experiments in governance; the Thomist theories, for example, appear innovative in their encouragement of a greater degree of power-sharing, while simultaneously expressing a distinct residue of distrust of the most critical third function, *negotium*, and thus of the population segment by which it is represented. His ideal of the mixed constitution finds expression along with other proposals where he grants sovereignty to the ruler or to the people according to differing constitutions. Even Marsilius, in his proposals of democratization and secularization, seems ambivalent when it comes to delineation of the omnipotent "pars valentior" which is the central component of his model; although the people are sovereign here, the societal function which each individual carries out is determined not by free choice, but by the somewhat nebulous notion of the "human legislator."

Surveying some of the intricacies of the latter '200 to mid '300 serves to focus more clearly on both particulars and generalities. Energies eager for change in systems of government vied with the resistant forces of established institutions; within these, other tensions compelled re-evaluation of ideologies previously unquestioned. Yet revaluation retained within the multiple models, both progressive and reactionary, is the fundamental notion of hierarchization. Not surprisingly, it remains the primary premise on which all order in the medieval community is based; however, as some theorists proposed, hierarchization, a sign of the imperfection of human nature, would be corrected, i.e., eliminated at the Second Coming. Globally viewed as part of natural, civic, and immutable divine law, it remained the prime divine structuring factor from pseudo-Dionysius through the evolutionary models from the eleventh to the fourteenth centuries. Synonymous with the notion of order itself, hierarchization conjoins with inequality and subjection as fundamental aspects of medieval social organization. In discourse decidedly more liberal than others, it is nonetheless as evident in Marsilius's distinctions between the *honorabilis* and *vulgus* as in the episcopal primacy of the Cambrai/Laon systems. That it should remain theoretically unchallenged except by groups condemned as heretical is not surprising in societies which were increasingly diversified and horizontally broadened, but united by a vertical religious ideology quite literally founded upon the principle of *unum regens* inclusion: one articulated whole, of which all beings are both parts and microcosms, a graduated system of partial bodies (Gierke 21).

Notes

1. Dionysius the Pseudo-Areopagite, *The Ecclesiastical Hierarchy*, trans. and annotated Thomas L. Campbell (Washington: University Press of America, 1981) 17.
2. It should be noted that there were other social models in circulation during the critical third decade of the eleventh century: three in competition with the Gerard/Adalbero model were the monastic, so-called egalitarian, and Peace of God. See Georges Duby, *Les Trois ordres ou l'imaginaire du féodalisme*, Bibliothèque des histoires NRF (Paris: Gallimard, 1978) 162-82.
3. For an excellent interpretation of Gerard's use of language, see Stephen G. Nichols, "Fission and Fusion: Mediations of Power in Medieval History and Literature," *YFS* 70 (1986): 30-41.
4. On the Augustinian determinacy of human nature, see Elaine Pagels, *Adam, Eve, and the Serpent* (New York: Random House, 1988) 99, 113:

> The work of his later years, in which he radically broke with many of his predecessors, and even with own earlier convictions, effectively transformed much of the teaching of the Christian faith. Instead of the freedom of the will and humanity's original royal dignity, Augustine emphasizes humanity's enslavement to sin. Humanity is sick, suffering, and helpless, irreparably damaged by the fall, **for that 'original sin,' Augustine insists, involved nothing else than Adam's prideful attempt to establish his own autonomous self-government.** Astonishingly, Augustine's radical views prevailed, eclipsing for future generations the consensus of more than three centuries of Christian tradition. . . . Augustine draws so drastic a picture of the effects of Adam's sin that he embraces human government, even when tyrannical, as the indispensable defense against the forces sin has unleashed in human nature. His analysis of internal conflict, indeed, leads directly into his view of social conflict in general. . . . (emphasis added).

5. In this exposition, his argument must be irrefutable, since Gerard is addressing a formidable group of opponents: some Frankish bishops, claiming to have received a letter from heaven wherein were expounded several social reforms which should be rapidly adopted before the imminent Second Coming. In the perfect society to be established at that time, all inequality would vanish,

because sin itself would cease to be. The bishops proposed three reforms for immediate enactment: equality of agreements (conjuration), by which one universal oath would serve for all human contracts; equality of penitence, by which a single law of fasting would redeem all sins; equality in peace, by which all warlike activity was to terminate (*Ordres* 53-61).

6. For theory, see Jurij Lotman, *The Structure of the Artistic Text*, trans. Gail Lenhoff and R. Vroon, Michigan Slavic Contributions 7 (Ann Arbor: U of Michigan P, 1977) 229; for discussion regarding medieval models, see Maria Corti, "Models and Antimodels in Medieval Culture," trans. J. Meddemmen, *NLH* 10.3 (1979): 341-57.

7. Dante takes particular exception to material wealth as a defining component of nobility. Inherently vile, wealth is also dangerous, in that it generates insatiable desire for increase; knowledge, likewise, arouses desire for further knowledge, but the spirit is nourished and satisfied, making it a source of good. By nobility:

> s'intende perfezione di propria natura in ciascuna cosa. Onde non pur de l'uomo è predicata, ma eziandio di tutte cose—ché l'uomo chiama nobile pietra, nobile pianta, nobile cavallo, nobile falcone—qualunque in sua natura si vede essere perfetta. . . .

And since mankind is all of one species:

> non si può per li principii ezzenziali la loro ottima perfezione diffinire, conviensi quella e diffinire e conoscere per li loro effetti. . . . (16).

Dante Alighieri, *Convivio*, ed. Gustavo Rodolfo Ceriello, Biblioteca Universale Rizzoli 483-486, 6th ed. (Milano: Rizzoli, 1952) 4.11-13, 4-16; 302-06.

8. Georges de Lagarde, *La Naissance de l'esprit laïque au déclin du moyen âge*, 5 vols. (Paris: Louvain, 1956) 1: 110-11:

> Tout pacte définit le 'statut' juridique d'un groupe, d'une collectivité, d'une association, d'une ville. . . . Tout individu faisant parti du groupe est ainsi inclus aux droits, . . . et possède un status, reconnaissance de la zone juridique correspondant à une condition, fonction, ou groupe social quelconque. L'état d'une personne c'est

> l'ensemble de ses prérogatives, ou de ses franchises; . . .
> il n'y a pas de droit commun, mais une série de droits
> juxtaposés . . . une hiérarchie de classes, de conditions,
> de situations sociales. . . .

9. In order to describe the dynamism of cultural semiotic models, Lotman identifies the following binary couples. It is the second element which is subject to "forgetting," or elimination from the system: 1. the systematic vs. extrasystematic; 2. the monosemic vs. ambivalent; 3. the nucleus vs. periphery; 4. description vs. non-description. "The Dynamic Model of a Semiotic System," trans. Ann Shukman, *Semiotica* 21. 3/4 (1977): 193-210.

10. See Gerhart B. Ladner, *The Idea of Reform: Its Impact on Christian Thought and Action in the Age of the Fathers*, revised ed. (New York: Harper & Row, 1967) 141:

> To the City of Saints, the city of God, corresponds the
> City of the World, the City of the Devil. The only
> thing that according to Augustine really matters in the
> history of man is the conflict between these two cities
> or societies . . . On earth the City of God is a stranger
> and pilgrim (*peregrinans* or *in peregrinatione*), but it
> exists also as the fatherland in heaven, Jerusalem,
> interpreted as *visio pacis*, the heavenly Jerusalem,
> which will descend to earth in the end, when heaven and
> earth are made new. Its counterpart is seen prefigured by
> Babylon, interpreted as *confusio*, a symbol of the
> 'worldly city.'

11. Aquinas mentions eight reasons for the perfection of the universe: 1. its multiplicity of species; 2. their accidental perfections; 3. their essential perfections; 4. the fact of a thing's being ordered to other things; 5. the order following accidental perfections; 6. the order following essential perfections; 7. the end to which things are ordered, God; 8. the order of the end, which follows from the goodness of the parts and their order to one another (1 *Sent.* d. 40 qu. 1, art. 2. ad 6um, cited in John H. Wright, S. J., *The Order of the Universe in the Theology of St. Thomas Aquinas*, Analecta Gregoriana 89, Series Facultatis Theologicae Sectio B (Rome: Universitatis Gregorianae, 1957) 7.

12. Marsilius is of particular interest because of his provenance, his work in France, and the likelihood that he was a contemporary of the *Entrée* poet. Rector of the University of Paris in 1313, he then served two of Lombardy's most prominent figures, Can Grande

della Scala and Matteo Visconti. Associated also with Pietro
d'Abano, Padua's leading Averroist, Marsilius was offered a
benefice in Padua by Pope John XXII, which he apparently did not
accept. Excommunicated for heresy after publication of the
Defensor pacis, he entered the service of Ludwig of Bavaria, aiding
in the latter's coronation. Named spiritual vicar of Rome by the
Emperor, Marsilius continued his criticism of the papacy and
clergy. He left Rome with the deposed Ludwig and died in 1342.
Alan Gewirth, *Marsilius of Padua and Medieval Political
Philosophy*. (Milan: Feltrinelli, 1960) 28. For translation and
editing of the text, see Marsilius of Padua, *Defensor Pacis*, ed. and
trans. Alan Gewirth, Mediaeval Academy Reprints for Teaching 6
(1956; New York: Columbia UP; Toronto: U of Toronto Press,
1980) xix. Citations from the *Defensor Pacis* are entered
preceeded by *DP*.

CHAPTER 4
DISCOURSE AND IDEOLOGIES

Citing Jean de Meung's *Roman de la rose* and Dante's *Divina Commedia* as quasi-encyclopedic works characteristic of the late Middle Ages, M. M. Bakhtin identifies their shared sense of the era's complexities, with a striving in both to expose "all the contradictory multiplicity of the epoch" (*Dialogic Imagination* 156). The *Entrée*, with its "interessi conoscitivi e ideologici vigorosi," is described by the late Alberto Limentani as a *summa* in its own right. I repeat his eloquent confirmation that:

> Il Padovano ha forzato al massimo il vecchio strumento formale della *chanson de geste* verso una strutturazione di poema: ne è risultato un 'poema sacro' con forma, spirito e scopi suoi propri, ben distinto in questo dagli antecedenti come dai posteriori sviluppi della materia carolingia. L'*Entrée* ha diritto a un suo posto di rilievo non solo nella storia culturale, ma al livello degli apprezzamenti qualitativi senza i quali questa storia non può che risultare deformata. Quella consistenza di poema stacca l'*Entrée* dalle *chansons* post-rolandiane, e le consente di accostarsi al gruppo delle opere poetiche tardo-medievali a carattere di *summa*, quali inanzitutto il *Roman de la rose* e la *Commedia* . . . ("Epica" 360).

Emerging within a climate of exceptional socio-political, economic, and cultural fermentation, the text in turn produces its own dialogical arena where a complex of languages and ideologies is deployed. From the opening verses, the text's Franco-Italian polyglossia signals the intersection of dual linguistic and cultural systems; "multiple" language itself, no longer either the traditional French medium of Rolandian material, nor yet the Italian of the *cantari* and *La Spagna*, serves to alter our expectations of content and meaning. Dialogic confrontation between national languages opens the text, as it were, preparing further confrontations of words and ideas.

The linguistic and ideological orientation of the *Entrée* should be examined as a series of discourse systems inseparable from the text in which they are produced. In its mediating function, literary language is a complex semiotic system capable of transmitting extensive volume and depth of information in an internal ideological structure. Literary texts in general, and the *Entrée* in particular, are "magnificently organized generators of languages of a special type" (Lotman, *Artistic Text* 4-12). In the *Entrée*'s first such system, the text may be seen in its relationship to the canons of the chanson de geste and its feudal ethos; it meets, for example, that part of reader/audience expectations which anticipates a chronological prologue to the *Chanson de Roland*. The sanctioned literary and political discourse of the French epic tradition posits itself within the *Entrée* as its "official," "correct," authoritative system of thinking and speaking the epic world. It not only represents established ways of looking at literature and social organization, but constitutes a centripetal force seeking to draw all discourse toward its epicenter. As a unifying discourse system, epico-feudal language provides a significant ground of shared comprehensibility for a public even minimally conversant with its codes. In the text, passages articulated around such issues as *orgueil* or chivalry in the service of lord and God fall within the conventions of such discourse and claim the authority of time and tradition.

Present within the text as well are other discourse systems viewing literature and the world in different ways. Thus romance, secular/courtly and hagiographical, provides another prominent example in several textual events following the Charles-Roland rupture; the influence of courtly romance is immediately evident in the hero's *planctus* as he departs the familiar world of epic collectivity and begins a solitary quest undertaken in the unknown wilderness of Spain and the exotic world of the Islamic Mideast. Further, the text reveals evidence of additional discourse elements throughout: most prominently, what we may call political discourse referring to questions of governance and civic authority, as well as elements of the language of the marketplace and schools. The pervasive discourse system of the Church will be examined in chapter 5.

Each of these internal languages comes from and in some way represents a social, political, or intellectual affinity group; each is a point of view, an opinion or judgment, and as such it anticipates contact, communication, and response (Bakhtin, *Imagination* 282).

These language systems constitute the *Entrée*'s heteroglossia, the presence and stratification of multiple linguistic codes within the Franco-Italian polyglossia. The discourse of the *roman* in Part Two challenges and undermines the primacy of the epico/feudal substratum in the text's first 9000 verses; the forces which it exerts thereafter seek to establish another discourse zone removed from the gravitational pull of the first. Throughout the *Entrée*'s nearly 16,000 verses, superimposed on its epic and romance discourse, there are, also, events, additionally, and language referring to extratextual issues of social organization pertinent to the world in which the text was composed and circulated. Each of these superimposed languages, related to the lexica of the political, commercial, and cultural, exert pressures which are centrifugal, decentralizing the text away from its principal infrastructures. While the literary languages of epic and romance are sequentially organized, the others are present in each of the *Entrée*'s major divisions and will be examined and evaluated within their specific textual contexts. Textual loci where such language and ideology appear include, for example, the political and commercial aspects of Charles's speech on the gift horse, and cultural discourse in the protracted debate on women, status and marriage in the Dionés episode.

Fundamental to the understanding of the verbal-ideological worlds represented in the *Entrée* is the perception that all words exist in a well-populated environment, in which they are continually in contact and communicating with other words. Their constant dialogic interaction renders each word sensitive to the influence of others in its semantic field at a given historical moment and creates a competitive environment where each seeks to prevail, to become the discourse of authority, absolute and unquestioned. Further, a word used by any given speaker is appropriated (frequently without his/her awareness) laden with all the allusions, implications, contradictions, and so on which it has accumulated over time. Examination of high-frequency words in the text demonstrates the effects of dialogic confrontation of characteristically epic terms such as *orgueil* when an agonistic discourse system encroaches on their space.

In what Bakhtin describes as a constant struggle between the forces of monoglossia (>centralization) and heteroglossia (>decentralization), it is the assertive presence of a second system which discloses the essence of the unitary language. Since we can best perceive one language as it interrelates with another, thorough comprehension of the infinite subtleties of words is achieved by viewing them within the arena of their dialogue with other words, from which all will emerge in some way altered (*Imagination* 272).

The *Entrée* text, then, with reference to literary and social models, produces a dialogue between systems of social organization and institutions which may coexist in relationships of relative accommodation or antagonism. Much of its epico-feudal material is of course drawn from, and dictated by, the Model I substratum. But to the late thirteenth to early fourteenth-century northern Italian public among which it initially circulated, such material was not timely or realistic in the sense of correspondence to the existential experience of that group— although, like the earlier chansons de geste, it might well be accepted as true.

The fundamental thematic of *Entrée* I is assignment of a task whose goal is the restoration of world order as conceived by Christian ideology. Since Spain is considered a member segment of the divinely-ordained Christian *communitas*, violation of its spatial integrity must be corrected so that social and spiritual order can be reinstated. The task involves recuperation of territory via military reconquest, hardly the ceremonial royal "entry" enunciated by the title; i.e., re-active action intended to vindicate wrongs perpetrated on the global community. Although it forms what Antoine Thomas called a "vaste prologue disproportionné et disparate" to the *Chanson de Roland* (Intro. xlii), the *Entrée*, too, presupposes previous texts narrating events at other sites leading to the shrine at Compostella. As stated earlier, the dual means by which the task is to be performed are themselves dialectical in their method: verbal in the *conseils*, military in the combats.

Yet superimposed on this subtext, surely remote in its ethos for a Trecento public, are signs of a new text in which a court and urban public may perceive the presentness of the past, elements which concern the real as well as the true. For example, in the language and events deployed to narrate the Charles-Roland conflict, the dominant structuring device of Part One, the Italian public might well perceive a dialectical forum on more contemporary issues regarding interaction between the communes, *signorie*, and empire; at a more general level, a dialectical presentation of the problematics of secular governance itself, both issuing from the global issues of authority and autonomy. The existence of encoded polysemy in the *Entrée* and other Franco-Italian works, with differing levels of signification accessible to differing levels of reader competence and ideological orientation, has received its most detailed examination to date by Henning Krauss. Suggesting a certain hermeticism in the *Entrée* absent from most chansons de geste, Krauss specifies the Paduan's narrative strategy as a "procedimento di parziale messa in cifra" in its referentiality to contemporary societies (*Epica* 230). A similar point is made by Peter Wunderli on the Franco-Italian restructuration of the *matière de France*:

> [N]ous avons maintenant affaire à un nouveau
> système de valeurs dont les mécanismes et les lois
> ont leur propre droit à l'existence et qui, dans leur
> fonctionnement, sont indépendants des structures
> antérieures. Ou, pour employer une métaphore
> linguistique: une synchronie antérieure a été
> remplacée par une synchronie ultérieure ("Roland
> théologien" 760).

My intention, however, is not to read the *Entrée* as a political allegory in which the epic and romance foundations are reduced to scaffolding. Instead, it is my belief that the text, characteristic of its geographical and chronological provenance, assumes the shape of a dialogical forum, raising, exposing, and disputing a series of questions; as such, it permits and invites multiple readings. The tension and, frequently, the friction arising from these confrontations produce what I see as the text's extraordinary vitality and may help to explain its wide dissemination.

Given the *Entrée*'s partial affinity with the French *baron révolté* cycle, it is interesting to speculate on analogous conditions behind the composition of these works. The pro-vassal French chansons de geste such as *La Chevalerie Ogier*, *Girard de Roussillon*, and *Renaud de Montauban* were composed in a period of a strengthening monarchy forging a revolutionary alliance with the bourgeoisie in order to reinstate its authority over a disruptive nobility perceiving its traditional privileges endangered. As presumed receptors of these works, adherents of the French nobility's *vision du monde* thus directed the literary rendition of their perceptions and aspirations. In some poems, a weak king (physically and/or morally), hesitant to assume the duties of his office and misguided concerning the use of royal authority over the nobility, deprives these same nobles of a degree of autonomy to which they feel entitled. In the *baron révolté* cycle, the feudal bond between king and noble vassal ruptures in disputes typically concerning land or marriage; the conflict may develop into open warfare and is usually resolved with the defeat and/or withdrawal of the vassal, who then enacts penance for his transgressive conduct and submits to royal authority.

In the Venetan-Lombard region during the Duecento and Trecento, a widespread *vision du monde* still included the idea of an emperor whose efforts to exercise significant control on the communes were still fresh in the collective memory. Although the death of Frederick II in 1250 neatly marked the end of an era of exacerbated commune-empire litigation, imperial potentates continued to pervade the operation of communal governments, as Ezzelino da Romano (1159-1259) and Can Grande della Scala (1291-1329), two of the most powerful imperial officers of the era testify. Reluctance to permit imperial entry into the urban commune was still sufficiently strong in 1310 to prevent Henry VII of Luxembourg, called King of Germany, from entering Florence. As Dante was to complain in *Paradiso* 30:137-41:

> . . . l'alto Arrigo, ch'a drizzare Italia
> verrà in prima ch'ella sia disposta.
> La cieca cupidigia che v'ammalia
> simili fatti v'ha al fantolino
> che muor per fame e caccia via la balia.

We should also recall that the regional Italian nobility perceived itself in a precarious position, whether in its fluctuating relationship with the empire or in its frequently agonistic transactions with the proliferating middle classes. In the *Entrée*, as in some of the forementioned French texts, we observe an inconsistent, sometimes ineffectual emperor, not infrequently questionable in the exercise of his office and possibly even abusive of his authority. He is paired with an indispensable vassal who, in the several readings which the *Entrée* invites, can plausibly be cast as the wronged hero justifiably resorting to the vindication of his honor and identity.

The Paduan's choice of Rolandian material is also to a significant extent a choice of language, of a largely foreign lexicon sanctioned by more than two centuries of written and oral usage. But the author has also made another language choice by adopting the Italian vehicle, a particularly sensitive choice which partially preselects a bilingual public competent in a second linguistic code; a public which, in the period 1300-1350, we may assume to have had access to some formal education, some acquaintance with the French chanson de geste, and to fit somewhere in the upper ranks of the socio-economic scale. The academic sector and clergy are to be included in this provisional delineation of the *Entrée* public.

Language as theme is particularly evident in Roland's ability to communicate in multiple codes, and is certainly an aspect of his *prouesse*; he is conversant in Latin, linking him to channels of official or traditional clerical culture, as well as in Islamic languages (11,522, 11,577), the importance of which was now clear in the intellectual and commercial worlds beyond the text. The hero, like the author, possesses skills which permit both to vary their means of communication according to their publics—quite literally, to speak the language comprehensible to differing narratees, thus to adapt, fit in, and ensure maximum receptivity within differing contexts. Maximal possibility of effective communication is thus assured. Despite the topical multilingualism of French epic heroes, the *Entrée's* polyglossia itself heightens our awareness of language as theme.

The Paduan's linguistic choices may be seen as a selection of heteroglot languages which integrate the text into "a complex hierarchy of artistic languages of an epoch, culture, and people" (Lotman, *Structure* 76). The *Entrée* is a generator of several stratified languages, each of which is somehow linked to the others, to the author, and to the socio-historical context in which they arose. As mentioned above, we are confronted with the extratextual languages of the mercantile, the legal, the intellectual, as well as with the literary language systems of epic, romance, and hagiography. Examination of the usage of textual languages informs the reader not only of how the text is part of other, larger literary groups, i.e. genres, but also how it is different, how it acquires singularity.

Labor/repois (locus *a*: 57-327)

The heteroglossia of late medieval discourse is well documented and an important aspect of the *Entrée*. In the opening *conseil*, we identify the morphemes *labor* and *travail* and their contraries *repois* and *"sbanoie"*, as initial examples of ideological dialogism. Subject of the debate is the advisability of undertaking the expedition to Spain: the passage thus stands in a specular rapport to the *Chanson de Roland*'s opening *conseil* debating the departure from Spain seven years later. The *Entrée* locus, in a broader sense, concerns the obligations of the individual to the community, and the community to its creators/Creator. Words once stained by association with punitive postlapsarian toil acquired more positive associations in the twelfth century. First, with the labor of the Pancreator: God as the first worker. To this was added a new perception of the blessed and joyful labor allotted to Adam and Eve before the Fall, the upkeep of Eden, free of all negative connotations. Further, the history of the medieval communes in general, and of the *popolo* in particular, must take into consideration the important role played by burgeoning labor markets and the association between labor and improved conditions of life. To a significant extent, communal society depended on a positive attitude toward various kinds of human labor, from that required for competent citizenship to the new professionalism of groups such as jurists, notaries, bankers, merchants, and academics. Within the new mentality of communal Prehumanist Italy, labor was the basis upon which both individual and society could create a better life. Thus words such as *labor* and *travail* illustrate the heteroglossia immanent in the *Entrée*'s language systems. Each enters in the text laden with associations from other texts, other speakers, other times, other contexts; once inserted, it is drawn into a dialogical relationship with other elements of the text's lexical system, in which the reader/public seeks to comprehend its meaning. "No words are shared by all; neither is there any word belonging to no one" (Bakhtin, *Imagination* 270ff).

In the *conseil*, a ritualistic structuring device of the chanson de geste, deliberative rhetoric is employed to formulate decisions in an environment reductively related to the *ars appondendi et respondendi* of the schools. Although all participants share the same ideological beliefs, or so we presume, each speaker addresses a narrative audience which will judge his argument according to the perceived probability of its chances for success. The authorial audience, however, receives the arguments with assumptions already formed: i.e., Roland will be hawkish and will ultimately prevail. In the *Entrée*'s initial ideological locus (dialogically related to its counterpart in the Oxford text regarding the role assumed by Roland), two thematic elements are elaborated which expand audience assumptions in the earlier text: the thematics of liberation and the polarity (+) *labor* opposed to (-) *repois* with their related semantic fields.

Their most prominent articulation occurs in the three "miracle" nocturnal visions which Charles experiences at the opening of the narrative. St. James had insisted on the necessity of liberating the entire pilgrim route, ordering that the emperor "afranche son chemins e sa droite santelle" (73) ("liberate his route and rightful road"); only then will that sacred space be restored to its rightful ideological status. The evocative initial presentation of Charles, hieratically enthroned as an icon of absolute authority, is, however, immediately marred by his explanation of why he is obliged to undertake the proposed mission. Banished from France many years ago following hostilities with Girard de Vienne (" 'Quant je fui forscacez de France por envie' " 94), the emperor only now recollects the oath then sworn to St. James for his victory over the rebellious baron: to liberate the pilgrim route to Compostella. Self-referentially, Charles's motivational axis can be traced back to that internal conflict:

"Forscacez de France" > sacred oath > "Je afranche son chemins"

The rebellious baron theme immediately introduced at a primary motivational level should alert us as to its possible recurrence and potential future functions. Girard himself, who abandoned Charles and the Christian cause to ally himself with the "pagan" king Marsile, establishes a dialogical link between the *Entrée* and a whole poetic corpus, several of whose texts will be alluded to by the Paduan.

More significantly, incorporation of this intertextual event alerts both narrative and authorial publics that conflicts within this (and other) texts arise ostensibly between groups of opposing (religious) ideologies, but also, and with more grave effects, between members of the same ideological group. This paradox, already latent in the *Roland*, suggests that a principal focus of the *Entrée*, to which its public can relate in an immediate way, is not the Moslem occupation of Spain, but rather the interplay of that external situation with discordant forces within a community confronting a crisis situation which can only be resolved if concord and unity are absolute. The crusader mission is the external crisis upon which all intratextual energy must be focused if it is to succeed. Yet in reality, the mission serves more to converge pretextual antagonisms on the internal crisis and to intensify tensions to the point of confrontation. Such confrontation not only jeopardizes the external mission, but threatens the destruction of the Christian *civitas* itself.

The lengthy debate (270 verses) involving the euphemistic "entry" into Spain is structured around war as labor, exertion, the necessary hardships of military action as opposed to the pleasures and leisure of peacetime. Of the seven opinions offered to Charles's proposition, it is the narrator's interpolation and the first two speeches which focus the debate on the dialectic of *travail* and *repois*. The narrator establishes the polarity in discourse directed beyond the text to his Italian audience: "Segnors, vos savez ben qe travail et repois/ Contralïent l'uns l'autre cumme triaqe e thois." (97) ("Lords/gentlemen, you well know that labor and leisure contradict one another like antidote and poison"). Galés de Vernandois thereupon makes the argument for *repois*, claiming the reconquest would be too difficult a task at present: if the decision is made according to "his law," let the next generation do the fighting for St. James! " 'Tard estes avehuz d'abatre lor bofois. / 'La conquise saint Jaqes, s'il sera par mon lois, / 'Laserez sor nos filz qe veniront depois; / 'E n'encargez tiel fais que vos morez del pois.' " (128-31) (" 'Belatedly you have noticed their arrogance. If action is taken according to my judgment, you will leave it to our sons who will come after us; and you will not take upon yourselves such a burden in such a way that you will perish from its weight' "). Galés acknowledges the pleasures of peacetime: " 'Si Deus me dona bien et grant pas e repois, / 'Je firai grant folie se je ne le conois' " (119-20) (" 'If God grants me wealth and leisure, I will commit great folly if I do not know it' "). Vigorous opposition is then expressed by Roland, for whom such disinclination to fight and attraction to a life of ease is tantamount to "criminaus pecez" (147). Since the informed reader, who enters the text aware of its dialogical relationship to the *Roland*, presumes the ultimate failure of any argument opposing Roland's, one of the text's major set of verbal and ideological polarities is established by the narrator in 98-109:

> Quant l'om a reposer s'est mis del jor al mois
> E qe il n'a sintiz ni afan ne sordois,
> Quant vient al chef de l'an, se metre le vorois
> A traval de labor, grant poine li avrois.
> Tot ensi la ferent e mostrerent François
> Que molt les agrevast la parole le rois.
> En desduit herent mis de rivere e de bois
> E a spendere et doner et diners et hernois,
> A donoier pulcelles e dames en secrois:
> Enruçunés herent lor acerez corois.
> Dex aing avoit pascez, ce nos conte el cronois,
> Qu'il n'avoient estez en guere n'en campois.

> When a man has begun to live a life of repose from a day to a month, and he has not felt/experienced either trouble or difficulty [effort]; when he comes to the end of the year [and] you will want him to put himself to work, you will have great difficulty [in doing so]. So did the French, and demonstrated that the king's word aggravated them very much. They had enjoyed the pleasures of river and forest, spending money, giving presents to maidens and ladies in secret, and let their steel horsewhips go to rust. Ten years had passed, so the chronicle tells us, since they had been at war or in camp.

This valorization of human endeavor finds its most significant referent in the narrator's exhortation that his audience expend sufficient effort to be(come) competent listeners/readers of his text. The tale will profit those willing to see "cum hom se doit pener / D'esamplir la loy Deu . . . " (22-23) ("how man must exert/force himself to glorify the law of God"). Thus, just as the expedition to Spain presents a military labor, the *Entrée* reader/listener should be prepared to strive to comprehend correctly the lessons provided. He, too, is a laborer.

Subsequent arguments relating the mission to liberation, *raison*, *droit*, and *honor* complete the configuration of counsel urging immediate obedience to the saint's exhortation. On the contrary, words associated with *courtoisie* are negativized. They belong to the lexicon of "les flabes Artu," incompatible with the Paduan's "gloriose cançun" extolled also in the authoritative discourse of Latin as "*canticum novon.*" While Arthurian tales are associated with worldly vainglories, the Paduan distinguishes and elevates his own literary effort in terms of both its quality and originality. "Gloriose" retains its religious resonance in the text's celebration of Roland as "le meilor Cristian," while the claim to originality in Prologue II ("ch'en sui estez houtor") is reiterated here in loftier Latin discourse to suggest that the *Entrée* should be considered among the ranks of highly authoritative documents.

Although the *Entrée* does fill in some narrative ellipses of the *Chanson*, it does not explain the much-debated source of the Ganelon-Roland antipathy. Prologue I alluded to the cause of the expedition's failure as "une difirnanze / que lor fist Gaenolonz, le sire de Maganze," (15-16) ("A difference/quarrel which Ganelon, lord of Mayence, brought upon them"). Thus only the authorial audience recognizes Charles's delegation of regent authority to Anseïs de Pontiu (locus b) as a bad choice, given the latter's relationship to Ganelon (his nephew) and the Italian penchant for identifying the Maganza/Mayence lineage as traitors. Anseïs is predicated here solely by his lust for power: "rois voust estre por son enging sotiu" (47) ("he wished to be king by means of his deceitful strategy"), distinguishing him from Roland, also a future king, but more hesitant than hasty for accession to the Spanish throne and insistent on meriting the privileges of kingship (see loci *e*, *i*.) Charles, of course, desires kingly privilege, yet proves at times recalcitrant in carrying out attendant responsibilities. While Roland understands that his coronation is among the goals of the Spanish mission, he at no time expresses an ambition to be king; rather, his volitional discourse is directed solely toward reappropriation of Spain for the Christian cause.

Of these three king—or king-to-be—figures, desire for power is the variable trait, each representing a different attitude regarding the link between the privileges and responsibilities of authority. The narrator expresses overt disapproval when depicting blatant, unbridled lust for power. Charles, having already fought a divisive war against one of his vassals, is now compelled to yield his imperial authority to someone who will emerge as another traitor in the Rolandian macrotext. The theme of issues associated with authority—its substance, uses, and problems—is foregrounded early in the *Entrée*, before the Spanish expedition is even begun. The dialectic of authority as political power, still in the background in the *Chanson*'s purportedly unified feudal-Christian community, shifts from the extra-systemic to the systemic in Charles's obligatory gesture of power-sharing.

Uses of Authority: The Thiois Rebellion (locus *b*: 7023-7165)

The *Entrée*'s Thiois Rebellion episode foregrounds the problematics of internal division and questionable uses of authority in two instances where Charles's authority is overtly resisted: first by the Thiois of Poland (also referred to as the "Alemans"); then by those ordered to repress them, eight thousand of the imperial troops including all the peers, under the leadership of Salomon. Resistance of the Thiois militia to perform menial tasks perceived as beneath their station and their decision to abandon Charles in protest opens a further dimension of the global textual dialogism. In the narrator's characterization of the Thiois "traïment" (6837), the *pairs'* discussion of the Thiois as internal dissenters, "traitors," and Thiois acknowledgement of their transgression when the ambush begins (" 'Chi son signor traïst, com la venjançe est preste!' " /. . . ./ 'Or nos apendra Carles, nostre franc roi honeste,' " 6998, 7000) (" 'He who betrays his lord, how quick is the vengeance! / . . . ./ Now Charles, our noble, worthy king, will hang us' "), a dialectical confrontation on the uses of power occurs between Naimon and Charles. Naimon begins by chastizing Charles for this unprecedented " 'mauvés labor' " (" 'evil piece of work' "): " 'une si grant folie ne feïstes ancor' " (7024) (" 'so great a folly you have/had not committed before/until now' "), the sage declares, in reference to Charles's deliberate deception in concealing the identity of the rebels and thus pitting relatives and *compagnons* against one another in the nocturnal ambush. When Salomon, leader of the imperial force sent to slaughter the Thiois, recognizes his Christian compatriots in the first light of dawn, he protests Charles's " 'grant vilanie' "; the emperor responds by condemning Salomon for ceasing the confrontation, thus disobeying orders and guilty likewise of " 'treçarie.' " The semantic center of the confrontation is ostensibly feudal, with terms such as " 'mesfeit' " and " 'defaut' " lending a pseudo-legalistic tone. Urging Charles to pardon the transgressors on moral as well as pragmatic grounds, Naimon's case is an eloquent response to the emperor's query whether his revenge was in fact " 'droit,' " or " 'oltrage' " and " 'folage' "; i.e., whether he acted within the parameters of his authority. Rhetorical, of course, the question evokes a textual *prise de position* pertinent to an extratextual society concerned with the uses of power, even when expressed in feudal language:

> 'Sor li sers doit avoir un avantaje
> 'Le grant baron chi ame signoraje:
> 'Plus rich doit estre e plus fort e plus saje.
> 'Se son baron, plen de aut vasalaje,
> 'Feit un defaut en trestoit sun aaje,
> 'Nel doit tantost destruir par un folaje,
> 'Mai segunt l'euvre li doit estre salvaje.
> 'Je nel di mie por metre mal usaje,
> 'Mai le venjance soit cum le cor vo imaje'
> (7120-28).

> 'The great baron/ lord who loves seigneury must have an advantage over the serf: he must be more rich/ powerful and more strong and more wise. If his baron/vassal, full of a sense of lofty vassalage, makes a mistake once in his life, [the lord] must not destroy him for one act of folly, but according to the particular case/ circumstances, he should be severe. I do not say this in order to introduce a bad custom; let the vengeance be according to what your heart conceives for you.'

The wielder of power, presumably prepared to honor its privileges, must possess additional qualities: he must be materially and morally superior to those whom he governs. The exercise of power is not merely a question of force, a point common to the many treatises on governance of the period. With specific reference to the transgressive party (vassal/citizen/commune), Naimon counsels a pragmatic approach well in keeping with the current revival of Roman law: legal consideration of the misdemeanor relative to the transgressor's previous service. Those joining Naimon include Hestout and Roland, who will ultimately find himself in a similar predicament at Roncevaux, as the narrator reminds us in an intertextual reference to the *Chanson* (7067-68). Roland's argument here is based on the advisability of satisfying the request of Naimon and his noble peers; the requirements of maintaining intra-community harmony must claim priority over the leader's personal desire for revenge.

Naimon's characterization of such inappropriate action on Charles's part is reinforced and extended by Salomon's declaration that the perpetrator or participant in such action renders himself transgressive ("home peccaor") on the spiritual as well as the legal level. Further, employing Aquinas's statement that a law which is not just or contradicts a higher authority is not binding and should be disobeyed, Salomon cites the obligatory disobedience of anyone commanded to perform an act which conscience and faith tell him is wrong:

> 'Se je seüse l'ovre che ensi gist,
> 'Un tot soul home vivant non estordist;
> 'Petit prisase se autrui m'en haïst.
> 'N'a home en l'ost, se au roi forfesist
> 'En tel mainere, e le roi me disist,
> 'Se je pooie, che je ne l'onciis.
> 'Mal fist mon sire quant il bien ne m'aprist,
> 'Car tot celor che pont deshobeïst
> 'A tort son sire, Deable ert ses minist' (7101-08).

> 'If I had known the task that lay ahead of us, a single living man would not have acted so foolishly. Little would it matter if others hated me on account of it. There is not a man in the host, if he violated the King's will in such a manner, and the King told me so, whom I would not kill, if I could. My lord acted wrongly when he did not inform me correctly, for he who does not disobey his lord when the latter is in the wrong—the Devil will be his advisor.'

Read in conjunction with Naimon's opinion on adjusting punishment to a specific crime, this statement advising the necessity of the individual conscience in matters of obedience in the governor/governed relationship is significant. Secular power and authority, whatever form they take, are no longer the absolutes which Model I stipulated, but are to be interpreted according to the context in which they are manifested. Charles eventually yields and grants to Naimon as his "justiser" whatever judgment he deems appropriate, but the problem is not fully resolved. As the Thiois return to the woodhauling "labor" befitting their physical abilities, their submission is due solely to fear of Charles's authority ("tant redotent le roi e son casti," 7165) ("so much do they fear the King and his punishment"). Naimon's characterization of the good ruler, morally superior and worthy of respect and love from those who serve him, is openly belied in the methods by which Charles has utilized his authority.

Well before Charles's less than exemplary revenge against the Thiois, the *Entrée* narrator has already compromised his position as epic king.[2] Nor was he the first: as Karl-Heinz Bender demonstrated in the first six chansons de geste transposed into the Franco-Italian idiom, the predication of Charlemagne as a mythical figure was relentlessly eroded. Tracing the process in the two Venetian versions of the *Roland*, the *Enfances* and *Chevalerie Ogier, Chanson de Karleto* and *Chanson de Macaire*, Bender perceives five elements of the transformation, in Charles's initial identity as feudal sovereign, *élu de Dieu*, hereditary monarch, defender of the faith, and the principal monarch of the West. He relates the Franco-Italian "rewriting" to the non-feudal Italian audience and to their differing concept of authority:

> . . . le passage des légendes épiques françaises en Italie n'a pas immédiatement fait naître une image tout à fait nouvelle de Charlemagne, . . . les traits essentiels et constitutifs du mythe du grand Carolingien n'ont été supprimés ou transformés en leur contraire que progressivement. Le Charlemagne des chansons de geste était un personnage mythique et doué d'un caractère normatif pour les rois de France. Comme ces normes féodales, royales et religieuses n'étaient plus valables pour un public italien, Charlemagne, personnage mythique, se métamorphosait en un personnage plutôt romanesque ("Les Métamorphoses de la royauté de Charlemagne dans les premières épopées franco-italiennes" 174, 164).

Doctrine and Cognition: Roland *Orator* (locus *c*: 3610-4050)

The introduction of new methods to approach issues familiar to epic ideology is well illustrated within the Roland-Ferragu combat, where the authority of religious doctrine is the subject of debate. In what initially appears to be the normative semiology of Islamic-Christian conflict, the assumptions shared by authorial and, to a lesser degree, narrative publics include Roland's ultimate victory and our expectation that his prayers for Divine aid will be answered. While honoring those expectations, the Paduan also introduces new elements which alter the focus of audience reception in order to signal different, new ways of perceiving faith and truth. Thus Roland is presented not only as courtly in offering a stone pillow for Ferragu to sleep upon during the "time out" granted to the exhausted giant (we note, however, that both engage in stone-throwing at other phases of the fight),[3] but, more significantly, as *orator* during the lengthy ideological debate in which he seeks to explicate several points of Christian doctrine. Noting Roland's rhetorical skills and erudition in matters theological, Ferragu comments: " 'Mult fus bon escoler / 'En ta jovente, tant sais bien predichier ' " (3879-80) (" 'You were a very fine student in your youth, you know so well how to preach' ").

It is his role as dialectician for his faith which most aptly depicts a Roland elevated to the function of *orator*; i.e., as in the primary models of society, interpreter and disseminator of Christian ideology. One might expect Turpin to assume such a function; instead, the archbishop fights honorably on the battlefields of Spain (where he is captured by Ferragu in the first conflict) and performs clerical duties such as saying Mass, baptizing the Noblians, and so forth. While included in many textual events, Turpin occupies a mainly chivalric, rather than religious rôle (In the Franco-Italian *Aquilon de Bavière*, Turpin's role is reduced and devalorized further still; as part of the text's elevation of Roland to an enunciator of the spiritual, Turpin becomes correspondingly less important. Wunderli cites the *Entrée* author as first to theologize Roland; it is the Paduan who clearly draws the model for Raphael of Verona ("Roland théologien" 761-79). Roland's first extended "sermon" during the three-day duel is termed "sa rasons," (3520) and constitutes a brief but eloquent questioning of why, since he has done penance for all past transgressions, divine assistance has not been granted him in the present combat: " 'E por quoi donque n'avez de moi merci? ' " (3508) (" 'And why, then, do you not have mercy upon me?' ").

As prologue to the debate, Ferragu expresses his willingness to convert to a faith which he can comprehend and know, concretely, through his reasoning faculty:

> 'Stu me savoies autre cose gehir
> 'Che je poüs conostre e asentir
> 'Qué chose est Diex, mout seroit da graïr.
> 'Se tu me sais dou toz bien esclarir,
> 'A ce qu puse le feu d'enfer fuïr,
> 'Aparilez me sui de convertir '
> (3629-34; emphasis added).

'If you know something else to inform me/ make me accept, which I could know and comprehend—what a thing is God—it would give me great satisfaction. If you know how to completely

> enlighten me well about it all so that I might escape
> the fire of Hell, I am prepared to convert.'

The ensuing more than five hundred verses explicate—or illuminate, as Ferragu requests—the doctrines of *Genesis*, the Triune Divinity and Immaculate Conception. Within this dialogic arena Ferragu, too, expounds Islamic doctrine: those junctures where the two ideologies share common ground, and where they part company (3635-4145).[4] The giant, repeatedly likened to Goliath, hurriedly assures Roland that they share the same "law" concerning the Creation and Fall (3647-65); surely the "tençons" between them can be resolved—immediately. Roland's oratory reveals a high frequency of terminology referent to human reason and natural causation as primary tools of faith (3761, 3764, 3812, 3844, 3847-48, 3858, 3940, 3992, 3996); as if to underline the pertinence of his argument, the locus opens with Roland's invocation of the recently-canonized "sant Tomais" (3538). Like any skilled dialectician, Roland is quick to reject Ferragu's too-eager acquiescence: no halfway, casual conversion will suffice here (" 'De Diex veus estre creant e non creant ' " 3683) (" 'You wish to be a believer and non-believer in God' "). Turning to the Trinity, Roland stresses that it exists by necessity and **by reason** (" 'Par estovoir sunt et reisnablement' " 3692). His "parole" here is the Word, and should be noted by authorial as well as by narrative audience: " 'or soit par toi ma parole notee' " (3698). Roland's explanation of order within the world is deployed via three similes and a metaphor, images of concrete, familiar objects such as the wheel and candle. He then invites Ferragu to hold his perforated shield against the sun, where, if he chooses three of those holes, he will think he sees as many suns, yet immediately recognizes via his rational faculty the error of appearances. Roland's "sermon" emphasizes that nature and reason are thoroughly compatible with Christian doctrine, a truth of considerable pertinence to a post-Aquinate Italian public.[5]

In an article entitled "Didactic Concerns in *L'Entrée d'Espagne*," Alfred Adler notes that Roland's argumentation resembles recently introduced methods of scientific empiricism to elucidate events heretofore accepted without explanation; what Roland does is "to explain phenomena as results of empirically ascertainable *causae proximae* and to search empirically for the many *causae proximae* which may exist between the event and its divine *causa prima* " (*EC* 108). Such methodology brings to mind Pietro Abano, the leading proponent of the Averroist movement in Padua in the late Duecento and early Trecento.

With Ferragu cast quite literally as the devil's advocate, Roland
then offers rational explanations for the *parturitio virginalis*: in one of
the *Entrée*'s most striking passages, Roland *orator* offers proof
accessible through observation of the natural world: " '. . . Mais qil te
provera / '**Naturelmant** e que droiz te parra, / 'Le creras tu? ' " (3760-
62; emphasis added). Analogies are offered: the ray of sunlight piercing,
yet not breaking the glass through which it shines, the emergence of
fruit from its flower:

> 'Tu ais, ce dist Rollant, 'bien veü le chucher
> 'Que feit la longue flor quant ele doit fruter:
> 'Tant i remaint les flors qe il se sant derier
> 'Nastre la chuche qe comance engroser;
> 'Lor chiet le flors, quant n'i puet plus ester;
> 'Le frut remaint sans et saus et entier;
> 'Tu n'i porois un sol pertus trover
> 'Dont fu isue la flors a commencer' (3862-69).[6]

> 'You have,' says Roland, 'certainly seen the formation
> that the long flower makes when it must produce
> fruit: the flower remains [inside] there until it feels
> behind it the fruit, forming and coming to life, and
> beginning to swell. Then the flower falls, when it can
> no longer stay inside; the fruit remains safe, sound,
> and whole. You could not find a single opening from
> which the flower emerged [to begin its process of
> growth].'

So it is: " 'il est le mestre, nos somes li escoler' " (2068). Roland's
"oraisun" displays an intellectual acumen which demonstrates new
means of valorizing the Word. There is no need to link the *Entrée*
directly with Averroism, described by Bruno Nardi and Paul Oskar
Kristeller as innovative tools of faith rather than heresies (Nardi, *Saggi
sull'Aristotelismo padovano* 19-74; Kristeller, "Paduan Averroism and
Alexandrism in the light of recent studies" 147-155). As Adler notes,
one ought simply to recognize the influence of the fertile intellectual
climate within which the *Entrée* was conceived. In a time of "scientific
independence," Roland as *orator* demonstrates a spirit of independence
here and throughout the text. While his methods for upholding and
serving his faith are different and admittedly "de stragne guise," there is
no question that his ends, to serve the *causa prima*, never waiver: "His
independence notwithstanding, the Roland of the *Entrée*—the prototype
for Pulci, Boiardo and Ariosto—is not a rebel. He remains the

champion of Charlemagne's ecumenical cause, but he explores this cause in his own ways, in new and unforeseen ways" (Adler 109).

Ferragu's inability or unwillingness to accept unconditionally Roland's explication of Christian doctrine renders him guilty of misinformed or deformed thinking. Still, addressing the giant as "Saracins frere " (3666), Roland likens Ferragu to the pilgrim who turns back when told that the road ahead is risky: " 'Cist desconfort que vient de mal senblant / 'Feit repentir de bien feir l'ignorant' " (3678-79); such a pilgrim soon renounces his good intentions. Initially, Roland lauds Ferragu for those good intentions (" 'Forment m'agré qe tu es entendant' " 3667) (" 'It pleases me greatly that you are comprehending [well-intentioned]' "). Subsequently, however, he chastizes Ferragu for failing to embrace Christian doctrine fully and finally (" 'De Diex veus estre creant e non creant, /. . . . / 'E ne veus croire en Diex debitemant, / 'En Pier, en Filz et en Espirit sant" 3683-3686) (" ' You want to believe and not believe in God. . . and you do not wish to believe as you should in God, in Father, Son and Holy Spirit' "). At the point when the Saracen's errors result from a refusal to conjoin his own will and intentionality with the Word, he is as guilty as Mohammed, or any of those condemned by Dante as "seminator di scandolo e di scisma" (*Inf.* 28:22-36).

Although Roland's arguments fail to convert his opponent, whom he concludes is an unnatural satanic being operating under the powers of magic (" 'Le cors me dit, se Diex me beneïe, / 'Che tu n'is home ne fais human vie, / 'Mais un Diable que vers Diex contralie' " 3997-99), his victory is written into the text as a sign of Divine justice; Roland can be seen here as the *puer senex* defending Christian ideology in a *mise en abyme* of the global text.

What Wunderli terms "la théologisation" of Roland is amply developed in the *Entrée*, subsequently borrowed (and modified) by Raphael of Verona in his *Aquilon de Bavière*:

> Les deux textes se situant vers la fin de la tradition franco-italienne, il semble donc que nous ayons affaire non seulement à une modification ponctuelle et individuelle de la *Matière de France* en Italie du Nord, mais à un développement plus général conditionné par des structures sociales et réceptologiques spécifiques ("Théologisation" 774).

Wunderli subsequently ascribes these contextual elements to authorial negativity towards the Church, an "élément anticlérical (ou plutôt: anti-église)" (780), readily identifiable in such disparate authors as Marsilius, Arnaldo da Brescia, and Cola da Rienzo. Wunderli attributes the idealization of Roland in the *Aquilon* to a "besoin d'un nouveau personnage d'identification, de la projection d'un souverain idéal qui réunit en lui toutes les qualités que les souverains réels n'ont que partiellement ou même pas du tout." Roland thus represents "les aspirations politiques de son époque" (779-80). Wunderli also explains the *Entrée*'s increased tolerance regarding Islam, attributable to growing commercial and cultural contacts. The *Entrée* author is "un innovateur idéologique," whose tendencies toward exaggeration can be explained, if not excused, by the role of pioneer and propagandist which the Paduan appropriates (780).

The Paduan *Orator* (locus *d*: 2763-2825, 10,939-10996)

An eloquent *apologia* of Christian ideology, the Roland-Ferragu duel is also inscribed with the narrator's *apologia* of his own textual authority; indeed, the interlacing of the two accentuates their interrelationship. As we shall see, both Roland and the *Entrée* poet are warriors/laborers for truth, struggling against those texts or tenets which present distorted versions of the word/Word. A lengthy interpolation toward the beginning of the combat is presented in a well-chosen dialogical arena:

> Par Diex, seignor qe **oiez la cançon**,
> Ne vos soit greu a oïr **por raison**
> L'aspre bataille dou duc a l'Esclavon,
> Che voiremant, se **mentir** ne devon,
> De dos sols homes, voilez li croir o non,
> N'oit tiel bataille ne tan longe **tençon**.
> Se longe fu **l'euvre** des dos barons,
> En breu **sentence** dir ne la vos puet hon;
> Anz s'aconvient **canter** l'aflicion
> Ch'a plain troi jors dura le niés Carlon
> Vers Feragu, por esmater Machon
> E par acroistre **la loi que nos creon**.
> **Se dam Trepin fist bref sa lecion**
> E **je di long**, blasmer ne me doit hon;
> Ce que il trova, bien le nos canteron.
> Bien dirai plus, a chi'n pois e chi non,
> Car **dous bons clerges, Çan Gras et**
>   **Gauteron,**

Çan de Navaire e Gauter d'Aragon,
Ces dos **prodomes** ceschuns saist pont a
   pon
Si come Carles o la fiere façon
Entra en Espaigne conquere le roion,
La començaile trosque la finisun
Dejusque ou point de l'euvre Guenelon.
D'iluec avant ne firect mencion,
Car bien conta Trepin la traïson
Que Guenes fist, li encresmé felon,
Com il vendi o roi Marsilion
En Roncival Rollant e se baron.
Ces **troi otor** che nomé vos avon
Se sunt trovez de voir dir compagnon,
Mais cil Gauter dist plus de nus autre on.
Chi donque veult intandre **par raison**,
Vienent avant, car je lor dirai com
Li ber Rollant, le filz al duc Milon,
Feragu oncist, que tant estoir prodon;
E les batailes che par cronice son
En vers François, n'i a mot Bergognon
Vos dirai totes **par bone intencion.**

Oï avez comant **le troi outor**
Sont en acord d'un dit a d'un labor;
L'uns ne contraire l'autre de nul collor.
Une novelle que viegne de longor
C'un home aporte o tri o quatre ancor,
S'adonc s'acordent les dos al prim ditor
El quart contraire, tenuz vient **fableor,**
Car bien savomes que devant un rector
Plus d'un sol home vienent creü ploisor.
Se dan Tripin e le dui troveor (AT seems to
   have period here)
Sont en acord **d'un ovre e d'un tenor,**
E par quoi donque **les foibles jogleor**
Cantent d'Espaigne e vont contre celor
Che **troverent l'estorie** . . . . ?
(AT suggests: o grant labor)
A **raisons droite** devroit un bon **pastor**
Far les **snarer** come **perjuraor,**
Car cil qe cante, s'il veult avoir **honor**

E ne veult estre apelez **mentior**
Ne doit canter cel dont il n'est letor;
E s'il ne soit respondre al proveor,
De lui se gabe **el bon escuteor.**
Leisons **bosdie** canter **al bosdeor;**
Chi les **eschute** remagnent avech lor,
Che pur dirai, a qui'n chant e qui'n plor,
Si com nos monstre **Trepin nostre**
        doctor. (2763-825; emphasis added)

By God, lords who are listening to the song, let there
be no opposition among you to hear, in the interests
of reason, the hard battle of the duke with the
Saracen; truly, if we should not lie, there never was
such a battle nor so long a contest between two men
alone, whether you want to believe it or not. If the
work/task of the two barons was long, one [I] cannot
tell it to you in a brief ("sentance": proverb/popular
saying; [n.b. this is *sententia* in its first-level
definition—see ch. 5]. Instead, it is fitting to sing of
the struggle which Charles's nephew endured a full
three days against Ferragu, to check Mohammed and
to increase [the glory of] the law in which we believe.
If lord Turpin made his tale/lesson/text short, and my
tale is long, one [you] must not blame me; that
which he found [wrote], we will sing well for you. I
will indeed tell more, to one of you [who is] at peace,
and another [who is] not, because two good clerics,
Jean le Gras and Gautier, Jean de Navarre and Gautier
d'Aragon, those two worthy men, each knew point for
point how Charles of the proud mien entered Spain to
conquer the kingdom from beginning to end, up to
the point of Ganelon's act/deed. From that point
forward they made no mention [of how the tale
continued], for Turpin narrated well the betrayal that
Ganelon committed, the criminal wretch: how he sold
Roland and his barons at Roncevaux to King Marsile.
Those three authors whom we have named for you
found themselves companions in [telling] the truth;
but Gautier told more than any other. Thus he who
wants to listen in a spirit of reason, let him come
forward, for I shall tell them how the valiant Roland,
son of Duke Milon, killed Ferragu, who was so

courageous a man. And [I shall tell the tales of] the
battles which are [written] in chronicles in French
verse, there is not [in my tale] a word of Burgundian
[dialect]; I shall tell all/the whole story with good
intentions. You have heard how the three authors are
in agreement regarding one tale and one task; one does
not contradict the other in any way. [Concerning] a
piece of news which comes from afar, which one man
brings/reports to three or four more; if the two agree
with the first teller and the fourth disagrees, he is
considered a teller of [false] tales; for well we know
that before a rector/judge/ judicial authority figure,
several men are believed more than one alone. If Sir
Turpin and the two writers are in agreement on the
act/deed and the method/text, why, then, do the
incompetent/untalented jongleurs sing about Spain
and go against those who found/wrote the story ...?
By all reasonable rights a good shepherd ought to
catch them like liars; for what he [the jongleur,
author] sings, if he wants to acquire honor and does
not wish to be called a liar, he must not sing that of
which he is not a reader [tales which he has not
read/seen in written form]. And if he doesn't know
how to respond to the man who puts his tale to the
test, the good listener makes fun of him. Let's leave
the charlatans to sing to [other] charlatans; let those
who listen to them stay with them, so that I will tell
[the tale], nonetheless, to one in joy and another in
tears, just as our teacher Turpin shows us.

The Roland-Ferragu combat is presented as the text's first major
encounter between hostile ideologies. It is both military ("bataille") and
verbal ("tençon"), a war of words and doctrine ("la loi qe nos creon"). As
his public enters the *Entrée*, the poet encourages them to employ their
own reasoning faculties in order to profit from a tale which is too
lengthy and complex to abbreviate or simplify ("en breu sentance dir ne
la vos puet hon"). It is this public, consisting not only of "gient
letree," but including the lesser literary and literate, with whom he
means to establish a dialogue. Henning Krauss judges that the Paduan's
public belongs to the wealthy protocapitalist north Italian bourgeoisie,
a class which in the early Trecento is separating itself from the lower
sectors of the middle classes both in its priorization of values and its

manner of existence, in an effort to emulate and assimilate with the aristocracy. The Paduan:

> si rivolge a quegli strati che sono economicamente in grado di dedicarsi a vasti studi e la cui auto-scienza richiede di cimentarsi intensamente con le opere letterarie considerate come le più dotte, riuscite e ambiziose deloro tempo (*Epica feudle* 229).

The point is interesting and well-taken, but seems to contradict the narrator's express affirmation that the literary contract which he accepted from Turpin stipulated that his text be read and sung to a public somewhat less erudite than those able to read Latin versions of the war for Spain. Krauss advises that "questa dichiarizione di intenzioni ci può aiutare solo fino a un certo punto a individuare 'il pubblico effettuale.' " The Paduan may wish to distinguish his public from the exclusively clerical readership implied by previous Latin texts; much of his public will belong to upwardly mobile individuals in the cultural/intellectual as well as in the economic sense, those who may well count literarity among their most important acquisitions.

The narrator assures his public that he, too, will act in good faith in his function as informant, "par bone intencion." Then, identifying his three sources for *Entrée* I, Turpin, Jean de Navarre and Gautier d'Aragon, the poet stresses their essential concurrence regarding content: Turpin has narrated the treason of Ganelon, while the other two texts did not. However, Gautier is said to have narrated more than Jean. The Paduan's text will surpass all three, since it will relate the complete story, improving on the segmented versions of his predecessors (see Limentani, "Epica" and *Entrée* 3214-16 on the complete story of Roland as told by Turpin). Yet in the events correlated in the Paduan's sources, the three authors were "companions in truth" (2791-92). Authorial accord is tantamount to assurance of authenticity where the traditional medieval respect for canonized texts still prevails.

It will be recalled that five epithets are employed to describe Jean de Navarre and Gautier d'Aragon: "dos baron," "ces dos prodomes," "bons clerges," "li due troveor," and "ces [troi] otor," the latter including Turpin's "lecion." The others are more arresting, even if unknown both to the medieval and modern public; it is not their existential reality which merits notice. The two are presented in feudal/chivalric, clerical, and poetic or performing functions: i.e., with what we would call impressive credentials meant to satisfy virtually any segment of the Paduan's public. What the poet means to establish here is the unquestionable quality of his sources and, consequently, of his own text. Like Turpin, Jean and Gautier expended great effort ("o grant labor" supplied by Thomas for 2814 *lacuna*) to compose their récits, whose accuracy and integrity are demonstrated by the simple law of multiple correlation. As an example, he writes, a "rector" (governor, director, figure of authority) will more readily accept as true the narration of an event told in the same way by three individuals out of four; the deviant text is generally rejected.

The word "rector" is entered in the Holtus *Lexikalische Untersuchungen* of words appearing in the *Entrée* and other Franco-Italian works as follows:
RECTOR s.m. G1 -, "recteur, gouverneur",

> RETOR s.m. G1 "recteur, gouverneur", It. RECTOR:
> 2808 Car bien savomes que devant un *rector* / Plus d'un sol home vienent creü ploisor, <:fableor, ploisor>, 956 Cil qi retreit plus a tarran *retor*, <:maor, flor>;
> 10963 *retors* pl. (*les - de tere*);
> *rector* "reggitore" Attila S XI-895; *retor* "reggitore, sovrano: Attila S XX-3199 (nicht 2199 G1); *retors* s.m.pl "rettori" EstVenL G1.
> TL VIII-511 *rector* "Leiter, Lenker (einer Schule, einer Kongregation u.a.)";
> GdfC X-508a *recteur*; FEW X-162a afr. *rector* (1424, Pans), b afr. *rector* 'supérieur ecclésiastique; prélat; directeur de certaines maisons religieuses"; Levy Vii-126a *rector*.
> Entlehnungen aus It. RECTOR; *rector* steht in archaisierendem Kontext (*dan Tripin e le dui troveor*); im Afr. nur vereinzelt belegt, meist im kirchlichen Gebrauch (Prälat" etc.); LEI mehrfach, cf. *rectore* "rettore" avic. Bortolan, *retor* "governatore" avenez. TestiStussi 13./Anf. 14 Jh., *retóre* reggitore" (-tt-) apad. Ende 14.Jh BibbiaFolena u.a.

For, according to the traditional, yet probably now-archaic conservatism of the chanson de geste, whoever departs from the canon is decried as "fableor," "perjuraor," "mentior," and "boisdeor": in short, a perverter of truth such as those "foibles jogleors." Similarly, the Paduan's three sources found themselves companions of truth (NB wordplay on "trover" and "voir dit"), whose texts are in agreement one with another regarding narrative material, theme, and the way in which the tale is told. Simple logic completes the case: the Paduan's version confirms and certifies his position as the author of the last—and best—word on the initial phases of the reconquest of Spain.

In order to win the credibility of his ideal public, "el bon escuteor," the author must be thoroughly conversant with written versions of his material (2817-19). Further, like the dialectician, the poet recognizes that words communicate with one another; thus he must be prepared to defend his text before anyone who might challenge its authority, such as the "proveor" of 2820, who may probe the surfaces of his text to try its merit. And if he does not know how to respond to those who test him, the competent reader will make light of him. The "proveor" are thus that segment of the public which asks questions, putting the integrity of the text to trial; in the additional meaning of the word, the "proveor" also, or then, becomes its advocate and defends it himself. (Larousse, *Dictionnaire de l'ancien français*: "celui qui sonde;" Godefroy, *Lexique*: "celui qui éprouve, qui sonde; défenseur, avocat"). An author unable to respond satisfactorily to the "proveor" in his public is ripe for mockery. Further, he must know how to use language correctly; hence the Paduan's claim of the quality of his French: he shall tell all ". . . en vers François, / n'i a mot Bergognon" (2801). (On the question of language, see Introduction and Bibliography.) As competent rhetorician, dialectician, and grammarian, the Paduan rightfully is the *orator*, authoritative disseminator of the word, of the "entrée en Espagne." As grammarian, rhetorician, and dialectician, he must be prepared to explicate his text to anyone who might question its authority.

The Paduan as *orator* acknowledges that the ultimate judgment between a good and bad text is made by the most important authority, which is of course its public. The "seignor" narratees mentioned at the opening are, or will be, so the poet hopes, the same good listeners evoked at its close. Meanwhile, woven into the passage are three allusions to the functions assumed by a public entering a text either as audience or reader. Impersonalized and abstracted into an exemplum, "un rector," "un bon pastor," and "el bon escuteor" are those to whom the *Entrée* is addressed and, according to whose judgment it will succeed or fail. The "rector" who hears the hypothetical four tales in 2804-09 is charged with the passing of judgment on those narratives: he is their "governor," "director," "ruler," or any manner of arbitrator. He is their public, thus their judge.

The "bon pastor" of 2815 likewise, and appropriately, exercises a necessary function regarding the *Entrée* or any literary work. He is its guardian, caretaker, and defender, protecting it from the "perjuraor," "mentior," and such who prey on the nascent, vulnerable text. In another heteroglot depiction of the reader/public juxtaposing Scriptural, literary, and legal discourse, it is his custodial function which safeguards the text. Momentarily dropping a studiously impersonal tone, the narrator injects a humorous note in the suggested punishment of discredited competitors, to have them "de-nosed" ("far les snarer" 2816). More important, he suggests an alliance of public and poet to eliminate such undesirables: "Let's leave the charlatans to sing to the charlatans" (2822). If they prey on one another, the good poet will be free to address the good public, "el bon escuteor."

Beyond the thriving protocapitalists, however, the Paduan addresses another, more significant public in Prologue II, at the very juncture where he is outlining Part Two, claiming authorship thereof, and specifying the corrective nature of his text:

> Por voloir castoier li coarz et li van
> E fer en cortoisie retorner li villan
> E les retors de tere encroire en consoil san,
> Me sui mis a trover dou meilor Cristian
> C'onque seüst canter jogleors en roman,
> Ni qi mais donast robes ni cheval ni teran
> (10,961-66).

> In order to chastize the cowardly and vain, and make
> the unworthy knight and rulers of the earth believe in
> sane counsel, I have begun to write about the best
> Christian that a jongleur ever knew how to celebrate
> in the Romance tongue, or who ever gave away
> clothing or horse or land.

The next few verses laud Roland's contribution to Islamic culture in introducing individual servings of food at table to replace the communal platter; they inject a note of levity (and perhaps irony) into a passage central to the cohesiveness of the global text. In the same laisse, he reiterates the apostrophe to one particular category of narratee, immediately before yielding the sole clue to his own identity:

> Oiez hom soveran!
> Je qe sui mis a dir del neveu Carleman
> Mon nom vos non dirai, mai sui Patavian,
> . . .
> De la citez qe fist Antenor le Trojan,
> En la joiose Marche del cortois Trivixan . . .
> (10,972-76).

> Hear ye, sovereign rulers! I who have begun to tell of
> Charles's nephew, will not tell you my name, but I
> am Paduan, from the city which Antenor the Trojan
> built, in the joyous march of the courtly region of
> Treviso.

The *Entrée*'s authorial "I" and addressee "you" is here at its most immediate: the Paduan's partial self-disclosure juxtaposed specifically in conjunction with those to whom he wishes to communicate—not in their function as textual publics, but in the extratextual world beyond. The repeated verbal phrase "se mettre a" in "me suis mis a trover" and "je qe suis mis a dir" suggests not just the continuation of a piece of writing, but the self-conscious undertaking of a commitment to associate the tale of Roland with those beyond the text, to whom are entrusted the governance of others. Thus "the project to which I have put myself" is to correct other narratives insofar as they do not relate the whole story, or the whole truth. With the Paduan's Roland stipulated as the best of Christians, real sovereigns would do well to see in him a model of Christian heroism. Thus while we are accustomed to view the behavior of fictional characters as alienating, escapist, even dangerous (as in Don Quixote and Emma Bovary), the fundamentally didactic medieval ethos still evident in the *Entrée* extends the reach of the text beyond the individual who reads, to the same individual who also lives what he reads:

> L'oeuvre littéraire est à la fois sa signification et la
> manière dont celle-ci est éprouvée. ... Le
> comportement romanesque n'est plus quelque chose de
> subjectif et de contingent à l'égard du texte et du
> monde, mais appartient à l'être même du roman. La
> critique traditionnelle tendait implicitement à refermer
> le roman sur lui-même. Au contraire, ce
> comportement ... est la finalité externe de l'accueil
> du roman ... et il naît à l'intersection du texte avec
> son public (Michel Stanesco, "Sous le masque de
> Lancelot: du comportement romanesque au Moyen
> Age" 48).

The "retors de tere" and "hom soveran" are one and the same: leaders, governors, holders of civic/legal/religious authority. Placed with their opposing terms "li coarz et le van" and "li villan," one sees the suggestion of the *ordines* of the primary social models: the latter as the *agricultores/laboratores*, the former as the apparently problematic *milites.* Thus the identification of rectors and sovereigns with those who rule: kings, emperors, *signori*, bishops, and such, those whose charge it is to lead the people. It is these individuals who must be made to believe in the wise counsel of this text ("encroire en consoil san"). The components of poetic authority are thus complete: a stipulated contract between public and poet, assurance of textual authenticity, identification of various sectors of that public. Authority of Church doctrine as the signified of the Roland-Ferragu duel is complemented by the Paduan's delineation of his own authority over his text. Both are comprehensible to the intelligent decoder, the "bon escuteor" in his various manifestations. Such an ideal audience utilizes its rational faculty as a necessary tool for entering this work, where models of religious knowledge, like social models and language systems, are in a dialogic process of change.

Hierarchy (locus *e*: 4454-4512)

Charles's elaborate argument for abandoning the mission following Ferragu's defeat of all the *pairs* except Roland comes within the text's characteristic irony on issues regarding political authority. Enhancing the intensity of his plea, Charles inserts a courtly note into the prevailing feudal discourse, perhaps ingenuously depicting his assessment of self and circumstances. He adds: " 'Par vos sui jé, biaus ami, fortunos / 'Et obëis et honorez de tos: / 'Se je vos pert, ensi remanrai sos / 'Cum pobre dame quant a perdu l'espos ' " (1593-96) (" 'On account of you, fine friend, I am fortunate, and obeyed and honored by all: if I lose you, then I shall be alone like a poor lady when she has lost her husband ' ").

The simile linking Charles with the (assumed) weakness of women engages the statement in heteroglossic dialogism, where the dominant discourse is diminished and exposed as vulnerable to usurpation. Since the disappearance of all the *pairs* benefits no one, Charles continues, it is better to take no further risks and return posthaste to France, " 'car cist païs commance estre anoios' " (1598) (" 'for this country is beginning to be annoying/troublesome' "). His less than noble discourse and style juxtaposed with the elevated tonality of Roland is aptly characterized by Krauss as the confrontation of "la limitata ed egoista concezione dell'Impero-Stato e l'idea dell'Impero universale responsabile di tutta la cristianità" (*Epica feudale* 220).

If such dubious logic appears odd in its admission that Charles's real authority comes not from his own merit but vicariously through his executor vassal, it seems the more so when his statement about whom they are in Spain to assist is reiterated first by Roland, then by the narrator. In acknowledging that the peers have undertaken the campaign "sol par moi" (1608), Roland himself assumes principle responsibility for its outcome. His *solidaire* reasoning, in stark contrast to the emperor's solipsism, is placed in high relief. Grave transgressions would result were Charles to abandon the expedition, Roland argues; the emperor could justifiably be accused of ruling uniquely for his personal benefit, i.e., tyranically, and would be disobeying the divine command which initiated the mission. The narrator's epithet of Roland as "li duc poesteïs" (4358) underscores the essential paradox of the relationship. Both characters and narrator recognize that Charles's authority is nominal only; it is his nephew whom all respect, trust, and desire to serve.

Both Roland and his public recognize in the Ferragu combat that divine force is indeed with him; as his victory affirms, it is he who appropriates the privileged role of *élu de Dieu*. In the *Entrée*'s nearly sixteen thousand verses, no such claim is made for Charles, although there are numerous positive characterizations of him, beginning with Prologue I's "le bons rois Carles." (The latter, incidentally, is mentioned immediately before the explanation of his procrastination in fulfilling the longstanding orders of St. James.) Increasing instability in the Charles-Roland relationship shifts reader/audience attention away from the traditional ways in which the *cycle du roi* material had been formulated. The feudal model is no longer a monolithic structure; the *Entrée*'s events, even when adopted from the epic repertoire, disturb conventional assumptions and compel questions to be raised. It is against a background of conventional narrative material that these innovations are introduced, precisely at those sites where the juxtaposition of dissonances can best be examined.

Further mention of hierarchy occurs following the death of Ferragu in a discussion of the Davidic Roland's triumph, evidence that mere force may not determine victory in the necessary labors of faith. An exemplary tale is told of two pupils, one small, the other bigger, who engage in swordplay under their masters' eyes; the smaller boy wins, much to the surprise of onlookers. The explanation? The larger boy's mentor failed to aid his pupil, thus " 'a soi fist onte et a cil mal e plor' " (" 'he brought shame upon himself and unhappiness and tears to the boy' "). The mentor of the smaller boy provided decisive aid and counsel and was awarded " 'joie et honor ' " (4269-70).

Shortly thereafter, Charles, in the flush of victory, declares that he will straightaway crown his nephew king. Roland reminds him that Nájera is only the first city on the road to Compostella and energetically declines coronation until the entire mission is accomplished through "force e de valor" (4462), all of Spain restored to Christendom. Basing his argument on the respective roles of "syre" and "serf," Roland extends the discussion of hierarchism:

> 'Ja ne prendroie d'Espaigne un cheitis bor,
> 'Car le bon serf qe n'aime desenor
> 'Ne qiert merit se il n'a feit son labor;
> 'E hom orgoilos, syre, feit gran follor
> 'Q'en l'altrui ort plante fruit ni aubor,
> 'Car au collir ça en ont li pluisor
> 'Englotis fruit de trop aigre sapor' (4454-60).

> 'I would not even claim a mere bourg in Spain, for the good serf who does not like dishonor does not seek reward if he has not completed his task; and an arrogant man, sire, acts in folly who plants fruit or trees in another's garden, for in gathering it (the fruit) several have swallowed fruit of a very bitter taste.'

Roland's heteroglossia introducing agricultural and perhaps Biblical terminology to describe the arrogant (superior) mingles somewhat uneasily with the dominant feudal discourse employed to portray the good serf. In another locus of discrete language systems, the contact forces the dialogism of feudal language, encroaching upon its increasingly jeopardized position of dominance. The metaphor sharpens differences pertinent to Roland's own relationship with Charles, becoming a thinly-veiled censure of the emperor's use of authority in this first critical battle:

Roland	vs.	Charles
"bon serf"		"hom orgoilos"
"honor"		"desenor"
"labor"		"follor"

Following close upon the above perspective on hierarchy, Charles enunciates a codification of vassal duties, addressed to a Roland whom he now wishes to chastize for excessive *otium* ("joie e li sbanoi," 4526) after the taking of Nájera. Perhaps ironically, the narrator introduces Charles's declaration:

> Mais li emperere, plein d'aut entendiment,
> Avoit son cor mis sor autre talent (4481-82).

But the Emperor, filled with [a] lofty understanding
[of the situation], had set his heart on another desire.

> 'Sire niés,' dist le roi; baron qe feit enprise
> 'D'autre terre conquerre vuelt sens e maïstrise
> 'E haïr le repos e sa pelice grise
> 'E costumer le cald e le froid e la bise.
> 'Quand il a un castel o une terre prise,
> 'Ne doit por vane glorie entre en druerise,
> 'Mais prés l'une vuelt estre mantinant l'autre
> asise,
> 'Car qi altrui offend penser doit por certise
> 'Qe le offendus porchaçe comant il l'en
> merise (4505-13).

'Sire, nephew,' said the King, 'the baron who
undertakes the conquest of another land requires good
sense and self-discipline, and needs to [should] detest
leisure and its [luxurious] grey fur, and to accustom
himself to heat and cold and wind. When he has taken
a castle or piece of land, he must not, out of vanity,
enter [into a spirit of] frivolous amusement, but must
immediately follow up the conquest with another
siege, for he who offends another man must consider
it certain that the offended party will hunt him down
[seek vengeance] as he merits.'

While both men specifically cite the obligations of the lesser, "in
service" party with its several possible interpretations by the *Entrée*
public, Charlemagne's allusion points to the labors of war. The "repos"
that he condemns specifies the dangerous leisure of courtly
environments; it may likewise signal equally dangerous texts, such as
the "flabes d'Artu," whose pleasures have tempted the morals and
spiritual fortitude of more than one knight, and blurred his vision of the
auxilium contracted in his vassalic oath.

Both medieval and modern reader recognize the narrator's dialogue
with the Oxford *Chanson de Roland* where Roland himself codified the
vassal's obligations:

> 'Bien devuns ci estre pur nostre rei:
> Pur sun seignor deit hom susfrir destreiz
> E endurer e granz chalz e granz freiz,

> Sin deit hom perdre e del quir e del peil.
> Or guart chascuns que granz colps i empleit
> Que malvaise cançun de nus chantet ne seit!
> Paien unt tort e chrestïens unt dreit.
> Malvaise essample n'en serat ja de mei.' AOI
> (1009-16).

> 'We must make a stand here for our king: One must
> suffer hardships for one's lord and endure great heat
> and great cold, one must also lose hide and hair. Now
> let's each see to it that he employs great blows, so
> that bad songs not be sung about us! Pagans are in
> the wrong and Christians are in the right. I shall
> never be cited as a bad example' AOI.

Beyond the obvious similarities between the two texts, the *Entrée* seems to assess the dangers of leisure and luxury as greater than lack of chivalric prowess centered in the Oxford text. "Sens e maistrise" are elements new to the obligations of the hypothetical knight. "Sens" appears to be related to the primary epic virtue of *mesure*, but with increased emphasis on the use of reason to determine behavior. The lesser party, in any hierarchical relationship, must maintain awareness of his place. "Maistrise" adds to that kind of intelligence traits not merely soldierly, but ethical and moral as well, suggesting self-mastery, that control of self which maintains the distinction between duty and pleasure and the tenets of hierarchism itself.

War and Ethics: (locus *f*: 5667-6274)

A dialogical zone probing the relationship between ethics and war within the Isoré episode becomes the site for locus *f*. Circumstances involve an exchange of prisoners: Hestout (Roland's cousin) for Prince Isoré, son of Malgeris. When Charles is unwilling to abide by the customary rules of such transactions, a lively discussion involving most of the *pairs* arises, which again broadens the debate beyond its immediate textual parameters. Insisting that he will hang Isoré whether Hestout is returned or not, Charles's militant autocracy mingles the discourse of feudal and matrimonial hierarchy, warning of the danger of allowing excessive self-expression to one's inferiors. In Charles's articulation of "liberté," it pertains not to the aspirations of the subordinate, but to the privilege of the superior. The emperor's use of multiple discourse systems delegates the seeker of autonomy to the ranks of the non-existent: here, the female. Indeed, the honor and freedom of the "chief" are defined by his ability to repress insubordination among inferiors:

> 'Home qui taise et sofre orguel sa hoisor,
> 'Si li met hon sor le chief le raisor,
> 'Car il subjete liberté et honor.
> **'Je l'ai dit, si le dirai ancor,**
> **'Tant com je vive n'avrai teran seignor**
> 'Por qoi le die, jel tais por le meilor (5693-
> 98; emphasis added).

> 'The man who is silent and suffers the pride of his wife places on his own head the razor for he is sacrificing his liberty and honor. I have said it (before) and will say it again, as long as I live I will have no earthly lord [superior]. Why I say so, I keep silent for the better.'

At stake is not Charles's authority here, although he tends increasingly to interpret virtually any issue in that light. In his misinterpretation of feudal ethics, Charles is unable to view the situation beyond the narrow confines of his own interests. He cannot see that the proper use of authority may require consideration of broader ethical standards. At issue in fact is one of the text's principal structuring concepts, honor, clearly articulated by a Roland who sees the fundamental interdependence on which their relationship must be based: " 'Mais si vos pri por la vostre douçor / 'Qe non facés, biaus sir enpereor, / 'Rien qui vos tourt ni a moi desonor ' " (5713-15) (" 'But so I beg you, for the sake of your kindness, that you not do anything, kind sir emperor, which brings dishonor to you or to me' "). Significant differences exist between each man's use of the word "honor," determined by his status. For Charles, honor belongs to the superior who retains absolute dominion over others with little regard to means; for Roland, it is the attribute of the individual who abides by ethical standards concomitant with chivalry and his own conscience. For Roland, who is emerging in the *Entrée* as a new model of knighthood on the one hand and as the representative of the "small" vs. the "great" in whatever extratextual guise the text may accommodate, the means by which acts are accomplished are as important as the deeds themselves.

Questions concerning Charles's response to the prisoner exchange continue to arise. His determination to execute Isoré is roundly condemned by Olivier: " 'Le roi feit vilanie: / 'Qui l'en conseile feit ancor plu folie ' " 5764-65) (" 'The king is conducting himself in a demeaning manner: he who advises him about it/counsels him to do so is committing still more folly ' "). Thus in another collision of Charles's imperial status vs. his less than royal behavior, he is here associated with the vulgarity of the lowest social order, the *villani*, *rustici*, *agricultores* and such of whom little better can be expected. While Roland insists that his own position as defender of chivalric ethics is not "estralois" (outside/beyond the law, illegal), a lengthy admonition by Richard de Normandie (5772-90) advises Roland that it is more important to obey Charles's "law," right or wrong:

> 'Celui a tort qui son droit contrelie
> '... Portés vostre oncle onor e cortesie;
> '... Dou roy avés feite une departie
> 'Dont mante gent endivinent envie;
> 'Venez abatre la lor malle pensie' (5777,
> 5782, 5787-89).

> 'He who resists rightful authority is in the wrong ...
> Bear honor and courtesy to your uncle; ... You have
> had a disagreement with the king, the cause of which
> many people see as envy; come, eliminate the bad
> thoughts.'

Honor here, of course, implies submission, while "cortesie" refers to the correct posture of unquestioning obedience essential to Model I hierarchism.

Efforts to moderate Roland's anger fail; he threatens to abandon the mission completely if a compromise cannot be reached. His condemnation of Charles's unethical behavior is shared by Isoré, who also perceives the prisoner exchange as a test of honor:

> 'Si le veult Carles de sa honor revestir
> 'Se ce ne feit, il m'aconvient morir.
> ....
> 'Ceschuns n'est daigne de prisons recoilir,
> 'Car qui promet et pués ne puet fornir,
> 'Plu bas en est et se feit eschernir:
> 'Ainsi en vait a le niés vostre sir' (5868-69,
> 5877-80).

'Thus Charles wishes to re-establish his honor; if he
does not do so, I must die. / . . . / Not every man is
worthy of retaining a prisoner, for he who promises
and then cannot keep his word, the more base he is
and makes a trap for himself/renders himself
impotent: so it goes [between] your lord and his
nephew.'

Isoré's remarks here serve to demonstrate the transcultural nature of
chivalric ideology. Like Roland, he is placed in opposition to his
father's refusal to respect ethical codes; for Malgeris, too, ends alone
count. The generational pairs abide by different standards, with the
younger men on the side of "droiture." In another confrontation of old
and new, simply put, perspectives regarding honor/dishonor constitute a
generational gap in both Christian and Saracen camps.

As the debate escalates, Hestout, whose florid declaration
brandishes allegorical embellishments suggesting ironic hyperbole,
defends the emperor's feudal integrity in discourse more appropriate to
the lexicon of courtly romance:

'Sire,' feit il, 'cil qui les Frans chadelle
'Non feroit chouse fors que raisnable et belle.
'Flor de vertu le vest et amantelle;
'Por ce le abrace la noble damoisselle
'(C'est la Droiture) sor sa franche rohelle,
'Et lui la baixe et ne la despulcelle.
'Carles me sanble le esperver qi oixelle
'Por autrui sempre; el si s'en enjoielle,
'Voir q'il en a por honor la cervelle:
'Einsi feit Carles, qui sol honor apelle'
(5937-46).

'Sire,' says he, 'he who leads the French would not do
anything but the reasonable and fine. The flower of
virtue clothes and swaddles him; on this account the
noble maiden (Righteousness she is) on her free-
moving wheel, he kisses but does not deflower her.
Charles seems to me the sparrow-hawk which hunts
birds, always for someone else; in this way he feels
joy. True it is that he has his mind on honor: so does
Charles act, who calls on/appeals to honor alone.'

The final phase of this prolonged debate on the lord's chivalric duties, forming a parallel with the earlier codification of vassal obligations, brings in *largesse* as another essential quality of the good ruler. Naimon's discourse specifies this fundamental virtue here as willingness to ransom an imprisoned compatriot, thus related to honor; failure to negotiate exchange is termed cowardice, contrary to the "barons chi veult a honor user sa vie" (6255) ("baron who wishes to employ his life in the cause of honor"). In a prophetic *sentence* reminding Charles that it is pragmatic to be benevolent, Naimon adds: " 'E bien savés, n'a mester chel vos die, / Che par lui soul signor ne moltiplie, / 'Mais veult pros estre et avoir compagnie' " (6270-72) (" 'And you well know without need of anyone telling you so, that by force alone a lord does not multiply [his power], but he needs to be worthy [of it] and have friends' "). Roland will give the same advice to the sultan in Part II.

Caveat: Heteroglossia (locus *g*: 6662-6671)

Charles's eloquently elusive declaration on the gift horse is placed at the core of the plateau phase, at a site where the text seems to pause and reflect on the growing momentum of the Charles-Roland discord. Viewed within the global text, we see that it comes before and follows a series of disagreements which will culminate in the blow. Yet at the moment when it is uttered, and perhaps received, with the ingenuous optimism of its intra- and extratextual narratees, everything still seems possible: reflection may lead to reconsideration, even to resolution.

Compromise, nonetheless, is not a termination point definitively resolving discordant perspectives; rather, it is a provisory moment in the text where the agent of authority reflects on another potential occasion of friction and utilizes that event to proffer, in discourse both event-specific and allusive, the possibility of accommodation between respective expectations of authority and autonomy. The specific occasion is unpretentious, even trivial; it centers around a magnificent horse given to Roland by Prince Isoré in a gesture of respect and admiration, followed by Hestout's apparently facetious suggestion that more than desirable fraternization took place at Nájera between the two youths. The ransom of Isoré has just been achieved, not without considerable resistance from Charlemagne. Although in theory Hestout should be a reliable narrator, himself a prisoner at Nájera and the only source for information concerning Roland's conduct in the negotiations, both narrative and authorial publics of Trecento Italy are sufficiently

informed to doubt the credibility of this character. As pretext to
Charles's statement, then, we have Roland's integrity apparently placed
in doubt, followed by Charles's defense of that integrity. Were the gift a
hunting-bird, says Charles:

> 'Je le prendisse; mai de vos entendons
> 'Feir come feit li mercheant prodons
> 'Quant oit noriç fil o niés grant o lons:
> 'Se il feit bien e ne le voit felons,
> 'Sa marchandise le met tot a bandons,
> 'Aler l'en laise e por vals e per mons;
> 'E cil porchace, chi bien soit sa raisons.
> 'Da Deu, bel niés, e de ma nuriçons
> 'Vos voi si feit che desor vos metons
> 'Les fais des armes che porter solions. (6662-
> 71).

> 'I would take it, but in your case we intend to do as
> the honorable merchant does, when he has raised a
> son or nephew for a long time: if he [the youth]
> behaves well and [the father /uncle] does not see in
> him an evil character, he [the merchant] grants him
> free disposition of/full authority over his
> merchandise/property. He lets him go both through
> valleys and mountains; and the youth goes his way
> freely, who well knows his reason [for his comings
> and goings]. By God, fine nephew, and as the young
> man whom I have raised, I see you formed/grown up
> in such a way that to you we grant the feats of arms
> which we (alone) were accustomed to bear ourselves.'

Primary among those elements specified in the text and pertinent to
ideological analysis is its declaration as statement of intent with the
inherent futurity of the speech act. If five occasions of conflict have
disturbed the Charles-Roland relationship thus far and resulted
ominously in Charles's recognition of further, perhaps more grave
possibilities of conflict, the onus is his to alter that course in the
interests of the entire mission. Not content with merely voicing his
acquiescence, Charles concretizes it by officially transferring the horse
to Roland's possession, control, and utilization. Further, by entrusting
the horse to Roland, Charles appears to grant something far more
significant: permission to carry out those kinds of chivalric acts which
until now only he has been entitled to enact.

In the two sociolects employed, the commercial ("merchant prodons," "marchandise") and familial ("fil," "nuriçons"), there is an element of abrasiveness between code and content in the use of a mercantile code as the transmitter vehicle for an apparently epico-feudal message. We do not generally associate such language with the Model I seigniorial system or the chanson de geste. Suggestion, then, of something referentially different results from the expression of the Charles-Roland feudal bond in the code of communal and post-communal societies, whose transactional language is more familiar and comprehensible to a fourteenth-century Italian public in its rather pragmatic ethos of reciprocity.

The parentage bond via which Charles chooses to enunciate the message adds its own intensifying elements. The older individual grants permission to the younger based on his longterm and informed knowledge of character and reliability. The simile reiterates the affective bond expressed by a paternal figure prepared to entrust his son with a valuable object and virtually all his "professional" possessions ("sa marchandise"); more significantly, however, the horse also represents the means by which the youth will be able to circulate more freely in the world (" 'Aler l'en laise e por vals e per mons' "). Discretion as to use of the mobility is granted to the son unconditionally. In adding the privilege of signing the horse with his personal coat of arms, Charles permits the youth to move about freely without the *congé* of traditional hierarchical relationships.

Relaxation of the merchant-father's control is, however, qualified by the stipulation of the youth's proper conduct as it is (and will be) judged by the older man; the critical " 'se il feit bien e ne le voit felons' " in effect preserves his judgmental privilege. Thus while the father figure of the first seven verses extends unlimited mobility/autonomy, there is no specificity in the last three verses that Charles himself hereby relinquishes his authority function irrecupably. This, of course, is the crucial point in the transaction, where the text enacts the increasingly "contradictory multiplicity of the epoch." What indeed is being said? How is it received?

Since it is the Nobles episode which most patently demonstrates Roland's enactment of the authority/autonomy theme, we can most effectively test Charles's declaration within that context (see ch. 1). Analysis of events related to Nobles, from Roland's decision to go there to his intense anger and shock when struck by Charles on his return, provide partial credibility to each of the following interpretational readings.

In an initial analysis, one may say that while Roland does not specifically relate Charles's discourse to his own decision to leave for

Nobles without *congé*, his reading creates a secondary, connotative text which Roland then implements to justify all aspects of his Nobles-related activities. Accordingly, Roland, narratee of a seven-verse récit, tells himself the merchant tale thus: since the emperor granted autonomy of both my person and projects by granting me possession of the horse: he thereby sanctions my departure. Evidence in support of such a reading is considerable: the youth's only momentary hesitation; reassurance to those accompanying him regarding the propriety of the undertaking; conviction that the act is in the interest of Charles and the reconquest; and afterwards, anticipation of approval upon his return.

However, in recognizing the centrality of this passage of the *Entrée*, we are obliged to acknowledge simultaneously its unusual complexity, perhaps not unrelated to an intertextual element inherent in the motif itself of the gift horse.

A second interpretation emerges whereby Charles's discourse is a monovalent gesture without applicability to textual events thereafter; it involves the granting of an object expressive of confidence concerning Roland's integrity in the Isoré negotiations at Nájera and thus should be seen principally as refutation of Hestout's suggestion as to how Roland acquired the horse. It can also be retroactively referential in the sense that Charles's present appraisal of Roland's character, logically founded on intratextual events heretofore, justifies his bequest of the horse. The obvious problem with this reading is its accommodation with five previous confrontations, in the course of which Charles has felt obliged to apprise Roland of the terms of feudal service, declared his unwillingness to brook "contrediçon", and levelled the charge of "orguel" more than once. It should be noted, however, that these are the confrontations in which Charles has yielded either to Roland or to those supporting him; permission to keep the gift horse may be simply another example of authoritarian largesse.

A third reading perceives Charles granting retention of the gift and freedom of movement to a Roland to whom he wishes to convey confidence and trust; his apparent largesse, probably conciliatory, includes the mobility and "marchandise" elements. However, Charles's use of figurative discourse distances him from the utterance and may signal his essential ambivalence on the authority-autonomy issue. His discourse merits close attention: on the one hand, an initial, unambiguous statement of intent utilizing two verbal forms of direct interlocutionary activity ("vos" - "nos" 6662). Yet the presumed self-referential narrator then adopts the absentee (*il*) voice in the next six verses to relate his merchant's tale. In the final three lines, he reverts to the morphology of direct communication in the implied *je* of the "vos voi," adjectival "ma," and pronominal "vos," and imperial (i.e., authoritarian) "nos" in the final two verbs "metons" and "solions."

Introduction and closure bear importantly on the récit: beginning and end are effected by direct communicative discourse, while the essence of content, the substance of the message, is couched in figural language. Both narrative and authorial narratees might well see evidence of evasiveness, intentional or not, in Charles's cautionary tale, an ambivalence which may both proffer and qualify the autonomy of his nephew.

In readings two and three, Roland fails to decode correctly Charles's message; in those instances, his Nobles enterprise is the act of a careless or incompetent reader. We see other instances of this charge both in the Oxford *Chanson* and in the *Entrée*'s Pamplona Reinforcement episode, dialogically related to the former. Yet in reading three, the onus of communication breakdown, toward which the global text is of course rushing headlong, is on Charles himself—if his message is insufficiently clear to assure comprehensibility. If the passage is ultimately open-ended, however, Roland's reading and subsequent acts are plausibly justifiable.

A narrative and authorial audience sense of ambiguity in Charles's words is not necessarily linked to speaker ambivalence or lack thereof. It seems, however, that connotative interpretations concerning feudal, communal (i.e., societal) ideologies are permitted once the intricacies of the passage are revealed. Contextually, then, a feudal reading of lord-vassal interaction applies, to the extent that feudal relationships still pertain in early Trecento northern Italy, to alternative methods by which the *auxilium-consilium* services were rendered. History amply documents such relaxation of seigniorial expectations, particularly in the *auxilium* realm, where monetary economies permitted the satisfaction of feudal duty through vassalic payment. If we see Charles here as *seigneur* relaxing some of the traditional feudal tenets, vassal Roland acquires increased mobility and autonomy within the parameters of the contract: that is, immanent hierarchism is lessened but not eliminated, while distance between *partenaires* is likewise reduced but not abolished. The caveat of " 'se il feit bien e ne le voit felons' " still pertains; vassal autonomy is granted conditionally, provided that its use—always defined by the superior figure—does not become abuse, turning vassal into *baron révolté*.

Where Charles may easily be seen by a Venetan-Lombard *Entrée* audience as representative of imperial interests and Roland as those of the commune, the brief historical outline in Chapter 3 attests the agonistic nature of those relationships since the first appearance of the communes. The sense of unwanted imperial involvement in communal affairs extends from the Lombard League through the *Entrée* period itself, directly following the Ezzelino tyranny and preceding the final Scaglieri takeover. Both these men were, of course, vehicles of imperial interests. In the Venetan-Lombard region, and particularly in Padua, the communes' struggle to achieve and maintain their autonomy is a leitmotiv of literary and documentary texts of the epoch. The empire, reluctant to release the communes from some measure of its authority, demonstrated considerable resourcefulness in its efforts to preserve that authority. Without detailing specific events, evidence frequently attests an official policy of non-intervention, while significant interference in communal affairs was more often the reality. The empire, at times paternalistic in its transactions with the communes, might affect a non-interventional posture provided that its own interests were not in jeopardy; nonetheless, should the "trusted offspring" show signs of transgressive behavior, the authoritarian presence was quick to reappear. Both Ezzelino and Can Grande assumed control over Padua and the surrounding region as a direct result of imperialist politics and in both cases proved disastrous to communal governance.

Orgueil Reconsidered (locus *h*: 7624-92)

The necessity to decode signs appears on the axes of both character and audience response in the dialectic of "onor," "orgueil," and "hobedience" of locus *h*. Situated within the Pamplona Enemy Reinforcement episode, this strongly intertextual site bears strong resemblance in its initial configurations to the *scènes du cor* in the Oxford *Roland* before it changes course to focus instead on ideological tensions. The issue of honor is immediately raised: assigned to prevent an *entrée* of Pamplona by approaching enemy troops, Roland declines to deploy his own militia: " 'Car l'apostoile me proia por amor / 'Che sa masnee, dunt me feit condutor,/'Ne amoinase o il aüst desonor' "(7550-52) (" 'For the Pope requested me, for love of him, that I not lead his army, of which he made me leader, where it might encounter dishonor' "). Roland and Olivier are dispatched with a modest army to confront enemy forces in far superior numbers, arriving around dawn near Estella. Because it is still too dark to see clearly, Roland can only attempt to identify the forces in front of his own, concluding, in a semiotic interpretation of evidence, that it is Maigeriz with a corps of soldiers coming to meet the reinforcements, for " 'cist sing le senefie' " (7642) (" 'this sign signifies it' ").

Just as the audience/reader must become a decoder of signs in this episode as it parallels, then diverges from the Oxford parent text, so Roland assumes the same role in his effort to comprehend still-unclear information. The two texts maintain their parallels through the next narrative segment when Roland angrily refuses to send for the reinforcements which Bernard suggests. His response recalls the four refusals in the _Chanson's_ laisses 83-86:

> Respunt Rollant: 'Jo fereie que fols!
> En dulce France en perdreie mun los.
> . . . .
> Respont Rollant: 'Ne placet Damnedeu
> Que mi parent pur mei seient blasmet,
> Ne France dulce ja cheet en viltet!
> . . . .
> Ne placet Deu', ço li respunt Rollant,
> Que ço seit dit de nul hume vivant,
> Ne pur paien, que ja seie cornant!
> Ja n'en avrunt reproece mi parent.
> . . . .
> Respunt Rollant: 'Mis talenz en est graigne.
> Ne placet Damnedeu ne ses angles
> Que ja pur mei perdet sa valur France!
> Melz voeill murir que huntage me venget.
> Pur ben ferir l'emperere plus nos aimet'
> (1053-54; 1062-64; 1072-76; 1088-92).

Roland replies: 'I would be behaving like a fool!
I would lose my good name in fair France.
. . . .
Roland replies: 'May it not please the lord God
That my kinsmen incur reproaches on my account,
Or that fair France should ever fall into disgrace!
. . . .
May it not please God, Roland replies to him,
That it be said by any man alive,
Nor by any pagan, that I ever sound the horn!
My kinsmen shall never incur reproaches.
. . . .
Roland replies: 'My determination is greater because of it.
May it not please the lord God nor his angels
That France lose its worth on my account!
I'd rather die than be disgraced.
The Emperor loves us more when we strike well.'

The *Entrée*, reducing the message to its essence, reads: " 'Honte n'avroie de ceste coardie, / 'Si feit l'avoie, en tretote ma vie; / 'Vos voleç bien che dan Hestous s'en rie' " (7648-50) (" ' I could not bear the shame of that cowardice for my whole life, if I had done it; you really want Sir Hestout to laugh about it' "). The last verse, however, deflects some of the gravity of the moment, while Roland's aversion to (the perception of) shame and cowardice is not insistently reiterated. The authorial assumption here, as in the previous codification of vassal obligations, is that his public remembers the earlier passage, and in sufficient detail, so that only cues need be repeated. And just as at Roncevaux, the narrator displays the paraphernalia of battle before us in bold, colorful strokes with a characteristic taste for anaphora. Numerous illuminations of Marciana XXI may have been inspired by:

> Tant banderes, tant penons colori,
> Tant blanc aubers, tant heum a or brusti,
> Tant bon çevaus e tant mul Arabi,
> Tant triés carjé de soie e de sami . . . (7659-62).

> So many banners, so many colored pennants, so many white [glistening] haubarks, so many gold-encrusted helmets, so many fine horses and Arabian mules, so many tents adorned with silk and precious fabrics. . .

Yet what we see initially is not through the eyes of Roland, but of Gérard, who looked at and saw ("garda e vi," 7652) the *res* rather than the *signum*. Like Olivier in the *Chanson*, Gérard's interpretation is correct because he has the advantage of direct vision. At this point, as readers of the earlier work, we anticipate Roland's refusal to blow the oliphant, and the ensuing tragedy.

Yet our skills as decoders must likewise be sharpened, for it is here that the Paduan once again alters the course of the narrative and the configurations of his principal character as well. Although Roland had mentioned his fear of " 'reporteur' " who might judge him harshly were he to accept the crown from Charles after the taking of Nájera, and thus apprehension of " 'malvaise cançun,' " the issue of his *orgueil* diminishes greatly. We shall have to reread his subsequent acts against the simple but striking fact that, despite his sense of dishonor when wounded and forced to cease combat (" 'Honiç me voi e tenuç a cohart' " 7857) (" 'I see myself shamed and considered a coward' "), Roland almost immediately summons reinforcements to aid his endangered men.

It is the deliberate play of one text against another which focuses our attention here on *inventio* and its ideological implications. J. Lotman writes that "if a text does not sustain the memory of traditional construction, its innovations will no longer be perceived" ("Structure of the Artistic Text" 22). The *Entrée* palimpsest must be read and decoded against the over two hundred year-old ancestral text; they are productions composed for widely different publics, yet bound to one another in profound, indelible relationships.

Like the medieval audience/reader, we enter the text aware of the several languages inherited from the *Chanson de Roland* and epic corpus. Those several languages, shared by Rolandian texts to some degree and convening them into a single macrotext, include languages of conflict, both intra-ideological (Charles's accusation of Roland's treason) and inter-ideological (Roland accuses Ferragu of treason against Christian doctrine), the language of adherence to or transgression of chivalric and religious codes, and of heroism (*prouesse*).

A passage such as locus *h*, with variants of its configurations, is essential to medieval epic morphology as an adaptation of the Aristotelian recognition scene, since it is here that the hero must confront his own limitations and come to terms with his mortality. In the *Chanson de Roland* as in the *Entrée*, the process consists of three phases:

1. Roland is placed in a military situation where his chances for victory are seriously jeopardized;
2. as an incompetent reader of signs, he initially refuses to acknowledge his vulnerability and resists a self-image counter to his ideal;
3. he is compelled to recode information and correct his error so that there is minimal dislocation between his perception of self and that shared by narrative and authorial publics.

While in the *Roland* , phase 3 is an agonistic one (Roland's quarrel with Olivier), the *Entrée* renders the accommodation consistent with the shape of the character as the text has developed him thus far: less driven by the *Chanson*'s rigidly hierarchical tenets.

There is one more factor to consider. In yet another shifting of the *orgueil* thematic from Roland>Olivier to Roland>Charles, the emperor accuses Roland of the same failure for not yielding sooner in order to prevent Christian losses. Yet given the sequence of events and point at which Roland permits the call for help, Charles's accusations lose their impact and emerge as less than cogent. By retaining the episode's basic segments but reordering their sequence, the Paduan orients us toward a significantly different interpretation. Rather than pursuing what has been the most controversial of debates regarding the *solitaire/solidaire*

aspects of heroic character, he in effect walks us through an episode
where he can contrast audience expectations with authorial innovations
in order to demonstrate that in a secular reading, the *Entrée*'s Roland is
not primarily motivated by *orgueil*. If we submit this information to
the later narrative chronology of events in the Oxford text, the same
argument might be reinforced. Audience appraisal of pride in Roland is
essential to the decoding of the following Nobles episode, where the
dialectics of "labor"/"repois," "honor"/"desonor," "largeçe"/"avarise,"
and "orguel"/"umbleté" are re-entered into the dialogic arena.

In what may be an ingenuous prophecy anticipating the tragedy at
Roncevaux, Charles reprimands Roland for sacrificing lives to his own
pride:

> 'Orguel fist ja mant pros homes morir,
> 'Sire Rolant; je vos voil descouvrir
> 'Une raisons che vos doit abelir
> . . . .
> 'Une sol home ne poit le munt conquir,
> 'Soit beus quant veult, fort e de grant haïr,
> 'Che s'il pur veult a l'orgueil consentir,
> 'La ou doit pros estre, orgueil li feit fuir.
> 'Por vos le di, ne vos en sai blandir:
> . . . .
> 'La vostre fam, chi tot cuide anglotir,
> 'Aprés mangier vos fera mal gesir' (7921-23; 7926-30;
> 7935-36).

> 'Pride has made many a man die, sir Roland; I want to
> reveal to you a reason which should be to your liking
> / . . . / One man alone cannot conquer the world, be
> he as fine, strong, and filled with hatred of the enemy
> as he likes, that if he wants to yield to pride, there
> where he should be courageous, pride makes him flee.
> For your sake I say so, I don't know how to flatter
> [illude] you about it / . . . / Your hunger, which
> thinks it can devour all things, after eating will make
> you lie [rest] uncomfortably.'

In strident tones and in discourse combining the sentential with
direct accusation, Charles compares Roland's desire for glory to
gluttony, deadly sin of excessive desire. A similar charge was levelled
earlier against Anseïs de Pontiu, whose "fam" for power led to an
attempted usurpation of the imperial throne. But it has likewise been

used by Roland in reference to Charles himself, in analogy of the arrogant individual who plants seed in another's garden, then harvests and gluttonously eats the bitter fruit. Association of pride with gluttony recalls the sin of Adam and Eve, increasing the resonant gravity of the charge.

Once again, reader/audience is invited to reexamine traditional feudal epic ideology. Hestout defends absolute hierarchism and established models of authority, reminding Roland: " 'Ver lui n'avrés ja drois' " (7962) (" 'Before [with regard to him] you have no right(s)/right [to resist]' "). Roland, as related by the narrator, represses his anger to demonstrate to Charles "che hobedïence senpre orgueil venqui" (7982) ("that obedience has always vanquished pride"), ironically praising the joys of subservience:

> 'Sire', dist il, 'or dites vos plaisir,
> 'Car je sui senpre a vos ire seguir:
> 'Quant che m'est greu a autre hom sofrir
> 'Me feit contant, soul par vos hobeïr' (7939-42).

> 'Sire, he says, now name your pleasure, for I am still
> yielding to your wrath. Everything that is difficult for
> me to tolerate from another man makes me happy,
> solely in order to obey you.'

The immediate crisis appears resolved. Not so the more fundamental questions regarding human behavior. What, after all, is pride? As presented here, can we describe it in terms of autocratic actions and/or challenges to their justifiability? Again, the text encourages reassessment of notions once unexposed to challenge.

Typologies Re-viewed (locus *i*: 10,399-434)

To underline the importance of largesse as a political virtue, the Paduan presents an iconographic representation of the archetypal benevolent monarch, Alexander the Great. In a formal ceremony baptizing Filidés as once-and-future lord of Nobles, Roland enters a magnificent chamber decorated with paintings depicting "l'estoire Platon," "le cours des estoiles" (10,939-40), and mural narratives of Alexander's battles and other feats. In this visual narrative of a model warrior-king, Roland studies scenes of Alexander crowning his "XII palatin," (10,425), quarrels with "mal voisin," (10,412), and inquiry as

to how his life was to end. Attributing the Macedonian King's triumphs
more to ethical virtues than mere military prowess, Roland comments:

> 'Veez qe feit largeçe, qi veit por son chemin.
> 'Cil conquist por largeçe la tere e le marin;
> 'Onques mais aveir homes n'ensira de topin.
> 'Qi volt honor conquere sor son felons vesin
> 'Apraigne d'Alixandre la voie et le train' (10,430-34).

> 'You see what largesse does, which goes its [own]
> way. This man conquered through largesse the land
> and the sea; never will earthly good follow men
> secretly. He who wishes to win honor over his evil
> neighbor, let him learn from Alexander the way and
> the means.'

While largesse in Charles is difficult to arouse, Roland's actions at
Nobles and restoration of the city to its converted ruler speak for
themselves. We should recall, too, that Roland has voluntarily
relinquished his fiefs to the empire. In another displacement of audience
assumption, the Paduan creates a typological rapport not between
Charles-Alexander, but between Roland-Alexander. The Paduan's only
comparison between Alexander and Charles is in terms of the great size
of their conquering armies (7664-66). He thus rewrites traditional
typologies, iconoclastically displacing Charles and replacing him with a
Roland steadily emerging as a model of the worthy secular leader. In
966-76, Charles's unannounced, thus unethical entry into Spain was
specifically opposed to Alexander's more correct military ethics. We
might also note the accusations by the Saracen ambassador Norbedrais
of pride and "traisons" in likening Charles to Judas Iscariot and to Paris,
whose reckless arrogance produced dire consequences, but did not go
unpunished. Henning Krauss cites this passage to comment on the
complexity of layers of meaning in the *Entrée* which, not infrequently,
"solo un intenditore può decodificare" (228-29). Warning Charles that
"mal en Espaigne entrais," the ambassador charges:

> 'Jameis lo fel Judais
> 'Del Diex qe vos orez tel traisons non fist mais
> 'Com sor la gient d'Espaigne, enperer, fete ais:
> 'Si les viens envaïr come corz font li gais.
> 'N'ais mie feit ensi com fist vers Nicolais
> 'Le boens rois Alexandre, li fiuz Olinpiais,
> 'Qe nel degna envaïr ne le desfiais;

'Parlamenter l'ala o ses Macedonais.
'Mais tu is furios e mal n'achaverais;
'Tant est grant ton orgoil, que tu resons te fais
'Meïme, sens alier por raisons de palais.
'Par mon chief, tu ais or encargiez plus grant fais,
'Ne fist Paris a prendre la fame Melelais,
'Car il en fu destruiz et oncis, bien le sais' (961-74).

'Never did the evil Judas commit such a betrayal of
the God whom you worship, as you have done to the
people of Spain: so you come to invade them like
braggart cowards. You have not done as the good
King Alexander, son of Olympus, did toward
Nicholas, whom he deigned not [considered unworthy]
to invade without official notification/challenge; he
[Alexander] went to discuss [the invasion] with his
Macedonians, but you are wrathful [mad] and you will
come to a bad end; so great is your pride, that you
invent reasons by yourself, without going by
[heeding] reasons of state. Upon my life, you have
now taken on a larger feat than Paris in taking the
wife of Menelaus, for he was destroyed and shamed,
as well you know.'

The paintings depicting Alexander's illustrious career offer a *mise
en abyme* of Roland's future as warrior-knight, and, presumably, king,
heir and successor to the Middle Ages's most celebrated monarch. By
proving himself a competent reader in the decoding of these murals,
Roland perceives his own role in the larger framework of world order.

Transgression Dialogized (locus *j*: Nobles episode *ad passim*)

Convergence of the *Entrée*'s dialectic of societal ideologies is
woven into the Nobles narrative. Unlike the Oxford poet, for whom
questions of ideology had generally clear and unproblematic responses,
the Paduan approaches such questions with a more relativist perspective
characterized likewise by an enthusiasm for inquiry from different, often
conflicting points of view. The text moves within the ideological
confines of Model I, maintaining in particular the feudal subsystem as a
closed verticality wherein authority is absolute and nonnegotiable. Yet
at the same time, it transgresses those boundaries, signalling the
pressures of new models still imperfectly articulated, but which in the

Entrée center upon pressures from heretofore excluded elements: the
"smaller player" seeking participation within the system and
confronting his superior with such demands. Tensions between Charles
and Roland escalating throughout *Entrée* I will culminate here. The
alteration of Charles-Roland roles in much of the Franco-Italian corpus
within the larger context of ideological implications is commented on
by Wunderli:

> Un tel surpassement du personnage de Roland, son
> évolution vers un héros idéal et le personnage
> intégrateur de tous les courants et contre-courants dans
> cette vaste matière épique implique en même temps
> une dévalorisation du personnage du roi, peu importe
> qu'il s'appelle Pépin ou Charlemagne. Nous avons
> sans aucun doute un effet du rôle lamentable que
> l'Empire et les empereurs allemands jouent en Italie
> au XIIIe et XIVe siècles; le représentant officiel du
> pouvoir central a perdu tout crédit et les espoirs, les
> aspirations idéologiques se tournent vers un nouveau
> personnage qui semble capable de donner une réponse
> satisfaisante aux défis qui lui sont lancés par un
> monde dont les structures, les centres de gravitation et
> les besoins ont complètement changé. Ainsi la
> modification du 'fondment dans la vie' de la Matière de
> France a pour conséquence une restructuration de cette
> matière elle-même: nous avons maintenant affaire à
> un nouveau système de valeurs dont les mécanismes
> et les lois ont leur propre droit à l'existence et qui,
> dans leur fonctionnement, sont indépendants des
> structures antérieures. Ou, pour employer une
> métaphore linguistique, une synchronie antérieure a
> été remplacée par une synchronie ultérieure ("Roland
> théologien" 760).

A review of the narrative elements of the Nobles episode, key to
the Charles-Roland rupture, helps to assess the dynamics of the process
and where transgression might logically be placed. If we (as external
observers) assign wrongdoing, intentional or not, to either individual, a
fairly extended list of "errors" emerges on both sides:

Roland at error
a. gives permission to scout for reconnaissance of Nobles without
   specific approval from Charles

b. conceals destination from Charles and from men accompanying him to Nobles
c. departs without permission
d. recognizes possibility of error en route to Nobles (" 'se folie ai fait' ")
e. Olivier speaks of " 'folage,' " " 'folloie,' " but yields nonetheless to Roland's will
f. The narrator comments on the "gentil conte Rolland qe ne garde a mesure, / comant il en porte bleisme, seguir vuelt sa nature" (4908-09) ("noble count Roland, who has no regard for moderation, how he bears [the] blame for it, he wants to follow his nature").

Roland at Nobles assumes the several functions of the epic authoritarian: generator, motivator, organizer, executor of events. Like Charles, whose role he virtually assumes here, Roland confronts internal opposition, but succeeds, through reasonable explanation of the undertaking, in maintaining authority over, and the allegiance of his men.

Charles at error
a. presumes that Roland has committed treason, passes judgment without allowing explanation or legal recourse
b. vows Roland's death and that of his kin, ordering his barons to execute his orders
c. asks for divine aid to punish Roland
d. strikes Roland himself (see discussion of *exfestucatio* below). In Prologue II, the narrator comments on condemnation of Charles's actions by his barons. Also, Charles himself recognizes his error and injustice immediately following Roland's departure: "Car repentis estois de cil folor" (11,185).
   Among the most problematic aspects of the Charles-Roland rupture is the blow itself as a signifying act. More devastating as a gesture of dishonor than physically injurious, the fact that Charles strikes with his mailed glove, symbol of his warrior-knight status more than his political function, may be relevant: the blow might have been dealt with the scepter or other instrument of imperial authority. The physical immediacy of direct bodily contact sharpens what we might call the communicative aspect of the blow—more so than other possible instruments such as the *Chanson*'s "bastun." In medieval Germanic law, a lord or vassal who strikes an individual to whom he is bound by oath automatically annuls that oath, liberating the victim from all further obligations and entitling him to go to war against the perpetrator of violence. Claims, reasonable as they seem, that a fourteenth-century

northern Italian community would neither have understood nor
appreciated an archaic feudal custom are nonetheless discredited by
Entrée 15,361-63, where two hundred of the emperor's men announce to
Charles that they renounce the mission and are returning to France:
" 'En Espagne venimes por conquir solemant / 'Por coroner dou regne le
fiuz Mille d'Anglant: / **'Le saigremant est qite por un ferir de
guant.'** " (" 'We came to Spain only to conquer, to crown as king the
son of Milon d'Anglant, **the oath/agreement is annulled by a blow of
the glove'** " (emphasis added). Neither is there any use in persuading
them to remain in Roland's absence, " 'Car nul ne doit secore qi soi
meiesme ofant' " (15,374) (" 'For no one is obliged to assist a person
who does offense to himself' ").

In his study of the evolution of Charlemagne in six early Franco-
Italian works, (*Chanson de Roland* V[4], V[7], *Enfances Ogier*, *Chevalerie
Ogier*, *Karleto*, and *Macaire*, Bender insists on the lack of interest in
feudalism in '200-'300 Italy:

> Cette conception des relations féodales propre aux
> mss. de Venise parle en faveur de la thèse, selon
> laquelle les modèles français de ces mss. datent d'une
> époque où les problèmes féodaux de la version
> d'Oxford n'intéressaient plus ou pour la thèse selon
> laquelle les remanieurs italiens ont profondément
> modifié leurs modèles français en vue de leur public
> qui ne s'intéressait guère aux problèmes féodaux.

Regarding physical violence between lord and vassal, he adds, in
reference to the *Chevalerie Ogier*:

> D'autre part, un tel châtiment corporel du seigneur
> aurait été inconcevable pour un public imprégné
> d'esprit féodal; car le code d'honneur de la féodalité ne
> permettait ni au seigneur de battre son vassal, ni au
> vassal de lever la main contre son seigneur
> ("Métamorphoses" 168-69).

The *Entrée*'s blow should be examined more closely. As bilevel
textual encoding, it can be read as a communicative act in several ways:
lord > vassal, governor > governed, Empire > commune. The Paduan's
recovery of waning archaic, but still-evident feudalism during the *Entrée*
era does not necessarily restrict either his contemporary or modern
audience in the interpretative process. In each case, a sanctioned

authority enacts its rejection of claims for autonomy issuing from its supposed inferior.

In order to judge the extent to which the *Entrée* may reflect feudal custom, the blow may also be examined from a sociological viewpoint within the context of the exit level of vassalage. The *festuca* (Lat. straw or small stick), was one of the symbolic objects given by the lord to his vassal in the investiture ceremony. Symbolic of the spear, it represented the knight's assumption of the lord's defense in return for protection. In the phrases "hominium exfestucare" or "dominium exfestucare," the "smaller" vassal literally throws off the object, thus renouncing homage and all attendant bonds.[7] Since examples of *exfestucatio* are rare in medieval documents, a definitive interpretation is difficult. Marc Bloch and Jacques Le Goff agree that the gesture essentially ruptured the feudal bond with all implications of hierarchism. Bloch adds that, in the renunciation, the vassal usually intended to maintain his fief, justifying his gesture of *exfestucatio* by the failure of the lord to merit the vassal's service and his rights over the fief. Le Goff takes issue with Bloch's interpretation as *déguerpissement* (defined as voluntary or forced yielding of property or inheritance < *de* + *guerpir*, "abandonner la propriété, la possession de (un immeuble) pour se soustraire à une servitude," *Petit Robert*): "Je crois plutôt que Chenon a raison en réservant ce terme à une *dévestiture* ou à un *déguerpissement* par accord entre les deux parties, le seigneur et le vassal, l'accord de divorce si j'ose dire étant scellé par un *osculum*." (Bloch, "*Les Formes de la rupture* de l'hommage dans l'ancien droit féodal," Nouvelle revue historique du droit français et étranger" (1912) 209; Le Goff, *Temps* 363-65).

The *Entrée* selectively utilizes aspects of the *exfestucatio*. Charles's blow, manual and thus part of a group of symbolic feudal acts (*immixtio, paumée*, etc.), does eliminate Roland's vassalage in a strictly feudal sense. Nonetheless, neither Charles nor Roland throws off a contract-associated object such as occurs in *Raoul de Cambrai*. There, Bernier remains loyal to his seigneur despite the destruction of his ancestral fief and his family; he renounces the feudal bond when, mourning the losses he has sustained, Raoul strikes him physically. Bernier removes three tufts from his mail, casts them at Raoul, declaring that he is legally revoking his feudal oath. Later, Bernier will slay Raoul.

Further, neither *Entrée* character announces that the contract is in fact broken. Charles initially claims that his condemnation of Roland is " 'segond l'euvre,' " punishment to suit the offense—just as Naimon advised him in the Thiois Rebellion episode. Roland's principal

" 'orguel,' " according to Charles, is the audacity to leave him without permission, jeopardizing his own safety and that of all his men.

As Roland merrily enters the emperor's tent ("chiere riant," 11,103), Charles extends a less than gracious welcome:

> 'Dan culvers mescreant,
> 'Avez nos vos encor trovez vivant,
> 'Qe v'en fuïstes de l'estor solemant,
> 'Por quoi morisent e moi el remanant.
> 'Par vestre orguel, qe demenez si grant,
> 'N'a estez manchise qe moi e ceste gent
> 'Ne somes mors, j'en sui bien conoissant.
> 'Mais segond l'euvre en avroiz loemant:
> 'Ferai vos pandre, par le cor sant Amant.'
> A cestui mot a levez le un guant;
> Ferir en veult li quens par mié le dant,
> Quant por le nés le consuet tot avant:
> Le sang en raie, q'en rogist l'açerant
> (ll,108-20).

'Sir faithless scoundrel, you have found us still alive, though you merely fled from the battle, on account of which I and the rest might have perished. Because of your pride, which you parade so grandly, I and these men nearly died, of that I am well aware. But according to the deed you shall receive your reward: I shall have you hanged, by the heart of St. Amant. At this word he raised a glove to him; he wants to strike the count on the tooth [mouth], when he hit him on the end of his nose, the blood gushes forth from it, so that it reddens the steel.'

Characteristic of the *Entrée*, this situation is more complex than it may appear. It will be recalled that Roland departed the field at Pamplona when he judged the day nearly won, with Charles protected by a full army. Although he was aware that his uncle might be momentarily displeased with his departure, Roland felt confident that a victory at Nobles would rapidly dispel any anger. Returning from Nobles:

> Rollant apelle Hestous tot in riant:
> 'Coisins,' dist il, 'je croi veraiemant
> 'Qe troverons le rois de mautalant.'

. . . .
                    'Ancor ne m'an repant,
        'Qe, merci Diex, nos feit avomes tant
        'Qe la merci mon oncle nos sera bien aidant'
        (11,010-12; 11,020-22).

Roland calls Hestout, laughing gaily: 'Cousin,' he says, 'I
truly believe that we shall find the king in bad humor. / . . . /
. . . Still I do not repent that, thanks be to God, we have done
so much that my uncle's thanks/mercy will surely help us/be
in our favor.'

Immediately following the blow, Roland is astounded that
" 'Queil aventure m'avient por bon ovragne!' " (11,147) (" 'What a
[mis]adventure befalls me for a good deed!' "). He is also consumed by
wrath and shame: "Honte le maine et hiror si tres grant / Ne lui
remambre d'ami ne de parant." (11,133-35) ("Shame leads him and
wrath so great / That he remembers neither friend nor relation.") An
impulse toward vengeance likewise enters his mind: "A grand onte se
tient qe creature humaine / Le oüst oseç ferir, se il non portast la paine"
(11,453-54) ("With great shame he considers that any human creature /
Would have dared to strike him, if he could not suffer the pain, were not
prepared to bear the risk"). However, the impulse to strike back is
checked by rational reflection as Roland remembers: "Qe il l'avoit noriz
petit enfant" (11,125-26) ("That he [Charles] had raised him since he
was a small boy").
    The blow propels Roland from the closed spaces in which he has
usually lived—military camp, the companionship of his fellow *pairs*,
Christianitas—with both their positive connotations (membership via
family, peers, faith, mission) and negative implications (censure of
well-intentioned acts from his superiors). His departure is doubly
intended as a vindictive and didactic gesture: " 'Miels veul morir qe je ni
li ensaigne / 'Se je riens li valloie en la gere d'Espagne' " (11,151-52)
(" 'I prefer to die if I do not teach him whether I was of any value in the
war for Spain' "). Roland perceives his departure not as voluntary
abandonment, but forced exile: " 'Gerpir me feit le rois ma douz
compaignie' " (11,150) (" 'The king is making me leave my gentle
companions' "). Thus at the two extremes of *exfestucatio*, manual
gesture of annulment and resultant separation, the *Entrée* follows feudal
custom; yet within those frames, it retains an independent voice.
    The Roland who now departs Pamplona is both a free agent and
potential *baron révolté*. He sees himself as a tragic figure since
boyhood: " 'Ai! hom gravez de paine et de tormant, / 'N'aviz jameis

repois a ton vivant, / 'E començais de mout petit enfant / 'A durer paine et estre travaillant.' " (11,158-61) (" 'Ah! Man burdened with pain and torment, you have never enjoyed repose in your lifetime, and you began as a very small child to endure pain and to be laden with travail' ").

Overturning the (+) *travail* (-) *repois* applicable throughout the text except in this single passage, the reversal illustrates textual violation of its own systems at the moment when we are asked to consider the character himself as a willful transgressor of established models. "Paine" and "estre travaillant" are associated here with well-intended exertion leading to suffering, rather than reward. Such acts are, like all human behavior, subject to erroneous interpretation and may thus lose their intended signification, as appears to have occurred here in Roland's efforts at Nobles to reinstate a degree of societal order in a chaotic world. If Roland's *travail* of battle, specifically at Nobles, is perceived as corruptive rather than corrective by the authority figure whom it intended to serve, then all those essential acts which identify him are rendered invalid. More desirable at this juncture, because signifying respite and possibly the tranquillity he has never enjoyed, is the same *"repois"* which Roland had condemned in locus *a*. Intertextual allusions to his *enfance* (narrated in French, Italian, and Franco-Italian works probably familiar to a large portion of the *Entrée* public) are rendered specific when Roland claims to have saved Charles "da mort" at the hands of the son of Agolant in *La Chanson d'Aspremont*. The *Entrée's* character calls upon other texts, then, to defend his action at Nobles (just as in the Oxford *Roland* Ganelon deploys the Nobles tale to discredit Roland's conduct at Roncevaux). Texts not only communicate among themselves, but may be called upon to defend or condemn one another.

The locus of ideological debate in the Nobles episode moves now to post facto discussion by the *pairs*. In the four exchanges appraising both Charles's and Roland's conduct, positions are articulated differing from those listed above as possible audience/reader response, which of course enjoys a certain distancing:

Speaker	Argument focus	For/Against Charles, Roland
1. Hestout	honor C. dishonors us by blow (11,190-95)	(+)R.
2. Gérard de Roussillon	"orguel" of C. " ' . . . Car por orguel qe sovant trop vos ard' " (11,213) (" ' . . . for the pride that often burns you too hotly' ")	(+)R.

3. Olivier	justice " 'Nuls sajes hom ni devroit mais errer / 'E plus doit estre sajes li justixer / 'Qe cil qe vient a lui droit demander.' " (11,235-37) (" 'No wise man must ever err, and the executor of justice must be more wise than he who comes to demand his rights [that justice be done].' ")	(+)R.
4. Salemon de Bretagne	Charles's absolute authority; the feud does not concern us. We are dependent on Charles " 'Karles est nostre syr e fa droit e raixon.' " (11,313) (" 'Charles is our overlord and is acting correctly and reasonably.' ")	(+) C.

Salemon delivers an eloquent defense of Charles, in which he reminds the Franks that their overlord accomplished many great deeds before Roland was born and that it is improper that he be judged by his inferiors (11,317-20).

If the above analysis seems to weigh judgment rather strongly on the side of the wronged vassal, it is still lacking one decisive element which will alter the majority opinion: the narrator's voice. The debate concludes with the latter's brief statement: "Adonques n'i oit quens ni duc ni aut baron / Qil desdixist, pour ce q'il dit raixon." (11,333-34) ("Thereupon there was neither count nor duke nor noble baron who contradicted him [Salomon], because he told the truth.") All the vassals ask forgiveness of Charles for their threat to abandon him unless Roland returns; they are forgiven.

Thus while the intratextual majority may condemn Charles's autocratic conduct, arguing for more democratic transactions, the narrator's authority, already vigorously asserted in reference to his text and to be reinforced imminently in Prologue II, carries more, or at least a different kind of weight. Justifying Charles's action on the basis of his kingly status is not tantamount to justification "segunt l'euvre," but here, both Salemon and narrator uphold the traditional sanctity of established authority. Within this view, those who trespass the boundaries of sanctified order, even in the form of verbal opinion, are as transgressive as Roland himself.

Two additional points should be made. In his argument, Olivier had stated in terms reminiscent of texts written for the education of future rulers, that execution of justice depends upon the moral integrity necessary to the good ruler. Charles, commenting on Olivier's words, reaffirms his authority in unambiguous terms: " 'Por vos, seignor baron, sui emperer e rois: / 'Vos m'aveis feit honor, ancor le me ferois./ 'Neporquant se je ai fet ver mon niés desrois / 'E j'en sui repanti, sor moi cheit li sordois.' " (11,350-54) (" 'For you [as far as you're concerned], lord barons, I am emperor and king. You have behaved honorably toward me, and shall do so again. Nonetheless if I have committed any misdeed toward my nephew and have repented of it, upon me the worst shall fall' "). In Charles there may be recognition of error and responsibility thereof, yet within the semantic field of *honor* due him, the expected enactment is submission and unquestioning obedience.

While one would exaggerate in saying that *Entrée* I's ideological debate concludes with the expulsion of the agent of change and restoration of traditional modes of social organization, it does close on an ambivalent, tentative note regarding the future direction which both hero and text are to take. In one sense, text and hero have liberated themselves from the confines of old models by the simple act of physical displacement. In fact, audience perception of change and the possibilities which it engenders are first aroused by spatial change as Roland leaves Pamplona. J. Lotman discusses the importance of spatial modeling in the literary text:

> Even on the level of supra-textual, purely ideational modeling, the language of spatial relations turns out to be one of the basic means for comprehending reality. The concepts 'high-low,' 'right-left,' 'near-far,' 'open-closed,' 'demarcated-not demarcated' and 'discrete-continuous' prove to be the material for constructing cultural models with completely non-spatial content and come to mean 'valuable-not valuable,' 'good-bad,' 'one's own-another's,' 'accessible-inaccessible,' 'mortal-immortal,' and so on. The most general social, religious, political, and ethical models of the world, with whose help man comprehends the world around him at various stages in his spiritual development, are invariably invested with spatial characteristics . . . (*Structure* 218).

As a sign of the new ideological and textual space which Roland is entering, close to fifty verses describe the magic fountain where he first arrests his centrifugal motion. Fashioned for a Saracen king, the fountain is presented as a masterpiece of artistry and, like the oriental world which it heralds, a temporary asylum.

Women, Marriage, Social Rank (locus *k*: 11,946-13,197)

Our concentration on ideological issues here is threefold: dialectic concerning women, attitudes regarding social standing, and the bond between governor/governed. The three are interrelated and yield interesting insights concerning what the Paduan will do with a text over which he has claimed full authority and apparently released from its epico-feudal infrastructure.

The Dionés episode, within which this locus appears, traces Roland's first phase of regeneration/reintegration after the blow. At issue is whether the princess will wed the old King Malquidant in a political marriage of convenience arranged by her father. Aligned against the girl's resistance are her parents and father's vassals plus Pélias, nephew of the elderly suitor, who opens with a vitriolic attack on women:

> 'Entendés, roi de Perse, que une feme chaca
> 'Adan dou Paradis, quant il por li peca.
> 'Quant le plus sage home c'onque fu ni sera
> 'As dis de une fame engigner se leisa,
> 'Dun n'est il mereveille se fames engigna
> 'Lot e Sanson le fort, que une bestosa;
> 'Davi e Salomon en lor croir araja.
> 'De l'ome ne vos di que il bien encontra;
> 'Je di que tut le mal qu'avient ni avenra,
> 'La feme en est chief, e ja coupe n'i a;
> 'Mais qui lor done oyë, chier le comperera'
> (12,017-27).

'Understand, king of Persia, that a woman chased Adam from Paradise, when he sinned because of her/for her. When the wisest man who ever was, or will be, let himself be tricked by the words of a woman, then it is no wonder that a woman tricked Lot and Samson the Mighty, whom a woman sheared. David and Solomon committed a mistake in believing them. Regarding man, I do not say to you that he found [any] good [in woman]. I say that of all the evil that occurs or will occur, woman is the cause and there is no end to it; but he who gives heed to them, dearly will he pay the price.'

As for Dionés herself, she is merely following the common destiny of her sex:

> . . . . .'ouvre e comencere d'un mal que devira.
> 'Dehé ait de ma part qi ja l'an blasmera.
> 'Ele feit ce que doit, e quant autre fera,
> 'Li seigles ert finis, plus jor non durera' (12,029-32).

> ' . . . the work and source of an evil which she will become [will come to pass because of her]. As far as I am concerned, may he who will blame her for it suffer grief. She does what she must, and when she will do otherwise, the world will end, not one day more shall it last.'

Such misogynistic discourse reinforces Model I exclusion of women, relegating them to the category of the non-classified. An acknowledgment of sorts to the ancillary appears in Gilbert of Limerick's *Liber de statu ecclesiae*. Outlining the trifunctional pyramid, he writes:

> Understand by those at the top of the pyramid the learned class, and since some of them are married, we have therefore mentioned both men and women. Truly, on the left of the pyramid are plowmen, both men and women. Also, on the right are the warriors, both male and female. Truly it is the position of women neither to speak [*orare*], plow, or certainly fight; nevertheless women are married to, and serve, those who speak, plow, and fight" (*PL* c. 997-98, cited in Corti, *Models* 343-44).

In the semiotics of textual space, Dionés's dual condition, royal and female, confer upon her differing and incompatible status. Against the elevated social rank normally associated with privilege and power, the annulling finality of gender prevails. Thus for Pélias, she is (-) low and (-) evil. Even among her family and subjects, her assigned role as political pawn (compared to her brother's apprenticeship for future assumption of power and heroism) imposes upon her a similar lowly status.

In these respects, Dionés bears a striking resemblance to Roland in his fallen state. He, too, is "non-existent"; i.e., without kin, friends, country, or even his rightful identity. The pseudo-identity as Lionés, "fil la fee" (12,138, to be discussed below), announces a radical denial of the past, selecting association instead with the world of the *merveilleux*, an ideological space in itself, generally not affiliated with either Christian or Moslem law. Such a change potentially alters reader perception and expectations of his conduct within the new Mideastern community.

Twelfth-century lyric and courtly romance offered a radical challenge to the non-personhood of women, yet the issue remained sufficiently controversial in the Trecento to become a focus of debate in the *Entrée*. That Roland undertakes Dionés's defense is no surprise, nor that he does so in the name of "honor" and "droit." Yet what Roland really defends is *her* right of free choice, *her* personal autonomy, and he will do so because reason, and right, as defined by the "new laws," mentioned below, may aid her cause. Before the duel, Roland seeks to clarify his own position and that of his opponent in the light of changing mentalities:

> 'Vasals,' feit il, 'avant que je te fere
> 'Je bien voudroie, se vausist ma proiere,
> 'Que tu aüses plus que n'ais rason çiere.
> 'A l'inforcer n'est pas zouse ligiere;
> 'Tu pois raison de ta memoire trere.
> 'S'au roi, tun uncle, promis sa file el pere,
> 'Necessités, cun je entant, li fist fere.
> 'Se a li non ploit, el non ha per ni mere,
> 'Selong les lois de hoi et de chi arere,
> 'Juger l'en poise, s'elle n'est consentere.
> . . . .
> 'Car de tot les vertuz est droiture banere' (12,684-93; 12,697).

> 'Vassal, says he, before I strike you I would very much like, if my request may be answered, for you to have a clearer reason than you [seem to] have. To force it [the marriage] [upon others] is not a light matter; you can draw upon reason from your memory. If the father promised his daughter to the king, your uncle, necessity, as I understand it, made him do it. If [the marriage] is not pleasing to her, neither her father nor mother, according to the laws of today and of those before, can pass judgment on it, if she does not consent. / . . . / For of all virtues, righteousness/justice is the banner.'

Signs of changing social models come to the fore in the debate on
social status in the Pélias combat. Having already offered his services to
the sultan in the sumptuous Persian court, Lionés acknowledges his
different background:

> 'M'apelle l'en Lionés, fil la fee;
> 'Onqe mon pere ne visqi de sodee,
> 'Mais marcheans de plus grant amasee
> 'Non fust trovei en Spagne la loee.
> 'Le grant richece ch'il avoit asenblee
> 'Me fist honour: a une Pasqe rosee,
> 'Avech qatorçes me fu cente la spee;
> 'Chevalier sui. Si est la cause alee,
> 'Or m'est richece on poverté tornee,
> 'Mais povertei non pris une deree
> 'Qant a vestre onbre ai ma vie amenee ' (12,138-48).

> 'My name is Lionés, son of the fee; Never did my
> father live as a solderer [artisan, common laborer]; but
> a merchant of greater wealth than he could not be
> found in well-celebrated Spain. The great wealth
> which he had amassed granted honor to me: on a
> Pentecost day, with fourteen [other young men] I was
> girded with the sword; I am a knight. So matters
> went; now my wealth has turned to poverty, but
> poverty I don't care about at all since the moment
> when I dedicated my life to your service.'

While class barriers in thirteenth and fourteenth-century northern
Italy were undoubtedly less rigid than elsewhere, one should keep in
mind the stratification of the Italian middle classes with differentiation
of major vs. minor *artes* and inherent inter-status tensions. The
commune system as discussed in ch. 3 encountered serious problems in
the accommodation of the *magnati* and *popolo grasso* with the *popolo
minuto*. Le Goff writes: "Si le travail en soi n'est plus la ligne de
partage entre catégories considérées et catégories méprisées, c'est le
travail manuel qui constitue la nouvelle frontière de l'estime et du
mépris" (*Temps* 106). And Villani, speaking of the defeat at Courtrai
(1302), comments:

> Di questa sconfitta . . . abassò molto l'honore, lo
> stato, e la fama dell'antica nobiltà e prodezza de'
> Franceschi, essendo il fiore della cavalleria del mondo

> sconfitta e abbassata da' loro fedeli, e dalla più vile
> gente, che fosse al mondo, tesserandoli, e folloni, e
> d'altri vili arti e mestieri, e non mai usi di guerra, che
> per dispetto, e loro viltade, da tutte le nationi del
> mondo erano chiamati conigli pieni di burro . . . "
> (Muratori, *SRI* 13,388, cited in *Temps* 106n37).

Although the Church initially joined the old feudal aristocracy in its scorn for trades, it subsequently recognized the impracticality of such a position and came to encourage and even protect merchants, providing new socio-professional groups with theoretical and spiritual justification of their condition and economic innovations. Yet the Church remained ambivalent toward the new classes, alternately condoning the aristocratic resistance to, and bourgeois enthusiasm for, social change. Although Rome came to admit that there were, finally, no "contemptible" trades, the Church was too close to the ruling classes to have a decisive influence on forces pressing for increasing commerce as part of a new way of life (Le Goff, *Temps* 106-107).

However, as historians generally acknowledge, the later Middle Ages see an increasing interpenetration of cultural models. The easiest to trace, according to Georges Duby, is the descendant movement, "la vulgarisation des modèles culturels," defined as "la tendance des formes culturelles construites pour les catégories supérieures de la société à se vulgariser, à se répandre depuis ses sommets, à descendre de degré en degré dans des couches de plus en plus frustes." Indeed, Duby finds this phenomenon the fundamental force in late medieval cultural history ("Valorisation" 194).

Krauss, too, identifies stages of evolution among the Italian middle classes, describing the early '300 rise of a protocapitalist bourgeoisie which clearly begins to imitate the nobility both in how people lived and conceived their lives.[8]

Popularization of aristocratic models is reflected in the present locus. The issue is not Lionés's social background in itself, but whether such a background renders him a suitable challenger to the noble Pélias. His merchant father, "gente nuova" in a society where his activities are of vital importance, has amassed great wealth and prestige to elevate his son to the ranks of knighthood.[9] The honor of chivalric ordination in *Entrée* II, as in reality, might be acquired with money; Lionés, then, has benefited from a more open social structure, but is still subject to the contempt—and confusion—of his opponent. While on the one hand calling him "villeins" (12,878) and fearing the shame of defeat from a social inferior, Pélias also thinks he recognizes in Lionés's conduct a nobly-born knight:

'Cist n'est villain ne de foible lignaige,
'Mais voiremant civalers de paraige
'Que por mostrer proesche et vassalage
'Vait ensi soul por estrainge regnaige'
(12,933-36).

'This man is neither a peasant nor of weak lineage, but truly a
knight of high rank who, in order to demonstrate his prowess
and vassalage, goes wandering about alone through foreign
kingdoms. '

Assuming the equalizing fraternity of chivalric ordination, Pélias
desires the consolation of knowing that his opponent does not issue
from the depths of the social register. As he requests a truce in the long
duel, he inquires:

'Cevallers frere,' ce a dit Pellias,
'Si Sarracins, Crestians o Judais
'Is, nel sai; més par la loi que tu ais
'Et par cil ordre dont civaler te fais,

. . . .
'Chuntente moi de voir dir, non de gais,
'De quel lignaze es tu nez et estrais,
'De roi, de quens, de duch ou de plus bais?
. . . .
'Bien sai tun peres non vit de vendre drais.
'Les crüels chols que insent de tun brais
'Me fait counostre ce que pués et que sais'
(13,086-89; 13,092-94; 13,099-100).

'Brother knight,' so said Pélias, 'If Saracen, Christian,
or Jew you are, I know not; but by the law that you
hold [worship] and by that order by which you make
yourself a knight, . . . Make me content by telling
the truth, not a lie: of what lineage were you born and
extracted, from a king, count, duke, or from someone
more humble? . . . I know well that your father did
not live by selling fabrics; the cruel blows that issue
from your blade inform me of what you can do and
what you know.'

In the Reggio Emilia fragment, whose second folio narrates an incident at the Persian court omitted in Marciana XXI, a somewhat different narrative posture is assumed regarding the issue of social standing. Roland, a foreigner at court, identifies himself once again as Lionés, the *bourgeois gentilhomme*. However, rather than the debates concerning his worthiness to enter this new community, the sultan immediately, and rather pragmatically, recognizes the importance of retaining the stranger: " 'Voirema(n)t, çe me croi por lui en aut mo[nte]r / 'E de fondre celour che nous cuide(*n*)[t] chaçer' " (" 'Truly, I think this in order to retain him in a high position / And to defeat those who are thinking of putting us to rout' "). Then, recognizing that it is time to initiate his son Samson into the unparalleled sanctity of knighthood ("Che n'est ordne si sant co(m) es[t]"), he announces that the ceremony will be celebrated next morning. And so it is: Roland dubs not only prince Samson, but a certain Candidus and others, offering them counsel on the importance of the obligations they are assuming. Roland then delivers the ceremonial *paumée* to Samson's chin, nearly knocking him over and causing the youth to wonder whether he has somehow offended the questing stranger (Specht, "Cavalleria francese" 491, 30-31, 53).

What is curious in the Reggio-Emilia fragment, even if we cannot know whether the episode comes before or follows another analogous to the Pélias class debate, is the monarch's readiness not only to accept Lionés's apparently non-noble extraction and *arriviste* knighthood, but the authoritarian function he immediately conveys upon his guest (following the ceremony, there are whispers at court that " 'cist n'est mie bo(r)çoy,' " Specht 161). The business-class chevalier anoints the prince without discussion or contention. Additionally, there is a water-immersion scene here which Specht suggests may represent Roland's secret baptism of the initiates ("Cavalleria" 498-99). It may well be that the redactor of this manuscript found the situation quite ordinary. Indeed, were it to occur following the Dionés episode in Marciana XXI, it would appear so as well.

In *La Prise de Pampelune*, the issue is approached with even greater candor. King Desiderio, whose valiant Lombard soldiers quickly conquer a Pamplona which all of Charlemagne's armies have failed to take, requests three concessions as rewards, the second of which is that chivalric ordination be accessible to all estates: " 'E che cescun Lombard, bien qu'il n'ait gentilie / 'Che remise li soit de sa ancesorie, / 'Puise etre civaler s'il a pur manantie / 'Qu'il puise mantenir à honeur civalerie' " (344-47) (" 'And let every Lombard, although he is not nobly-born, be considered apart from his ancestry, so that he can be a knight if he has the domain/wealth and can maintain knighthood honorably' "). As noted by Krauss and others, the traditional literary vilification of the Lombards was related to aristocratic bias against their merchant status and association with popular communal armies (*Epica feudale* 234-35).

In the primary model the bourgeoisie was unrecognized, non-existent; in latter thirteenth-century formulations of new models, as Humbert of Romans unwittingly discloses, it was entered into the system, but assigned an ambiguous place. Ambivalence, though of a less innocent nature, also characterizes the *Entrée* episode. When five hundred Persians praise Roland by exclaiming " 'Preus est nostre paisant' " (12,730), they are ascribing (+) chivalric, i.e., noble traits to a (-) *laborator/rusticus* in a semantic contradiction revealing their tacit acknowledgement that chivalric virtues are not totally class-linked. Roland's claim to "knighthood of the purse," however, does not improve his social image among the Persian noblemen. Knighted son of a merchant, "vilein" or "paisant," the appellations are used interchangeably as if no differentiation existed. All come under the same mantle of scorn, diametrically opposed to and incompatible with the old nobility. Thus Roland's assumed social status still represents transgression for the old Persian nobility, unsanctioned upward movement to be sure, but prophetically youthful, vigorous and committed to a cause. Dionés's cause, the removal of outdated authorities restricting her personal autonomy, is of course a *mise en abyme* of Roland's own.

In a curious variant of this mentality, Roland hurls the unflattering " 'glotuns villains' " (13,073) at Pélias and declares that the Persian's rejection of women's autonomy is a transgression of aristocratic ideology:

> 'Car n'avez fait a loi de gentyls hon.
> 'Cant por droiture mantenir et ses non
> 'Vais travalant por estranges rouyon
> 'E prant bataille et trai a fenysson,
> 'Mais vos n'avés en li nulles braisson,
> 'Huei est le jors que n'avreis geherdon,
> 'Char de droiture voil estre cunpaignon' (12,755-61).

> 'For you have not behaved according to the law of a
> gentleman. When to maintain righteousness and its
> qualities I go about laboring in foreign lands and I
> undertake battle and carry through to its conclusion,
> but you do not have any glimmer [indication?
> *braisson*: Thomas, unknown; Holtus, possibly from

OF *braison, cri*, or *brason, étincelle*] of it. Today is
the day when you shall have your reward, for I wish
to be the companion of justice.'

While Lionés may be a " 'fils de borcoi' " who behaves like a
knight, Pélias is a prince who behaves like a peasant, likewise
transgressing the strictures of Model I conduct and social rank.

As the *Entrée*'s agent of social mobility, Roland has, in a literal
and social sense, crossed the border into another textual space. As he
was in Moslem-occupied Spain, in Islamic Persia he is in the space of
the other, of the "they" rather than the "we"; such space is characterized
by the risks inherent in all error, literal and figural. In this major
textual event, Roland is a violator of primary model class prohibitions,
but his transgression, in the new world of the Middle East, proves
pragmatically justifiable by the simple fact that he wins the duel. One
perceives a significantly more pragmatic attitude on the part of Roland's
Persian benefactors, one which recalls the Franco-Italian *enfances*
poems of Marciana XIII. There, too, the rise of the three youths,
Charles, Roland, and Ogier, is presented as the natural result of their
individual capacities, without restrictions either on account of birth or
social origins. Krauss comments: "Par ce processus 'libéral' avant la
lettre, les jeunes héros peuvent devenir figures d'identification pour la
bourgeoisie qui s'élève contre une classe de droit s'assignant à priori une
qualité ontologiquement supérieure" ("Analyse sociologique" 790).

Lionés's chivalric (and linguistic, i.e., communicative) superiority
redefines the class issue significantly. His triumph will not only grant
him a place in the social system of the Mideast, but render him central
to its efficient functioning and very survival. In previous confrontations
with Charlemagne in Spain, the old world, Roland had repeatedly
attempted to cross borders of the Model I lord-vassal paradigm. His
movement had either been contested or blocked. Now, as agent in a
more open and pragmatic environment where the individual can thrive
on his own skills and merit, Roland/Lionés is granted the autonomy—
and even the authority—which his new benefactor willingly offers.

Emphasizing the necessity to recognize and reward Lionés, Prince
Samson advises his father: " 'Peres, ces home est de valors' " (13,006).
Then, insisting on reciprocity in the vassal/lord relationship, the youth
adds: " 'Proier vos vuel, par le vestre honor, / 'Se bien nos fait, qu'il
non soie pezor.' " (13,007-08) (" 'I want to beg you, on your honor, if
he behaves well for our sake, that he not be the worse off for it' "). The
young prince likewise recognizes in Lionés the questing *chevalier
errant*, embarked on a mission the nature of which he cannot

comprehend: " 'Il vait honor querant, et honor li faizon' " (13,386)
(" 'He travels about seeking honor; honor let us grant him' ").

Yet the fact that Lionés "truly" is nobly born finally hedges the
question between the narrative, uninformed aristocratic public and its
authorial, informed counterpart, the latter comprised of both aristocratic
and bourgeois elements. Each will interpret the situation somewhat
differently. The narrator ultimately resolves the issue by what Lotman
calls "dominating the new," the process whereby the extra-systemic is
absorbed into, and eventually becomes institutionalized within the
official model ("Artistic Text" 236-38). Thus each group can find some
element with which to define and defend its particular interests.

Incorporated within the downward movement of cultural behavior
apparently enacted in this locus is another, more conservative
infrastructure. If the aristocratic, courtly portion of the narrative
audience decodes the Lionés-Pélias verbal exchanges in terms of what
we call social codes, it is confronted with serious discrepancies between
appearance (as judged by the opponent) and reality. Roland purports to
be a " 'fils de borcoi,' " but within the reality of the global text enjoys a
considerably more prestigious pedigree. Pélias, on the other hand,
conducts himself like a " 'glotuns villains' " (according to Roland), not
at all like the " 'gentyls hon' " and nobleman that he is. Yet this
polarization of what is, and what seems to be, is mere simulation. One
need hardly repeat Roland's status as count, nephew to the emperor, and
future king of Spain; we readily recall Pélias's equally lofty status as
nephew to King Malquidant, would-be son-in-law to the sultan of
Persia, and heir apparent to the sultan. In terms of social status, the two
are more or less equals.[10]

A similar dialectical approach toward social rank and mobility
occurs when a Persian council tries to determine a suitable reward for
the young foreigner who has saved the kingdom. The first speaker
perceives it as a class issue; Lionés should be remunerated in terms of
his original class values. Thus the suggestion is to pay the
impoverished youth suitably for his services, then dispatch this " 'home
estraigne' " back home to Spain.

King Clador, on the other hand, wishes to make the remuneration a
test of Lionés's true social status. Accordingly, he argues that the
young man's reaction to an offer of matrimony to Princess Dionés will
disclose whether he is truly a nobleman's son in disguise or the " 'fils
de borcoi' " that he claims to be. From the aristocracy's perspective, it
is one thing to offer one's military services to a community torn apart
by the marriage of the king's daughter, quite another to marry the young
woman, who is quite enamoured of the mysterious stranger. Since

Lionés has already proven his military skills, the test is whether his ethical standards are equally honorable.

If Lionés accepts the royal bride, the "traditional" element of the narrative audience will see him as a violator of Model I sanctions. If he declines, his refusal reassures those whose convictions dictate that as " 'paisant' " or *bon bourgeois*, he prefers not to transgress vertical social barriers. Roland's response, among the *Entrée's* most eloquent passages, opens by thanking the sultan for such an honor, then continues:

> 'Mais non acunvient a home de si zative aire
> 'Choment je sui, a prendre tels doiare
> 'Chant il i avroit honor un grant Cesaire.
> 'Se j'ai oncis ancué sun aversaire,
> 'Ce fu Justise quel moi cunsanti faire.
> 'Il n'a si foibles borgois, tant cun clut l'aire,
> 'Non l'aüst mort, se raison non desquaire.
> . . . .
> 'Non doit vilain porter pellice vaire,
> ' E a gentil dame doit païsans desplaire.
> 'Par moi le di, que conois mon afaire'
> (13,450-56; 13,459-61).

'But it does not befit a man of such lowly background as I to take such a dowry when a great Caesar would be honored to accept it. If I slew her adversary just now, it was Justice which permitted me to do so. There is no bourgeois so weak [humble], as long as a hair shirt may cover him, who would not have killed him, if reason [right] does not violate its boundaries./ . . . / The peasant must not wear variously-colored furs, and to a noble lady a peasant must be displeasing. Of my own will I say this, I who know my affairs [my place].'

Then, anticipating his decision as subject to the judgment of his superiors, including arbitrators of the structures of language, Lionés expresses such transgressive vertical movement as a mythological *exemplum*:

> 'Non voil voler sor si haut abitaire
> 'Que, au devaler, li saiges de gramaire
> 'En lor escrit moi faicent rementaire,
> 'Ensi cun fist Dedailus et Ychaire' (13,462-65).

'I do not wish to fly unto so lofty a realm that, in coming
down, the wise men of grammar [of language] may make a
[negative] mention of me in their writings as they did with
Daedalus and Icarus.'

Universal acclamation of Lionés's " 'nobles refusee' " (13,470)
ultimately reinforces Model I hierarchism. All the prowess in the world
cannot replace noble birth, by the admission of the knighted bourgeois
himself. (Dionés eventually marries the French Anseïs de Blois, who
becomes ruler of a reconquered and reconverted Jerusalem, and is
elevated to queen of the Holy City, a particularly felicitous ending to
her story.)

Thus Daïre, acting on his son's counsel, names Lionés " 'baillis de
tote Perse' " (13,494-95). The term clearly indicates a position of
prominent leadership. Although an exact description is unclear here,
Roland's first assignment is to travel the kingdom in search of the
finest warriors to serve in the imminent war declared by a disgruntled
Malquidant. Thomas mentions only the substantive *ballior* as
"conducteur"; *Larousse* lists *bail* and *baillie*, defined as "tutelle,"
"pouvoir," "domination," "juridiction," and *bailier* as "gouverneur" and
"gardien." Godefroy: *bail* as "gouverneur, régent," and *bailli* as "tuteur."
The Holtus *Entrée* lexicon traces the word to *bailir*, v. tr., "donner" and
It. bajulare, bajulus.

In a ceremony of fealty (*infestucatio*) where Lionés receives the
symbolic "bastun," Daïre charges him " 'a governer bien ma tere toi
don' " (13,522). Through his services to Daïre and his people, Lionés
has acquired a position of high authority and has acquired a role in the
governance of the state. The narrative (Persian) audience universally
approves the appointment.

**The New *Bellator*, Warrior and Leader (locus *l*: 12,293-13,622;
segments of locus *k*)**

The Persians, "the great and the small," subsequently comment on
Lionés:

'Etre poit verité
'Que cist soit le meldre home de la Paieneté.
'Pué que le cors insenble e le cuer sunt fermé
'E qu'il sunt d'ardiment et de sens inflamé,
'Bien li est convenable une grant dignité ' (13,792-96).

> . . . 'It may be true that this is the finest man in pagandom.
> Since his body and heart are firm and are inflamed by courage
> and good sense, a position of great dignity is surely
> appropriate for him.'

In the final locus, Roland incarnates the new warrior, initiates the
organization of a new citizen warrior sector in Persia, and demonstrates
that the viability of the military sector depends on the example set by
the warrior king/leader. Empowered by the more open, flexible Persian
community, the new leader now offers similar opportunity to those
enlisting in the Malquidant conflict. Roland's criterion for selection of
men to defend their country is simple: decisions are made strictly
according to individual merit and desire to serve. The new "baillis"
demonstrates a pragmatism characteristic of a new social order:

> Chant Roland i trovoit un rice ome d'arzant
> Que fust foibles de cors et trop viels et ferant,
> Il non le voloit mie en son asenblemant,
> Mais si li fait trover uns pobre om desirant
> De cunquer honor d'armes, se d'avoir ert pusant:
> Diner, cevaus et armes il i fait douner tant
> Qu'il poit an l'ost venir bien honorablement (13,828-34).

> When Roland found a man rich in money who was weak of
> body and too old and grey-bearded, he did not want him at all
> in his armies. But if he finds a poor man desirous of winning
> honor in arms, if capable of doing so, he has such a man given
> so great a quantity of food, horses, and weapons that he can
> enter the army very honorably.

Perhaps more important, the interests of all segments of the
society are accommodated in the making of the new *bellator*: " 'Si que
le rice el poubres disent: 'Je m'en contant.' " (13,835) ("So that the rich
say to the poor: 'I am happy with it [the new system].' ") Thus the
text's dialogue between the old and new warrior order appears to relax
Model I rigidity to a degree, while at the same time remaining sensitive
to traditional aristocratic/clerical views. Such conservatism:

> est plus vigoureux peut-être que partout ailleurs au
> sein des clergés de toutes sortes, attachés au maintien
> des visions du monde et des préceptes moraux sur
> quoi se fondent l'influence qu'ils exercent et les

> privilèges dont ils jouissent. . . . L'effet de
> semblables glissements est de prolonger très
> longtemps la vitalité de certaines représentations
> mentales et des comportements qu'elles gouvernent, et
> de maintenir en contrebas d'une modernité de surface
> où les élites trouvent leur satisfaction, une solide
> assise de traditions sur quoi peuvent trouver appui les
> aspirations au conservatisme (Duby, "Systèmes de
> valeurs" 17).

Like the Roland-Ferragu duel in *Entrée* I, the Pélias combat is a
locus of multiple-issue ideological debate, closing with comments on
the governor/governed relationship. Having noted that Daïre appeared to
lack men ready to defend Dionés, Lionés offers some well-considered
advice:

> 'E vos, biaus sire', feit il, 'me resenblé
> 'Avoir de gient bone grant poverté.
> 'S'il ont raisons vers vous, ce ne sai jé.
> 'Seignor aver et cruaus et ingré,
> 'Quant devroit estre acheris et amé,
> 'Par son defaut vient dou sers esloigné:
> 'Maint de aut omes n'ont estez debasé' (12,293-99).

> 'And you, fine lord, said he, you seem to me to have a great
> poverty of good people. Whether they are right [in their
> opinion] toward you, I know not. A greedy and cruel and
> terrible lord, when he ought to be cherished and loved, by his
> own failings alienates himself from his serf: many highly-
> placed men have been brought down in this manner.'

Reference to the abuse of power, of which Roland considered
himself a victim under Charles, recalls (recovers) what Naimon and
others counselled the Emperor-*bellator* in the Thiois episode, here by a
negative corollary. The lord/governor or government which rules
tyrannically, achieving obedience solely through fear, risks the refusal
to serve on the part of its vassal/subject/citizen. "Par son defaut," the
perpetrator of abusive authority jeopardizes his own position. To his
comments on the obligations of the "bigger" party, Roland, "loial
servior" of the sultan, adds a brief codification of vassal/subject/citizen
fidelity to the deserving superior. Dismissing even the humorous
caution that causes Daïre to remove Roland from the temptations
presented by the proximity of his beautiful daughter, Roland declares:

'Home qe de tel delit seroit trop intazé,
'Le cris d'onor doit estre de li mout eslunzé.
'Qui de sun bons segnor panse desloiauté,
'Diables li governe tant qu'il ert perilé' (13,619-22).

'A man who would be too tempted by such a crime
must be very far from the voices of honor. He who
considers disloyalty toward his good lord, the devil
governs him in such a way that he will be in danger.'

Yielding to Pélias's insistent questions as to his identity (" 'Bien
sai tun peres non vit de vendre drais' "), Lionés finally discloses who he
is. " 'Mon nom dirai,' " he declares, adding that he is the son of Milon
D'Anglant and nephew of the Emperor Charlemagne. Further,
" 'Rollant, jel sui, de Rome justiser / 'Et chanpion et maitre tresorer' "
(13,116-17). The latter epithet is new to the portrait, while the judicial
function claim repeats a consistent preoccupation with justice, honor,
and law, both secular and sacred.

One notes immediately the striking syntactic parallel to the
narrator's "Mon nom vos non dirai, mai sui Patavian" of Prologue II.
Just as that authorial pronouncement introduced the poet's *prise de
position* regarding control over his text, so Roland's revelation leads
immediately to his physical control over Pélias. In *Entrée* II both poet
and protagonist have entered uncharted territory, after departing from
well-known, much-travelled spaces. Both strive to establish authorial
and Christian leadership in the world of the new text. The narrator's
conclusion at the death of Pélias fulfills the sultan's hope that Roland's
humble appearance might conceal substance and meaning of great
worth. Prior to the duel, he had said:

'A le semblance de la couse celee
'Fust huei l'ensaigne por vos desvolupee,
'Qe le cors deinz respondist a l'entree,
'Encué avroie une bone jornee' (12,133-36).

'In the semblance of the thing concealed, today the
sign was unveiled by you in such a way that the heart
within did correspond with the entry therein [the
bodily form], and so I would enjoy a fine day.'

Thus Roland's triumph over the injustices of Malquidant and Pélias
is accomplished in his own name, reidentifying him as the hero of the

new eastern world. The narrator can now reveal the significance of his victory:

> Ce senefie que ceschuns fait infance
> Que contre droit motre orgoil ne bubance.
> Chant a ce fait le niés au roi de France,
> Non par orgoil, mais por senefiance,
> Dout brant essue sor le Païn le brance (13,173-77).

> This signifies that any man behaves like a child who displays pride or self-inflation against the law/what is right. When the nephew of the king of France accomplished this [victory], not out of pride, but in the service of meaning/significance, he wiped his sword blade on the Pagan.

Roland as the nemesis of Pélias's pride adds to—and may alter— our decoding of past events, in a process of reading which does not close the individual narrative segment upon itself, but leaves it dialogically open, potentially modifying reader response in the constant play of one textual element against another. Thus the same Clador who challenged Lionés's respect of class restrictions can now deliver unqualified praise of the " 'meldre home' " in Persia, the Roland who combines "prowess with sense and moderation." Clador has, by seeing Roland in action, altered his initially negative assumptions. The text suggests that further reconsideration of characters' judgment of one another, and/or audience judgment of Roland *et alia*, may be in order to correct premature, reductionist readings. Concerning Roland and Pélias, one can now recognize a motivational polarity: Roland has acted in the interests of *droit*, while his opponent was motivated by, and died because of *orgueil* and *démesure*.

It is now clear that there is an important "senefiance" between this victory of Roland's and the sum of his previous acts in *Entrée* II. He has accomplished this feat as a performative lesson for the ultimate benefit of Charles, as he vowed upon leaving Pamplona long ago: " 'Mielz veul morir qe je ni li ensaigne / 'Se je riens li valloie en la gere d'Espagne' " (1151-52). Again, as in the Ferragu duel, Roland assumes the role of instructor imparting information and wisdom.

Roland's triumph over Pélias, which appears to the authorial public as an internal ideological conflict similar to those dominating *Entrée* I, further advances the exoneration of pride in the hero. Locus *h* (*Orgueil* Reconsidered) recast the problem and invited a more open reading of his previous and subsequent actions. The Pélias victory, Roland's last in the extant manuscript, casts a retrospective view on those same deeds. The youth's actions in the past, present, and presumably in future, are almost without exception motivated by *droit*, so that he can rightfully present himself as " 'justiser de Rome.' " His character is, as pronounced by Clador, one of " 'prouesce et sens et nature atenpre.' " Such is the new *bellator*; such is the agent of leadership as well.

The sequel *Prise de Pampelune* carries on the *Entrée's* narrative project of the conquest of a critical city on the road to Compostella, yet cannot approach the parent text in terms of conceptualization and artistry. It is interesting, nonetheless, that Nicolò da Verona, who composes his text on the single *sensus litteralis* far more than the Paduan, summarizes early in his work several fundamental elements of the *Entrée*. Thus King Desiderio, leader of the Lombard armies who have just succeeded in conquering a city which Charles had been fruitlessly assailing for years, announces his countrymen's requests for remuneration of their military service. They are three: a. their guaranteed liberty; b. the guaranteed accessibility to knighthood of all Lombards, regardless of social origin, provided the order be maintained "à honour"; c. their guaranteed right to bear arms before the emperor.

Once again, we witness in a direct, unequivocal manner, the thematics of liberty and autonomy which run throughout the ideological strata of the *Entrée*. Like Roland, the Lombards request only what they have earned, in order that the association lord/vassal, governor/governed, or simply bigger/smaller be permitted to reflect a less hermetically hierarchical rendering of that relationship. Convinced by Naimon of the importance of the requests, Charles grants all three without hesitation.

Notes

1. "This is the unforgiveable sin for Dante, that Florence in its arrogance should not only rival Rome, but should oppose the divinely ordained destiny of the empire, the only hope, as he saw it, for all of Italy. . . . Florence also treated Henry as a foreign intruder, addressing him in letters as 'King of Germany' in 1311 and solemnly banning him, . . . making it clear that it was concerned not so much with the foreign element as with the imposition of authority. . . . " Joan M. Ferrante, *The Political Vision of the Divine Comedy* (Princeton: Princeton UP, 1984) 63-64.

2. For an excellent account of the elevation of the historical Karolus, see Stephen G. Nichols, Jr., *Romanesque Signs: Early Medieval Narrative and Iconography*, especially chapter 3, "Charlemagne Redivivus: From History to *Historia*," 66-94. Nichols traces the process from the discovery of Charles's tomb in the year 1000 to the rapidly ensuing mythification evident in historical texts, art, and literature, which increasingly "refer to Charlemagne in terms of an expressive system usually reserved for Christ" (New Haven and London: Yale UP, 1983) 76.

3. The motif is borrowed from the *Pseudo-Turpin* and has been traced to *Gen.* 28: 17. As explained by Nichols, a typological reading interprets the stone as the altar of sacrifice upon which the Saracen will presently die; within the global Rolandian narrative, it is the site of Roland's own immolation at Roncevaux. *Romanesque Signs* 137-38.

4. In *Aquilon de Bavière*, Islamic doctrine is proselytized by the caliph, who rejects the divine nature of Christ and the Immaculate Conception, but offers what Peter Wunderli terms a "contribution oecuménique": differeces between Judaism, Islam, and Christianity are minimized, ultimately reduced to the point where the three are seen as variants of a single universal faith, with ideological differences attributable to historical, social, and cultural contexts. "Roland théologien dans l'*Aquilon de Bavière*," *Essor et fortune de la chanson de geste dans l'Europe et l'Orient latin*, Actes du IXᵉ Congrès international de la Société Rencesvals pour l'étude des épopées romanes: Padoue-Venise, 29 août-4 septembre 1982 (Modena: Mucchi, 1984) 2: 76:

5. The "sermon" reads:

    'Or soit par toi ma prole notee:
    'La Deité qu'en troi part est sevree
    'Et en un seul stablie et ordonee

211

'Est tot ensi come roie dolee:
'Par troi parties est fete e complee,
'Chescune part est en sa part nomee,
'Rais e muçeil e gante par seignee;
'Quant ces troi coses ont la roie adornee,
'Lor est complie; mais se nulle en desgree,
'Adonc ne est roe e ne puet estre ovree.
'Tot ensi est la candele alumee,
'Que par trois coses est de lus aparee:
'Feu e cotons e cire sorgitee.
'Se feu n'i a par ele estre atochee,
'Ne rend clarté plus come une ramee;
'Coton sans cire ne ars a la duree:
'Il fera feu e calor e fumee,
'Mais il ne giete granmant nulle flamee;
'Ne cire n'ard se ne est enstopinee,
'De feu de flanbe enprise e luminee.
'E se tu metes ta grant targe rohee
'Que j'ai de piere e fraite et pertusee,
'Prant troi pertus, de ceus que plus t'agree,
'Devant le sol soit ta targe tornee,
'Verais troi sol; e quant tu l'ais hostee,
'Un sol remant, ce est cose provee.
'En cest gise te soie demonstree
'La Tirnité en un seul Diex sclaree' (3698-725).

Now may you note my word(s): the Deity, which is divided into three parts, as well as established and ordered in One alone, is just like the flattened wheel; it is made and fashioned into three parts, each named within its own function: spokes and hub and rim by designation. When these three things have been fitted to the wheel, then it is complete; but if any is lacking, then it is not a wheel and cannot function. Just the same is the lighted candle, which is endowed with light by three things: fire, cotton wick, and wax applied to it. If there is no fire to be touched by it, the candle no longer gives brightness like a [burning] branch; a wick without wax does not burn for long. It will produce fire and heat and smoke, but it does not cast any flame for long, nor does wax burn if it is not fitted with a wick, lighted and illuminated by flame. And if you place your large round shield, which I have split and pierced with stones, and put three holes (any that you like), in front of the sun, and let your shield be turned [in different directions], you will see three suns. And when you have taken it away, one sun remains; this is a proven matter. In this manner may the Trinity in one God be clarified to you.'

6. *Aquilon de Bavière* adopts the same images. Wunderli, "Roland théologien" 159.

7. The annulment of all feudal obligation was also part of the excommunication of Frederick II in 1245, when the pope decreed that no imperial subject should henceforth provide any feudal service or obey any of Frederick's decrees.

8. "La ricca borghesia, che era uscita dalla sua fase rivoluzionaria grazie ai suoi successi economici e politici, non sentiva più la visione del mondo propugnata fin allora—razionalistica, orientata sul successo, ostile al lusso—come adeguata alla propria condizione attuale, e si sforzava di emulare la nobiltà, di cui continuava a riconoscere la superiorità culturale. . . " *Epica feudale* 218.

9. A recognizable discourse of mercantilism can be traced to the twelfth century, called *navigatio* and treated with some respect by Hugh of St. Victor: "This art is beyond all doubt a peculiar sort of rhetoric—strictly of its own kind—for eloquence is in the highest degree necessary to it. Thus the man who excels others in fluency of speech is called a *Mercurius*, or Mercury, as being a *mercatorum kirrius* [kyrios]—a very lord among merchants." *Didascalicon: de studio legendi*, ed. Charles Henry Buttimer, trans. Jerome Taylor (Washington: Catholic UP, 1939), *The Didascalicon of Hugh of St. Victor* (New York: Columbia UP, 1961) 91-92.

10. Cf. Krauss: "Il fatto che il Padovano combina il conflitto di ceto con quello religioso . . . attesta (al pari della scelta di Rolando quale esponente dell'autoscienza della nobiltà di denaro) la sua chiara presa di posizione a favore della grande borghesia protocapitalistia." *Epica feudale* 221.

CHAPTER 5
SIGNS OF *SENTENTIA*

From a tropological point of view, *Entrée* II demonstrates that the "grant/minor" relationship need not be agonistic. However, it is worth noting that the successful model is placed beyond the confines of the usual Western European geographical sites and *consueditudines*, habits or customs, where events occur which are foreign to the French epic repertoire. By concentrating on three motifs in *Entrée* II, the forest, voyage(s) and the hermit, my purpose in this chapter is to demonstrate how the poet's *causa finalis* is given form: i.e., how these particular elements function to provide the final configuration of the text. I shall then try to reveal how the Paduan utilizes this triad to complete the educative odyssey of his hero, finally to suggest that his appropriation of *sententia* involves a *correctio* of both epic and secular romance.

> En honor et en bien et en gran remembrançe
> Et offerant mercé, honor et celebrançe
> De Celui che par nos fu feruç de la lançe
> Par trer nos e nos armes de la enfernal
>   poissançe,
> Et de son saint apostre, qi tant oit penetançe
> Por feir qe cescuns fust en veraie creançe
> Que Per e Filz e Spirt sunt in une sustançe
> C'est li barons saint Jaqes de qi faç la mentanze
> ....(1-8).

In honor and in good and great remembrance and offering thanks, honor and celebration of Him who was struck by the spear for our sake, to bring us and our souls out of the infernal power, and of his holy apostle, who felt so much penitence, to bring it about that every man might be [live] in the true belief that

215

Father and Son and Holy Spirit are in one substance
it is the baron Saint James of whom I make mention
. . .

A rhetorically ornate dedication to the martyred Christ opens a text
wherein the initial premise stipulates the Crucifixion as willed sacrifice
enacted to preserve mankind from unwilled martyrdom to the powers of
evil. Dedication is likewise made to St. James, whose function as the
first apostle martyr and disseminator of Trinitarian doctrine in the West
also serves to assure the efficacy of an expedition organized to
recuperate his "plus mestre habitançe" (12) at Compostella. Allusion is
to the privileged relationship of James to Christ via the saint's
witnessing of the Transfiguration, whereby, according to Maximus the
Confessor, James was granted "the grace of participating in dialogue
with the deity" and an understanding of the monologic text of the world
and the Word, "a conjoint discourse focused on a single meaning: the
manifold made one" (Nichols, *Signs* 15).
      The story of the entry into Spain will thus be well-heeded by a
public concerned with the ethical/moral self-correction necessary to
achieve "veraie creançe" in both the specifics of Trinitarian doctrine and
of "la loy Deu" announced as a global textual thematic. The following
verses concern textual form and authorial intention:

> Vos voil canter e dir por rime e por sentençe
> Tot ensi come Carles el bernage de Françe
> Entrerent en Espagne, et por ponte de lançe
> Conquistrent de saint Jaqes la plus mestre
>   habitançe.
> Ne laserent por storme ne por autre pesanze:
> S'il n'aüsent leisié par une difirnanze
> Que lor fist Gaenelonz, le sire de Maganze,
> Coronez eüsent, n'en soiez en dotançe,
> Roland, par chi l'estorie et lo canter
>   comanze,
> Li melors chevalers que legist en sianze.
> Ben le vos dirai jé, s'un poi fetes sillanze (9-19).

I wish to sing and tell you in [by means of] rhyme
and "sentençe," (see below) the whole tale of how
Charles and the barons of France made their entry into
Spain, and by the point of the sword conquered the
greatest dwelling [shrine] of Saint James. They would
not have abandoned [the mission] on account of a

> battle nor for any other power if they had not ended it
> because of a difference [quarrel] which Ganelon, the
> lord of Mayence, brought upon them; they would
> have crowned Roland, have no doubt about it,
> concerning whom the story and song begin, the best
> knight whom men read about when they gather
> together. Indeed I shall tell it to you, if you grant
> [me] a bit of silence.

The narrator outlines a four-part approach to his text: the articulation of authorial intention predicated in direct locutionary action, then specificity of dual modalities of compositional activity.[1] Focus then turns to the form in which the text is to be cast. Revised from Turpin's prose "istorie croniquee" (48), the poet uses the term "rime" in the broad medieval sense which includes assonance, again reflecting the text's epic ancestry. The final "por sentençe" anticipates elements of form, content, and meaning as we shall see in exploring the polyvalency of the term.

A brief discussion of the word _sententia_ and its evolution to the latter Middle Ages is necessary in order to assess its application to Prologue I; we shall also look at the word used in other _Entrée_ passages. Nominal form of the verb _sentire_ with reference to the internal mental process by which cognition is acquired, _sententia_ came to be associated also with resultant opinions and judgments, as in Terence, "quot homines, tot sententiae." In this sense, it came to refer to the content or meaning of one's thoughts or opinions, differentiated from their form, i.e., the words used to express meaning (C. S. Lewis, _Words_ 138, 139).

By extension, the term designated the "sense, meaning, signification, idea, notion" of a literary text, and was used in this way by Cicero and Lucretius (Lewis-Short). Cicero also used the word with reference to profound meaning or meaningfulness (as in _Laws_ I, xxii, 58), where he says that the maxim "know thyself" must have been formulated by a god because it contains so much _sententia_ (Lewis, _Words_ 140).

The term then came to indicate a "minimal unit of speech or writing which has a complete meaning," as in aphorisms, maxims, saws, or apothegms, where _sententia_ can be a universal, impersonalized enunciation (Lewis, _Words_ 139). Thus Priscian's definition: "Sententia est oratio generalem pronuntiationem habens, hortans ad aliquam rem vel dehortans vel demonstrans qual sit aliquid" (_De pre-exercitamentis rhetoricis_ 553f.) ("_Sententia_ is discourse containing a general proposition/judgement, encouraging or discouraging something, or demonstrating what something may be").

In the twelfth century, the Ciceronian use of *sententia* as a more profound level of meaning contained in the nucleus conjoins with related notions concerning the external appearance of texts, their cortex, *integumentum*, or *involucrum* ("Integumentum est genus demonstrationis sub fabulosa narratione veritatis involvens intellectum: unde et involucrum dicitur" (B. Silvestris in Commentary on the *Aeneid*, cited in De Bruyne 2: 280) ("*Integration* is a kind of demonstration of truth beneath a fictional narrative, involving use of the intellect; whence it is also called *involucrum*"). Hugh of St. Victor describes a three-part process of textual explication:

> Expositio tria continet, litteram, sensum, sententiam. Littera congrue ordinatio dictionum, quod etiam constructionem vocamus, sensus est facilis quaedam et aperta significatio, quam littera prime fronte praefert. Sententia est profundior intelligentia, quae nisi expositione vel interpretatione non invenitur. In his ordo, ut primum littera, deinde sensus, deinde sententia inquiratur, quo facto, perfecta est expositio (*Didascalicon* 88; emphasis added).

> An exposition contains three elements: letter, sense, deeper meaning. The literal sense is the correct ordering of words, that which we also call 'construction.' Sense is facile and apparent meaning, which a literal reading initially offers. *Sententia* is deeper understanding, not found except by exposition or interpretation. In this respect, order consists of seeking the literal level first, then the sense, and finally, the profound meaning. With this achieved, the exposition is complete.

After the twelfth century, when the use of *sensus* and *sententia* became more widespread and distinctions less clear, the latter was commonly adopted to refer to the import of any text, sacred or profane: "The result of allegorical interpretation might be called either sense or sentence," with the latter more prevalent during the fourteenth century (D. W. Robertson, "Terminology" 316).

In *Entrée* II, the *sensus* relates to those multiple questions of order and governance in the rapidly-changing world discussed in chapters 3 and 4. The *sententia* or *profundior intelligentia* communicates ethical/moral and spiritual levels of meaning for those able to perceive them and to receive the wisdom of the text, "se Diex vos soit eidant" (15,354). One reaches deeper levels of meaning only after passing through *littera* and *sensus*, both of which retain their own identity and integrity.

Augustine and Rabanus claim that the nucleus of a secular or pagan text is usually a verbal convention linked to *allegoria*, and the latter warns readers to avoid "signa pro rebus accipere." Nonetheless, twelfth-century authors such as Alain de Lille confirmed that levels of deeper meaning were encoded in their works, using "things" to signify, as they do in Scripture, because "the values for things which are signs of other things in the Bible have a kind of absolute quality." Thus:

> In a poem by a well-educated Christian author we should not be surprised to find an extremely complex *cortex* made up of signs stemming both from the traditions of Scriptural exegesis and from the traditions of literary exegesis. A poet might well use signs from Scripture and figures from conventional interpretations of Vergil and Ovid in the same poem. At the same time, there was nothing to prevent him from making new allegorical inventions of his own, based on etymologies, on conceptions of natural history, or on new combinations of traditional elements. His ingenuity and enterprise in this respect were limited more by the character of his audience than by any theoretical considerations (Robertson, "Terminology" 679, 682-83).

Entrée II's forest and voyage motifs introduced as Roland departs Pamplona are semiotic indices of the text's *profundior intelligentia*. They distance the text from the traditional Rolandian and romance repertoire and signal its participation in more profound signifying activity. Thus we readily accept the phrase "por sentençe" in Prologue I as anticipating the numerous maxims, proverbs, and so forth sown throughout the *Entrée*'s 15,805 verses, such as " 'Qi a soi meïsme feit onte et mespreison, / L'en le devroit pandre come leron' " (11,067-68) (" 'He who brings shame and mistakes upon himself ought to hang like a thief' "); or, describing the misguided Ferragu preparing to do battle with Roland as a sheep who has strayed from the flock, "Ha! lor dolant en le novisme jor, / Que tard pentir torne a duel et a plor" (3,098-99)

("Ha! Those grieving on the final day, whose belated repentance turns to pain and tears").

In the second instance, however, we can already see that the poet himself distinguishes between this type of "sentençe" and another relating the narrative to further meaning. Immediately following the parenthetical commentary above regarding Ferragu, he returns to the more serious matter of the Roland-Ferragu duel, the text's first major ideological encounter: "A ma santançe m'aconvient feir retor" (3102) ("It is fitting that I return to my story and its meaning"). It is such narrative material of a deeper signifying nature which the poet will fully relate in a text which he admits will be rather lengthy, precisely because "En breu sentance dir ne la vos puet hon" (2770) ("In brief form (i.e., via proverbs, maxims, etc.,) one cannot tell you [the whole tale]").

As we saw in Chapter 1, the Paduan perceives his narrative undertaking as a kind of contract via which he has promised to recover ("recovrer") those aspects of the French expedition in Spain heretofore understood only by "gient letree." He offers, then, a literary *correctio* to the *Pseudo-Turpin* parent text in a language presumably affording greater opportunity of comprehension and dissemination. Parallel to this *correctio* is Charles's own promise to militarily "recovrer" the road to Compostella. We should not forget the seriousness with which vows and agreements drawn up between cooperating parties were taken in the Middle Ages. The Paduan's vow is not so profoundly engaging as Charles's to St. James; yet it is not difficult to believe that he labored with his text with a similar sense of mandate that in some important way his scriptural "labor" was vitally important.[2]

In *Entrée* I, character presentation, themes, and episodes reveal a general correspondence to late medieval epic norms and, in the schematic manner of the genre, to a feudal ethos. All of these elements, as we have seen, are exposed to considerable scrutiny. Roland is still the unconquered hero, though no longer unquestionably invincible; the Ferragu encounter and Pamplona Reinforcement episodes have rendered him more aware of human limitations. Charles has diminished dramatically in stature. Opening episodes depict him as defeatist, erratic, impulsive, even unethical. His authority is neither absolute nor unquestioned, as demonstrated in the five initial confrontations with Roland, where he is more or less compelled to yield, and in Naimon's chastizing "sermon" on the responsibilities of leadership. The blow culminating *Entrée* I does violence not only to Roland, but to the epico-feudal ethos upon which the text's first ten thousand verses are founded.

Displacement

The disorientation and "mespreison" of the Roland who rides away from Pamplona are not elements common to the *cycle du roi* hero. Lost in the thick forest which will open and close *Entrée* II, he brings to mind Arthurian and Dantean characters and metaphors.[3] Like Chrétien's *chevaliers errants*, Roland's passage into the forest introduces a critical new experiential phase, the onset of adventures apparently gratuitous in nature but which may contain signs of deeper meaning. The forest functions as a border space of transition between the radically different worlds of East and West. Void of signs associated with the epic world, it is, like the sea, a non-domesticated zone of unpredictable events which must be experienced in order to reach, or return to, the civilized spatiality of the Middle East or Spain. The forest is the hero's transformational space, where he must relinquish modes of behavior familiar to his epic conduct and prepare to learn the codes of an uncharted, initially menacing new world.

Just as the narrative is reorienting itself from an epic to a romance plane, Roland's disorientation reflects the hero's hesitant transition from the known epic community to the mysterious world before him. Having abandoned—or, as Roland himself claims, been forced to abandon—the world of the chanson de geste (11,150), he passes into a forest semiotically marking the alienation, despair, and disorder which such loss arouses.

In the first segment of the bipartite *planctus* (11,145-71), Roland's reaction to the blow, governed by wrath and shame, is self-defensive and self-pitying:

> 'E Diex!' dist il, 'qe is de tot cavataigne,
> 'Queil aventure m'avient por bone ovragne!
> 'Tiel honte n'ai au cors et tiel desdaigne
> 'Qe je ni sai cum l'arme ou cors remaigne.
> 'Gerpir me feit le rois ma douz compaigne;
> 'Miels veul morir qe je ni li ensaigne
> 'Se je riens li valloie en la gere d'Espagne.
> . . . .
> A soi meïsme se guermente disant:
> 'Ai! hom gravez de paine et de tormant,
> 'N'avis jameis repois a ton vivant,
> 'E començais de mout petit enfant
> 'A durer paine et estre travaillant.

'Par le vertus dou Roy omnipotant,
'Pois je bien dir qe da mort fui aidant
'A cestui roys vers li fils Agolant,
'Ke hui moi laidi ensi vilainemant'
(11,146-152; 11,157-65).

'Ah God!' said he, 'who are the leader of all things,
what a [mis]adventure in return for a good deed! I feel
such shame and disdain [anger, scorn] in my heart that
I know not how my soul remains within my body.
The king has made me abandon the sweet
companionship [of my friends]; I would rather die
than not to teach him whether I was of no value to
him in the Spanish war.' / . . . . / To himself he
laments, saying: 'Ah! Man burdened with pain and
torment, never have you had rest in all your lifetime,
and you began as a very small child to endure pain
and to labor. By the virtue of the all-powerful God, I
can say that [in protecting Charles] from death I
helped that king in his conflict with the son of
Agolant, [Charles] who today humiliated me so
villainously.'

The second part of Roland's *planctus* (11,443-69) stresses not
consciousness of transgression or readiness to repent, but again, anger
and shame regarding the blow and a sense of loss of worldly status.
Divesting himself of his armor and thus of his epic identity at the
fountain, Roland composes and glosses a micro-autobiography:

Membre lui de son pere, qe jadis fu la graine
De tot buens chevaler, quand fu mort en Ardaine;
De son aiol li mambre, de sa geste anciaine;
De ce qe i estoit feit ire ne li lontaine.
A grand onte se tient qe creature humaine
Le oüst oseç ferir, se il non portast la paine.
La couse qe tot jor un poi li fu germaine
L'a visitei e dir i fist parole vaine:
'Rollant, or estes sol en gaudine selvaine,
'Qe soliés avoir en le vostre demaine
'Vint mile chevaler por la glesie Romaine!
'Ni soloie descendre ni in camp ni en taine
'Q'as estriver n'aüse mant fils de castelaine:
'Or sui ci cum ermite qe fa la treduaine.

'Fortune de ces siegles ai bien la plus sotaine;
'Ja me cuidoie seoir bien prés la soveraine.
'Mais poi qe vostre roe me vuelt estre vilaine,
'Verés moi trepaser outre la mer autaine.
'Je sai bien le langaje de Perse e l'Aufricaine,
'La Greçoise, la Hermine, e sai la Suriaine:
'Se chevaler deu segle doit vivre en terre straine,
'Ne dot q'a mon cival poise falir l'avaine' (11,448-69).

He remembers his father, who formerly was the seed
[essence, model] of all good knights, when he died in
the Ardennes; he remembers his grandfather, his
ancient family clan; he does not go far beyond [in his
thoughts] of what made him angry. In great shame he
considers that any human being dared to strike him,
unless that man should bear the brunt of it/pay the
price. The thing /trait that was always was a little
germane to him /in his blood visited him and made
him say vain words [empty, worthless, wrong]:
'Roland, now you are alone in the wild wood, you
who used to have in your domain twenty thousand
knights for the Roman Church! Nor were you
accustomed to dismount in camp in a manner
unsuited to your station, unless there were many a
chatelain's son at your stirrup: Now I am like a
hermit who goes without food for three days. I have
[suffered] the worst fortune of any man in this world;
just a short time ago I thought I was sitting very
close to the top. But since your wheel [of Fortune]
wishes to be cruel to me, you will see me cross
beyond the high seas. I know well the language of
Persia and Africa, Greek, Armenian, and I know
Syrian: if a knight of today is obliged to live in a
foreign land, it doesn't mean that my horse must lack
hay.'

Outraged that any man had dared strike him, scion of illustrious
forbears, Roland attributes his fall to the caprices of Fortune. All those
(presumably) fixed truths of the epic knight are rendered void; Roland
has been dislodged from that canonic world. Contrasting the *solidaire*
quality of his life thus far to his present hermit-like solitude, Roland
marks the hermit status with the negative sign of exclusion from epic
collectivity. Later, toward the end of his odyssey when he encounters

the hermit Samson, Roland will recode the word with different connotations.

The text, too, has reached an impasse, revealing where the epic ethos can lead if taken to its extremes. The poet demonstrates here, *figuralitur et grosse*, that those virtues which constitute epic heroism may come into conflict with other institutionalized forms of authority, reiterating the fundamental paradox underlying the trajectory of the quasi-oxymoronic Christian hero. Further, the text in/of this idealized world is immobilized by the apparent exhaustion of its epic energies. After ten thousand lines narrating *conseils*, chivalric feats, single and mass combat, and the continuing failure to retake Pamplona, the story cannot move ahead. Having deployed, and in some instances magnified traditional epic themes and events, traced the activities of the most illustrious of its knights and emperor, the *Entrée*'s stylized epic discourse has lengthened, but the story stands still.

More important, those canons comprising our expectations as readers of the chansons de geste, i.e., what such personages do and say in a *cycle du roi* text, have not always been respected. As for the Charles-Roland situation, it appears that all possibilities of resolution have been played out in vain; the text has offered all the episodes, dialogues, and so forth that it can evoke—and it is not enough. The *Entrée*'s chanson de geste is arrested in the staticity of its own modalities.

That few voyages in medieval literature are gratuitous of meaning is a commonplace: "Il signifie toujours quelque chose; il a toujours . . . un rôle à jouer, une valeur à révéler" (Jean Subrenat, "L'attitude des hommes en face du voyage d'après quelques textes littéraires" 409). Here, Roland's act conjoins the topoi of both the Augustinian *homo viator* and Arthurian *chevalier errant*. His voyages take him from France to Spain, then to Persia, Mecca, and Jerusalem, finally returning him to Spain. They function as an exciting force literally and metaphorically to make and mark change.

The initial situation of departure thus complete, Roland begins his voyage: "Seigne son vis, a Diex se commanda; . . . Mais vil se tient qe ne sa o il va" (11,494-96) ("He makes the sign of the Cross upon his face, to God he entrusts himself; . . . But vile he considers himself who does not know where he is going"). This "vileness" is principally a deprecating self-judgment, a "mespreison" relative to Roland's sense of alienation and exclusion. Formulated proverbially and stated by the narrator within the *planctus*, the enunciation suggests further meaning to be examined below.

Following the first night spent at the magic fountain, Roland wanders aimlessly without food or drink for three days and nights.

Arriving at the sea, he meets two Saracen merchants, who see in his
disordered appearance a thief: " 'rubeor estes naturel de chamin' "
(11,542) (" 'You are a natural-born road thief' "). Offended by the
"vilenie" (11,545) imposed on him so arbitrarily, Roland refutes their
arrogance founded merely on wealth (11,544-50). The confrontation
quickly erupts into violence, in which Roland slays both Saracens. The
senseless killing of unarmed men startles a Roland who hardly
recognizes what he has become:

> 'Roland, or es vengié.
> 'Ei! cheitis home e plain de crualté,
> 'Com ais ici ton mautalent monstré!
> . . . .
> 'Sainte Marie, roïne mer de Dé,
> 'En quel desgrace sui de vos fils entré!
> 'Tuit les honor deu siegle ai oblié' (11,568-70;
> 15,574-76).

> 'Roland, now you are avenged. Ah! wretched man and
> full of cruelty, how you have demonstrated your
> wrath here! / . . . . / Holy Mary, Queen Mother of
> God, for what disgrace of your son have I set out! All
> the honors of the world have I forgotten.'

The segment closes with the narrator's comment on the dangers of
language: " 'Por ce dit voir dan Caton li Roman, / 'Grant vertus est a
metre a la lengue le fran' " (11,562-3) (" 'For this reason Sir Cato the
Roman tells the truth, it is a great virtue to apply the brake to the
tongue' ").

But voyage is also education, the etymological leading out and
away from the known, without suggestion of return; in *Entrée* II it is
progress toward destinations initially unknown. From the familiar epic
sites of Spain, Roland travels to two holy cities: Mecca, which he will
lead back from its ideological errancy, and Jerusalem, which he will
"recovrer" for the Word. In the course of these long journeys, Roland
will enter realms of experience unfamiliar to the epic character and will
rise above the gravitational force of human imperfection. Had the text
closed with Roland's departure from Persia, its *sententia* would have
remained at the levels of the *quid credas* and *quid agas*. The addition of
the Hermit episode not only alters that course, but requires an additional
rereading of *Entrée* I.

Intratextual judgments of the Charles-Roland conflicts in *Entrée* I
were consistently posited with reference to secular standards of order.

Particular interests were disputed: the timeliness of coronation, prisoner ransom, assignment of military tasks, and so on. Analysis of who prevails in each of the confrontations does little to resolve the reader's questions concerning this iconoclastic rendering of the Charles-Roland relationship. One can claim that Roland manages to prevail in conflicts 1, 2, 3, and 5, just as Charles appears to do so in 8, 9, and, possibly, 4. As for the final Nobles confrontation, Roland can be held responsible for not requesting *congé* at Pamplona, yet at the same time pardoned for abandoning Charles after the blow according to the text's rendering of the *exfestucatio*. Likewise, feudal law may excuse Charles's blow, as a justifiable response to his perception of vassalic treason, while judging less generously his denial of even a minimal defense.

When consistent, unequivocal assignation of liability for the failures of *Entrée* I is also denied by a narrator who advertised in Prologue I an educative tale, those elements must be sought elsewhere. The very failures of *Entrée* I formulate their own message, readily perceptible to a public known to champion secular governance in the '200 and '300. The several failures of such social experiments, all of which sought separation and autonomy of the lay sector, were judged by the Church as threats to sacralized hierarchism and condemned as heresy. Proliferating theories of the secularization of the human community varied from those, like Dante's, endorsing universal empire ultimately subject to Church authority, to Marsilius and William of Ockham, whose theories radically reduced Church authority and submitted it to the aegis of secular government .[4]

The repeated ambiguities, impasses, and breakdowns of *Entrée* I's secular order are the work of a narrator who presents them as inevitable and necessary in a community distracted from the essential Pauline dictum then recently reiterated by Aquinas: "Let every soul be subject unto the higher powers, for there is no power but of God." At fault within the text, in varying degrees, are all those who fail to model their actions on the immanent authority of "la loy Deu" posited in Prologue I. Admission that he has poorly used his position in power struggles within the Christian community was stated by Charles on the eve of his departure for Spain:

> 'Longemant a je feit ce qe ne funt li los,
> 'Qe totes autres cars manjue fors lui sols:
> 'A destruir Cristians ai stez trop afaros.
> 'Or entand d'esanplir la loi cil Glorios
> 'Qe par la gient humane fu stendu en la cros' (529-33).

'For a long time I have done what does not make for
praise, of all other meat [sustenance] I have eaten
[partaken] save Him alone. I have been too zealous in
destroying Christians; now I intend to observe the
law of that Glorious One who for humankind was
stretched out upon the Cross.'

Nonetheless, at the close of *Entrée* I, it is clear that he has failed to
accomplish the recovery of Christendom by embroiling himself once
again in internal conflicts: in this sense, it is Charles himself who has
created the stalemate at Pamplona, for which the price will be high.

The narrator wastes few opportunities to find Charles at fault in
these confrontations with Roland and others. Likewise, all his barons
hold him accountable for Roland's departure. Olivier speaks for them
regarding Roland's conquest of Nobles:

'Se il a bien fait, est ce donc li loer
'Qe vos l'avés ferus au retorner?
'Se il vos ennoie de Paiens geroier,
'Por qoi nos feistes de France desevrer?
. . . .
'Aler men voil; le congié vos requer.'
(11,267-70; 11,273)

' If he acted well, is this then the reward, that you
have struck him on his return? If you don't like to
fight pagans, why did you make us leave France? / . .
. ./ I want to leave; I request permission to take leave
of you.'

Olivier and the others subsequently change their minds and remain,
but toward the end of Roland's several years' absence, they again
threaten to abandon Charles unless Roland returns immediately. And in
fact, Charles himself recognizes the error of the blow almost
immediately following Roland's disappearance. Shortly thereafter,
Charles offers a qualified apology to the mutinous barons: "'Neporquant
se je ai fet ver mon niés nul desrois / 'E j'en sui reparti, sor moi cheit li
sordois' " (11,352-53). (" 'Nonetheless if I have committed any injustice
toward my nephew, and have repented of it, let the burden/responsibility
fall on me' "). When the narrator reminds us that we will comprehend
his text only "se Diex vos eidant," it is in part Charles's failure to
properly enact his own authority which is impugned.

Again toward the close of *Entrée* II, a Charles humbled by his inability to honor his pledge to St. James recognizes that his own salvation depends on the good will and collaboration of his nephew. "Con umble vois," he addresses Roland: " ' . . . Je conois / 'Qe senz vos bras non valdroie un pois . . . ' " (15,799-800) (" 'I know that without your arm [support] I would be worth nothing . . . ' ").

On the literal and *sensus* levels, one perceives what seems to be an intratextual bias which occasionally juxtaposes Roland's excessive discourse or action with valiant chivalry, generally to the advantage of the latter. However, judged by the higher laws of faith, those acts in *Entrée* I which set Roland against a superior appointed by the Divinity are violations of a hierarchism which is not open to compromise. We are reminded that in most fictional medieval texts, "la loy Deu" may not be stated, but it is not to be ignored nor misunderstood. (Lagarde cites the hierarchy of laws according to Aquinas: *lex aeterna*, *lex naturalis*, *lex humana positiva*. A second hierarchy is added: *lex aeterna*, *lex gratiae* ("loi de grâce"), *lex divina positiva* . While all other laws exist in relation to something else ("ad aliquid") eternal law is immutable. Accordingly, *lex aeterna*

> n'est que la norme suivant laquelle l'univers tout entier et chacune de ses parties s'ordonnent à la fin suprême qu'ils poursuivent. Cette loi éternelle, vue du côté de l'Etre pur, n'est autre que la sagesse divine elle-même considérée sous l'aspect des fins qu'elle a imposées à la création . . . . Vue du côté de l'être créé, elle est l'ensemble des forces qui guident le monde de la matière et les êtres vivants que n'éclaire pas la lumière de la raison. En chacun d'eux, la loi est présente comme un esprit secret, qui anime toute la création (Lagarde 1: 65-66).

When in Prologue II the poet announces that his subsequent text means "to praise all Roland's works," (10,991) precisely for their exemplary value: "Car la bontié Rollant ne feit bien a tesir" (10,994) ("For it is not proper to [leave in] silence the goodness of Roland"), he signals the Roland embarking on a corrective odyssey, who will emerge in *Entrée* II: Spain as a quasi-hagiographical figure. The expiation process is realized in the narrative vehicles of the Dionés and Malquidant episodes, where Roland re-forms the "grant"/"minor" relationship in the *consilium* and *auxilium* he offers to the sultan. In the course of the extant text, both character and public reaffirm the truth that "quiconque en effet s'insurge, même à bon droit, contre un mauvais souverain, s'attaque moins à un homme indigne qu'à une fonction sainte" (Jean-Charles Payen, *Le Motif du repentir* 165). Behind this stands the Biblical "He who defies authority condemns himself." The transgression is *superbia*.

But in order to comprehend the corrective process, we must look back to its inception as Roland leaves Pamplona. As the *planctus* indicates, Roland is entirely absorbed by a wrath and shame which the narrator characterizes as "mespreison" and "parole vaine." He is not utilizing the "raison e droit" which the text commonly ascribes to him. On the contrary: "Mais tant vient cumbatuz des autres esperis / Que cunfortent venjance sor ce que i est mespris" (11,768-69). ("But he is assailed by other thoughts which lend comfort to the vengeance concerning which he is mistaken").

Even on the return from Nobles, advised by Hestout that Charles might not approve his decision, Roland defends his " 'bon ovragne' " and declares " 'Ancor ne m'an repant.' " He adds, however: " 'E se folie fais, ancor amendrai.' "

But if Roland does not readily recognize the gravity of his error now, it is important the the *Entrée* public see more clearly. From the perspective of a higher law, it is not merely the unannounced departure of which Charles accuses him nor any single event, but the accumulation of conflictual situations in which Roland fails to honor his similarly sacralized functions. At times in both the Middle Eastern and Spanish segments of II, a tropological reading of the text seems like those "dense mists" in Scripture about which Augustine wrote:

> I do not doubt that this situation [complexity of the Word] was provided by God to conquer pride by work and to combat disdain in our minds, to which those things which are easily discovered seem frequently to become worthless (*OCD* 2, 6, 7).

A somewhat oblique reference to Roland's *superbia* is made by the narrator introducing his second *planctus*. If we read the subject of 11,454-55 ("La couse qe tot jor un poi li fu germaine / L'a visitei e dir i fist parole vaine"; emphasis added) as the flaw or trait which was always "a little germane to him," thus somewhat inherent to Roland's character, we can see that the "parole vaine" is the empty, erroneous discourse immediately lamenting the loss of status, and decrying the cruelty of Fortune. It then becomes clear that some nature of *orgueil* is the flaw in question. The issue of pride, always an element in a Rolandian text, encourages him to decry an unmerited exile, protest his innocence, deny even partial responsibility for the rupture with Charles.

Thus the narrator's predication of the *planctus* as futile, vain language casts a different judgment on Roland's acts and the more problematic self-righteous discourse Roland has employed to justify them.[5]

Just as Roland must overcome "la couse qe tot jor un poi li fu germaine" and come to understand his errors, the reader/public must labor to comprehend the *sententia* of this text. If the effort is greater, so are the pleasures, for "no one doubts that things are perceived more readily through similitudes and that what is sought with difficulty is discovered with more pleasure" (*OCD* 2, 6, 8).

Accordingly, on the feudal/vassalic axis, Roland's resistance to and criticism of his seigneur's will in the Isoré, Thiois, and Pamplona Reinforcement conflicts become verbal acts of progressively strident insubordination. If Charles, as the sacralized leader of the mission, is to exercise his directive function, he must be presumed to possess the requisite rational faculty to ensure professional competence and moral authority. Summarizing the link between reason and leadership, Aquinas wrote: "Rationis est imperare et ordinare " (*S.T* la, 2ae, qu.17, art.1). Should he, as Aquinas's "persona publica," judge opportune the execution of a royal prisoner, that judgment is to be obeyed. Likewise, Charles may justifiably quell the Thiois mutiny by whatever means he deems appropriate. At fault, according to the *lex aeterna*, are the Thiois and those who refuse to cut them down. In each case, the underlying premise is that these, and all Charles's decisions, are made in the interests of the collective good of the global mission, the needs of which he understands better than anyone else, and of which he is the living enactor. Society's mission, as stipulated by Aquinas, is to realize the *bonum commune* of the *multitudo*. From its smallest familial unit to the city, nation, and world community, "Tout bien commun sera action, volonté, tension de personnes vers le bien d'un ensemble de personnes" (Lagarde 2: 69-72). The fact that several of Charles's judgments do not seem reasonable to his vassals does not sanction disobedience. Roland's unauthorized leavetaking based on an independent reading of the battle for Pamplona is the most grave of a series of defiant words or actions for which he is to be held accountable.

Similarly, at the *figuralitur* level, communal resistance to imperial will appropriately exercised in the secular realm is erroneous in the sense that all law concerns moral issues and the maintenance of order. Incessant friction in the multiple interrelationships operating within any commune may summarily indicate what occurred, but in those instances where the Church sanctioned imperial participation and regulation of communal affairs, the latter had an obligation to respect justifiable use of authority. The text's figural play of authority-autonomy between commune and empire reiterates necessary cooperation if the common good is to be served. A commune claiming absolute independence from established institutions fails to recognize political and economic realities. The medieval *civitas* is always bound to larger social configurations and to its Creator: "la cité a beau être un 'tout.' Elle n'est jamais souveraine, au sens moderne du mot, car elle trouve toujours au-dessus d'elle un tout plus vaste, au regard duquel elle ne vaut que comme partie" (Lagarde 2: 85). At the same time, an imperial vicar or edict denying any self-regulation of communal affairs violates his function as "retors de tere."[6] Maintenance of order within these diversified communities, where several authorities must accept one another's "raison e droit," is the basis of the Thomist theory of pluralism:

> En sympathie profonde avec l'ordre politique de son temps, saint Thomas professe que le 'pluralisme' assurant le jeu d'innombrables 'droits' à l'intérieur du Droit, de multiples sociétés à l'intérieur de l'Etat, de divers 'régimes' à l'intérieur de l'ordre, est l'application naturelle de la loi fondamentale de multiplicité qui est dans la nature profonde de l'ordre. . . . La centralisation unificatrice tue. L'ordre vivifie. La centralisation égalise. L'ordre différencie. La centralisation anémie les sociétés secondaires. L'ordre les suscite et les fait s'épanouir en floraisons, de plus en plus denses (Lagarde 2: 80).

The forest which Roland now enters realizes the pathless wastes of spiritual error. Rejected by the epic world by Charles's death sentence, Roland in turn vindictively rejects that same world. At the same time, although rent by conflicting feelings "d'amer et desamer" (11,763), Roland prays for the emperor's well-being.

Regarding the transition from medieval epic to romance literature, Bakhtin comments:

> The epic wholeness of an individual disintegrates in a novel. . . . A crucial tension develops between the external and internal man, and as a result the subjectivity of the individual becomes an object of experimentation and representation . . . . Co-ordination breaks down between the various aspects: man for himself alone and man in the eyes of others. This disintegration of the integrity that an individual had possessed in epic [and in tragedy] combines in the

novel with the necessary preparatory steps toward a
new, complex wholeness on a higher level of human
development (*Imagination* 37-38).

Now Roland, and his reader/public, must re-view a world in which
the dangers of pride are always more grave than those of the battlefield.
Roland's task henceforth will be to correct that vision which led him to
question and finally defy the authority of the *lex divina*. His lighthearted
remark to Hestout returning from Nobles (" 'E se folie fais, ancor
amendrai' ") now may be read as more serious, if still subconscious,
intentionality, if indeed he is judged to be in error. That judgment, as
stipulated in the gift horse speech, will always be subject to Charles's
perception: mobility, autonomy, and the like are granted " 'se il [the
subordinate] feit bien e [the superior] ne le voit felons' " (6665;
emphasis added).

Roland prefaces his voyage with an *assimilatio* in a prayer relating
the fall of God's angels for their *superbia*—and a reminder that the
Creator delivered explicit orders to man on the perils of violating the
divine *Ordo*. The prayer concludes with an(other) oblique acknowledge
of transgression: Roland hopes that he may utilize this voyage to better
learn the tenets of a higher law: " 'Et cest çamin me faites en tal gise
fornir / 'Que mielz me soit a l'arme par le vos loi emplir / 'E onor n'ait
sainte Glise, qe devons mantenir ' " (11,761-63) (" 'Help me to make
use of this journey in such a way that it may make me better armed to
fulfill your law, and may Holy Church, which we must maintain,
acquire honor from it' ").

It is pertinent that the Roland entering Part II has at his disposal
knowledge of other languages beyond the now-devalorized French epic
lexicon. "Apris de maint latin," Roland will find need first for his
linguistic, rather than chivalric skills in his *errance* (11,522-23). He
will presumably be able to replace the language of *orgueil/superbia*
with the superior language of "la loy Deu" and to participate in the
dialogue with the Creator in which every man may engage as a member
of the universal order. Roland's linguistic competence is more than a
touristic convenience. It will facilitate his mobility and, more
important, ensure his comprehension of foreign social codes through
which the corrective process will emerge.

Augustinian sign theory emphasizes the importance of a knowledge
of languages for the beginning exegete seeking the will of God in
Scripture, "lest he be impeded by unknown words and locutions" (*OCD*
3, 1, 1) in the corrective speculum of *Entrée* II. Roland's success in his
quest will depend significantly on his ability to interpret both language
and human behavior in the semiotically fertile experience which lies

ahead. For the reader/public, forest and voyage are the marker points where, in our effort to interpret Roland's experience in this strange new world, we begin to "think beyond the impression the thing itself makes upon the senses;" i.e., to apply the Augustinian definition of sign (*OCD* 1, 1). Roland's first gesture is to impose semioticity upon all his future experience when he "seigne son vis," thus marking his person with the immanence of his faith.

Both forest and voyage were signs familiar to a Trecento public, *signa translativa* of courtly romance, yet also of texts such as the *Divina Commedia*. The transference necessary from a secular romance interpretation to Roland's spiritual self-correction is readily made; Augustine, again, repeatedly stresses the polyvalence of language and the possibility that a word may signify differently (i.e., water to signify people in Apoc. 17.15; 19.6 and the Holy Spirit in John 7.38; *OCD* 3, 25, 36). Further, a word may signify contrary, even incompatible things in Scripture (i.e., the lion as Christ in Apoc. 5.5 and Satan in Pet. 5.8). Context will determine the positive or negative signifying activity of words used as signs: "Thus one thing signifies another and still another in such a way that the second thing signified is contrary to the first or entirely different" (*OCD* 2, 1).

Transference of this kind will govern *Entrée* II: Spain. The hermit evoked in Roland's *planctus* (" 'or je sui cum hermite' ") foreshadows the "real" Samson. Initially marked by isolation, separation from the collectivity of the epic world, Samson will materialize in the final episode as the living sign of human sanctity, Roland's final teacher and model. In a tropological reading, then, epic discourse belongs to the old language and old world of secular values and systems of authority.

Entrée I, culminating in the failure of the military task and pseudo-death of the hero, also demonstrates the limitations and potential dangers of the genre. To the ethical *correctio* of customs and beliefs, we may add a metatextual parallel. The poet has written a chanson de geste about the genre as textual production, the correction (but not annulment) of which will form the point of departure for *Entrée* II.

The next phase, then, is for Roland to move into the next literary world of romance. In 367, the narrator had pronounced his negative opinion of Arthurian narrative, dismissed those "flabes d'Artu" popular in the elegant courts of the "joyeuse Marche." Such literary frivolity stands opposed to his own "gloriose cançons," the full significance of which has not yet been revealed. We thus become aware that Roland's *entrée* into the world of secular romance can only be part of a longer journey; unlike some medieval heroes, he will not complete his

trajectory at the stage of *romanisation*. His presence amidst amorous
princesses and luxurious courts is doubly educational: Roland, like the
reader/public, must enter and experience this somewhat dazzling,
seductive world in order to appraise its flaws according to a higher law.
Thus, just as he did in *Entrée* I, the Paduan composes a model romance
text in order to demonstrate the limitations of the genre. He integrates a
Roland therein who will utilize the experience to recognize and correct
previous failings. Yet once Roland *becomes* the ideal romance hero in
the Persian court, he must reject that model, too, as incomplete and
imperfect.

Progress in the internal voyage manifests itself in the first major
episode of *Entrée* II when Roland offers to defend the Princess Dionés.
In an axiomatic *sententia* advocating the new language of humility and
moderation which he is acquiring, Roland explains how one's discourse,
in both content and delivery, becomes a sign of the propriety of one's
acts:

> 'Por trop mus estre n'est nul home sené
> 'E por trop dir ne vient il pais lohé.
> 'Home qi veult parlant estre honoré
> 'Dou poi, dou trop doit estre amesuré.
> . . . .
> 'Voulez, segnor, conoistre un tort prové?
> 'Quant cil qi a droiz oul tort vient apelé,
> 'Il senpre parle paisible et atempré,
> 'E le tort huche con se fust forsené:
> 'Senefiance est qu'il se sent dané' (12,280-83; 12,287-
> 91).

> 'No wise man is too silent, and the peasant does not
> win praise by saying too much. A man who wishes
> to be praised in his speech must measure his words so
> as not to say too little or too much. / . . . . / Lords,
> do you want to recognize a proven wrong? When he
> who is right is called wrong, he always speaks in a
> calm and temperate manner, and the man in error yells
> as if he were out of his senses: the meaning is that he
> feels himself condemned/ judged guilty. '

Following Roland's victory over Pélias, the narrator comments on
"desmesurance" as the cause of the Persian's demise: "Ce senefie que
ceschuns fait infance / Que contre droit motre orgoil ne bubance"
(13,173-74)   ("This signifies that a man behaves like a child who,

contrary to [what is] right/law, demonstrates pride or an inflated ego"). According to the *profundior intelligentia* in the following verses describing Roland acting "Non par orgoil, mais por senefiance" (13,176), we may recode "droit" as divine law, which only the unformed child and uninformed proud are rash enough to challenge. In a more overt statement, the deeper text seems to condemn any act of rebellion against rightful authority.

Progress in the ethical sphere is likewise evident in Roland's refusal of rewards in the opulent Persian court, insisting that, unlike Icarus, he has no desire to challenge divine Order. Such transgression, the mortal's assumption of his right to approach the source of power and perhaps appropriate (some of) it for himself, would, in Roland's words, merit the condemnation of the learned, wise men of this world, " 'li saiges de gramaire' " (13,463). It is these sages who know the rules of language and how they are connected to the larger ordering of men in society. Once again, the uses of language are at issue, for to accept reward would be to revert to the "parole vaine" of pride. The proliferation of languages (polyglot and heteroglot) plays an important role in the *Entrée*. While Part II: Middle East challenged the epico-feudal discourse of Part I, Part II: Spain reinstates, i.e., recovers the language of faith as the primary authority of human thought and expression.

Thus as Roland prepares to leave the Mideast, his fellow knights seek to detain him with the suggestion that he lead an attack on the Tower of Babel. "La tor ou des langajes fist Nembrot les divis" (14,145) ("The tower by which Nimrod brought about the separation of languages"), sign of communicational disorder and division of men, must be brought down. Its appropriate conqueror would be the Roland who has lived these confusions himself. Since he is now better equipped to defend and disseminate the Word, it is Roland whom the text proffers as restorer of correct language. It is indeed true that "language reports the world . . . and language constitutes the world."[7]

We may now concur with Prince Samson that Roland possesses " 'proesce et sens et nature atenpree.' " Of these qualities, the first is most evidently epic, while "sens" may allude to the ethico-moral implications of common sense and knowledge of the order of things in *Entrée* II. "Nature atenpree" stands in direct contrast to earlier statements regarding the Roland "qe ne garde a mesure / vuelt seguir sa nature." Roland has rechannelled his epic energies to recognize their proper source and end, the *lex aeterna*.[8] He can now reformulate his conquest of Nobles and attribute his victory to "l'aute Vertu qui li avoit donee" (13,504).

The culmination of Roland's expiational quest, along with the final shifting of the narrative axis, appears in the Hermit episode. The text now accommodates the anagogical, generally acceptable in application to fictional texts by the fourteenth century. Delineated by J. B. Allen, it is:

> . . . not the text, but something extra-textual which may be assimilated. Biblically, the anagogical level is prophetic—it evokes heaven, last things, ideal possibilities. . . . In medieval terms, the probable best term for this anagogy is figural prosopopoeia. Ideal doctrines, concepts, or possibilities for existence, taken not propositionally (that would be allegorical merely) but as if materially existing in their ideal form—these are the anagogy of a nominalist world, which has given up philosophical realism without yet being able to give up the need for the real presence of the true (*Ethical Poetic* 214).

The hermit Samson is an ancient holy man whose introduction into the narrative adds the thematic of asceticism to that of militant faith. The hermit in medieval literature functions as a presence on the knight's voyage, to stop the fallacious quest or adventure and to aid him to see the truth (J. - P. Perrot, "Le Sens de l'errance" 487). He is counsellor, judge, and restorer of order to/in the mind of the chevalier. In terms of the Word, he is one of " 'li saiges de gramaire,' " whose example can provide beneficial structure to quest experience.

Logically, as penitent seeking the best modality of human existence, Roland reveals his name and status to Samson (14,768-69), who in turn discloses their meaning and mandate:

> 'qant Rolant ais en non,
> 'Fais adonch q'il ne mante dou nom l'antencion,
> 'Car roe de siance dois estre por raison;
> 'Mais qi a Deu ne sert n'est saje ni prodon' (14,781-84; emphasis added).

'When you have Roland for a name, behave (live) in such a way that your conduct does not belie the intention of the name, for you are rightfully to be a wheel of wisdom/knowledge/science; but he who does not serve God is neither wise nor worthy.'

This curious pseudoetymology is based on the (erroneous) Latin form ROTHOLANDUS, and is probably borrowed from an apocryphal letter of Pope Calixtus II. Commonly appended to *Pseudo-Turpin* manuscripts, the letter reads: "Rotholandus interpretatur rotolus scientiae, quia omnes reges et principes omnibus scientiis imbuebat." (Thomas, 2: 303n, notes, cited from *Pseudo-Turpin, Hist. Karoli magni et Rotholandi,* ed. Castets 65).

Thus the name itself is replete with *sententia* which its bearer is charged to enact. Endowed almost with a will of its own, the name intends to identify a man of consummate learning and wisdom, the new ways of learning via the faculty of reason.[9] "Reason" is a high-frequency word in the *Entrée*; indeed, Roland based his *apologia* on Christian doctrine on the compatibility of faith and reason. In the Latin definition, Roland as the wheel of knowledge, learning, and wisdom, instructs the "reges et principes," the "retors de ter" and "hom soveran"; extratextually, these would be the old, "grant" authorities, feudal or imperial, to be enlightened in innovative methods of governance. As king-to-be, Roland must be, in the sense of both obligation and destiny, a paradigm of learning and intelligence; mindful, however, that all secular authority serves its divine superior.

The wheel of "sciance" as the determining force directing human behavior annuls the random rotation of the wheel of Fortune charged in Roland's *planctus* with his fall from grace. In the text's fullest *expositio* of his response to Charles's blow, Roland tells Olivier that he was so consumed by shame and wrath (" 'ontance' " and " 'irance,' " 15,559, 15,561):

> 'Qe je perdi de tot bien conosançe;
> 'De vos ne d'autre n'avoie remembrançe,
> 'Tan che non fu torné in ma siançe,
> 'Car vos savez, bien vore est la sentançe
> 'De celu saje che en son dir comançe:
> '*Cum furor in cursu,* e quand ire t'avançe,
> '*Currenti cedi furori,* et abstinançe
> 'Si feit t'amer; de li seit recordançe' (15,562-69).

> 'That I lost the knowledge of all good; of you or of anyone/anything else I had no memory, until I returned to my senses, for you know well that the proverb is true of that wise man who begins in his saying: *Like madness in a race* [out of control], and when wrath pushes you forward, *racing yields to madness,* and thus abstinence [from such madness,

control of wrath, temperance] makes you be loved; let
there be remembrance of this.

"Loss of knowledge of all good"—rhetoric which recalls the sinners
of Dante's *Commedia*. Initially aware merely of losing knightly
prestige and its trappings, Roland now recognizes the greater
significance of " 'tot bien.' " It is acceptance and submission to law,
human and divine, which constitute the hierarchy binding him to
Charles, and both to God. *Ira* is one of Dante's sins of incontinence
(after Aristotle's *Ethics*), aptly characterized here as a sin of excessive
movement which seizes the mind and runs away with it. It is the
contrary of action directed "por raison." Roland now expresses the
achieved goal of his internal voyage: he has " 'torné in [ma] siançe,' "
nearly ready for reconciliation with Charles. He has reacquired the
mind's mastery of informational learning, and the existential knowledge
of immanent order.

Of past errors, Roland wants no mention: " 'Cangiez cestu latin' "
(15,700): efface that language of "parole vaine," of failings now
overcome. Roland here cites Dionysius Cato in the language of " 'tot
bien' ":

> '*Post inimiciciam* a remenbrer le iror,
> 'Est la costume, frere, de malditor.
> '*Litis preterite*, dit le nostre autor
> 'Non doit saje hon estre remenbreor' (15,707-10).

> '*After a quarrel*, to remember the wrath is the custom,
> brother, of the slanderer/gossip. *Past hostilities*,' says
> our author, 'a wise man does not remember.'

Remembrance is reserved for the good events; the rest should be left to
oblivion as occurs at the summit of Dante's *Purgatorio* in the waters of
Lethe.

Intertextually, the verse (" 'Mais qi a Deu ne sert n'est saje ni
prodon' ") evokes the Oxford *Chanson*'s much-discussed 1093: "Rollant
est proz e Oliver est sage." Recuperating the two epithets, the *Entrée*
affirms that neither epic *prouesse* nor *sagesse* alone is sufficient to
portray the hero of his corrected text. "Mais" invalidates the secular
semantic field of both terms, which must henceforth be interpreted and
enacted as components of the more clearly predicated *miles Christi*.

He is also "preux et sage" in the chanson de geste compilation of
Marciana XIII (Krauss, "Analyse" 790). Wunderli observes that in the
Franco-Italian *Aquilon de Bavière*:

> Cette idéalisation, ce 'perfectionnement' du personnage de Roland a pour conséquence qu'il réunit en lui, à partir d'un certain moment, toutes les qualités qu'originellement étaient réparties sur plusieurs protagonistes. Ainsi Roland, dans l'*Aquilon*, n'est pas seulement *preu*, mais il est aussi *sage*: il a ainsi assimilé la fonction d'Olivier. ...

While most scholars have commended the eloquence and erudition of *Entrée* II's prayers and religious debates, Wunderli finds those aspects of the "théologisation" of Roland exaggerated, repetitious, and too long: "Nous avons affaire à une sorte de propagande en faveur du protagoniste" ("Roland théologien" 2: 760, 775).

In the phrase " *'Ecce servus Domini,'* " Roland adopts the linguistic system of " 'li saiges de gramaire,' " or Dante's " 'coloro che sanno,' " the wisest of men. His new language marks his reaffirmation of the Church's *auctoritas*, and informs us how to interpret his remaining acts. Self-predicated " *'servus Domini,'* " Roland at last publicly discloses his true identity. The two pseudo-identities assumed in the East (Bacharauf and Lionés) were fabricated personae with personal and ideological animosities toward Charlemagne. They were, and were not Roland, serving both to enact his alienation, yet preserving the essence of his bond (*vinculum*) with Charles for future reconstitution.

The schematic autobiographical text which Roland composes in answer to Samson's queries tells of the expedition to Spain, conquest of Nobles, and of Charles's angry blow (14,765-79). Of these events, "[d]e la prise de Noble e dou roi corocé / Con le feri dou guant i dist la verité" (14,773-74) ("Of the capture of Nobles and how the enraged king struck him with the glove"), the narrator remarks only that Roland tells the truth. Acknowledgement of error occurs somewhat elliptically when Roland says he is doing what is in his power to extinguish the evil of Islam and asks God: " 'Qu'il m'otroit mieus a fere que n'ai jusqu'a cist pon ... ' " (14,790-91) (" 'that I be allowed to do better than I have until this point' "). Roland, and presumably the *Entrée* public, have by now learned the " 'liçon' " of the third epistle of John paraphrased here: " 'car ja nos dit l'Apostre en une sa liçon / 'Qui por autrui feit bien en a bon geardon,' " (14,794-95) (" 'He that doeth good is of God: but he that doeth evil hath not seen God' ").

The more extended and glossed autobiography that Samson now narrates constitutes the last—and best—exemplary tale of Roland's voyages (14,799-931). The hermit prefaces his text with counsel: " 'Entand e met en ovre, se avrais gran merite, / 'Car le queison de l'ovre non est mie petite' " (17,804-05) (" 'Listen and put to work, if you

would have great merit, for the issue [question, subject] of the work is
hardly insignificant' "). If Roland listens, understands, and puts into
practice what he hears, " 'le uns poroit de l'autre aucune profit traire' "
(14,698) (" 'the one can benefit from the other' "), where "the other"
indicates authorial audience, such as the narratee himself. Samson is
expressing one of the principal aspects of the ethical poetic, that:

> a medieval person who wishes to be ethically good
> could achieve that condition by acting as if he were in
> a story—that is, by submitting to the assimilatio of
> becoming the story's tropology, or its letter, or (very
> occasionally), its anagogy (Allen, *Ethical Poetic*
> 292).

Admonishing Roland to avoid " 'pechié criminaus,' " (14,806),
Samson reveals the three transgressions, each in defiance of paternal
authority, that led him to this life of penitent solitude. As a prideful
boy, son of a Roman senator and raised in a privileged environment,
Samson stole and gave to friends his father's weapons, clothing and
horses (" 'Les armes a mon pere, si dras e si chevaus' " 14,817).
Discovered one day by his father, who slapped him in anger, the youth
became so enraged that he killed the count, and when they surprised
him, his mother and brother as well. Under the power of " 'le angle
faus' " (14,831), Samson fled to the forest without food or drink, where
he recognized his error and began immediately to repent. He then
confessed directly to the pope in Rome. Granting absolution, the pope
chose not to impose a specific penance, but to let the " 'vergonios e
faus' " (14,833) devise his own. Thus Samson removed from his body
all vestimentary signs of his status and identity, living " 'a guise
d'animaus' " in a desert (14,869). Then, setting out for the shrine of St.
James at Compostella, he encountered a hermit, to whom he again
narrated his transgressions. He remained with the hermit until the
latter's death, when a celestial voice told him that his food, bread and
apples, would henceforth be provided. When he saw a sword on the
chapel's altar and was tempted to use it against the "pagans" who
interrupted his constant reading of the Word, a voice again counselled
him: " 'Ja non soies doutans' " (14,890) (" 'Be not doubtful' ").
Thereupon Samson took up the sword and has been slaying the heathen
giants roaming the forest ever since.

" 'Se Diex vos seit aidant,' " Roland and the *Entrée* public will see
that the hermit's narrative is a *mise en abyme* of his own trajectory, and
will comprehend the *sententia* culminating here. In the first of his sins,
the prodigal son Roland repeatedly abused filial privilege and defied

Charles's natural authority. Secondly, desertion after the blow was tantamount to killing the emperor. Indeed, Charles says to Roland at their reunion: " ' . . . resuresi m'avois / 'Da mort a vie; . . .' " (15,792-93) (" ' . . . You have resurrected me from death to life' "). Finally, Roland's desertion destroyed the chances for imminent victory at Pamplona, preventing further progress toward Compostella.

A further series of parallels assimilates the misuse of three specific possessions of Samson's father to elements central to *Entrée* I's gift horse speech. The "dras" recall the "marchandise" of the hypothetical merchant of the conflict structure's plateau phase; the "chevaus" of Samson's father recovers the gift horse itself. Finally, " 'les armes a mon pere' " denote his father's weaponry, which the boy took and put to poor use, but plausibly connote independent activities ordinarily permissible only with parental authority, which had evidently not been granted. Samson describes his habitual conduct with three verbs in the imperfect: "Anbloie" means both "to steal" and to apply a given equestrian gait (a brisk walk); " 'I used to steal, or amble about with his horses.' " " 'I engaged in ribaldry and debauchery' " issues from "ribaudoie," and " 'I used to spend, or dispensed his possessions among my friends' " translates " 'despandoie entr' aus.' " Application of such blatant delinquency may at first seem hyperbolic—but might well likewise describe Charles's judgment of his nephew's behavior upon his return from Nobles.

It is thus by the hermit's narrative that we are able to see the full extent of Roland's transgressions and to comprehend the long "penitançe" he has undergone. Seen tropologically or anagogically, he was wrong to resist "la loy Deu" sanctioning Charles's authority. Wrong to abuse the emperor's largesse, wrong to leave Pamplona. Samson's immediate remorse is more clearly conveyed than Roland's; yet it is by the clarity of Samson's determination to repent that we see like-minded intentionality beyond Roland's initially self-righteous posturing. Roland, like Samson, wandered in the forest divested of his chivalric trappings. He, too, independently devised the enactment of his own penance, expiating his errors by behavior " 'fort e ardi' " (14,862). If equally explicit acknowledgement of guilt and penance are less clearly articulated in Roland's *planctus* and tale of his life, it is the poet's preference that the long journey of moral and spiritual correction be narrated *grosse et figuraliter* in the events of *Entrée* II. Reunited at the close of the text, Roland and Charles both fall to their knees and ask one another for forgiveness. By the example of Samson *viator*, the *Entrée* public finally comprehends Roland's own experience; by the introduction of an assimilative narrative, the *sententia* of Roland's experience is clarified. The strategy is not uniquely literary: in medieval

legal proceedings, lawyers told and retold the story of the case until its
form, content, and meaning were clear. Then it was judged (Allen,
Ethical Poetic 279).

From repeated insubordination to alienation from the community
and ensuing retribution, the hermit's narrative recovers the *profundior
intelligentia* of Roland's own. In fact, Roland says, he has already heard
Samson's story—in the form of a cautionary tale told by priests in
church. Roland's only difficulty is that, " 'en dit qe,' " people said that it
happened a century ago, a recollection which Samson confirms. Roland
and the *Entrée* public are now entering the world of the Christian
merveilleux where time and truth rise to the higher planes of anagogy.
The facts of Samson's récit are verifiably "true," although the man who
lived them has transcended, and will enable Roland to transcend, that
limited world.

To enhance the credibility of the mission by which he has slain the
Saracen giants impinging on his meditation, Samson tells Roland that
to see them was to believe in the books we know about the heroes of
old:

> 'Tu bien avroies dit de croire les romans
> 'E de Rome e de Troie e dou tens ancians
> 'E q'il fust verité la force des jaians,
> 'D'Erculés e d'Antheu e de Febus le grans' (14,914-
> 17).

> 'You would have done well to believe the romances
> both of Rome and Troy of days gone by and that the
> might of the giants was the truth, of Hercules and
> Antenor and Phebus the great.'

Samson's narrative has twice entered Roland's life; only after the
second telling, having in some ways lived it himself, can he understand
its meaning for him. For the medieval listener/reader, "when one
understands a real event, it is because one has seen it in the shape of a
literary event" (Allen, *Ethical Poetic* 261).

Roland "marvels in the way of a wise man who strengthens his
courage beyond the impossible" ("se merveille a guise d'ome sage /
qi desor l'inposible n'aferme son coraje" 14,918-19). The wisdom which
he has acquired opens him to experience beyond the merely human.
Now, he will believe those heroic tales told by priests and written in
books (" 'Or cro gie bien d'Ector e dou bon duch d'Archaje' " 14,925). In
the medieval sensibility, boundaries between fact and fiction, history,
legend, and myth, are, as we now know, far less rigidly drawn. The
world itself, simultaneously and eternally comprehensible and full of

marvels, is a book waiting to be opened and read, as the well-cited statement by Hugh of St. Victor indicates: "Universus enim mundus sensibilis quasi quidam liber est scriptus digito Dei . . . et singulae creaturae quasi figurae quaedam sunt, non humano placito inventae sed divino arbitrio institutae ad manifestandam invisibilem Dei sapientiam"(*Didasc.*, 7, c. 814). Perhaps even better known:

> Omnis mundi creatura
> quasi liber et pictura
> nobis est in speculum;
> nostrae vitae, nostrae mortis,
> nostri status, nostrae sortis
> fidele signaculum
> (cited in De Bruyne 3: 338, attribution uncertain).

Every creature of this earth is like a picture or a book: it is a mirror of ourselves. It is a faithful mark of our life and of our death, of our state and of our fate.

As Allen affirms:

> The basis, of course, is the conventional medieval authority of books, which supports, not the truth which can be verified, but the truth of 'fama,' the truth which is believed because everyone has said it . . . . Apparently it is possible for history to be at once true, and the story of events which possess a canonical shape—as if history, in spite of its bewildering and at times absurd variety, will subject itself to a kind of medieval Proppean analysis . . . (*Ethical Poetic* 257, 260).

The narration of these stories by Samson and Roland has been carried out in "leur Roman lengaje" (14,930), another curious bit of linguistic ambiguity as to the old or new languages.

The Roland who now asks Samson to reveal how long he will live in " 'cist pechable mon' " (14,943) indicates awareness of the hermit's figural significance to his own heroic career. In place of direct response, the hermit counters with another question: " 'Nen ais tu mie point lit les vers de cançon?' " (14,945) (" 'Have you not read at all the verses of the song?' ") The prophetic texts immediately coming to mind of course are the *Chanson de Roland* and Turpin's (prose) chronicle. What we see here is a clever bit of authorial play, first on textual vs. "real" temporality: according to textual chronology, Roland cannot have read a text narrating his own death, while in supratextual time, both the *Roland* and *Pseudo-Turpin* parent texts appeared nearly two centuries before the Paduan's *Entrée*. The intertextual web binding these works one to another permits a "real" personage in one to (fore)see his future in another. It is already inscribed in the book of the world, where human notions of temporality are transcended. All of Roland's life is already known somewhere; Samson is able to read that book.

Additionally, the passage raises the question of who/what is real, what is literature; what is true, what *fabula*. In this medievally precocious segment, the *Entrée* extends the dialogue which began with the "true" story of Roland's life at 14,765. The most comprehensible response regarding this text has been formulated by J. B. Allen:

> The relation between literature and life is not mimetic, but assimilative—reciprocal. We do not move from life to words to meanings as from concrete to abstract; rather, we move within a web of words, some literal, some figural, some in the natural language of the book of the creatures, some historical, so that what is now literal may become meaning and commentary, and what is now commentary may exist as letter (*Ethical Poetic* 270).

In answer to the hermit's question, Roland prays to a God of " 'ombleté, pïeté e charité divine,/largece pardurable' " (14,952-53), virtues which he has learned and which render him, at last, " 'le ome beneoit' " (15,039). Now empowered to comprehend and participate in the transcendant, Roland's request that his two companions be attended to in " 'charité' " is answered by an angel who reproduces a living image of Roland ("image Rolant" 14,976) to pass the night with them.

The first sign of Roland's sacralization lies in a "santisme odor" emitted when he is able to receive into his hands the hermit's reliquary cross (14,717), which only a "friend of Christ" may touch. Roland's " '*Ave* ' " as he accepts the cross pursues interweaving of language both sacred and secular, as the chapel bells spontaneously render a *Te Deum Laudamus*. The two men share at this moment the solitary existence of the self-named exile, both seeking a perfection greater than the secular world, that of epic and romance, is able to offer. The episode continues with the appearance of an angel bearing bread and two apples (NB negative and positive polysemy of the apple). Here we can say that all the Rolandian texts conjoin in a single sense of time: ". . . the 'earlier,' and 'later' of earthly temporality are replaced by the synchrony of eternal time, which alone can reveal the significance of all. Events have moved beyond time, diachrony has been synchronized, as it is in the *Divine Comedy*" (Bakhtin, *Imagination* 157).

Addressing the hermit, the angel says:

> 'Ce soit
> 'Por le tien compagnons qi est chevalers droit;
> 'Bien a feit e fera, tant con vie li croit;
> 'Por eshalcer la loi onqes son per non oit.
> 'Fa li onor, car c'est le ome beneoit
> 'Qi pechié de luxurie ni nul mal non feroit'
> (15,035-40).

> 'Let this be for your companion who is a righteous knight; he has done good and will continue to do good, so long as he grows with life; to carry out the law there never was an equal [to Roland]. Do honor unto him, for he is the blessed man who would never commit the sin of lust nor any evil deed.'

The problematics of secular heroism have yielded to a higher law, in which the narrator dissipates any remaining ambiguities. "Droit" no longer signals authority toward which Roland has an agonistic relationship, but is henceforth his own attribute, absorbed and appropriated in the quest. In future, he will accept and act for " 'la loi de Cil qi fu pendus' " (15,119), recognizing that human law is always subject to question, though rarely open to permanent resolution. The process of self-correction complete, Roland is a holy man to whom honor is due. No longer will the secular tensions of authority/autonomy cloud our response to his conduct. This is the *Entrée*'s moment of Rolandian *theosis*, when the increasing sanctity raising him heavenward encounters, mystically, the Divinity descending to the level of man.[10]

Since the veracity of a medieval narrative, even in the form of prophecy, increases with repeated recitation/reading, the story of Roland's destiny will be twice told: first by the angel to Samson (15,035-57), then by Samson to Roland (15,126-37). He will continue, as a knight who would never transgress rightful authority, to labor via *lex humana* for the supreme *lex aeterna*. After conquering the city " 'which France now fears,' " Pamplona:

> 'Set ans vivra, non plus, en le humain destroit;
> 'Mout joians pora estre s'onques France revoit;
> 'Traïs ert en Espagne, ou coroner se croit,

'E teil le traïra qi il mout ame e croit' (15,044-47).

'Seven years will he live, no longer, in the human
condition; very joyous will he be if he ever sees
France again; he will be betrayed in Spain, where he
believes he will be crowned, and such a man will
betray him whom he loves and believes [trusts].'

Thus "la cançon," Roland's own book which he has not read,
follows the present text, although not necessarily immediately. It is the
Entrée's audience, medieval and modern, who can fill in the elliptical
tale with names and places. Roland will die joyfully, a martyr in the
service of God. All this and Samson's death next morning have already
been foreseen (" 'con prevoire sera' " 15,056).

When the prophecy is recounted by Samson to Roland, he twice
enunciates Roland's future function, like his own, as a servant,
laborator of God (15,130, 15,135: " 'en le servise Deu' "), the
transformation from "orguel" to "onbleté" undoubtedly being the
Entrée's most critical ethical lesson. Thus the remuneration of eternal
salvation likewise foreseen is dependent upon one condition examined
in locus *a*: " 'Se tu por Deu travailes' " (15,126) (" 'If you labor for
God' "). The *Entrée* glosses the *Chanson's* death of Roland.

The recoded forest-voyage motifs recur at the end of Marciana XXI.
Disembarking on the return voyage on an unrecognized shore in Spain,
a voice tells Roland not to be afraid; he then encourages his
companions: " 'Je sai bien ou je sui venus et arivés' " (14,423). The
apparent circularity of his travels yields to a perception of the deeper
significance of the internal voyage when one recalls the narrator's
depiction of him departing Pamplona: "Mais vil se tient qe ne sa ou il
va" (11,496). Hence the *Entrée's* ideal knight possesses a double text in
his own mind. He voyages, on the *littera* level, to seemingly random
destinations, undergoing apparently gratuitous adventures. Yet without
consciously knowing where he is going or the meaning of his
experience, he possesses also a *profundior intelligentia* of his own
experience; he possesses his own *sententia*.

The text marks this new state of self-knowledge (i.e., the
instrument of knowledge of immanent Order) in the path which now
opens miraculously before Roland in the darkness of the forest. He can
now see clearly and proceed without obstruction. Within a short time,
he is reunited with the French near Pamplona.

The *Entrée* recognizes the particular dangers of heroic pride: other
sins find their vent in the accomplishment of evil deeds, but pride lies

in wait for the good deeds, to destroy them. If the numerous Church fulminations concerning new secular literatures reached their peak in the condemnations of 1277, Aquinas himself expressed tolerance of jongleur arts as a manifestation of man's need for *ludus* and *solatium*. He warned, nonetheless: "Ludus est necessarius ad conversationem humanae vitae et ideo etiam officium histrionum quod ordinatur ad solatium hominibus exhibendum non est secundum se illicitum" (*ST* 2a, 2ae, qu. 168, art. 3, ad 3um). The *Entrée* heeds both admonitions; it maintains our desire to know the story of Roland, while offering a *correctio* of the dangerous pleasures of the text.

The Roland who returns to Pamplona will carry on the fight, putting "en ovre" what he has learned. He will fulfill what Guillaume de Conches specified as the *raison d'être* of creature and Creator: Roland's sanctity, like God's, is a living sign that "all good radiates with greater beauty when it is shared and spread throughout a community of men." If the *Entrée*'s Roland has undergone theosis and transcended ordinary earthly experience, he will not complete the hermit typology by renouncing the world. His will be the *via activa*, reintegration with the human community fittingly marked with the collective pronoun he employs: " 'a service de nus' " and " 'por nostre salus.' " The Christian armies in "un cri plus de mil a un ton" welcome "le ome beneïs" and the final victory they know will be theirs:

> 'Cantate Domino canticum novon,
> Que nos remaine la nostre garison,
> Le douç, le onble, le per de pobres hon;
> Veez la conquisse de tuit ceste regnon'
> (15,638-41).

> 'Sing to the Lord the/a new song, may our protector remain with us, the gentle, the humble, the equal of the poor man; you see the conquest of this whole kingdom.'

The *Entrée* reexamines the dialectic between feudal and religious heroism and carries on the medieval debate of hero-definition. Topical invention has combined elements of form and content to construct what the poet terms his "gloriose cançons." In accordance with the Thomist thesis that art is based on principles of spiritual activity and its goal is to produce perfect forms, the poet has endeavored to demonstrate the process by which perfected forms are created. Art, for Aquinas as for the Paduan, "n'est donc pas l'ensemble des créations artistiques; il est un principe d'activité spirituelle. . . . L'art a pour but non point de réaliser la perfection de l'artiste mais celle de l'oeuvre" (*ST* 1a, 2ae, art.3, 4 cited in De Bruyne 3:326).

Thus in his hero and in the text woven around him, the poet adheres likewise to Aquinas's three-part classification of human behavior in its participation with the spiritual:

> . . . l'homme manifeste trois activités principales, celles du savoir, de l'agir et du faire. Le savoir est réglé de la manière la plus apparente par la science, l'agir par la prudence, le faire par l'art. Il s'ensuit que la création artistique est avant tout un phénomène de l'esprit au même titre que l'action morale ou la recherche scientifique (De Bruyne 3: 318; emphasis added).

Still more critical is the text's realization of a human ideal evolved in three phases within one text, within one character. Roland is not prepared to profit from his encounter with the hermit until he has experienced and corrected the failings of his epic and epico-romance manifestations. Likewise, the poet does not offer the definitive, tropological and anagogical text until he has created and put into question two imperfect forms-as-texts. Nonetheless, the textual voyage presented here has not been myopically assembled. Its destination was postulated from the beginning.

The Paduan's claim to authorial originality in the Prologue to *Entrée* II lies here. By serving Thomistic and rhetorical prescriptions, he has composed his work with a conception or *sens* of the processes (voyages) necessary to its perfect realization, to the specific contingencies of literary form and the inclinations of his public. The idea of its final perfection governs each aspect of the structuring process. Just as the Roland of forest and voyage is engaged in a quest, the text, too, proceeds with a sense of immanent order in search of its own perfect form.

Notes

1. Although both "canter" and "dir" suggest orality alone, a literate audience is subsequently evoked in "leu" and elsewhere. See my Introduction and ch. 4.

2. In a discussion of contract vs. status societies as related to fourteenth-century England, Judson Boyce Allen finds both terms incapable of accurately describing reality because:

    > . . . they inadequately account for the presence of language to Chaucer's society, by which, because of the presumed existence of the Incarnate Word, vows can be far more than contracts, and stories far more than fictions. For the Middle Ages, a vow was more than a contract, because it is made of words which, under medieval definition, constitute reality rather than merely refer to it, and which have, as pronounced, a sacramental dimension which makes their betrayal a sin. To break a contract involves loss of credit; to break a vow, the loss of both honour in this life and soul in the next . . . .

    The Ethical Poetic of the Later Middle Ages (Toronto: U of Toronto P, 1982) 305.

3. Alberto Limentani was much interested in similarities between *La Divina Commedia* and the *Entrée*, considering that the Paduan may have known, at least in part, Dante's masterpiece. We know, of course, that Dante's latter years of exile were spent with the Scaglieri in Verona in the time period compatibile to current dating of the *Entrée*, it is more than likely that he was familiar with other literary, scientific and Prehumanist centers of the region, such as Mantua, Ferrara, and of course Padua; See Hyde, *Padua in the Age of Dante*. Limentani notes that "il senso di una missione morale-letteraria può far pensare al più vicino poeta della *Commedia*," plus a considerable quantity of

    > espressioni e immagini, che richiamano alla mente versi danteschi, siano davvero derivati dalla *Commedia* . . . . Ora, il Padovano. . . dà alla comparazione uno sviluppo che, in taluni episodi, è

249

quantitativamente paragonabile a quello della
Commedia, e si presenta dotato di varietà nelle
strutture e nell'impiego contestuale. . . .

Concerning the Roland-Ferragu duel:

Dal canto suo, l'autore si inserisce ripetutamente con
interventi di vario ordine, con bella prova di quella
tecnica d'innalzamento del livello stilistico di cui, in
altra chiave, ha dato gli esempi sommi Dante
dall'inizio del *Purgatorio* al *Paradiso*.

"L'epica in 'lengue de France': L' 'Entrée d'Espagne' e Niccolò da
Verona," *Storia della cultura veneta: il Trecento* (Vicenza: Neri
Pozza 1976) 2: 339-56. See also Limentani, "L'Art de la
comparaison dans *L'Entrée d'Espagne*, "*Actes du VIe Congrès
international de la Société Rencesvals*, Aix-en-Provence, 29 Août-
4 Septembre 1973 (Aix-en Provence: Université de Provence,
1974) 353-71.

4.   The emergence of a markedly lay mentality in the period 1270-
      1350 is the subject of Georges de Lagarde's study *La Naissance de
      l'esprit laïque au déclin du moyen âge*, 5 vols. (Paris: Louvain,
      1956) 2: 141 and *ad passim*; 2: 169 and *ad passim*. Important
      among the multiple forces at work in Italy was the revival of the
      Justinian Code, by which the concept of law devoid of
      metaphysical referentiality gained considerable support. Also, the
      constitution of Frederick II's empire established strict control over
      the clergy (2: 127). Subsequently, many of Italy's new sovereign
      city-states and principalities assumed a specifically secular system
      of operation: "Philosophes et juristes, en donnant à l'état nouveau-
      né ses titres, l'élévaient à la dignité de la nature rationnelle et lui
      permettaient du même coup d'entrer dans la lice des grands
      'tournois spirituels' dont l'Eglise avait été jusqu'alors le champion
      incontesté" (2: 138). Lagarde considers also a sometimes-virulent
      anticlerical current at work. The Church condemned numerous
      statuaries challenging its secular authority: for example, the 1258
      edict warning "milites, communitates et barones, rustici et
      burgenses" of the perils of insubordination. It was most notably
      in the communes, of course, that the "esprit laïque" was most
      actively engaged.

5.   Thomas notes this reference to *orgueil* as a "péché mignon."
      Entrée 2: 299n.

6. There were, of course, many instances in which the Church permitted, even encouraged, communal resistance to imperial intervention in their affairs: most notably, the Lombard League. See ch. 3.
7. See Conclusions.
8. A quotation from Seneca taken from an English version of the *Secreta secretorum* well summarizes the relationship between human and divine law: "Iusticia divina lex est, et vinculum societatis humane" ("the divine law is justice and the bond of human society"). J. B. Allen applies the citation to an examination of medieval law as it appears in Langland. If one sees the text as a series of questions concerning what a human being is capable of doing, thinking, knowing:

> the answer, crucially, has to do with language, with sermo which binds, which is a vinculum, supremely in the activity of right law under pietas, but also in one's own name, and in all the metaphors and relations of nomen and res in between proper naming and legal judgment. . . . The goliard is explicitly concerned for the relation between words and things, the angel for the spirit in which legal formulae should be applied, and the commons for the relation between legal authority and what the king says. All three, in complementary ways, are concerned to define language, and to define it for that crucially operative and powerful case, the law. . . .The law and legal process are verbal procedures which render the world true by describing it. In medieval pleadings, opposing lawyers would tell and re-tell the story of the case at issue until it could be decided what kind of story it was, and then judgment could be rendered. . . . Thus law is a language which seeks to be absolutely descriptive, and absolutely performative, and at the same time (*Ethical Poetic* 279-81).

9. The *Entrée* Roland's unusual capacity for wisdom, knowledge, and reason seems to find precedence in a late tenth-century French historian, Richer, who describes his native land and peoples in very complimentary fashion. Richer traces the name "Gallia," meaning "whiteness," to Isidore of Seville, who found the Gauls more fair of complexion than other peoples of the world:

What appears to be simply an external set of facts
instead lays the groundwork for metaphorical and
metaphysical constructions. For Richer transforms
the eponymous color symbolism from an externally
distinguishing trait to a metaphor for inner qualities
which assert the special relationship of the Gauls
with the Logos. Although the Gauls share with all
humans the capacity for unruly behavior, says Richer,
they are more readily persuaded to conduct themselves
according to the rules of reason. In other words, to
place themselves under the rule of the Logos, the
conventional language enunciated by the divinity for
the rational ordering of the world. . . .

Still earlier, St. Jerome had written that:

'Gaul is the only country which has not produced
monsters, but has always illuminated the world by
wise and learned men.' . . . In Richer's intellectual
world, humans who understood and construed by their
actions the grammar and syntax of the Logos more
completely would, inevitably, demonstrate their
greater evolution toward the celestial order of
Revelation . . . (cited in Nichols, *Romanesque Signs*
2).

10. The term *theosis* was used by Scot Eriugena in his "philosophical
     anthropology" for the "mystical conjunction of the ascending
     individual with the descending godhead." Initially applied only to
     prelates, saints, kings, and emperors, the concept was extended to
     heroes such as Roland. The *Pseudo-Turpin,* according to Nichols,
     develops him into a *figura Christi* more clearly, for example, than
     the Oxford *Chanson*:

... the matrix of Roland's spiritual role derives from
his prominent textual association with Charlemagne,
Turpin, and, by extension, Saint James, for whom he
will ultimately stand as recapitulation. . . . Like
Turpin and Charlemagne, he defines himself as
exemplary being in a manner that transforms *historia*
by means of a *theoria* predicated on the passion
model, which he voluntarily articulates and assumes.
. . .

Nichols, *Romanesque Signs* 11, 135, and ch. 5, "Roncevaux and the Poetics of Place/Person in the Song of Roland" 148-203.

11.   Semper finis factionis est aliquid alterum ab ipsa factione sicut finis aedificationis est aedificium constructum. Ex quo patet quod bonum ipsius factionis non est in faciente sed in facto. Sic igitur ars quae est circa factiones non est circa hominis bona vel mala sed circa bona vel mala artificiatorum. . . . Ars nihil aliud est quam ratio recta aliquorum operum faciendorum quorum tamen bonum non consistit in eo quod appetitus humanus aliquo modo se habet, sed in eo quod ipsum opus quod fit in se bonum est.
(ST 1a, 2ae, qu. 57, art. 6) cited in De Bruyne 3: 327.

CONCLUSIONS

As "baillis" appointed to recruit and command the sultan's armies, thereby participating in the leadership of the kingdom, Roland accedes to the ranks of the "retors de tere" entrusted with ordering of the restored *Christianitas* of the Mideast.[1] But such had already been predicted. Earlier in the battle for Pamplona, one of his companions warned an enemy knight:

> 'De tant bien vos conseil
> 'Que vos ne fetes onques au quens Rolant revel.
> 'Maugré le roi Marsile et de tot si bidel
> 'Avra Rolant corone dunt d'or ert le cerclel;
> 'En son dimin avra tot le reing de Castel
> 'E neïs oltre mer, jusque la Tor Babel (8417-8422).

> I advise you in your own interests not to ever rebel against/resist the authority of Count Roland. In spite of King Marsile and all his soldiers, Roland will have a crown encircled with gold; in his domain he will have all the kingdom of Castille and even beyond the sea, as far as the Tower of Babel.

Where Charles's intentions were to crown his nephew king of Spain, Roland's fellow-knights, who have undertaken this mission more out of love and loyalty to him than to the emperor, prophesy a more glorious future: Roland sovereign of a vast world-space extending west and east up to, and including, the Tower of Babel.

Much of the prophecy is realized. *Entrée* II's Roland does conquer vast expanses of those lands eastward beyond the sea, including Jerusalem (in *lacuna*). After recovery of the *civitas Dei*, the converted Persians implore Roland to remain with them and pursue the mission further, into lands yet unknown. As his "homes e jurés e plevis":

255

> Aiderunt li conquere li estranjes païs,
> Babilone e Chaldee, les bos e les laris,
> La tor ou des langajes fist Nembrot les divis,
> Tote tere d'Egit e Sidonie neïs (14,142-45).

> As men sworn and pledged to his service, they will
> help him to conquer foreign lands, Babylon and
> Chaldea, forests and plains, the tower where Nimrod
> brought about the separation/division of languages,
> all the land of Egypt and even Sidon.

Under his leadership, Roland's Persians also envision new Christianized space to the east and south—including once again the Tower of Babel, more specifically predicated now as the site of a major event in the history of mankind. They wish to "conquere," either to reclaim, retake, or perhaps to destroy the structure where men suddenly became incomprehensible one to another, to undo the nefarious work of Nimrod.[2]

In Gen. 10.8-10 and 11.1-9, Nimrod is "a mighty one in the earth," "mighty hunter before the Lord," whose kingdom originated in Babel (and three other sites). With other descendants of Noah desiring to "make us a name" greater than that of all other men, Nimrod conceived the construction of a great tower and city tall enough to reach heaven itself. Such incursion upon divine spatiality incurred punishment more devastating than the simple dismantling of the tower: annihilation of their power to comprehend what another was saying, a primary requisite for survival of the species. *Confusio*: suddenly, the perfect Adamic language binding together those raising the tower and all men on earth, was silenced.[3] *Superbia* punished: for such is the power of language, that if all men could understand one another's speech, "nothing will be restrained from them, which they have imagined to do."

Dante, blaming the ignominy of Babel's "turris confusionis" on "culpa presumptionis humanae," renders the tale critical to his explanation of negatively-marked proliferation of human languages (*DVE* 1. 6, 20-30, 64). Irrevocable human shame caused by "superbam stultitiam"(*DVE* 1.7, 11-12, 64). His tone is harsh, his reading of the Biblical text provocative. Seen from a human perspective, the "confusio linguarum" occurred without direct warning, unlike man's first Fall. Its "victims," the diversified groups of workers (architects, masons, bricklayers, haulers, etc.), found themselves inexplicably incapable of communication with anyone except those engaged in the self-same task.[4] As many and as varied were the workers' groups, so became the quantity and diversification of human tongues: "And now as many languages separated the human race as there were different kinds of work; and the more excellent the type of work, the more crudely and barbarically did they now speak" (*DVE* 1. 7, 29-32, 66).

An excellent article by Maria Corti further explores the Dantean reading of the Babel narrative. From its initial symbolism of pride, the tower acquired additional negative associations specific to the later Italian Middle Ages. Babel became a "topos anticittadino" identified with the communes, their new men and new notions of social order ("Dante e la torre di Babele" 251-52). In doing so, the notion of city not only threatened the Model I tripartite order/Order, but "ha reso impossibile l'istituzione di un nuovo modello gerarchico che sacralizzasse la società, cioè la nascita di strutture semiotiche che fossero insieme nuove e coerenti con l'ideologia feudale, . . ." ("Dante e Babele" 248).

Nimrod himself, creator of new social structures, was surely among the first to lose the privilege of language communication. Half-immersed in Inferno 31 with the living towers whom Dante calls "orribili giganti," Nimrod has indeed made a name for himself. He babbles: "Raphèl maí amèche zabí almi" (67), utterances meaningless to his two addressees, not improbably to himself as well, "ché cosí è a lui ciascun linguaggio/ come 'l suo ad altrui, ch'a nullo è noto" (80-81). The "mighty hunter's" initial attempt to address Virgil and Dante erupted like a horn-blast which the narrator likens to Roland's oliphant call to Charles beyond the mountains during the massacre at Roncevaux: "Non sonò sí terribilmente Orlando" (16-18). In the *Chanson de Roland*, it is the same call by which Ganelon tried to dismiss Charles's anxiety regarding his nephew commanding the rear guard, and to which he related his tale of Roland's disobedience at Nobles (see ch. 2).

Nimrod associated with Roland in the *Entrée* and *La Divina Commedia*, both with *superbia*. Is there a *Roland> Entrée> Commedia* intertextuality with a common theme? The question arises: was the issue of Roland's pride sufficiently familiar to Dante to associate somehow the French knight with the incomprehensible languages of Babel? If the *Inferno* 31 passage raises the question of Roland as *figura superbiae*, recognizable to Italians of the fourteenth century, resolution in a negative form is provided in *Paradiso* 18:43. There, the Dantean pilgrim sees Roland (and Charles) among those who fought and died for their faith. The earlier Roland-Nimrod comparison would appear to be (simply?) a reference to the volume of the sound emitted by similar instruments; there may also be allusion to the futility of the act. (We should remember that Roland's oliphant message in the *Chanson* was correctly understood by Charles; it was Ganelon who destroyed the connection). The *Entrée* recalls the *Roland* in its Nobles episode; it also utilizes Babel as a *signum* to synthesize Roland's long trajectory. Hyperbolic as it may seem, the *Entrée*'s Roland has evolved from a speaker of "parole vaine," like Nimrod, to the text's principal agent of Language restoration: " '*ecce servus Dei.*' "

Nimrod's noise, applied to Jakobsen's speech event grid, is as impotent as the giant himself. Code, contact, and message elements responsible for describing such utterances in terms of a shared language system, establishing linkage between speaker and addressee, encoding of *parole*, discourse, text, are impossible to carry out ("Linguistics and Poetics" 18-51).

For Nimrod and virtually all men ("siquidem pene totum humanum genus ad opus iniquitatis coierat" (*DVE* 1. 7, 21, 66), the essential transgression was abuse of human intelligence ("mal coto" < *cotare* or *coitare* < Lat. *cogitare*; Sapegno, *Inferno* 344n.77) that led from Babel to the infernal city of Dis: the reasoning of an "anima sciocca" (*Inferno* 31:70) whose city and tower were, like all postlapsarian human enterprises, unstable and corruptible. For the new languages, like the new cities, communes and "new men," trace their origins to man's attempts "to surpass by his skill not only Nature, but even Nature's creator, which is God" (*DVE* 1.7, 14-15, 64). There are two exceptions: (Adamic) Hebrew and Latin, the latter "perpetuo e non corruttibile" (*Conv.* 1.5, 7-14). For Dante, like all Christian medievals, Latin, even if crafted by man, is the language of the Word and of universal human communicability, amidst the proliferating *vulgari*. Latin is, and must remain the world's monoglossia.

It is within the complex associative system briefly outlined here that we should read *Entrée* I's prophecy that Roland will reign over the land of Babel, *Entrée* II's encouragement that he "conquere" the infamous tower. Metonymically, it would be Roland's "best work," enacting the power of human labor (locus *a*) put to its correct(ed) purpose. Adam and Eve transgressed in claiming to establish their own autonomous governance, liberated from subordination to what they came to see as oppressive hierarchism (see Pagels 105ff). Not dissimilarly, the builders of Babel quite literally denied hierarchism, presuming their human *artes* limitless—not, as in Eden, by transgression of a specific nature, but by the "superbam stultitatem" which clouded their understanding of unspoken boundaries. That act, begun as a collective undertaking in a monophonic world, was to destroy the requisite harmonization of diverse human elements, the Augustinian *compactam*. Human creation to challenge the highest reaches of Creation.

In order to fulfill the significance of his name (Rotholandus), Roland will have to "conquere," to "recovrer" that unity through military and spiritual activity, both in the service of the restoration of the Word. Roland is to remove the polyglossia of other doctrines throughout the world, beyond the erroneous discourse of Islamic Spain and the Middle East to "strange countries" settled by the descendants of Nimrod. Each, like the divided builders of Babel, are able to communicate only among their small affinity groups. It is not a question of eliminating either the new tongues or new kinds of human communities each is continually developing, but of restoring Christian monoglossia to its proper supremacy. In the Ferragu combat, Roland had failed to convince the giant of Trinitarian unity-within-multiplicity at Nájera; his labor as *orator* proves more successful in the Middle East.

Yet the more complex problem is to correct the heteroglossia dividing the Christian community itself, the proliferation of post-Babelic discourse which has led to innumerable intra-community ideolects comprehensible only to those bound to their particular doctrines. Those who govern are undoubtedly among the disseminators of secular ideolects; Aquinas complains of politicians that "their public activities seem to be performed more from an aptitude or a kind of habit acquired from custom and experience than from intellectual discernment, that is, reason or science" (*Commentary on The Ethics,* Lesson 16, 294). A chastening of "retors de tere" and "om soveran," no doubt, whose "languages" of empire, communes, *signorie* compete incessantly for dominance. Amidst the Babelic din described by Dante and the *Entrée*, each speaker hears only his own case, quite deaf to the words of others, and so to the Word. The text's conflict structure tracks the increasing noise of uncontrolled ideoloects, a shouting match terminating in the virtually inevitable communicational breakdown. Retaining the "grant e petit" binarism inscribed throughout the text, the *Entrée*'s secular dialogism enters the discourse of commune and *signoria* into an arena already disputed by empire and Church. For Dante, it is the smaller systems and institutions which bear much of the blame (i.e., his negative depiction of the new urbanism in Florence in the Cacciaguida *canti*, Paradiso 15-17); for Mussato in the *Ecerinide* the tyrannical *signore*, for the anonymous thirteenth-century author of the *Oculus pastoralis* and many others, the empire.

While some scholars have argued the *Entrée*'s pro-bourgeois, protocapitalist ideology, others that it is pro-feudal, anti-imperial, or anti-clerical, I have expressly avoided what I consider over-reductionist readings. Multiplicity there is, at times ambiguous, even apparently contradictory; the polemical complexities of the text are among its finest qualities. Far more than one ideology pitted against another—to the point of violence—the text's moment of intra-ideological violence marks the culmination of a confusion etymologically *ad absurdum*, almost inevitable, as one recognizes in hindsight, of more fundamental communicational disorders.

In their initial representations, the languages of authority and autonomy are presented in discourse sufficiently clear so that narrative and authorial publics can at least comprehend one another's position. Radical disruption of communicability occurs with the intertextually-marked gift horse speech; words pertaining to the feudal, chivalric, mercantile, communal and familial, each a self-absorbed microcosm seeking to "make for itself a name," crowd into a ten-verse passage further complicated by the commingling of an apparently exemplary récit with direct interlocutionary activity. Linguistic pluralism, heteroglossia *ad confusionem*. Given the midpoint position occupied by Charles's remarks on the gift horse in the text's conflict structure and the public(s) to which the *Entrée* is addressed, it is difficult to perceive the selection of this particular object and gesture as a random issue over which a brief dispute arises regarding the propriety of accepting presents from an enemy. If one recognizes the *Entrée*'s intertextual communication with the *Iliad*'s gift horse stratagem, the episode begins to acquire some logic. In the Homeric text, object and gesture were not the disinterested largesse that they appeared to be; a misreading, "mespreison" of their content brought down the walls of Troy. Apparent donor generosity proved misleading. What the medieval public in general, and the *Entrée* public in particular, might retain from the Homeric text was the necessity of careful, well-reasoned interpretation of human activity, including linguistic activity.

Nor will the imagery be lost on Trecento Paduans, who proudly inhabit "la citez qe fist Antenor le Troian," as the poet reminds us of the *Aeneid*'s claim concerning the city's illustrious founder (see Introduction). Or, more immediately, as anyone was reminded as he passed by the imposing *tomba di Antenore* erected in central Padua in 1284, still standing today. Brunetto Latini's *Trésor* likewise testified to the illustrious founder of the city: "[. . .] et enchor i est son sepulture" (see Limentani, "Virgilio" 291).

Ironically, the *Entrée*'s most concentrated example of post-Babelic verbiage is uttered by the voice of imperial authority, the "grant" secular participant in the text's polyphonic dialogism. Whether a well-intentioned but misguided effort to ameliorate communication by adopting discourse he supposes comprehensible to his "petit" interlocutor, a case of excessive, careless, ambivalent encoding, or, more trivially, a poor choice of words, I do not find it possible to

determine unequivocally what Charles intends by the words he utters to
Roland concerning the gift horse.

There is no narratorial interpolation to clarify the confusion. But
the passage is eloquent in its elusiveness, for what it does is to move
the text decisively closer to the violence erupting thousands of lines
later, which forms the *Entrée*'s most significant contribution to the
Rolandian macrotext.

Although one can speculate indefinitely regarding accountability in
the conflicts following the gift horse speech, the text suggests
multiple, frequently incompatible interpretations as it goes forward.
Even narrative progress is confusing: the military expedition is
stalemated at Pamplona, while the only real narrative activity issues
from the increasingly strident confrontations between its two principal
agents as they race toward the final confrontation. We might well
ascribe to both men Roland's recollection of language and actions
incomprehensible to the other:

> '. . . je perdi de tot bien conosançe;
> 'De vos ne d'autre n'avoie remembrançe,
> 'Tan che no fu torné in ma siançe,
> 'Car vos savez, bien vore est la sentançe,
> 'De celu saje che en son dir comançe:
> '*Cum furor in cursu*, e quand ire t'avançe,
> '*Currenti cedi furori*. . . (15,562-68).

> 'I lost the knowledge of all good; of you, nor of
> anyone did I have any recollection, until I was
> returned to my wisdom/knowledge. For you know,
> the proverb of that wise man is indeed true, which
> begins: *Like madness racing headlong,* and when
> anger pushes you forward, *those running yield to*
> *madness . . .* '

When language yields to violence, the text pauses (at Prologue II)
before setting off again to explore further the results of multi-language
secular cacophony. Threatened by mutiny, the voice of imperial
authority quickly recognizes the error of violence ("Car repentis estoit
de cil folor" 11,185). While refusing to negotiate his authority, Charles
does express regret, even repentance for striking Roland (" 'e j'en sui
repanti . . .' ").

However, it is not Charles's fortunes which the text then pursues;
rather, the odyssey of the new, younger voice, whose correction claims
virtually all textual space in *Entrée* II. To some degree Roland's regret,

but more significantly his repentance, are to require much time before it becomes clear that his "parole vaine" protesting the injustice of the blow is, in fact, any discourse denying the sacralized hierarchism of all earthly authority. The narrator intervenes to address the voices of change among his readers/public, whatever form they may assume:

> Exanple en pragne cil de joven ahité
> Che pur desirent seguir volenté.
> Hei! quant en sunt mort e desarité
> Por treir a chief les emposibleté! (7413-16)

May the young learn their lesson from this, those who desire at any cost to pursue their own will. Alas! How many have died or been disinherited by such thinking/behavior, in order to carry out the impossible! [5]

Paramount among the *Entrée*'s "emposibleté" must be the dissonance of post-Babelic languages; ultimately responsible is that trait which Roland shares with all men, "la couse qe li fu senpre un poi germaine." Once more, *superbia*.

But Roland is also "justiser" of Rome. At both the secular and sacred levels, he is charged with the maintenance and restoration, if necessary, of law as the instrument of civic order, and the monoglossic "loy Deu." Roland is to conquer the metonymic Babel and overcome "parole vaine" in the human community, then to reinstate the true "*canticum novon*." The privilege of correction is granted to him, not to Charles; Roland, not Charles, will be hailed as "le meldre Cristian" and "le ome beneoit." From his initial vindictive determination to teach Charles the order of things as he saw it (" 'mielz veul morir qi je ni li ensaigne/ 'Se je riens ne li valloie 'en la gere d'Espagne' "), Roland finds that he, too, must learn what happens when one resists hierarchism. The "new song" will be composed for the most part of distinctly venerable elements concerning hierarchism sacralized by Pseudo-Dionysius, thundered by Augustine as the "inescapable necessity of enforced order" (Pagels 34), and, more optimistically, entrusted by Aquinas to human reason, another "couse qi . . . fu un poi germaine" to mankind. In Part I, Roland occasionally recognizes the necessity of hierarchism in facile aphorisms such as " 'cil a tort qi son roi contrelie' " and " 'hobedience senpre orgueil venqui;' " their true *sententia*, however, is incomprehensible to him until his encounter with the hermit.

Literary hierarchism is critical as well. Since, in a literary text, "that which negates does not annul what is negated" (Lotman, *Structure* 248), the *Entrée*'s chanson de geste yields to the higher order of its particular rendering of the *roman*, which in turn rises to the hagiographical tones of the Hermit episode. Like Dante in the *Commedia*, the Paduan reserves a place of high honor in the celestial hierarchy for Roland. According to the cognitive labors of its public(s), the text's several language systems will be received and retained; new languages and literatures have their function in the pluralistic order of things characteristic of the late Middle Ages. Ultimately, however, its "*canticum novon*" narrates a tale of *lex aeterna* created by the first *Auctor*. The *Entrée* as *summa* acknowledges the changing nature of human social and literary discourse, while demonstrating the necessary hierarchism between words/the Word and between books/the Book.

Notes

1. The Holtus *Lexikalische Untersuchungen* enters "baillis" as past participle used as noun < *bailir*, "donner" and *bailior*, "conducteur"; Gdf and FEW add "gouverner." Larousse, *Dictionnaire de l'ancien français*: OF *baillier*, v. "avoir à sa charge, protéger; gérer. Tote aures Engleterre desos moi a baillier" (*Chev. cygne*). n. *baillie*: "tutelle, pouvoir, domination, empire." "Tote sa terre ot en baillie" (*H. de Camb.*); "juridiction, administration." *Baillier*: n.m. (13th c.) "gouverneur." (227-28). Limentani interprets the word as "bailo dell'esercito": Roland in Persia appointed to a strictly military function. In that case, as commander-in-chief, Roland would still rank among the leaders of the realm. ("Il comico nell'*Entrée d'Espagne* e il suo divenire: una preghiera 'en la lois aufricaine,' *Interpretation: Das Paradigma der Europëischen Renaissance-Literatur: Festschrift für Alfred Noyer-Weidner zum 60 Geburtstag* (Wiesbaden: Franz-Steiner Verlag GMBH, 1983) 76.

2. I am assuming that the communication and languages referred to in *Gen.* 10-11 are in oral form; extension of the *confusio* to the written word is implicit, but not specified here.

3. See *Gen.* 11.1: "And the whole earth was of one language, and of one speech;" 11.5: "And the Lord said, Behold, the people is one, and they have all one language." 11.7: "Go to, let us go down, and there confound their language, that they may not understand one another's speech." Dante describes Adamic language as a:

> certam formam locutionis a Deo cum anima
> prima concreatam fuisse. Dico autem
> 'formam' et quantum ad rerum vocabula et
> quantum ad vocabulorum constructionem et
> quantum ad constructionis prolationem; . . .
> Hac forma locutionis locutus est Adam; hac
> forma locutionis lucuti sunt omnes posteri
> eius usque ad edificationem turris Babel, que
> turri confusionis interpretatur; ha[n]c
> formam locutionis hereditati sunt filii Heber,
> qui ab se dicti sunt Hebrei. . . . Fuit ergo
> hebraicum ydioma illud quod primi loquentis
> labia fabricarunt. *DVE* , ed. Panvini, 1. 6,
> 20-30, 64.

certain form of speech together with and for the first soul. I say 'form' with reference to the words for things, and the construction of these words, and their grammatical pronunciation; 1 . . . this form of speech was used by Adam and by all his descendants until the building of the Tower of Babel, which is translated as Tower of Confusion. This form of speech was inherited by the children of Heber, who were known as Hebrews . . . . Thus Hebrew was the language formed upon the lips of the first speaker (trans. Shapiro, 52).

The only people who retained Adamic Hebrew were those who recognized the transgressive nature of the Babelic tower and refused to involve themselves in it:

> . . . Quibus autem sacratum ydioma remansit, nec aderant, nec exercitium commendabant; sed, graviter detestantes, stoliditatem operantium deridebant. Sed hec minima pars quantum ad numerum fuit de semine Sem, sicut conicio, qui fuit tertius filius Noe; de qua quidem ortus est populus Israel, qui antiquissima locutione sunt usi usque ad suam dispersionem. *DVE*, ed. Panvini, 1. 7, 32-37, 66.

> . . . . But those to whom the sacred language remained had not been present nor did try to condone the work, but profoundly condemning it, derided the stupidity of the builders. Yet as I conjecture, this minority was of the seed of Sem, the third son of Noah; and from it arose the people of Israel, who continued to use the most ancient language until their dispersion (trans. Shapiro, 53-54).

4. Solis etenim in uno convenientibus actu eadem loquela remansit: puta cunctis architectoribus una, cunctis saxa volventibus una, cunctis ea parantibus una, et sic de singulis operantibus accidit. Quot quot autem exercitii varietates tendebant ad opus, tot tot ydiomatibus tunc genus humanum disiungitur; . . . *DVE*, ed. Panvini, 1. 7, 27-31, 66.

5. Limentani cites these verses concerning the failed war-machine "invention" raised by a group of young soldiers in Charles's army determined to take Pamplona more rapidly with their new technology:

> . . . . Faccio . . . osservare il carattere astratto, filosofico-giuridico, di quel termine (*les*) *enposibleté:* un plurale, come indica l'articolo, inesistente nella documentazione del francese antico . . . ; ed è mio parere che, superando la prospettiva puramente linguistica di tale trattazione, si debba far conto della natura intellettualistica del conio, e del carattere sentenzioso dell'intera espressione che lo include: nella quale è da ravvisare una rielaborazione o messa a partito di un'antica regola giuridica, a un certo momento fissata nella forma del broccardo. *Ad impossibilia nemo tenetur.* . . .

Limentani also cites similar phrases in Quintilian and Justinian ("Virgilio" 285-86).

Appendix

Summary of the Plot of *L'Entrée d'Espagne*

Prologue I. 1-19: The poet begins his work on Charlemagne's entry into Spain and "recovery" ("recovrer " 29, "recovree" 39) of the St. James pilgrim route to Compostella. Had it not been for a "difirnanze" caused by Ganelon, Charlemagne and his barony would have crowned Roland king of Spain. The story beginning now is about Roland, the finest knight about whom people read. The work will be dedicated to Jesus Christ and St. James. 20-34: The "cançons," addressed to "segnors," is good to hear for anyone who wishes to mend his ways ("son cors amender"); it informs its public how man must exert himself to carry out the law of God ("la loy Deu"), help the poor, visit impoverished knights, and assist orphans and widows. Charles had made an oath to undertake the mission but had forgotten it and did not wish to go. St. James himself appeared to him in a vision, warning him that there would be trouble ("engombrer") if he did not. 35-56: Now you will be able to hear truly how the council made an oath to conquer the route, which had been taken away from pilgrims, but was "challenged" ("chalonçee") by Roland. Ferragu received the first attack when they fought for three days; Roland slew him by a blow in the navel. The poet has undertaken his tale because Turpin, who fought so valiantly, wrote a "chronicled history" ("istorie croniquee") of the expedition: it was not well understood except by literate people ("gent letree"). One night Turpin appeared to me (the narrator), while I was sleeping; he commanded me, for love of St. James, to write the story in rhyme ("l'estorie rimee"), for my "arme" would constantly be assisted. And so I have begun the story for you, so that it may be both read and sung/recited orally. (end of Prologue I).
57-131: At his court in Aix-la-Chapelle, Charles informs his knights of the intended expedition. A *conseil* discloses that many knights prefer to extend a decade of leisure rather than undertake another military campaign. 132-75: Roland emphasizes the necessity to undertake the mission, noting Marsile's treachery. He will command a militia of 20,000 men granted to him by the pope. 176-337: Ganelon wishes to send a message to Marsile ordering him to surrender; the proposal is vetoed and the expedition agreed upon. 338-78: Secret preparations are initiated. Roland and Olivier travel to Rome, returning with Roland's

269

private army. 379-640: A Saracen *conseil* is held in Saragossa; Marsile, learning by divination that invasion is imminent, sends a letter to Charles expressing outrage regarding the undeclared war the French are about to initiate. He is advised to fortify Nájera; his nephew Ferragu will be in command there, and sends a contingent of men to ravage French territory. 641-54: Charles appoints Anseïs de Pontieu, Ganelon's nephew, regent during his absence; the narrator alludes to Anseïs's subsequent treason in attempting to wed the queen and seize the throne. 655-805: The pope and other Christian rulers organize defenses. Charles's army departs France, Roland as marshal. At the Spanish border, Roland is in the front guard. The 100,000-man army arrives in sight of Nájera. 806-95: Portrait of Ferragu: young, tall, handsome, chivalric. 896-1112: He proposes to Charles single combat to decide the fate of Nájera; Roland and Olivier volunteer, but Charles refuses. Ogier le Danois rides off to do battle with Ferragu. 1113-631: Ogier is defeated and taken prisoner, followed by Oton, Bérenger, Anseïs, Engelier, Sanson, two of Naimon's sons, Turpin, Girard de Roussillon, Hestout, and Olivier. Roland, who sees that the fate of all depends on him, again requests permission to fight Ferragu. Charles reluctantly agrees, after proposing that they instead abandon the expedition and return to France. 1632-2014: Day 1 of the Roland-Ferragu combat. Prayers of each; Roland's horse is killed, he himself thrown to the ground in a faint. Ferragu carries him off, thinking Roland dead; the latter regains consciousness and resumes combat. Roland affirms trust in God. Returning to Charles at the close of the day, Roland swears he will not return to France until the prisoners are freed. In their respective camps, Roland and Ferragu praise the chivalry of the other. 2015-965: Day 2: Roland hears Mass. Ferragu orders that the prisoners be well treated; reaction of the Christian prisoners. Roland decides to fight on foot, starts to leave the field when he realizes he cannot wound Ferragu; the latter reminds him that such is not chivalrous conduct. Roland kills Ferragu's horse with a stone; combat continues with stone-throwing. The narrator says he is following three sources: Turpin, Jean de Navarre, and Gautier d'Aragon; he scorns the "faibles jongleurs" who do not know the story as well as he. 2966-4204: Day 3: Roland prays again and allays Charles's fears for his safety. Charles lets him wear his personal helmet. Ferragu and Roland meet at the bridge; Roland is astonished that he cannot wound the giant, although he does fell him. Stone-throwing continues. Ferragu mocks Roland when he flees. Requesting a rest period, Ferragu falls asleep upon a stone pillow provided by Roland. Both praise the other's *courtoisie*. Ferragu offers Roland his sister's hand in marriage if he will convert; Roland begins his long *apologia* of Christian doctrine. Ferragu reveals that he is vulnerable only in the navel; Roland strikes him there and kills him. Roland thanks God for victory. 4205-536: The Nájerans agree to convert to Christianity; Olivier appeals to Charles for mercy towards them, and it is granted. The keys to the city are brought to Charles, who enters triumphantly and wishes immediately to crown Roland king of Spain. Roland refuses, claiming that it would be premature; he will accept the crown only when all Spain is retaken. Festivities at Nájera, baptisms. Charles becomes irritated and demands immediate departure for Pamplona. 4537-5339: Charles sends Roland to Pamplona to fortify positions, instructing him not to fight until the rest of the forces arrive. Roland leaves, guided by three converted Saracen merchants. A scouting party massacres a group of local cowherds, some of whom flee back to Pamplona to sound the alarm. Corsabrin decides to remain in the city. The "pagans" launch an attack against the Christian scouts, which develops into major combat. Battle between Prince Isoré, son of King Maugeriz, and Turpin; Isoré is captured by Olivier, but will surrender only to Roland. 5340-626: Isoré is sent to Charles with instructions that he be well treated. Hestout is taken prisoner by Maugeriz who, upon learning of the capture of his son, orders the city gates closed and drawbridges raised. The queen's despair. 5627-6681: Charles threatens to hang Isoré; Roland threatens to leave the army if he carries out the execution. Charles yields, agrees to request Maugeriz to convert or that he return Hestout. The latter, meanwhile, tries to deny his noble status in order to convince Maugeriz to release him. Gautier d'Orlin arrives to relate to Maugeriz the first part of Charles's message regarding his conversion; the king refuses, suggesting instead a prisoner exchange. Gautier, to gain the advantage, claims that this is not really Hestout, to which Hestout now protests angrily. Charles entrusts the transaction to Roland; Roland releases Isoré, who agrees to return as prisoner if promises are not honored on his side. Maugeriz is joyful to see his son, but now reluctant to free Hestout, whereupon Isoré threatens to join the Christian forces against his father. Queen Géophanais agrees with Isoré's protest, threatening to join her brothers if her husband does not release Hestout. Maugeriz yields Hestout, who returns to the French with a magnificent horse given to Roland by Isoré as a gesture of admiration and respect. Upon his return, Hestout suggests that the gift horse is the result of improper fraternization between Roland and Isoré; Roland says he will not keep the gift if Charles considers it wrong. Charles insists that Roland keep the gift horse. 6682-767: News arrives that the front guard at Nobles has been attacked. A *conseil* is held; Ernaud de Baslandé, Olivier's uncle, suggests that a party be sent to besiege Nobles, regarding which there is general agreement. First, however, fortifications at Pamplona will be solidified so that the Christian position there will not be weakened by dividing the army prematurely. Charles agrees that Nobles must be taken, due to its strategic location, wealth, and power. 6768-7167: To fortify their position at Pamplona, Charles orders various national groups to carry out different tasks: the Thiois, a Germanic or Polish contingent, are ordered to carry wood from the forest. Humiliated by an assignment which they consider an insult to their dignity, the Thiois draw up secret plans to desert. Charles is informed, and orders Salomon de Bretagne and a group of soldiers to pursue the escaping group, which he does not identify, at midnight, leading Salomon to believe the enemy are Saracens. A moonlight pursuit, battle and massacre of many Thiois. Salomon recognizes his error at first light, returns to Charles and reproaches his cruelty. Others join the condemnation of Charles's act. 7168-91: Bernard de Meaux, one of Roland's private militia, asks Roland if he may go to Nobles to recconoiter; Roland grants permission. Bernard leaves disguised as a pilgrim. 7192-397: Charles has a master craftsman construct a mobile "castel" war-machine for the assault of Pamplona. Without authorization, a group of 6,000 young Christian knights take the war-machine to the city walls, intending to gain quick entry. They are discovered by Maugeriz's men, who attack and burn the "castel," killing many of the youths. Charles's grief. 7398-976: Maugeriz learns that Marsile is dispatching reinforcements to Pamplona under command of Baligant; the troops are already at La Stelle. Charles sends Roland with 8,000 men to prevent the reinforcements from reaching Pamplona and to halt Turquin de Tortelose. Roland is forced to do battle not only with Turquin, but with 80,000 Saracens commanded by Maugeriz. Quickly recognizing his disadvantage, Roland sends to Charles for reinforcements. Large-scale battle; Roland is wounded by twenty blows. The Christians retreat, leaving the Saracen reinforcements to enter Pamplona. Charles arrives with reinforcements, but too late. Charles's anger with Roland that he did not fall back sooner; Roland's anger that Charles was so slow in arriving. 7977-8345: "Pagan" *conseil* in Pamplona, where it is decided to launch a full-scale attack. The French also prepare for battle. Roland refuses Charles's assignment as marshal, declaring he will take charge only of his own troops. Angrily, Charles sends him to the rear guard and draws up strategy. 8346-975: Battle exploits ; Ganelon is captured, then released. Isoré wounded. Baligant joins the fray. 8976-9409: Bernard de Meaux returns from Nobles when battle at Pamplona seems to be going well for the French; he convinces Roland that Nobles can be taken tomorrow, since the city is presently undefended. He urges secrecy, that Roland not inform Charles nor reveal to his men where they are going. All the *pairs* agree to go with Roland, leaving five hundred of his men behind to guard the *oriflamme*. A German informs Charles of Roland's departure, which the emperor interprets as desertion. Panic among the French, confusion on the field as they flee, unnerved by the news that Roland is not with them. Charles's fury; he declares he will hang Roland as a traitor. 9410-10,434: Roland and company leave for Nobles at night. Strategy is drawn up by Bernard, who divides the troops into four groups, one to attack each gate of the city. Olivier will be at the Porte Paris; Ogier and Turpin at Porte Clause; Girard and Hestout at Port Vals; Roland at Porte Lice. Olivier is first to penetrate the walls of Nobles, followed by Ogier, Girard and Hestout. Bernard is killed at the Porte Lice, which Roland is unable to force, but which he takes by entering via another gate and attacking Porte Lice defenders from within. Street-fighting inside Nobles; use of Greek fire. Citizens throw stones, but plea for mercy when fires frighten them. Girard is wounded by Felides, lord of Nobles. Englier enters the palace, is trapped inside with fifty men; Felides surrenders to Englier and opens the palace gates. The city apparently won, Roland "gives" it to Olivier, who turns it over to Felides on condition that he convert. Roland raises Charles's flag over the city along with his own banner. Description of the palace room painted with the story of Alexander the Great. 10,435-938: Felides is made count of Nobles. Folquenor of Nobles arrives with an army initiating a second battle for the city. Felides is wounded, given to the care of Roland's doctors along with Girard. Saracens receive reinforcements from Chalaste and Melias, who are killed by Anseïs and Hestout. Olivier slays Folquenor. Nobles is won; two weeks of baptisms, recuperation of the wounded. Roland leaves Nobles to rejoin Charles at Pamplona. 10,939-996: Prologue II: The poet outlines episodes to follow, from the blow Charles will deliver to Roland, to the latter's departure for the Middle East and eventual return years later. The poet declines to identify himself by name, but says he is from Padua, declaring that he discovered a copy of the Latin chronicle of Turpin in Milan and that he is the author ("houtor") of the remaining narrative. 10,997-11,137: Roland arrives in Pamplona; Charles immediately orders the barons to slay him, which they refuse to do. Charles erupts in rage against Roland and strikes him on the face with his mailed glove, drawing blood. Roland, infuriated and humiliated, controls his impulse to strike back by remembering how the emperor raised him from childhood; he determines that his vengeance shall be "de stragne guise," depriving Charles of his aid in the battle for Pamplona. Roland rides away. 11,138-384: Roland wanders aimlessly across the countryside and enters a thick forest. *Planctus* when he recalls his present predicament and past. Meanwhile at Pamplona, Hestout, Girard

and Olivier deplore Charles's act and request release from service to him;
Hestout threatens to ravage imperial territory. Salomon convinces the
three to remain. Charles defends his action and orders a search for
Roland, but abandons his vow to have him slain. 11,385-764: Roland
spends the night at a magic fountain constructed by the pagan Clariel.
After three days of wandering, he comes to the sea, where he encounters
two Saracen merchants; a fray ensues in which Roland slays them both.
The shipcaptain Baudor, grateful to Roland for saving him, offers to
take Roland to the East in his ship. Roland accepts; they sail. Baudor
offers his daughter Salomé to Roland in the hope of producing a mighty
grandson. Roland prays. 11,765-913: They arrive in Syria, sailing up
the River Jordan to a lake on which is situated "La Mecque," capital of
Persia. Roland invents a new identity as the Saracen Bacharuf. He
disembarks at Mecca, saying he wishes to visit the shrine of
Mohammed. 11,914-13,171: Roland arrives at the sultan's tent, where
debate is raging over whether the Princess Dionés will be forced to wed
Malquidant, whom her father needs as an ally. His nephew Pélias,
declaring that all women are evil, demands that she be burned alive and
challenges anyone who dares to oppose him. Roland is presented to the
sultan; now he calls himself Lionés, recently-knighted son of a "fee"
and Spanish Saracen merchant. Roland asks to defend Dionés;
preparations for combat. Her beauty troubles Roland, who determines to
remain faithful to Aude. An informer tells Daïre that "Lionés" is
actually Roland, but is not believed. Combat; Roland dismounts in
order not to claim unfair advantage when he kills Pélias's horse. Pélias
asks Roland who he really is, convinced he must be a nobleman by his
chivalric valor. Roland reveals to Pélias his true identity, then slays
him. 13,172-676: Celebrations for Roland; admiration on the part of
all, especially Dionés. Her brother Samson admires Roland and
becomes a protégé. An infuriated Malquidant vows to avenge the death
of Pélias by invading Persia. *Conseil* to decide on how to reward
Roland and retain his services; he is offered Dionés in marriage, but
declines, claiming that his bourgeois background makes him an
unworthy husband for her and that he does not merit such a prize. He
accepts the sultan's appointment as "bailis" of Persia. Dionés, who is
versed in astrology, predicts that Roland will bring them victory in the
war with Malquidant, which will end in Jerusalem. Roland is given a
palace of his own where he may entertain. 13,677-991: Roland becomes
mentor of all the young Persians in the arts of chivalry. He suggests,
then leaves on a tour of the realm to assess the sultan's military
strength, taking Samson with him. They visit Gog and Magog, but
avoid Sidoigne, where the citizens offer their wives to visitors. Return
to Mecca, where Roland announces that an army of 100,000 can be

raised. A banquet is held during which Roland instructs the Persians in table manners.

LACUNA (possibly up to 5,000-6,000 verses).

13,992-14,293: The narrative resumes at the wedding of Anseïs de Blois and Dionés in Jerusalem. Anseïs has been named king of Jerusalem, Dionés has become Christian, as has Aquilant, who will accompany Roland back to Spain. Roland announces his wish to return to Spain rather than to pursue the Christianization of the Mideast, especially to lead an attack on the Tower of Babel. Samson asks to accompany him, and is given permission by his father. Roland promises to return to the Middle East after Spain is won if the sultan still needs his aid. Roland visits the holy sites in Jerusalem. Preparations for departure. 14,294-427: Roland departs with three companions, the third being Hugues de Blois. At sea, a storm comes up and forces landing in enemy Spain. 14,428-647: They enter a wild forest strewn with decapitated giants. Encounter with three Saracen brigands; Roland pretends he is Saracen to avoid a fight, but when they demand horses and weapons, a fight breaks out. Aquilant is slain along with the thieves. 14,648-15,250: Roland comes upon a chapel inhabited by an old hermit, Samson of Rome, who first threatens to kill him, thinking Roland another of the Saracen giants. He hands Roland his sacred cross, which only a good man can touch, then welcomes Roland. The hermit relates his life story; he was a Roman noble, a senator's son, who defied paternal authority and culminated a degenerate youth by killing his family. Repentant, he went to Rome to seek papal pardon, and determined to spend the rest of his life doing penance. He lived with another hermit for fourteen years; since then he has lived alone, armed with a miraculous sword which permits him to slay the local heathen giants. Food is brought to them by an angel. In the meantime, Roland's two companions are visited by another angel in the form of Roland himself; the angel gives them food and promises they shall see Charles the following day. The first angel reveals to Roland that he will live only another seven years, and will die a martyr betrayed by someone he loves and trusts. He also reveals that the hermit will die before daybreak, and that Roland is to keep vigil and bury him. Both are initially frightened by the prophecies, but accept and resign themselves. Roland thinks of all the heathens he can slay in the years remaining to him. Confession, death, and burial of the hermit. Roland rejoins his friends. 15,251-332: The magic apples that Hugues and Samson had been eating suddenly turn sour, a sign that the miracles have ended. But another occurs when a large path opens before Roland in the thick forest. They sight Pamplona and the Christian camp. 15,333-805: Rainier de Nantes recognizes Roland and hurries to tell Charles. At the same time, the emperor's barons are threatening to

abandon the siege of Pamplona unless Roland returns immediately.
Charles's grief and regret at his earlier brutality toward Roland. Olivier
asks that he be allowed to ask Roland to rejoin the army and resume the
rear guard position. Rainier announces that he has seen Roland.
Reunion of Roland with Rainier, Olivier, Salomon, and others. Charles
arrives, is about to kneel before Roland to beg pardon when Roland
instead kneels, submitting himself to the emperor's justice. Charles
embraces Roland; great joy of both. The whole Christian army weeps
with emotion.

Selected Bibliography

Principal Primary Literary Sources

Alighieri, Dante. *Convivio*. Ed. Gustavo Rodolfo Ceriello.
Biblioteca universale Rizzoli 483-486. Milan: Rizzoli, 1952.
—. *La Divina Commedia*. Ed. Natalino Sapegno. 3 vols. Florence:
La Nuova Italia, 1957.
—. *La Divina Commedia*. Ed. and trans. Charles S. Singleton. 6
vols. Bollingen series 80. Princeton: Princeton UP, 1975.
—. *De vulgari eloquentia*. Ed. and trans. Bruno Panvini. Palermo:
Andò, 1968.
Bédier, Joseph, ed. *La Chanson de Roland, publiée d'après le
manuscrit d'Oxford et traduite par Joseph Bédier*. Paris: L'Edition
d'Art H. Piazza, 1937.
Brault, Gerald J., ed. and trans. *The Song of Roland: An Analytical
Edition*. 2 vols. University Park and London: Pennsylvania State
UP, 1978.
Catalano, Michele, ed. *La Spagna: poema cavalleresco del secolo XIV*.
3 vols. Collezione di opere inedite e rare. Bologna: Carducci,
1939.
Jenkins, T. Atkinson, ed. *La Chanson de Roland, Oxford Version*.
2nd. ed. Boston: Heath, 1924.
LIBER INTROITUS YSPANIE. Manuscript Codice Marciana francese
XXI (=257). *L'Entrée d'Espagne*. Biblioteca Marciana, Venice.
Meredith-Jones, George, ed. *Historia Karoli Magni et Rotholandi ou
Chronique du pseudo-Turpin*. Geneva: Droz, 1936.
Mortier, Raoul, ed. *Les Textes de La Chanson de Roland*. 10 vols.
Paris: Editions de la geste francor, 1940-1944.
Mussafia, Adolfo, ed. *La Prise de Pampelune. Ein altfranzösisches
Gedichte aus venezianischen Handscriften. I. La Prise de
Pampelune. II. Macaire*. Vienna: Druck und Verlag von Carl
Gerold's Sohn, 1864.
Pseudo-Dionysius the Areopagite. *The Ecclesiastical Hierarchy*. Ed.
and trans. Thomas L. Campbell. Washington: UP of America,
1981.
Queirazza, Giuliano Gasca, S. J., ed. and trans. *La Chanson de Roland
nel testo assonanzato franco-italiano*. L'Orifiamma: Collezione di
testi romanzi o mediolatini. Turin: Rosenberg & Sellier, 1952.
Robertson-Mellor, Geoffrey, ed. *The Franco-Italian Roland (V4)*.
Salford: U of Salford Reprographic Unit, 1980.
Ruggieri, R.M., ed. *Li fatti di Spagna*. Modena: Mucchi, 1951.
Segre, Cesare, ed. *La Chanson de Roland*. Documenti di filoligia 16.
Milan: Riccardo Ricciardi, 1971.

Thomas, Antoine, ed. *L'Entrée d'Espagne: chanson de geste franco-italienne, publiée d'après le manuscrit unique de Venise.* 2 vols. SATF. Paris: Firmin-Didot, 1913.
Whitehead. F., ed. *La Chanson de Roland.* Blackwell's French Texts. Oxford: Blackwell, 1970.

Studies of *L'Entrée d'Espagne*

Included in this section are works not entirely nor explicitly on the *Entrée*, but which provide important information regarding the text.

Adler, Alfred. "Didactic Concerns in the *Entrée d'Espagne.*" *EC* 2.2 (1962): 107-09.
Aebischer, Paul. "Ce qui reste d'un manuscrit perdu de *L'Entrée d'Espagne.*" *Archivum Romanicum* 12 (1928): 233-64.
——. "Deux récits épiques antérieurs au *Roland* d'Oxford: *L'Entrée d'Espagne* primitive et le *Girart de Viane* primitif." *Etudes de Lettres* 3rd ser. 1 (1968): 4-35.
——. *Préhistoire et protohistoire du Roland d'Oxford.* Biblioteca romanica, series prima, manualia et commentationes 12. Berne: Francke AG, 1971.
——. *Rolandiana borealia: la Saga af Runzivals Bardaga et ses dérivés scandinaves comparés à la Chanson de Roland. Essai de restauration du manuscrit français utilisé par le traducteur norrois. Université de Lausanne Publications de la Faculté des lettres 11.* Lausanne: F. Rouge et Cie., 1954.
——. *Rolandiana et Oliveriana: recueil d'études sur les chansons de geste.* PRF 97. Geneva: Droz, 1967.
——. "Le Rôle de Pampelune lors de l'expédition franque de 778 en Espagne d'après l'histoire et l'épique médiévale." *Schweiz. Zs. für Geschichte: Revue suisse d'histoire* 9 (1959): 305-33.
——. *Textes norrois et littérature française du moyen âge.* 2 vols. PRF 54 and 118. Geneva: Droz, 1954 and 1972.
Arnaldi, Girolamo. "Il primo secolo dello studio di Padova." *Il Trecento.* Ed. Gianfranco Folena. 6 volumes (projected). *Storia della cultura veneta.* Modena: Neri Pozza, 1976. 2: 1-18.
Avesani, Rino. "Il preumanesimo veronese." *SCV* 2: 111-41.
Baldelli, Ignazio. "Un glossarietto francese-veneto del Trecento." *Studi linguistici italiani* 2 (1961): 155-62.
Barberini, Andrea da. *I Reali di Francia.* Ed. Giuseppe Vandelli and Giovanni Gambarin. Bari: Laterza, 1947.
Beckmann, Gustave A. "L'Identification Nobles = Dax." *MA* 28.1 (1973): 5-24.

Bédier, Joseph. *Les Légendes épiques. Recherches sur la formation des chansons de geste.* 3rd ed. 4 vols. Paris: Champion, 1908.

Beretta, Carlo. "Les Prières épiques de l'*Entrée d'Espagne.*" *Actes du XIᵉ Congrès international de la Société Rencesvals (Barcelone, 22-27 août 1988).* 2 vols. Barcelona: Real Acad. de Buenas Letras, 1990. 2: 65-74.

Bertoni, Giulio. Rev. of *L'Entrée,* ed. Thomas. *Giornale storico della letteratura italiana* 65-66 (1915): 426-34.

Billanovich, Guido. "Il preumanesimo padovano." *SCV* 2: 19-110.

Bradley-Cromey, Nancy. *L'Entrée d'Espagne: Elements of Content and Composition.* Ph D Diss. U of Wisconsin, 1974. Ann Arbor: University Microfilms, 1975.

—."Roland as *Baron Révolté*: The Problem of Authority and Autonomy in *L'Entrée d'Espagne* ." *Olifant* 5.4 (May 1978): 285-97.

—. "Signs of *Sententia*: Forest and Voyage in *L'Entrée d'Espagne.*" *Romance Epic: Essays on a Medieval Literary Genre.* Ed. Hans-Erich Keller. Studies in Medieval Culture 24. Kalamazoo: The Medieval Institute, 1987. 203-11.

Branca, Daniele Delcorno. *Il romanzo cavalleresco medievale.* Florence: Sansoni, 1974.

Brugnolo, Furio. "I Toscani nel Veneto e le cerchie toscaneggianti." *SCV* 2: 369-439.

Callu-Turiaf, Florence. "Les Versions franco-italiennes de la chanson d'*Aye d'Avignon.*" *Ecole française de Rome. Mélanges d'archéologie et d'histoire* 73 (1961): 391-435.

Constans, Léopold. "*L'Entrée d'Espagne* et les légendes troyennes." *Romania* 43 (1914): 430-32.

Delcorno Branca, Daniela. *L'Orlando furioso e il romanzo cavalleresco medievale.* Florence: Olschki, 1973.

Dionisotti, Carlo. "*Entrée d'Espagne, Spagna, Rotta di Roncisvalle.*" *Studi in onore di Angelo Monteverdi.* 2 vols. Modena: Mucchi, 1959. 1: 207-41.

Fabio, F. *Materia cavalleresca prima dell'Ariosto.* Naples: Libreria Scientifica Editrice, 1972.

Ferrero, Giuseppe Guido. "Astolfo (storia di un personnaggio)." *Convivium* 24 (1961): 513-30.

—. *Poemi cavallereschi del Trecento.* Turin: UTET, 1965.

Finoli, Anna Maria. "Personalità e cultura dell'autore dell'*Entrée d'Espagne.*" *Cultura Neolatina* 11 (1961): 175-81.

Flöss, Lidia. "Le fonti dei *Fatti de Spagna.*" *Medioevo Romanzo* 15 (1990): 115-37.

Folena, Gianfranco. "La cultura volgare e l'umanesimo cavalleresco nel Veneto." *Umanesimo europeo e umanesimo veneziano.* Florence: Sansoni, 1964. 111-58.

Fontana, Giovanni. "Le Problème des remaniements dans les textes épiques et dans les cantari italiens du XIV⁰ et du XV⁰ siècles." *Au Carrefour des routes d'Europe: la chanson de geste. Xᵉ Congrès international de la Société Rencesvals pour l'étude des épopées romanes.* 2 vols. Aix-en-Provence: Publications du CUER MA, 1987. 1: 513-30.

Franceschetti, Antonio. "On the Saracens in Early Chivalric Literature." *Romance Epic.* 203-11.

Gargan, Luciano. "Il preumanesimo a Vicenza, Treviso e Venezia." *SCV* 2: 1142-70.

Gautier, Léon. "*L'Entrée en Espagne,* chanson de geste inédite, renfermée dans un manuscrit de la bibliothèque de Saint-Marc à Venise. Notice, analyse et extraits." Bibliothèque de l'Ecole des Chartes 19th ser., 4 (1858): 217-70.

Guiette, Robert. "L'Entrée de Charlemagne en Espagne et la tradition des croniques et conquestes de Charlemaine (1458)." *CN* 21 (1961): 206-13.

—. "Notes sur 'La Prise de Nobles.' " *Romanica Gandensia* 4 (1955): 67-80.

Holtus, Günter. *Lexikalische Untersuchungen zur Interferenz: die franko-italienische "Entrée d'Espagne."* Tübingen: Niemeyer, 1979.

—. "Quelques aspects de la technique narrative dans l'*Entrée d'Espagne." Essor et fortune de la chanson de geste dans l'Europe et l'Orient latin. Actes du IXᵉ Congrès international de la Société Rencesvals pour l'étude des épopées romanes. Padoue-Venise, 29 août-4 septembre 1982.* 2 vols. Modena: Mucchi, 1984. 2: 703-16.

Huet, G. Busken. "*L'Entrée d'Espagne." Neophilologus* 3 (1918): 241-47.

Krauss, Henning. "Aspects de l'histoire poétique de Charlemagne in Italie." *Charlemagne et l'épopée romane. Actes du VIIᵉ Congrès international de la Société Rencesvals (Liège 28 août-4 septembre 1976).* Bibliothèque de la Faculté de Philosophie et Lettres de l'Université de Liège 225. Paris: Les Belles Lettres, 1978.

—. "Cenni sull' 'Entrée d'Espagne' e sulla 'Prise de Pampelune.' " *Epica feudale e pubblico borghese. Per la storia poetica di Carlomagno in Italia.* Ydioma Tripharium. Collana di studi e saggi di filologia romanza diretta da Alberto Limentani 6. Ed. A.

Fassò. Trans. F. Brugnolo, A. Fassò, M. Mancini. Padua: Liviana, 1980. 217-40.

Lazzarini, Lino. "La cultura delle signorie venete e i poeti di corte." *SCV* 2: 477-516.

Lejeune, Rita and Jacques Stiennon. *The Legend of Roland in the Middle Ages.* Trans. Christine Trollope. 2 vols. London: Phaidon, 1971. 1: 243-60.

Limentani, Alberto. "Anticipation épique et chanson dans la chanson. Notes sur le *Cantar de mio Cid* et sur l'*Entrée d'Espagne*." *Atti del VIII ⁰ Congresso de la Société Rencesvals.* Pamplona: 1981. Goolena: Societa tipografica modenese, 1983. 281-90.

——. "L'Art de la comparaison dans *L'Entrée d'Espagne*." *Actes du VIᵉ Congrès international de la Société Rencesvals (Aix 1973)*. Aix-en-Provence: Université de Provence, 1974. 353-71.

——. "Astronomia, astrologia e arti magiche nell'*Entrée d'Espagne*." *Medioevo e Rinascimento veneto, con altri studi in onore di L. Lazzarini.* 2 vols. Padua: Antenore, 1979. 1: 129-46.

——. "Il comico nell'*Entrée d'Espagne* e il suo divenire. Una preghiera 'en la lois aufricaine.' " *Interpretation. Das Paradigma der europäischen Renaissance-Literatur. Festschrift für Alfred Noyer-Weidner zum 60. Geburtstag.* Ed. K. W. Hempfer and G. Regn. Wiesbaden: Franz-Steiner GMBH, 1983. 61-82.

——. "*Entrée d'Espagne* e *Milione*." *Scritti linguistici in onore di Giovan Battista Pellegrini.* Ed. P. Benincà. 2 vols. Pisa: Pacini, 1983. 2: 393-417.

——. "L'epica in 'lengue de France': l'*Entrée d'Espagne* e Niccolò da Verona." *SCV* 2: 339-56.

——. "Epica e racconto: osservazioni su alcune strutture e sull'incompiutezza dell'*Entrée d'Espagne. AN* Classe di scienze morali, lettere ed arti 133 (1974-75): 393-433.

——. "Presenza di Virgilio e tracce d'epica latina nei poemi franco-italiani?" *Lectures médiévales de Virgile. Actes du Colloque organisé par l'Ecole française de Rome (Rome, 25-28 octobre 1982).* Rome: Ecole française de Rome, 1985. 285-311.

——. "Venezia e il 'pericolo turco' nell'*Entrée d'Espagne*." *CN* 40 (1980): 165-81.

Mandach, André de. "Les Blasons des grandes familles padouanes dans l'*Entrée d'Espagne*." *CN* 2-4 (1989): 179-202.

——. *Chronique dite saintongeaise: texte franco-occitan inédit "Lee." A la découverte d'une chronique gasconne du XIIIᵉ siècle et de sa poitevinisation.* Beihefte zur Zeitschrift für Romanische Philologie 120. Tübingen: Neimeyer, 1970.

—. "Le Destinataire de l'*Entrée d'Espagne* de Venise (Marciana fr. XXI): Francesco il Vecchio da Carrara?" *AIV*. Classe di scienze morali, lettere ed arti 148 (1989-90). In press.

—. "Les Destinataires du *Tacuinum sanitatis in medicina* de Vienne (Oesterr. Nationalbibliothek N. S. 2644): la Casa Cerruti de Vérone ou le couple Sperone Speroni degli Alvarotti de Padoue? A propos du principal miniaturiste de l'*Entrée d'Espagne*." *de Venise*. In press.

—. "L'*Entrée d'Espagne*: six auteurs en quête d'un personnage." *Studi Medievali* 3rd ser. 30.1 (1989): 163-208.

—. *Naissance et développement de la chanson de geste en Europe*. 5 vols. Geneva: Droz, 1961-1983.

—. "La Prise de Noples et de Gormaise par Roland." *Essor et fortune*. 2: 717-28.

—. Rev. of *Epica feudale e pubblico borghese* by Henning Krauss. *CCM* 30 (1987): 169-71.

—. "Sur les traces de la cheville ouvrière de l'*Entrée d'Espagne*: Giovanni di Nono." *Testi, cotesti e contesti del franco-italiano*. *Atti del 1° simposio franco-italiano (Bad Homburg, 13-16 aprile 1987)*. Ed. Günter Holtus, Henning Krauss, Peter Wunderli. Tübingen: Niemeyer, 1989. 48-64.

Moisan, André. "L'Exploitation de l'épopée par la *Chronique du Pseudo-Turpin*." *MA* 95 (1989): 195-224.

Monteverdi, Angelo. "Un fragment manuscrit de l'*Entrée d'Espagne*. (Résumé)." *CCM* 3 (1960): 75.

Ninni, Franca di. "La formazione del lessico in Nicolò da Verona." *Testi, Cotesti*. 202-08.

Paris, Gaston. *Histoire poétique de Charlemagne*. Paris, 1865.

—. "Notice sur *L'Entrée d'Espagne*." *Rom.* 10 (1881): 456.

—. Rev. of "*Nouvelles recherches sur L'Entrée d'Espagne*, ed. Antoine Thomas." *Rom.* 11 (1882): 147-49.

Paris, Paulin. "Chanson de geste." *Histoire littéraire de la France*. 30 vols. Paris, 1873. 26: 350-60.

Petrobelli, Pierluigi. "La musica nelle cattedrali e nelle città ed i suoi rapporti con la cultura letteraria." *SCV* 2: 440-68.

Renzi, Lorenzo. "Per la lingua dell'*Entrée d'Espagne*." *CN* 30 (1970): 59-87.

Richthofen, Erich von. "La 'Entrée d'Espagne' y el 'Poema del Cid.' " *Tradicionalismo épico-novelesco*. Barcelona: Editorial Planeta, 1972. 37-38, 79-82.

—. *Sincretismo literario. Algunos ejemplos medievales y renacentistas*. Madrid: Alhambra, 1981.

——. "Théorie de la genèse du *Roland* confirmée par l'analogie de celle du *Cid*." *La Chanson de geste et le mythe carolingien. Mélanges . . . René Louis, publiés par ses collègues et ses élèves à l'occasion de son 75e anniversaire*. Ed. André Moisan. 2 vols. Bibliothèque du Musée Archéologique Régional: Saint-Père-Sous-Vézelay, 1982.

Roncaglia, Aurelio. "Les quatre eschieles de Rollant." *Atti del 2° Congresso della 'Société Rencesvals*. *CN* 21 (1961): 191-205

——. "Petit vers et refrain dans les chansons de geste." *La Technique littéraire des chansons de geste. Actes du colloque de Liège (sept. 1957)*. Paris: Les Belles Lettres, 1959. 141-59.

Ruggieri, Ruggero M. "Dall'*Entrée d'Espagne* e dai *Fatti di Spagna* alla 'materia di Spagna' dell'inventario gonzaghesco." *CN* 21 (1961): 182-90.

——. *Lirica, epica, romanzo cortese nel mondo neolatino. Studi e ricerche*. Matera: Montemurro, 1973.

——. "Les Lombards dans les chansons de geste." *Société Rencesvals: IVᵉ Congrès international . Heidelberg, 28 août-2 septembre 1967. Actes et mémoires*. Studia Romanica. Heidelberg: C. Winter, 1969. 37-45.

——. "Nuove osservazioni sui rapporti tra il frammento di Roncesvalles e la leggenda rolandiana in Francia e in Italia." *Coloquios de Roncesvalles (agosto 1955). Disputación Foral de Navarra*. Zaragosa: Institucíon Principe de Viana, 1956. 173-88.

——. "Temi e aspetti della letteratura franco-veneta." *Dante e la cultura veneta*. Ed. Vittore Branca and Giorgio Padoan. Florence: Olschki, 1966. 143-56.

——. "Il titolo e la protasi dell'*Entrée d'Espagne* e dei *Fatti de Spagna* in rapporto alla materia della *Chanson de Roland*. " *Mélanges de linguistique romane et de philologie médiévale offerts à M. Maurice Delbouille*. 2 vols. Gembloux: Duculot, 1964. 2: 615-33.

——. *Umanesimo cavalleresco italiano da Dante al Pulci*. Rome: Ateneo, 1962.

——. *Umanesimo classico e umanesimo cavalleresco italiano*. Biblioteca della facoltà di lettere e filosofia. Catania: Università di Catania, 1955.

Specht, René. "Cavalleria francese alla corte di Persia: l'episodio dell'*Entrée d'Espagne* ritrovato nel frammento reggiano." *AIV*. Classe di scienze, lettere, ed arti 135 (1976-77): 489-506.

——. "L'Etat actuel des recherches sur l'*Entrée d'Espagne*." *Essor et fortune*. 2: 791-94.

—. "Il frammento reggiano dell'*Entrée d'Espagne*: raffronto filologico col codice marciano francese XXI (=257)." *AIV*. Classe di scienze, lettere ed arti 136 (1977-78): 407-24.

—. *Recherches sur Nicolas de Vérone*. *Contribution à l'étude de la littérature franco-italienne du quatorzième siècle*. Publications Universitaires Européennes ser. 13. Langue et littérature françaises 78. Berne, Francfort/M: Peter Lang, 1982. 25-110.

—. "La tradition manuscrite de l'*Entrée d'Espagne*. Observations sur le fragment de Châtillon." *Essor et fortune*. 2: 749-58.

Stengel, Edmund Max. "*L'Entrée d'Espagne*." *ZRP* 5 (1881): 379-81.

Thomas, Antoine. Avant-propos and Introduction to edition of *L'Entrée d'Espagne*. 1: i-cxxxvi.

—. *Nouvelles recherches sur l'Entrée d'Espagne, chanson de geste franco-italienne*. Bibliothèque des Ecoles françaises d'Athènes et de Rome 25. Paris: Thorin, 1882.

Toesca, Pietro. "Le miniature dell'*Entrée de Spagne* della Biblioteca Marciana." *Scritti vari di erudizione e di critica in onore di Rodolfo Renier*. Turin: Fratelli Bocca, 1912. 747-53.

Torraca, Francesco. "*L'Entrée d'Espagne*." *Studi di storia letteraria*. Florence: Sansoni, 1923. 164-241.

Viscardi, Antonio. *Storia della letteratura d'oc et d'oïl*. Milan: Nuova Accademia Editrice, 1959. 401-13.

Voigt, F. Theodore A. *Roland-Orlando dans l'épopée française et italienne*. Leiden: E.J. Brill, 1938.

Wunderli, Peter. "Roland théologien dans l'*Aquilon de Bavière*." *Essor et fortune*. 2: 759-81.

Yocca, G. Stefano. *Saggio su L'Entrée d'Espagne ed altre canzoni di gesta medievali franco-italiane*. Rome, 1895.

Franco-Italian Sources

Adler, Alfred. "Adenet's *Berte* and the Ideological Situation in the 1270's." *Studies in Philology* 45 (1948): 419-31.

—. *Epische Spekulanten*. Versuch einer synchronen Geschichte des altfranzösischen Epos. Munich: W. Fink, 1975.

Alessio, Franco. "Filosofia e scienza. Pietro da Abano." *SCV* 2: 171-206.

d'Arcais, Francesca. "Les Illustrations des manuscrits français des Gonzague à la Bibliothèque de Saint-Marc." *Essor et fortune*. 2: 585-616.

Avesani, Rita. "Il preumanesimo veronese." *SCV* 2: 111-41.

Arnaldi, Girolamo. "Il primo secolo dello studio di Padova." *SCV* 2: 1-18.

Arnaldi, Girolamo and Lidia Capo. "I cronisti di Venezia e della Marca trevigiana." *SCV* 2: 272-337.

Bartoli, Adolfo. *I codici francesi della Biblioteca Marciana di Venezia.* Venice: Marco Visentini, 1872.

Baüml, Franz. "Varieties and Consequences of Medieval Literacy and Illiteracy." *Speculum* 55 (1980): 237-65.

Bekker, Immanuel. "Die Altfranzösische Roman der St. Marcus Bibliotek." *Abhandlungen der königlich preussischen Akademie der Wissenschaften. Deutsche Akademie der Wissenschaften zu Berlin. Philologische-historische Klasse.* Berlin, 1839.

Bender, Karl Heinz. *König und Vassal: Untersuchungen zur chanson de geste des XIII Jahrhunderts.* Heidelberg: Carl Winter, 1967.

——. "Les Métamorphoses de la royauté de Charlemagne dans les premières épopées franco-italiennes." *CN* 21 (1961): 164-74.

Bertoni, Giulio. "L'epopea francese in Italia e le leggende italiane." *Il Duecento. Storia letteraria d'Italia.* Milan: Vallardi, 1911. 37-59.

——. "Nota sulla letteratura franco-italiana a proposito della *Vita* in rima di S. Maria Egiziaca." *Studi su vecchie e nuove poesie e prose d'amore e di romanzi.* Modena: Mucchi, 1921. 227-40.

——. *I trovatori d'Italia.* Rome: Multigrafica Editrice, 1967.

Billanovich, Guido. "Biblioteche di dotti e letteratura italiana tra il Trecento e il Quattrocento." *Studi e problemi di critica testuale* 2. (1971): 335-48.

——. "Il preumanesimo padovano." *SCV* 2: 19-110.

Binni, Walter. "Veneto." *Storia letteraria delle regioni d'Italia.* Florence: Olschki, 1968. 168-70.

Bolisani, Ettore. "Un importante saggio padovano di poesia preumanistica latina. *Accademia patavina di scienze, lettere ed arti. Atti e memorie* 66 (1953-54): 61-77.

Boni, Marco. "Reminiscenze della 'continuazione' franco-italiana della *Chanson d'Aspremont* nell'*Aquilon de Bavière*." *Miscellanea di studi romanzi offerta a Giuliano Gasca Queirazza.* Ed. Anna Cornagliotti, Lucia Fonanella, et al. 2 vols. Turin: Orso, 1988. 1:49-74.

Bradley-Cromey, Nancy. Rev. of *Aliscans,* ed. by Günter Holtus. *Olifant* 11 (1986): 244-49.

——. Rev. of *Recherches sur Nicolas de Vérone. Contribution à l'étude de la littérature franco-italienne du quatorzième siècle* by René Specht. *Olifant* 9 (1981): 70-74.

——. Rev. of "Zur Edition der franko-italienischen Fassung von Aliscans" by Günter Holtus. *Olifant* 8.1 (1980): 104-05.

Braghirolli, Willelmo, Paul Meyer, Gaston Paris. "Inventaire des
    manuscrits en langue française possédés par Francesco Gonzaga I,
    Capitaine de Mantoue, mort en 1407." *Rom.* 9 (1880): 499-514.
Branca, Daniela Delcorno. "Il cavaliere delle arme incantate:
    circolazione di un modello narrativo arturiano." *I cantari: struttura
    e tradizione.* Ed. M. Picone e M. Bendinelli Predelli. Florence:
    Olschki, 1984.
——. "Fortuna e trasformazioni del *Buovo d'Antona.*" *Testi, cotesti.*
    285-306.
——. *I romanzi italiani di Tristano e la Tavola Ritonda.* Florence:
    Olschki, 1968.
Branca, Vittore, ed. *Mercanti scrittori. Ricordi nella Firenze tra
    Medioevo e Rinascimento.* Milan: Rusconi, 1986.
Calin, William. "Problèmes littéraires soulevés par les chansons de
    geste. L'exemple d'*Aspremont.*" *Au Carrefour.* 1: 333-350.
Callu-Turiaf, Florence. "Notes sur une version disparue de 'Renaut de
    Montauban' en franco-italien." *MA* 68 (1962): 125-36.
——. "Les Versions franco-italiennes de la chanson d' 'Aye d'Avignon.' "
    Ecole française de Rome. Mélanges d'archéologie et d'histoire 73
    (1961): 391-435.
Cappelli, A. "La biblioteca estense nella prima metà del secolo XV."
    Giornale storico della letteratura italiana 14 (1889): 26-27.
Cassola, Nicolò da. *Attila: poema franco-italiano di Nicolò da Casola.*
    Ed. Giulio Bertoni. Fribourg, 1907.
Castellani, Carlo. "Sul fondo francese della Biblioteca Marciana, a
    proposito di un codice recentemente ad esso aggiunto." *AIV.*
    Classe di scienze letterarie ed arti 85 (1892-93): 56-94.
Castets, Ferdinand. "Recherches sur les rapports des chansons de geste
    et de l'épopée chevaleresque italienne." *Revue des langues
    romanes.* 3rd ser. 13 (1885): 5-15.
Ciampoli, Domenico. *I codici francesi della reale Biblioteca nazionale
    di San Marco in Venezia.* Venice, 1897.
——. "Due indici inediti dei codici francesi nella Marciana." *Nuovi studi
    letterari e bibliografici.* Rocca S. Casciano, 1900. 399-418.
Ciarambino, Gerardo C. A. *Carlomagno, Gano e Orlando in alcuni
    romanzi italiani del XIV e XV secolo.* Pisa: Giardini, 1976.
Colliot, Régine. "Structure de la trahison dans les diverses versions de
    la légende de Berte aus grans piés." *Essor et fortune.* 2: 663-78.
Contini, Gianfranco. "Le Début de la *Mort Charlemagne.*" *Mélanges
    René Louis.* 1: 303-11.
——. "La canzone della *Mort Charlemagne.*" *Mélanges . . . Delbouille.*
    2: 105-26.
——. *Poeti del Duecento.* 2 vols. Milan: Ricciardi, 1960.

Cremonesi, C., ed. *Berta e Milon. Rolandin. Codice Marciana XIII.* Milan: Istituto editoriale Cisalpino-La Goliardica, 1973.

——, ed. *Le Danois Ogier: enfances-chevalerie.* Codice Marciana XIII. Milan: Istituío editoriale Cisalpino-La Goliardica, 1977.

——. "Note di franco-veneto." *Studi di lingua e letteratura lombarda offerti a Maurizio Vitale.* 2 vols. Pisa: Giardini, 1983. 1: 5-21.

Crescini, Vincenzo. "Di una data importante nella storia dell'epopea franco-veneta." *AIV. Classe di scienze lettere, ed arti.* 8th ser. 54 (1895-96): 1,150-74.

Cracco, Giorgio. *Società e stato nel Medioevo veneziano (secoli XII-XIV).* Florence: Olschki, 1967.

Delbouille, Maurice. "L'Origine franco-vénitienne des chants épiques yougoslaves." *Venezia e il Levante fino al secolo XV.* 2 vols. Florence: Olschki, 1973-74.

Fabio, F. *Materia cavalleresca prima dell'Ariosto.* Naples: Libreria Scientifica Editrice, 1972.

Fabris, G. "La cronaca di Giovanni di Nono." *Bollettino del Museo Civico di Padova.* New ser. 8 (1932): 1-33; 9 (1933): 167-200; 10-11 (1934-39): 1-30.

Fasoli, Gina. "La 'Cronique des Veniciens' di Martino da Canale." *SM* 3.2 (June 1961): 42-71.

Ferrari, Giorgio, ed. *Codici marciani ed edizioni italiane antiche di epopea carolingia: catalogo di mostra in occasione del II Congresso della Société Rencesvals in Venezia (settembre 1961), dedicato all'epopea francese, con particolare riguardo all'epopea franco-italiana.* Venice: Biblioteca Nazionale Marciana, 1961.

——, ed. *Documenti marciani e principale letteratura sui codici veneti di epopea carolingia.* Venice: Biblioteca Nazionale Marciana, 1961.

——. "La tradizione di studi dei codici marciani francesi, preludio ad una bibliografia analitica." *CN* 21 (1961): 105-15.

Ferrero, G. *Poemi cavallereschi del 300.* Turin: UTET, 1965.

Folena, Gianfranco. "Tradizione e cultura trobadorica nelle corti e nelle città venete." *SCV* 1: 453-562.

Fontana, G. "Le Problème des remaniements dans les textes épiques et dans les cantari italiens du XIVe et du XVe siècles." *Au Carrefour.* 2: 513-30.

Gardner, Edmund G. *The Arthurian Legend in Italian Literature.* London: J. M. Dent & Sons, 1930.

Giovanna, Giuseppe della. "S. Francesco d'Assisi, giullare." *Giornale storico della letteratura italiana* 25 (1895): 1-7.

Girolla, Pia. "La biblioteca di Francesco Gonzaga secondo l'inventario del 1407." *Atti e Memorie della Reale Accademia Virgiliana di Mantova,* New ser. 14-16 (1921-23): n. pag.

Guessard, Francis, ed. "*Macaire*: chanson de geste, publiée d'après le manuscrit unique de Venise, avec un essai de restitution en regard du texte." Bibliothèque de l'Ecole des Chartes 5th ser. 5 (1864): 489-551.

Hills, Elijah Clarence. "Irregular Epic Metres. A Comparative Study of the Metre of the Poem of the *Cid* and of certain Anglo-Norman, Franco-Italian and Venetian Epic Poems." *Homenaje a Menéndez Pidal*. 2 vols. Madrid: Libreria y casa edicional Heinando, 1925. 2: 759-77.

Holtus, Günter. "Approches méthodiques d'une description linguistique du franco-italien." *Festschrift für Kurt Baldinger zum 60. Geburtstag*. Ed. Manfred Höfler, Henri Vernay, Lothar Wolf. Tübingen: Niemeyer, 1979. 854-75.

——. "Aspects linguistiques du franco-italien." *Essor et fortune*. 2: 802-06.

——. "Etimologia e lessico franco-italiano." *Etimologia e lessico dialettale. Atti dell XII Convegno per gli studi dialettali italiani (Macerata, 10-13 aprile 1979)*. Pisa: Pacini, 1981. 153-63.

——. "L'influsso del francese sull'italiano settentrionale antico." *Elementi stranieri nei dialetti italiani. Atti del XIV Convegno del CSDI (Ivrea 17-19 ottobre 1984)*. Pisa: Pacini, 1986.

——. "Lessico franco-italiano=lessico francese e/o lessico italiano." *Medioevo romanzo* 10 (1985): 249-56.

——. "La 'Matière de Bretagne' en Italie: quelques réflexions sur la transposition du vocabulaire et des structures sociales." *Actes du 14e Congrès international arthurien. Rennes, 16-21 août 1984*. Rennes: Presses universitaires de Rennes, 1986. 325-45.

——. "Sulla posizione del franco-italiano nella dialettologia italiana." *Scritti linguistici . . Pellegrini*. 63-71.

——. "Lo stato attuale delle ricerche sul franco-italiano." *La dialettologia italiana di oggi: Studi offerti a Manlio Cortelazzo*. Ed. Günter Holtus, Michele Metzeltin and Max Pfister. Tübingen: Narr, 1989. 209-19.

——, ed. with Henning Krauss and Peter Wunderli. *Testi, cotesti e contesti del franco-italiano. Atti del 1º simposio franco-italiano (Bad Homburg, 13-16 aprile 1987)*. Tübingen: Niemeyer, 1989.

——. "Zur franko-italienischen Sprache und Literatur. Forschungsbereicht 1959-1974." *ZRP* 91.5/6 (1975): 491-533.

——. Zum Verhältnis von Oralität und Schriftlichkeit im Franko-Italienischen." *Testi, cotesti*. 75-79.

——, ed. *La versione franco-italiana della 'Bataille d'Aliscans': Codex Marciana fr. VIII [=252]*. Tübingen: Niemeyer, 1985.

Hope, T. E. *Lexical Borrowing in the Romance Languages: A Critical Study of Italianisms in French and Gallicisms in Italian from 1100 to 1900.* Oxford: Oxford UP, 1971.
Jacoby, David. "La Littérature française dans les états latins de la Méditerranée orientale à l'époque des croisades: diffusion et création." *Essor et fortune.* 2: 617-53.
Krauss, Henning. "Analyse sociologique du Ms. Venise 13." *Essor et fortune.* 2: 789-90.
—. "Der Artus-Roman in Italien." *Grundriss der Romanischen Literaturen des Mittelalters* 4 Heidelberg: C. Winter, 1978. 667-75.
—. *Epica feudale e pubblico borghese. Per la storia poetica di Carlomagno in Italia.* Ed. Andrea Fassò. Trans. F. Brugnolo, A. Fassò, M. Mancini. Ydioma Tripharium. Collana di studi e saggi di filologia romanza diretta da Alberto Limentani 6. Padua: Liviana, 1980.
—. "Ezzelino da Romano-Maximo Cudé. Historische Realität und Epischer Strukturzwang in der frankoitalienischen *Chevalerie Ogier.*" *CN* 30 (1970): 233-49.
—. "Metamorfosi di Orlando nell'*Aquilon de Bavière.*" *Atti e Memorie dell'Accademia Patavina di Scienze, Lettere ed Arti* 95 (1982-83): 425-40.
—. "Ritter und Bürger - Feudalheer und Volksheer. Zum Problem der feigen Lombarden in der altfranzösischen und franko-italienischen Epik." *ZRP* 87 (1971): 209-22.
—. "Roland et la richesse des Florentins dans *Aquilon de Bavière.*" *Au Carrefour.* 2: 777-95.
—. "La Spéculation épique et le problème de l'histoire." *Testi, cotesti.* 225-31.
—. "Von Varocher zu Ispinardo. Anmerkungen zur Rearistokratisierung der Chanson de geste im Italien des 15. Jahrhunderts." *Das Epos in der Romania. Festschrift für Dieter Kremers zum 65. Geburtstag.* Ed. S. Knaller and E. Mara. Tübingen: Niemeyer, 1986. 193-205.
Latini, Brunetto. *Li Livres dou tresor.* Ed. Francis J. Carmody. Berkeley and Los Angeles: U of California P, 1948.
Lazzarini, Lino. "La cultura delle signorie venete e i poeti di corte." *SCV.* 2: 477-516.
Levi, Ezio. "I cantari leggendari del popolo italiano nel secolo XIV e XV." *Giornale storico della letteratura italiana.* Supp. 16 (1914): 1-159.
—. *Francesco di Vannozzo e la lirica nelle corti lombarde durante la seconda metà del secolo XIV.* Reale Istituto di Studi superiori

pratici e di perfezionamento in Firenze. *Sezione di Filosofia e filologia 32*. Florence: n.p., 1908.

Limentani, Alberto. "Appunti sulle traduzioni dalle letterature d'*oc* e d'*oïl*." *Critica e storia letteraria. Studi offerti a Mario Fubini*. 2 vols. Padua, Liviana, 1966. 1: 240-72.

——. "Cinque note su Martino da Canal. *1. Federico II e tre legati veneziani; 2. Una nave dei Templari; 3. Alcuni testimoni altolocali; 4. Menolesso e i suoi compagni; 5. Martino e i Chioggiotti.*" *AIV*. Classe di scienze morali, lettere ed arti 124 (1965-66): 261-85.

——, ed. with M. Infurna. *L'epica*. Strumenti di filologia romanza 3. Bologna: Mulino, 1986.

——, ed. *Martin da Canal. Les Estoires de Venise. Cronaca veneziana in lingua francese dalle origini al 1275*. Civiltà veneziana, fonti e testi 12. ser.3.3. Florence: Olschki, 1973.

——. "Les Nouvelles méthodes de la critique et de l'étude des chansons de geste." *Chanson de geste und höfischer Roman. Heidelberger Kolloquium, 30 Jan. 1961*. Studia romanica 4. 2 vols. Heidelberg: C. Winter, 1963. 2: 295-334.

——. Problemi dell'epica franco-italiana: appunti sulla tecnica della lassa e della rima." *Atti e Memorie dell'Accademia patavina di Scienze, Lettere ed Arti* 95.3 (1982/1983): 159-74.

——. "Tradizione letteraria e funzione pubblicistica nella preghiera a San Marco di Martino da Canal." *CN* 24 (1964): 142-96.

Lomazzi, A. "Franco-veneta, letteratura." *Dizionario critico della letteratura italiana*. Ed. Vittore Branca. 2 vols. Turin: UTET, 1986. 2: 285-91.

Mandach, André de. "A la découverte d'un nouvel *Aspremont* de la bibliothèque des Gonzague de Mantoue." *CN* 21 (1961): 116-22.

——. "Les Manuscrits uniques de la *Passion* et de la *Pharsale* de Nicolas de Vérone sont-ils des 'manuscrits princips'?" *Testi, cotesti*. 232-44.

——. *Naissance et développement de la chanson de geste en Europe*. 4 vols. Geneva: Droz, 1961-1980.

——. *La Tapisserie de Trajan et Archambault. A la découverte d'une galerie internationale de portraits du XVᵉ siècle*. Berne: Benteli, 1987.

Mann, Nicholas. "Petrarca e la Cancelleria veneziana." *SCV* 2: 517-35.

Massart, Robert. "Contribution à l'étude du vocabulaire de Nicolas de Vérone." *Mélanges . . . Delbouille*. 1: 421-50.

Melli, Elio. "Rapporti fra le versioni rimate del 'Renaut de Montauban' e il 'Rinaldo' in versi del manoscritto palatino 364." *Giornale storico della letteratura italiana* 141 (1964): 369-89.

Meneghetti, Maria Luisa. "Ancora sulla *Morte (o Testamento)* di Carlo Magno." *Testi, cotesti.* 245-84.

Menéndez Pidal, Raymon. *La Chanson de Roland et la tradition épique des Francs.* Trans. Irénée Cluzel. 2nd ed. Paris: Editions A. et J. Picard et Cie., 1960.

Meyer, Paul. "De l'expansion de la langue française en Italie au moyen âge." *Atti del Congresso internazionale di scienze storiche* 4 (1904): 61-104.

Meyer [Lübke], Wilhelm. "Franko-italienische Studien." *ZRP* 9 (1885): 597-640.

Moisan, André. *Répertoire des noms propres de personnes et de lieux cités dans les chansons de geste françaises et les oeuvres étrangères dérivées.* Geneva: Droz, 1986.

Monfrin, Jacques. "Fragments de la chanson d'*Aspremont* conservés en Italie." *Rom.* 79 (1958): 237-52, 376-409.

——. "*Le Roman de Belris, Le Bel Inconnu, Carduino.*" *Testi, cotesti.* 161-76.

Monteverdi, Angelo. "Lingua e letteratura a Venezia nel secolo di Marco Polo." *La civiltà veneziana del secolo di Marco Polo.* Florence: Sansoni, 1956. 21-35.

——. "Regolarità e irregolarità sillabica del verso epico." *Mélanges... Delbouille.* 2: 531-44.

Morgan, Leslie Zarker. "Evidence of Oral Interference in Franco-Italian." *Canadian Journal of Linguistics / Revue canadienne de linguistique* 30 (1985): 407-14.

——. "Text and Non-text: For a Standard Lemmatization of Franco-Italian." *Testi, cotesti.* 209-22.

Ninni, Franca di. "La formazione del lessico in Niccolò da Verona." *Testi, cotesti.* 202-08.

——. "La *Passion* di Niccolò da Verona fra traduzione e tradizione." *Studi francesi* 75 (1981): 407-23.

——. "Techniche di composizione nella *Pharsale* di Niccolò da Verona." *Medioevo Romanzo* 10 (1985): 103-22.

Novati, F. "Poeti veneti del trecento." *Archivo storico per Trieste, Istria e Trentino* 1 (1881-82): 130-41.

Paccagnella, Ivano. *Le macaronee padovane: tradizione e lingua.* Padua: Antenore, 1979.

Palermo, Joseph. "Aspects 'romans' des 'Enfances Hector.' " *Mélanges offerts à René Crozet à l'occasion de son 70ᵉ anniversaire, par ses amis, ses collègues, ses élèves.* Ed. Pierre Gallais et Yves-Jean

Rion. Cahiers de civilisation médiévale. 2 vols. Poitiers: Société d'études médiévales, 1966. 2: 1283-92.

———. "La Langue franco-italienne du *Roman d'Hector et Hercules*." *Actes du Xe Congrès international de linguistique et philologie romanes. Strasbourg, 1962.* 2 vols. Paris: Les Belles Lettres, 1965. 2: 687-95.

———. *Le Roman d'Hector et Hercule. Chant épique en octosyllabes italo-français. Edité d'après le manuscrit français 821 de la Bibliothèque Nationale de Paris avec les variantes des autres manuscrits connus.* TLF 190. Geneva/Paris:Droz, 1972.

Paris, Gaston, ed. "*Mainet*. Fragment d'une chanson de geste du XIIe siècle." *Rom* 4 (1875): 305-37.

Pellegrini, Giovan Battista. "La canzone di *Auliver*." *Studi mediolatini e volgari* 5 (1957): 95-131.

Peron, Gianfelice. "Cultura e pubblico del *Boèce* franco-italiano (Paris, B.N. ms. fr. 821)." *Testi, cotesti*. 143-60.

Pertusi, Agostino. "Maistre Martin da Canal, interprete cortese delle crociate e dell'ambiente veneziano del secolo XIII." *Venezia dalla prima crociata alla conquista di Costantinopoli del 1204.* Florence: Sansoni, 1965-66. 103-35.

Ponchiroli, Daniele, ed. Il libro di Marco Polo detto Milione. Turin: Einaudi, 1974.

Queirazza, Giuliano Gasca. "A trenta anni dall'edizione di V4. Riflessioni su questioni di metodo e revisione dei risultati." *Testi, cotesti*. 115-27.

Rajna, Pio, ed. *Codici francesi posseduti dagli Estensi nel sec. XV. Rom.* 2 (1873): 49-58.

———. "Le origini delle famiglie padovane e gli eroi dei romanzi cavallereschi." *Rom.* 4 (1875): 161-83.

———. "I rinaldi o i cantastorie di Napoli." *Nuova antologia* 13 (1878): 557-79.

———. "La rotta di Roncisvalle nella letteratura cavalleresca italiana." *Il Propugnatore* 3.2 (1870): 384-409; 4.1 (1872): 52-78, 333-90; 4.2 (1872): 53-133.

Renzi, Lorenzo. "Il francese come lingua letteraria e il franco-lombardo. L'epica carolingia nel Veneto." *SCV* 1: 563-89.

———. "Stratificazione provenzale-franco-veneta nella 'Canzone dei desideri' marciana." *AIV*. Classe di scienze, lettere ed arti 126 (1967-68): 39-68.

———. "Gli ultimi studi sulla 'Chanson de Roland' et la redazione franco-veneta (ms. V⁴)." *Lettere italiane* 16 (1964): 324-39.

Riccoboni, Daniele. "Studi sul dialetto veneto. Intorno alla lingua di Nicolò da Verona, trovero del secolo XIV." *AIV. Classe di scienze, lettere ed arti* 7th ser. 55 (1896-97): 1,239-46.

Richthofen, Erich von. "Théorie de la genèse du *Roland* confirmée par l'analogie de celle du *Cid*." *Mélanges . . . René Louis*. 2: 379-88.

Riquer, Martín de. *Les Chansons de geste françaises*. Trans. Irénée Cluzel. 2nd ed. Paris: Nizet, 1968. 288-96.

Robertson-Mellor, Geoffrey, ed. *The Franco-Italian Roland (V4)*. Salford: U of Salford Reprographic Unit, 1980.

Roncaglia, Aurelio. "La letteratura franco-veneta." *Il Trecento. Storia della letteratura italiana*. Ed. E. Cecchi and N. Sapegno. Milan: Garzanti, 1965. 2: 725-59.

——. "Les Quatre eschieles de Rollant." *Atti del 2⁰ Congresso internazionale della Société Rencesvals*. CN 21 (1961): 191-205.

Rossellini, Aldo. "Analisi critica della 'Prise de Narbonne.' " *Studi francesi* 5.13 (1961): 1-13.

——. "*Codici Marciani di epopea carolingia (Richerche bibliografiche)*. Dispensa prima*. Udine: n. p., 1979.

——. "Il cosìdetto franco-veneto: retrospettive e prospettive." *Filologia moderna* 2 (1977): 219-303.

——. "Etude comparative des manuscrits de Châteauroux et de Venise VII de la 'chanson de Roland.' " *MA* 66 (1960): 259-300.

——, ed. *La 'Geste Francor di Venezia.' Edizione integrale del Codice XIII del fondo francese della Marciana*. Brescia: La Scuola, 1986.

——. "Di nuovo sul valore della traduzione della 'Chanson de Roland' nel ms. di V⁴." *Studi francesi* 4 (1960): 1-10.

——. "Onomastica epica francese in Italia nel medioevo." *Rom.* 79 (1958): 253-67.

——. "Sul valore della traduzione della 'Chanson de Roland' contenuta nel ms. franco-italiano di V⁴." *ZRP* 74 (1958): 234-45.

Ruggieri, Ruggero M. "La cosìdetta infecondità epica del popolo italiano: sguardo retrospettivo e riflessioni critiche." *Capitoli di storia linguistica e letteraria italiana*. Rome: Ateneo, 1971. 9-24.

——. "Cronaca: Studi italiani sulle epopee medievali (1962-64)." *CN* 25 (1965): 139-45.

——. "Expressivité et polymorphisme dans l'onomastique de l'ancienne littérature chevaleresque française et italienne." *MA* 71 (1965): 275-88.

——, ed. *L'influsso francese in Italia nel Medioevo*. Rome: DeSanctis, 1969.

——. "Origine, struttura, caratteri del francoveneto." *Saggi di linguistica italiana e italo-romanza*. Florence: Olschki, 1962. 159-68.

—. "Un Problème de langue mixte aux origines de la littérature italienne." *Actes du 13ᵉ Congrès international de linguistique et philologie romanes (Québec 1971).* 2 vols. Quebec: Presses de l'Université de Laval, 1976. 2: 433-42.

—. "Temi e aspetti della letteratura francoveneta." *Atti del Convegno di Studi "Dante e la cultura veneta," Venezia, Padova, Verona 30 marzo-5 aprile 1966.* Florence: Olschki, 1966. 143-56.

—. *L'umanesimo cavalleresco italiano, da Dante al Pulci.* Rome: Ateneo, 1962.

Segre, Cesare. "Il codice V⁴ della *Chanson de Roland.* Presentazione (con riflessioni sul francoveneto)." *Testi, cotesti.* 128-30.

Simone, Franco. "Cultura medievale francese e umanesimo italiano." *La rassegna della letteratura italiana* 58 (1954): 212-31.

Stäblein, Patricia Harris. "Patterns of Textual Shift and the Alien Hero: Ogier the Dane in the Europeanization of the Old French Epic." *Olifant* 12 (1987): 47-61.

Stiennon, Jacques and Rita Lejeune. "La Légende arthurienne dans la sculpture de la cathédrale de Modène." *CCM* 6 (1963): 281-96.

Stocchi, Manlio Pastore. "La biblioteca del Petrarca." *SCV* 2: 536-65.

Tartaro, Achille. *Forme poetiche del Trecento.* Bari: Laterza, 1971.

Tyssens, Madeleine. "Poèmes franco-italiens et *Storie Nerbonesi.* Recherches sur les sources d'Andrea da Barberino." *Testi, cotesti.* 307-24.

Viscardi, Antonio. "Arthurian Influence on Italian Literature from 1200-1500." *Arthurian Literature.* Ed. R.S. Loomis. Oxford: Clarendon P, 1959. 419-29.

—. "Letteratura epico-storica di corte e poesia cortese." *ZRP* 81 (1965): 454-75.

—. *Letteratura franco-italiana.* Istituto di Filologia Romanza dell'Università di Roma. Testi e manuali a cura di Giulio Bertoni 21. Modena: Società Tipografica Modenese, 1941.

—. "Lingua e letteratura." *La civiltà veneziana del Trecento.* Florence: Olschki, 1956. 181-205.

—. "Poesia 'collettiva,' poesia giullaresca, letteratura epica." *Filologia e letteratura* 8 (1962): 143-92.

—. *Storia della letteratura d'oc et d'oïl.* Milan: Nuova Accademia Editrice, 1959.

Wahle, Hermann, ed. "Die Pharsale des Nicolaus von Verona." Ausgaben und Abhandlungen 80. Marburg, 1888.

Wunderli, Peter. "Un Modèle d'intertextualité: l'*Aquilon de Bavière.*" *Au Carrefour.* 2: 1153-92.

—, ed. *Raffaele da Verona: Aquilon de Bavière. Roman franco-italien en prose (1379-1407)*. 2 vols. Tübingen: Niemeyer, 1982.
— and Günter Holtus. "La 'renaissance' des études franco-italiennes: rétrospective et prospective." *Testi, Cotesti*. 3-23.
—. "Rolandus epilepticus." *Das Ritterbild in Mittelalter und Renaissance*. Düsseldorf: Droste, 1985. 105-30.
Zanetti, Antonio M. *Latina et italica D. Marc. Biblioteca codicum Manuscriptorum. Per titulos digesta*. Venice, 1741.

General Primary and Secondary Sources

Alighieri, Dante. *Convivio*. Ed. Gustavo Rodolfo Ceriello. Biblioteca Universale Rizzoli 483-486. 6th ed. Milan: Rizzoli, 1952.
—. *De monarchia*. Ed. Gustavo Vinay. Florence: Sansoni, 1950.
Allen, John Robin. *Index de la chanson de geste romane et textes apparentés du moyen âge*. Manitoba: St John's College, 1984.
Allen, Judson Boyce. *The Ethical Poetic of the Later Middle Ages: A Decorum of Convenient Distinction*. Toronto/Buffalo/London: U of Toronto P, 1982.
—. *The Friar as Critic: Literary Attitudes in the Later Middle Ages*. Nashville: Vanderbilt UP, 1971.
d'Alverny, Marie-Thérèse. "Pietro d'Abano et les 'naturalistes' à l'époque de Dante." *Atti del Convegno di Studi "Dante e la cultura veneta." Venezia, Padova,Verona: 30 Marzo-5 Aprile 1966*. Ed. Vittore Branca and Giorgio Padoan. Florence, Olschki, 1966.
Appelt, H. "La politica imperiale verso i comuni italiani." *I problemi della civiltà comunale. Atti del Congresso storico internazionale per l'VIII centenario della prima Lega Lombarda (Bergamo, 4-8 settembre 1967)*. Ed Cosimo Damiano Fonseca. Bergamo: Cassa di Risparmio delle provincie lombarde, 1968. 23-32.
Aquinas, Thomas. *Opera omnia*. Ed. Roberto Busa. 7 vols. Stuttgart, 1980.
—. [*In decem libros Ethicorum Aristotelis ad Nicomachum expositio.*] *Commentary on the Nicomachean Ethics*. Ed. Angelo Pirotta. Taurini: Marietti, 1934.
—. [*De rege et regno, ad regem Cypri.*] *On Kingship: To the King of Cyprus*. Trans. Gerald B. Phelan. Ed. I. Th. Eschmann, O.P. Mediaeval Sources in Translation 2. Toronto: Pontifical Institute of Mediaeval Studies, 1982.
—. [*Summa contra Gentiles.*] *On the Truth of the Catholic Faith*. Trans. Vernon J. Bourke. 2 vols. New York: Doubleday, 1956.

—. *Summa theologiae. Latin text and English translation.* 60 vols.
  Ed. and trans. Thomas Gilby, O.P. and T. C. O'Brien, O.P.
  Cambridge: Blackfriars, 1966.
Aristotle. *The Nicomachean Ethics.* Trans. H. Rackham. Loeb
  Classical Library. Cambridge: Harvard UP, 1962.
—. *The Poetics. "Longinus," On The Sublime. Demetrius. On
  Style.* Trans. W. Hamilton Fyfe and W. Rhys Roberts. Loeb
  Classical Library. Cambridge: Harvard UP, 1965.
—. *Politics.* Trans. H. Rackham. Loeb Classical Library.
  Cambridge: Harvard UP, 1967.
Arnaldi, Girolamo and Lidia Capo. "I cronisti di Venezia e della Marca
  Trevigiana." *SCV* 2: 272-337.
Augustine. *City of God.* Ed. David Knowles. Trans. Henry Bettenson.
  London: Penguin Books, 1976.
—. *De doctrina christiana.* Ed. M. Amelia Klenke. Washington:
  Catholic UP, 1943.
—. *On Christian Doctrine.* Trans. D. W. Robertson, Jr. The Library
  of Liberal Arts. Indianapolis: Bobbs-Merrill, 1981.
Badel, Pierre=Yves. "Rhétorique et polémique dans les prologues de-
  romans au Moyen Age." *Littérature* 20 (1973): 81-94.
Bakhtin, M. M. *The Dialogic Imagination. Four Essays.* Ed. Michael
  Holquist. Trans. Caryl Emerson and Michael Holquist. U of Texas
  Slavic Series 1. Austin: U of Texas P, 1981.
Bender, Karl Heinz. "Un Aspect de la stylisation épique: l'exclusivisme
  de la haute noblesse dans les chansons de geste du XIIe siècle."
  *Actes et mémoires du IVe Congrès international de la Société
  Rencesvals 1967.* Studia Romanica 14. Heidelburg: C. Winter,
  1969. 195-205.
Bezzola, Reto R. "A Propos de la valeur littéraire des chansons
  féodales." *La Technique littéraire des chansons de geste.* Paris: Les
  Belles lettres, 1959. 183-95.
—. "De Roland à Raoul de Cambrai." *Mélanges . . . Hoepffner.* 195-
  213.
Blanchard, Joël. "Les Entrées royales: pouvoir et représentation du
  pouvoir à la fin du Moyen Age." *Littérature* (May 1983): 3-14.
Bloch, Marc. *La Société féodale.* 2 vols. Paris: A. Michel, 1940.
Bloch, R. Howard. *Medieval French Literature and Law.* Berkeley: U
  of California P, 1977.
Brett, Edward Tracy. *Humbert of Romans: His Life and Views of
  Thirteenth-Century Society.* Studies and Texts 67. Toronto:
  Pontifical Institute of Mediaeval Studies, 1984.
Brezzi, Paolo. "Gli uomini che hanno creato la Lega Lombarda."
  Popolo e stato in Italia nell'età di Federico Barbarossa: Alessandria

e la Lega Lombarda. Relazioni e comunicazioni al XXXIII Congresso storico subalpino per la celebrazione dell'VIII centenario della fondazione di Alessandria. Alessandria 6-9 ottobre 1968. Turin: Deputazione subalpina di storia patria, 1970. 249-61.

Brugnolo, Furio. "I Toscani nel Veneto e le cerchie toscaneggianti." *SCV* 2: 369-439.

Burgess, Glyn Sheridan. *Contribution à l'étude du vocabulaire précourtois.* PRF 110. Geneva: Droz, 1970.

Calin, William C. *The Epic Quest: Studies in Four Old French Chansons de Geste.* Baltimore: The Johns Hopkins UP, 1966.

——. *A Muse for Heroes: Nine Centuries of the Epic in France.* Toronto: U of Toronto P, 1983.

——. *The Old French Epic of Revolt: Raoul de Cambrai, Renaud de Montauban, Gormond et Isembard.* Geneva: Droz, 1962.

Cerquiglini, Bernard. *La Parole médiévale.* Paris: Les Editions de Minuit, 1981.

Chrétien de Troyes. *Le Chevalier au lion. Les Romans de Chrétien de Troyes, édités d'après la copie de Guiot (Bibl. nat. fr. 794).* Ed. Mario Roques. CFMA. Paris: Champion, 1963.

Cluzel, Irénée Marcel. "La Culture générale d'un troubadour du XIIIe siècle." *Mélanges . . . Delbouille.* 1: 91-104.

Corti, Maria. "Culture as text in the thirteenth century." *Semiosis: Semiotics and the History of Culture.* No trans. Michigan Slavic Contributions 10. Ann Arbor: U of Michigan P, 1984. 53-64.

——. "Dante e la torre di Babele: una nuova *allegoria in factis.*" *Viaggio testuale.* Turin: Einaudi, 1978. 243-56.

——. "Ideologie e strutture semiotiche nei *Sermones ad status* del secolo XIII." *Viaggio testuale.* 221-42.

——. "Il genere *disputatio* e la transcodificazione indolore di Bonvesin da Riva." *Viaggio testuale.* 257-88.

——. "Models and Antimodels in Medieval Culture." Trans. John Meddemmen. *NLH* (1979): 339-66.

Cracco, Giorgio. "La cultura giuridico-politica nella Venezia della 'Serrata.' " *SCV* 2: 238-71.

——. *Società e stato nel Medioevo veneziano (secoli XII-XIV).* Florence: Olschki, 1967.

Curtius, Ernst Robert. *European Literature and the Latin Middle Ages.* Trans. Willard Trask. 1953. Harper Torchbooks. The Bollingen Library. New York and London: Harper & Row, 1963.

De Bruyne, Edgar. *Etudes d'esthétique médiévale.* 3 vols. 1946. Geneva: Slatkine, 1975.

Delany, Sheila. *Medieval Literary Politics: Shapes of Ideology.* Cultural Politics. Manchester: Manchester UP, 1990.

Dessau, Adalbert. "L'Idée de la trahison au moyen âge et son rôle dans la motivation de quelques chansons de geste." *CCM* 3 (1960): 23-26.

Dionysius The Pseudo-Aeropagite. *The Ecclesiastical Hierarchy.* Ed. and trans. Thomas L. Campbell. Washington: UP of America, 1981.

Duby, Georges. *Le Chevalier, la femme et le prêtre: le mariage dans la France féodale.* Collection Pluriel. Paris: Hachette, 1981.

—. "L'Histoire des systèmes de valeurs." *History and Theory: Studies in the Philosophy of History* 11.1 (1972): 15-25.

—. "La Vulgarisation des modèles culturels dans la société féodale." *Niveaux de culture et groupes sociaux: actes du colloque réuni du 7 au 9 mai 1966 à l'Ecole Normale Supérieure.* Paris/La Haye: Mouton, 1967. 33-41.

—. *Les Trois ordres ou l'imaginaire du féodalisme.* Bibliothèque des Histoires NRF. Paris: Gallimard, 1978.

—. *La Société chevaleresque. Hommes et structures du Moyen Age.* 1979. Paris: Flammarion, 1988.

Duggan, Joseph J. *A Concordance of the Chanson de Roland.* Columbus: Ohio State UP, 1969.

—. "Performance and Transmission, Aural and Ocular Reception in the Twelfth and Thirteenth Century Vernacular Literature of France." *RP* 43 (1989): 49-58.

Eco, Umberto. *Art and Beauty in the Middle Ages.* Trans. Hugh Bredin. New Haven: Yale UP, 1986.

—. ed., with Costantino Marmo. *On the Medieval Theory of Signs.* Trans. Shona Kelly. Amsterdam: John Benjamins Publishing Co., 1989.

—. *Il problema estetico in Tommaso d'Aquino.* Milan: Bompiani, 1970.

—. *Segno.* Enciclopedia filosofica. 1973. Milan: Mondadori, 1980.

—. *A Theory of Semiotics.* Advances in Semiotics. Bloomington: Indiana UP, 1976.

d'Entrèves, Alessandro Passerin, ed. *Aquinas: Selected Political Writings.* Trans. J. G. Dawson. Blackwell's Political Texts. Oxford: Blackwell, 1948.

Fasoli, Gina and Francesca Bocchi. *La città medievale italiana.* Florence: Sansoni, 1973.

Ferrante, Joan M. *The Political Vision of the Divine Comedy.* Princeton: Princeton UP, 1984.

Foulet, Alfred. "Is Roland guilty of 'desmesure'?" *RP* 10 (1957): 145-48.

Freeman, Michelle A. The Poetics of *Translatio studii* and *conjointure*: Chrétien de Troyes's *Cligés*. French Forum Monographs 12. Ed. R. C. La Charité and V. A. La Charité. Lexington, Kentucky: French Forum Publishers, 1979.

Gabrieli, Francesco. "Cultura araba nelle Venezie al tempo di Dante." *Atti "Dante e la cultura veneta."* 143-56.

Gallais, Pierre. "Recherches sur la mentalité des romanciers français du Moyen Age." *CCM* 7 (1964): 479-93.

Gautier, Léon. *Les Epopées françaises*. 5 vols. 2nd ed. Osnabrück: Otto Zeller, 1878.

Gennari, Giuseppe. *Annali della Città di Padova*. Historiae urbium et regionum Italiae 63. Bologna, 1804.

Gewirth, Alan. *Marsuius of Padua and Medieval Political Philosophy*. New York: Columbia UP, 1956

Gierke, Otto. *Political Theories of the Middle Age*. [sic] Trans. Frederic William Maitland. 1900. Cambridge: Cambridge UP, 1987.

Gilson, Etienne. Reason and Revelation in the Middle Ages. New York: Scribner's, 1966.

Greene, Thomas M. *The Descent from Heaven: A Study in Epic Continuity*. New Haven: Yale UP, 1963.

Greimas, A. J. and Roman Jakobsen. *Sign, Language, Culture*. The Hague: Mouton, 1970.

Guiette, Robert, ed. *Croniques et conquestes de Charlemaine de David Aubert*. Brussels: Palais des Académies, 1940-51.

Hackett, Winifred Mary. "La Féodalité dans la *Chanson de Roland* et dans *Girart de Roussillon*." *Actes IVᵉ Congrès . . . Société Rencesvals 1967*. Studia Romanica 14. Heidelburg: C. Winter, 1969. 22-27.

Hardison, O. B., Jr. and Alexander Preminger, Kevin Kerrane, Leon Golden. *Medieval Literary Criticism: Translations and Interpretations*. New York: Frederick Ungar, 1974.

Hiestand, Rudolf. "Aspetti politici e sociali dell'Italia settentrionale dalla morte di Federico II alla metà del '300." *Testi, cotesti*. 27-47.

Hugh of St. Victor. *De studio legendi*. Trans and ed. Charles Henry Buttimer. Washington: Catholic UP, 1939.

—. *The Didascalicon of Hugh of St. Victor: A Medieval Guide to the Arts*. Trans. Jerome Taylor. New York: Columbia UP, 1961.

Hyde, John Kenneth. *Padua in the Age of Dante*. Manchester: Manchester UP, 1966.

Jakobsen, Roman. *Questions de poétique*. Paris: Editions du Seuil, 1973.

—. *Verbal Art, verbal sign, verbal time.* Ed. Krystyna Pomorska and Stephen Rudy. Minneapolis: U of Minnesota P, 1985.

Jauss, Hans Robert. "Chanson de geste et roman courtois." *Chanson de geste und höfischer Roman.* 61-77.

John of Salisbury. *Policraticus: the Stateman's Book.* Ed. C. C. I. Webb. 2 vols. Oxford: Oxford UP, 1909.

Keller, Hans Erich. *Autour de Roland: recherches sur la chanson de geste.* Paris Champion. Geneva: Slatkine, 1989.

—. "Changes in Old French Epic Poetry and Changes in the Taste of its Audience." *Olifant* 1.4 (1973-74): 48-56.

Kelly, Douglas. *Medieval Imagination: Rhetoric and the Poetry of Courtly Love.* Madison: U of Wisconsin P, 1978.

—. "Obscurity and Memory: Sources for invention in medieval French literature." *Vernacular Poetics in the Middle Ages.* Ed. Lois Ebin. Studies in Medieval Culture 16. Kalamazoo: Medieval Institute Publications, 1984.

Kennedy, A. J. "The Hermit's Role in French Arthurian Romance." *Rom.* 95 (1974): 54-83.

Kibler, William. "Relectures de l'épopée." *Au Carrefour.* 1: 103-40.

Kleinhenz, Christopher. "Biblical Citation in Dante's *Divine Comedy.*" *Annali d'Italianistica* 8 (1990): 346-59.

—. "Dante and the Bible: Intertextual Approaches to the *Divine Comedy.*" *Italica* 63.3 (Autumn 1986): 225-36.

Köhler, Erich. "Quelques observations d'ordre historico-sociologique sur les rapports entre la chanson de geste et le roman courtois." *Chanson de geste und höfischer Roman.* 21-36.

Kristeller, Paul Oskar. *Iter italicum.* 2 vols. London: Werburg Institute, 1967.

—. "Paduan Averroism and Alexandrism in the light of recent studies." *Byzantium* 17 (1944-45): 553-85.

Ladner, Gerhart B. *The Idea of Reform: Its Impact on Christian Thought and Action in the Age of the Fathers.* Revised ed. New York: Harper & Row, 1967.

Lagarde, Georges de. *La Naissance de l'esprit laïque au déclin du moyen âge.* 5 vols. Paris/Louvain: Nauwerlaerts, 1956.

Lausberg, Heinrich. *Handbuch der literarischen Rhetorik: Eine Grundlegung der Literaturwissenschaft.* 2 vols. Munich: Hueber, 1960.

Lazzerino, Lino. "Sulla cultura e la civiltà veneziana del Trecento." *Lettere italiane* 51 (1958): 60-77.

Le Gentil, Pierre. "La Rédemption du héros." *Technique littéraire des chansons de geste.* 59-70.

Le Goff, Jacques. *L'imaginaire médiéval: essais.* Bibliothèque des Histoires NRF. Paris: Gallimard, 1985.
—. *Pour un autre Moyen Age Temps: travail et culture en Occident: 18 essais.* Bibliothèque des Histoires NRF. Paris: Gallimard, 1977.
Lewis, C. S. *Studies in Words.* 2nd ed. 1967. Cambridge: Cambridge UP, 1981.
Lomazzi, Anna. "Primi monumenti del Volgare." *SCV* 1: 602-32.
Lotman, Juri. "The Dynamic Model of a Semiotic System." No trans. *Semiotica* 21.3/4 (1977): 193-210.
—. "On the Metalanguage of a Typological Description of Culture." No trans. *Semiotica* 14.2 (1975): 97-123.
—. "The Origin of Plot in the Light of Typology." No trans. *Poetics Today* 1.1-2 (1979): 161-83.
—. The Sign Mechanism of Culture." Trans. Ann Shukman. *Semiotica* 12.4 (1974): 301-06.
—. *The Structure of the Artistic Text.* Trans. Gail Lenhoff and Ronald Vroon. 2nd ed. Michigan Slavic Contributions 7. Ann Arbor: U of Michigan P, 1977.
Lusignan, Serge. *Parler vulgairement: les intellectuels et la langue française aux XIIIe et XIVe siècles.* 2nd ed. Etudes médiévales. Montreal: Presses de l'Université de Montréal, 1987.
Mandach, André de. "La Vie de la chancellerie épique des Gonzague de Mantoue." *Bibliothèque d'humanisme et renaissance* 29 (1964): 621-33.
Marsilius of Padua. *Defensor pacis.* Ed. and trans. Alan Gewirth. Columbia UP 1956. Mediaeval Academy Reprints for Teaching 6. Toronto/Buffalo/London: U of Toronto P, (see also Gewirth). 1980.
McNamee, Maurice B. *Honor and the Epic Hero: A Study of the Shifting Concept of Magnanimity in Philosophy and Epic Poetry.* New York: Holt, Rinehart and Winston, 1960.
Migne, Jacques-Paul, ed. *Patrologiae cursus completus series latina.* 222 vols. Paris, 1844-1890.
Monumenta Germanica Historiae. Scriptores 26: Ex rerum Francogallicarum scriptoribus. Ex historiis auctorum Flandrensium Francogallica lingua scriptis. Supplementum tomi 24. 1882. Munich: Gesamtverzeichnis, 1975. [*MGH*].
—. *Scriptores 31. Annales et chronica Italica aevi Suevici.* 1903. Munich: Gesamtverzeichnis, 1980.
Mussato, Albertino. *Ecerinide. Tragoediae duae et alia auctoris poemata, epistolae, elegi, soliloquia. RIS* 10: 786-800. Milan, 1727.

302   Selected Bibliography

—. *L'Ecerinide*. Ed. and trans. Manlio Dazzi. *Mussato preumanista (1261-1329): l'ambiente e l'opera.* Vicenza: Neri Pozza, 1964. 140-58.

—. *De gestis Italicorum post Henricum VII Caesarem.* Ed. J. G. Graevius. *Thesaurus antiquitatum et historiarum Italiae* 6.2. Leiden, 1722. *Antiquitates italicae.* 6 vols. Bologna: Forni, 1965.

—. *Historia augusta de gestis Henrici VII Caesaris.* Ed. J. G. Graevius. *Thesaurus antiquitatum et historiarum Italie* 6, pt. 2. Leiden, 1722. *Antiquitates italicae.* 6 vols. Bologna: Forni, 1965.

Nardi, Bruno. *Saggi sulla cultura veneta del Quattro e Cinquecento.* Padua: Antenore, 1971.

Nichols, Stephen G., Jr. "Fission and Fusion: Mediations of Power in Medieval History and Literature." *YFS* 70 (1986): 30-41.

—. *Romanesque Signs: Early Medieval Narrative and Iconography.* New Haven and London: Yale UP, 1983.

Niemeyer, Sister Mary Fredericus, O.P., M.A. *The One and the Many in the Social Order According to Saint Thomas Aquinas.* Washington: Catholic U of America P, 1951.

Nolthenius, Hélène. *Il Duecento: The Late Middle Ages in Italy.* Trans. Darton. New York: Longman & Todd, 1962.

Oculus Pastoralis, sive libellus erudiens futurum rectorem populorum. Anonymo auctore conscriptus circa annum 1222. Antiquitates italicae medii aevi. Ed. L. A. Muratori. Milan, 1723-51. 95-132.

Pacaut, M. "La Papauté et les villes italiennes (1159-1253)." *Probemi della civiltà comunale.* 33-46.

Pagels, Elaine. *Adam, Eve and the Serpent.* New York: Random House, 1988.

Payen, Jean Charles. *Le Motif du repentir dans la littérature française médiévale (des origines à 1230).* PRF 98. Geneva: Droz, 1967.

Perrot, Jean-Pierre. "Le Sens de l'errance dans la plus ancienne version française de *La Vie de saint Julien l'hospitalier. Voyage, quête, pèlerinage dans la littérature et la civilisation médiévales.* Sénéfiance 2 (Cahiers du CUER MA). Aix-en-Provence: Université de Provence, 1976. 473-88.

Priscian. *De pre-exercitamentis rhetoricis.* Ed. Bruno Keil. Leipzig, 1860.

Quillet, Jeannine. *La Philosophie politique de Marsile de Padoue.* Paris: Vrin, 1970.

Rajna, Pio. "Contributi alla storia dell'epopea e del romanzo medievale." *Rom.* 14 (1865): 398-420.

Robertson, D. W., Jr. "Some Medieval literary terminology, with special reference to Chrétien de Troyes." *Speculum* 48 (1951): 669-92.

Rolandino, (Patavino). *Cronica in factis et circa facta Marchie Trivixanie.* Ed. A. Bonardi. *RIS* 8.1. Città di Castello, n.p., 1905-08.

Segre, Cesare. "What Bakhtin Left Unsaid: The Case of the Medieval Romance." *Romance: Generic Transformation from Chrétien de Troyes to Cervantes.* Ed. Kevin Brownlee and Marina Scordilis Brownlee. Hanover and London: Dartmouth College, UP of New England, 1985. 23-46.

Siraisi, Nancy G. *Arts and Sciences at Padua: The Studium of Padua before 1350.* Studies and Texts 25. Toronto: Pontifical Institute of Mediaeval Studies, 1973.

Stanesco, Michel. *Jeux d'errance du chevalier médiéval. Aspects ludiques de la fonction guerrière dans la littérature du Moyen Age flamboyant.* Brill's Studies in Intellectual History 9. Leiden: Brill, 1988.

Starn, Randolph. *Contrary Commonwealth: The Theme of Exile in Medieval and Renaissance Italy.* Berkeley: U of California P, 1982.

Subrenat, Jean. "L'Attitude des hommes en face du voyage d'après quelques textes littéraires." *Voyage, quête.* 395-412.

Tabacco, Giovanni. *Egemonie sociali e strutture del potere nel Medioevo italiano.* Piccola Biblioteca Einaudi 379. Turin: Einaudi, 1974.

Todorov, Tzvetan. *Mikhail Bakhtin: The Dialogical Principle.* Trans. Wlad Godzich. Theory and History of Literature 13. Minneapolis: U of Minnesota P, 1984.

Uitti, Karl D. *Story, Myth and Celebration in Old French Narrative Poetry (1050-1200).* Princeton: Princeton UP, 1973.

Vance, Eugene. "The Differing Seed: Dante's Brunetto Latini." *Vernacular Poetics.* 129-52.

—. *Reading the Song of Roland.* Englewood Cliffs: Prentice-Hall, 1970.

—. *From Topic to Tale: Logic and Narrativity in the Middle Ages.* Theory and History of Literature 47. Minneapolis: U of Minnesota P, 1987.

Vasoli, Cesare. "Marsilio da Padova." *SCV* 2: 207-37.

Villani, Giovanni. *Cronica.* Ed. F. G. Dragomanni. Florence, 1844-45.

Vinaver, Eugene. "From Epic to Romance." *Bulletin of the John Rylands Library* 46 (1964): 476-503.

——. *The Rise of Romance.* Oxford: Oxford UP, 1971.
Waley, Daniel. *The Italian City-Republics.* 3rd ed. London and New York: Longman, 1988.
Wetherbee, Winthrop. "Per te poeta fui, per te cristiano." *Dante, Statius, and the Narrator of Chaucer's Troilus." Vernacular Poetics.* 153.76.
Weiss, Robert. "La cultura preumanista veronese e vicentina del tempo di Dante." *Atti . . . Dante e la cultura veneta.* 263-72.
——. "Lovato Lovati (1241-1309)." *Italian Studies* 6 (1951): 3-28.
Wright, John H., S.J. *The Order of the Universe in the Theology of St. Thomas Aquinas.* Analecta Gregoriana 89. Series Facultatis Theologicae, Sectio B. Rome: Apud Aedes Universitatis Gregorianae, 1957.
Zumthor, Paul. *Essai de poétique médiévale.* Paris: Editions du Seuil, 1972.
——. "Introduction à la poésie orale." Paris: Editions du Seuil, 1983.
——. *Langage de la chanson de geste.* Università di Urbino: Centro internazionale di semiotica e di linguistica, 1971.
——. "Literatus/illiteratus: remarques sur le contexte vocal de l'écriture médiévale." *Romania* 106 (1985): 1-18.
——. "Observations sur l'écriture médiévale." *CN* 45 (1985): 149-70.

INDEX

Adler, A., 151, 152-53
Aebischer, P., 27, 67-69, 71,
    73, 74, 76
Aeneid, 13-14, 55n
Aimeri de Narbonne, 62
Aiol, 62
Alain de Lille, 107-10, 124,
    127, 219
Aliscans, 9
Allen, J.B., 236, 240, 241-42,
    243, 244, 249n.,
    251n
Ansëis de Carthage, 10
Appelt, H., 94, 96, 98
Aquilon de Bavière, 10,
    25n, 42-43, 211n
Aquinas, Thomas (Saint), 108,
    110-18, 123, 125,
    126, 127, 128, 129,
    130, 131, 133n, 148,
    151, 226, 228, 230,
    231, 247, 248, 253n,
    259, 262
Ariosto, 5, 152
Aristotle, 45, 92, 113, 118,
    122, 126, 238
Arthurian Literature, 9, 145,
    166, 221
Aspremont, 9, 45, 55n, 72
Augustine of Hippo (Saint),
    81, 110, 112, 125,
    127, 131n, 219, 224,
    229, 232-33, 253,
    262
Authority / autonomy as
    thematic, 32, 33-34,
    42-49, 53, 55n, 115,
    139, 146-49, 154-63,
    167-71, 171-76, 224

Bakhtin, M.M., 7, 11, 135,
    136-37, 231-32, 2/.5
Beckmann, G., 71
Bédier, J., 70
Bender, K. H., 75, 77, 149,
    186
Bloch, M., 187
Boiardo, 5, 152
Brault, G., 21 n.1, 76, 79 n.1

Calin, W., 48
Canale, Martino da, 7
Can Grande Della Scala, 11-12,
    102, 106-07, 135,
    140, 176
Chanson de Roland, La:
    canonic text, as, 55n
    characterization of Charles,
    30, 71-72, 74-75
    characterization of Roland
    in, 27, 37-39, 74-75,
    142, 166-67, 175,
    142, 166-67, 175,
    176-81, 238, 244

Ganelon in, 44, 58-62, 73,
    75; 257, 258
language in, 136, 141
Nobles récit in, 57-62, 76
    V⁴, 9, 63, 65, 80n,
    186
    V⁷, 63, 186
Chanson des Saisnes, 62
chansons de geste
    baron révolté cycle, 48,
        50, 51, 139
    movance to Italy, 6-7
    known by Paduan, 15
    conflict between Charles
        and Roland in, 55n,
        74, 163-64
    language in, 136
    reception in Italy, 6
Charlemagne
    demythification of, in
        Franco-Italian chansons de
        geste, 75-76
    legends regarding, 6
    mythification of, 211n
Chaucer, 12
Chevalerie Ogier, 50, 139, 186
chivalry, 30, 33, 36, 88, 166-
    67
Chrétien de Troyes, 221
Chronique dite Saintongeaise,
    63
Cicero, 217
Commune as system of
    governance, 12, 53, 95-96
    and Church, 94-96
    and empire, 96-99
    failure of, 105-06
    formation of, in
        northern Italy, 89-90
    internal dissension in,
        99-101
Corti, M., 108, 109, 111, 194,
    257

Croniques et conquestes de
    Charlemaine, 70

Dante Alighieri
    Convivio, 92, 94, 132n
    Divina Commedia, 10-11,
        92, 93, 103, 135,
        140, 153, 211n, 221,
        233, 238, 239, 245,
        257, 258, 259, 263
    De monarchia, 123, 129,
        276
    De vulgari eloquentia, 9,
        12, 256-58, 265-66
D'Entrèves, G. P., 112, 115,
    116
Dionisotti, C., 28
Duby, G., 83, 84, 85, 86, 87,
    88, 89, 108, 110,
    112, 197, 206

Ecerinide, see Mussato, A.
Enfances Ogier, 186
Entrée d'Espagne, L'
    authorial strategies in, 3-5
    authorship of, 14-16, 71-
        72, 154-157, 158
    baron révolté theme in,
        75, 139, 142-43
    blow, Charles's, 42, 43,
        47, 51, 53, 186-89
    chanson de geste, elements
        of, 5, 27, 47, 50,
        159, 220
    Charlemagne in, 27-49,
        140, 142, 145-49,
        163-64, 168-71, 176,
        185, 220, 226-27,
        228, 260-61
    conflicts between Roland-
        Charles in, 57-81,

164-71, 171-176,
184-86, 188, 190-92,
220, 226, 239
correctio, as, 215, 220
dating of, 10, 12, 17, 23n,
26n
dialogic forum as, 12,
136-39, 144, 167-71,
183-84, 204-210,
247-48, 259
discourse systems in, 33-
34, 135-41, 142, 151,
153, 167-68, 232,
239, 260, 263
Ganelon in, 3-4, 5, 145,
155-56
hagiographical elements
in, 224, 239-48, 263
hermit Samson in, 215,
225, 233, 236-46
honor, 31, 167-71
horse, gift, episode in,
3-34, 171-76, 232,
241, 261
iconoclasm of, 10, 12, 27,
47-48, 50, 149, 164,
182, 183-84, 208-09,
224, 233
ideological aspects of,
143, 186-87, 192,
193-204, 206, 259-60
intertextuality in, 3-4, 37-
39, 45, 141n, 176-81,
221, 225, 238, 244,
246, *see baron
révolté* cycle,
Chanson de Roland;
sources
lacunae in, 50, appendix
language as theme in, 171-
76, 225, 234, 238,
243, 244, 258, 259-
61, 262

loci, as dialogic sites in,
23,137
a. labor/repois, 141-
46
b. Thiois Rebellion,
146-49
c. Doctrine and
Cognition:Roland
orator; 149-54
d. Paduan *orator*,
154-63
e. Hierarchy, 163-67
f. War and Ethics,
167-71
g. Caveat:
Heteroglossia,
171-76
h. Orgueil
Reconsidered, 176-81
i. Typologies Re-
viewed, 181-83
j. Transgression
Dialogized, 183-92
k. Women, Marriage,
Social Rank, 193-
204
l. New *Bellator*,
Warrior and Leader,
204-09
manuscripts, 12-14, 26-
28n20, 26n23, 51,
52, 199
mouvance of, 6
narrator in, 43, 44, 143,
154-63, 178, 186-87,
191, 193-204, 206,
217, 220, 227, 259-
60 *See also* Paduan
Nobles, city of,in, 40-42,
57-80, culmination of
conflict structure as,
40-42, 173-74, 175,
184-85, 188-90, 227,

235, 239, source,
72, 77, 78
polysemy in, 138, 172-76,
259
Prologue I, 3-4, 164, 215-
17, 219, 226
Prologue II, 47, 73, 75,
145, 161, 228, 261
prologue to *Chanson de
Roland*, as, 138
public, 4, 6, 53, 138, 143,
151, 157, 159-63,
175, 216, 260
Roland in:
abandons Charles,
169-70, 189-90, 221-
23; autobiography of,
221-23, 239; named
bailis of Persia, 50,
204, 255, 265n;
baron révolté, as, 27-
56, 189; bourgeois
knight, 196-203, 206-
07; "capitaine de
l'Eglise," 40;
champions autonomy
for women, 193-98;
compared to Alexander
the Great, 181-83;
conflicts with
Charles, 27-49;
creator of pseudo-
identities, 57, 201-04,
236-37, 239; death
predicted by hermit,
243-46; death,
symbolic in, 47; in
Mideast, 49, 193-204;
démesuré, 44, 208;
dialectician, 149-54,
165, 211-13n;
multilingual, 140-41,
232, 236; new model

knight, 33, 50-52,
145, 164, 168, 170,
204-210, 228, 235,
246-48, 262; name
Rotholandus, 22,
24, 236-37, 259;
orgueil in, 176-81,
188, 208, 229, 232,
235, 246; personal
army of, 40, 79n,
176, 81n; "senator de
Rome," 39, 42;
speaker of "parole
vaine," 235, 238,
262; traitor,
condemned as, 41;
Tower of Babel, urged
to conquer, 23, 235,
255-56; transgressive,
53, 184-85, 201, 229,
237, 239, 261; would-
be king of Spain, 3-4,
28, 165, 237
romance elements in, 23,
221, 233-34
sententia in, 45, 215, 217-
53, 262
sources of, 69-74, 154-59
structure of, 27, 45-47
summa, as, 9-10; 263
title, 4, 143, 155
Tower of Babel in, 255
Veneto-Lombard region, as
context, 24n, 47, 89-
106
Ezzelino da Romano, 98, 101,
103-05, 128, 140

Fasoli, G., 90
Fatti de Spagna, Li, 28n
Ferrante, J.M., 211n
Finoli, A.M. 70
Floire et Blancheflor, 62

Francis da Assisi (Saint), 7
Franco-Italian
    evolution of texts in, 8-
        9, 21n
    first international
        conference, 4
    Francophilism in Italy as,
        6, in Dante, 9
    identification of, 9-10
    language, 5-6, 8, 140-41
    in northern Italy, 6
    orality, 6
    polyglossia, as, 135
    predicated in *Entrée*, as
        pure French, 155
French language, beauty of, 7

Gaydon, 62
Gautier, Léon, 14
Gewirth, A., 119, 120, 122
Gierke, O., 123, 124, 125,
    127, 130
Girard de Roussillon, 139
Girard de Vienne, 47
Gonzaga, dynasty of, 12
    library of, 15, 28n
governance, 113, 129
    law as factor in, 113-14,
        126
Greene, T, 47, 52
Gregory the Great, (Pope), 82
Gui de Bourgogne, 62
Gui de Nanteuil, 62
Guiette, R., 70
Guillaume de Conches, 247

Hector et Hercule ,Roman de,
    10
Hieatt, C., 66-68, 74, 76
hierarchism, 85, 88, 113-15,
    129-30, 163, 167,
    181, 226, 228, 238,
    258, 262, 263. *See*

    also locus *e, and*
        Pseudo-Dionysius.
Holtus, G., 8-9; 24, 25n, 50,
    69, 70, 159, 204,
    265n
Homer, *Iliad* , 260
houtor, 70, see also Prologue
    II
Hugh of St. Victor, 213n, 218,
    243
Humbert of Romans, 108-10,
    200
Hyde, J. K., 93, 101

Intertextuality: *see Entrée
    d'Espagne*
Jackson, W. T. H., 55n
Jakobsen, R., 258

Karlamagnus Saga, 62, 64-66,
    69, 71, 74
Karleto, 186
Kibler, W., 5, 55 n
Krauss, H., 15, 24n, 44,
    69, 70, 94, 96, 138,
    157-58, 163, 182,
    197, 200, 213n,
    238

Ladner, G. B., 133n
Lagarde, G. de, 126, 128,
    132n, 231, 250n
Latini, Brunetto, 9, 104-05,
    124, 260
Le Goff, J., 85, 87, 187, 196,
    197
Lewis, C.S., 217
Limentani, A., 10, 11, 12, 14-
    15, 18, 69, 70, 249-50n,
    260, 265, 267n
    Entrée d'Espagne as
        summa, 9, 135
Limerick, Gilbert of, 194

Loci as dialogic sites in *Entrée*,
        see *Entrée d'Espagne*
Lombard League, 97-99, 102
Lotman, J.M., 107, 109, 111,
        133n, 136, 141, 179,
        192, 263
Loveti, Lovato, 11,13, 91

Macchiavelli, 116
Macaire, 10, 186
Mainet, 27
Mandach, A. de, 15,16-17, 19,
        26n, 29, 63, 69, 70,
        71, 72
Marsilius of Padua, *Defensor
        Pacis*, 118-23, 125,
        126, 129, 131, 133-
        134n, 226
Meredith-Jones, G., 79n; *see
        also Pseudo-Turpin*
mespreison, 23, 48, 221
Meyer, P., 14
Models of medieval society
    evolution of, 106-130,
        197-98, 215
    French, Primary Models,
        81-88, 131n, law and,
        128-31
    northern Italian, 91-93
    others in eleventh century
        France, 131n
    Pseudo-Dionysius, 83-84,
        85-91, 133-34n, 183,
        200, 257
    See also Alain de Lille
        Aquinas, Thomas
        Jacques de Vitry
        Humbert of Romans
        Marsilius of Padua
Monteverdi, A., 17
Mort Charlemagne, La, 63
Mussato, A., 11, 91, 101
    chronicles, 11, 104-05

Ecerinide, 11, 99, 103,
        106, 259
father of Renaissance
        tragedy, 11

Nichols, S., 131n, 211n, 216,
        252-53n
Nicolò da Verona, 9,10, 17,
        28n, 202. *See also
        Prise de Pampelune,
        Passion du Christ,
        Pharsale*
Nobles, city of, 44-45, 57-80,
        181
    lost poem on, 71, 72, 74-
        75

Ockham, William of, 128
Oculus pastoralis, 27n, 105,
orality, 3-4, 249n, 265n
order, 81-89, 107, 111-12,
        118-23, 138, 151,
        190, 232, 246
orgueil, 37, 38-39, 246-47

Pacaut, M., 94, 95-96
Padua
    autonomy, desire for, 101-
        105
    Europe's fourth oldest
        University in, 10
    golden age of, 101
    legendary founding of,13,
        260
    political history of, 12,
        16, 103-07, 176
    Studium, 10, 91
Paduan, the, supposed author
        of *Entrée*, 11, 12, 44,
        53, 73, 76, 140, 160-
        61, 181, 207. *See*
        narrator
Pagels, E., 125, 131n, 262

Palermo, J., 26n
Paris, Gaston, 14, 70, 73-74
Passion du Christ, 10, 17
Payen, J. C., 229
Perot, J. P., 236
Petrarch, 11, 13, 128
Pharsale, 10, 17
Poeta Saxo, 63
Polo, Marco, 8
Prehumanism, 13, 91, *see also*
    Padua, Mussato, Lovati
Priscian, 217-18
Prise de Pamelune, La, 10, 14,
    17, 199, 209
Pseudo-Dionysius, 81-82, 262
Pseudo-Turpin chronicle, 28,
    63-64, 72-73, 74,
    21n, 81n, 220, 244
Pulci, 5, 152

Quatre fils Aymon, 55n, 72
Quillet, J., 118, 120

Raoul de Cambrai, 47
recovrer, military term, 4
    literary term, 5, 220
"retors de tere," 112, 159, 162-
    63, 237, 255, 259
Renaud de Montauban, 47, 139
rhetoric, 142, 160
Robertson, D. W., 218, 219
Robertson-Mellor, G., 6
Rolandian macrotext, 5, 12,
    15, 53, 201
Rolandian material in Italy, 7
Rolandino, 27
Rolandino Patavino,
    chronicler, 103
romance genre, 136, 219,
    233, 242
Roman de la Rose, 10, 12, 135
Roncaglia, A., 70

Ruggeri, R.M., 28, 29, 70,
    72,   73
Ruolantes Liet, 62, 73

Salisbury, John of, 116, 119,
    125, 128
Salutati, C., 128
Seneca, 251n
Sententia, 3 ("sentençe"), 215-
    53
Silvestris, B., 218
Spagna, La, 28n
Specht, R., 28n, 51, 199
Stanesco, M., 162

Tabacco, G., 87, 94, 95, 96,
    97, 98, 100, 106
Thomas, A., 21n, 27n, 39,
    50, 69, 70, 72-73,
    138, 237, 250n

Veneto-Lombard region, 7, 139
Verona, Nicholas of, 7, 14
Villani, Giovanni, chronicler,
    103, 196-97
Virgil, 11, 260
Vitry, Jacques de, 108

Waley, D., 90, 91, 92, 97
Wunderli, P., 25, 42-43, 71,
    138-39, 150, 153-54,
    184, 211n, 238-39